W9-BJT-882

FLORIDA STATE
UNIVERSITY LIBRARIES

SEP 25 1995

TALLAHASSEE, FLORIDA

Canada

WORLD BIBLIOGRAPHICAL SERIES
General Editors:
Robert G. Neville (Executive Editor)
John J. Horton

Robert A. Myers   Ian Wallace
Hans H. Wellisch   Ralph Lee Woodward, Jr.

John J. Horton is Deputy Librarian of the University of Bradford and currently Chairman of its Academic Board of Studies in Social Sciences. He has maintained a longstanding interest in the discipline of area studies and its associated bibliographical problems, with special reference to European Studies. In particular he has published in the field of Icelandic and of Yugoslav studies, including the two relevant volumes in the World Bibliographical Series.

Robert A. Myers is Associate Professor of Anthropology in the Division of Social Sciences and Director of Study Abroad Programs at Alfred University, Alfred, New York. He has studied post-colonial island nations of the Caribbean and has spent two years in Nigeria on a Fulbright Lectureship. His interests include international public health, historical anthropology and developing societies. In addition to *Amerindians of the Lesser Antilles: a bibliography* (1981), *A Resource Guide to Dominica, 1493-1986* (1987) and numerous articles, he has compiled the World Bibliographical Series volumes on *Dominica* (1987) and *Nigeria* (1989).

Ian Wallace is Professor of Modern Languages at Loughborough University of Technology. A graduate of Oxford in French and German, he also studied in Tübingen, Heidelberg and Lausanne before taking teaching posts at universities in the USA, Scotland and England. He specializes in East German affairs, especially literature and culture, on which he has published numerous articles and books. In 1979 he founded the journal *GDR Monitor*, which he continues to edit.

Hans H. Wellisch is Professor emeritus at the College of Library and Information Services, University of Maryland. He was President of the American Society of Indexers and was a member of the International Federation for Documentation. He is the author of numerous articles and several books on indexing and abstracting, and has published *The Conversion of Scripts* and *Indexing and Abstracting: an International Bibliography*. He also contributes frequently to *Journal of the American Society for Information Science*, *The Indexer* and other professional journals.

Ralph Lee Woodward, Jr. is Chairman of the Department of History at Tulane University, New Orleans, where he has been Professor of History since 1970. He is the author of *Central America, a Nation Divided*, 2nd ed. (1985), as well as several monographs and more than sixty scholarly articles on modern Latin America. He has also compiled volumes in the World Bibliographical Series on *Belize* (1980), *Nicaragua* (1983), and *El Salvador* (1988). Dr. Woodward edited the Central American section of the *Research Guide to Central America and the Caribbean* (1985) and is currently editor of the Central American history section of the *Handbook of Latin American Studies*.

VOLUME 62

Canada

Ernest Ingles
Compiler
With an Introduction by James Pitsula

CLIO PRESS
OXFORD, ENGLAND · SANTA BARBARA, CALIFORNIA
DENVER, COLORADO

© Copyright 1990 by Clio Press Ltd.

All rights reserved. No part of this publication may be reproduced, stored in any retrieval system, or transmitted in any form or by any means, electronic, mechanical, photocopying or otherwise, without the prior permission in writing of the publishers.

British Library Cataloguing in Publication Data

Canada. — (World Bibliographical Series, 62).
1. Canada – Bibliographies
I. Ingles, Ernest B.   II. Series ·
016.97296

ISBN 1-85109-005-3

Clio Press Ltd.,
55 St. Thomas' Street,
Oxford OX1 1JG, England.

ABC-CLIO,
130 Cremona Drive,
Santa Barbara,
CA 93117, USA.

Designed by Bernard Crossland.
Typeset by Columns Design and Production Services, Reading, England.
Printed and bound in Great Britain by
Billing and Sons Ltd., Worcester.

THE WORLD BIBLIOGRAPHICAL SERIES

This series, which is principally designed for the English speaker, will eventually cover every country in the world, each in a separate volume comprising annotated entries on works dealing with its history, geography, economy and politics; and with its people, their culture, customs, religion and social organization. Attention will also be paid to current living conditions – housing, education, newspapers, clothing, etc.– that are all too often ignored in standard bibliographies; and to those particular aspects relevant to individual countries. Each volume seeks to achieve, by use of careful selectivity and critical assessment of the literature, an expression of the country and an appreciation of its nature and national aspirations, to guide the reader towards an understanding of its importance. The keynote of the series is to provide, in a uniform format, an interpretation of each country that will express its culture, its place in the world, and the qualities and background that make it unique. The views expressed in individual volumes, however, are not necessarily those of the publisher.

VOLUMES IN THE SERIES

For Erin,
May she come to know her country,
May her country come to know her.

Contents

Contents

x

Contents

Introduction

Geography

Canada is a country dominated by geography. It has the second largest land mass of any country in the world (9,215,438 square kilometres), but a population that ranks only twenty-eighth (about 25.3 million in 1986). Politically, Canada is a federation consisting of ten provinces and two territories. From west to east, the provinces are: British Columbia; the three prairie provinces of Alberta, Saskatchewan and Manitoba; the two central provinces, Ontario and Quebec; and the Atlantic provinces of Nova Scotia, New Brunswick, Prince Edward Island, and Newfoundland. North of the province of British Columbia is the Yukon Territory; the remainder of the northern lands belong to the Northwest Territories.

Canada's geography is highly diverse. Although there are an almost infinite number of regions and subregions, six principal geographical areas can be identified.

The Canadian Shield covers nearly half the total area of the country. A region of forest, lakes, muskeg bogs and Pre-Cambrian rock, it extends across most of Quebec and Ontario, northern Manitoba, northern Saskatchewan and into the Northwest Territories. The Shield does not support a large population, but it contains an abundance of valuable natural resources – minerals, timber, and hydro-electric power.

South of the Shield lies the region of the Great Lakes-St. Lawrence lowlands, one of the smallest but also one of the most prosperous regions of Canada. Occupying part of southern Ontario and the valley of the St. Lawrence River in Quebec, it is characterized by intensive agriculture and a highly developed manufacturing industry. Despite its relatively restricted area, the Great Lakes-St. Lawrence lowlands holds more than half of Canada's population and produces about three-quarters of the value of the nation's manufactured goods.

The Atlantic provinces are dominated by the Canadian Appalachians, ranges of gently rolling hills and low mountains. The succession of highland and lowland and the indented coastline result in the distribution of the population in a number of valleys and small coastal areas.

The Interior Plains cover most of Alberta and the southern parts of Saskatchewan and Manitoba. The region is bounded on the west by the Rocky Mountains and on the east by the edge of the Shield. The broad, flat plains are ideally suited for grain farming. But while it is true that much of the region is flat, the land forms also include hills, escarpments and entrenched river valleys.

The Western Cordilleras, roughly congruent with the province of British Columbia and the Yukon Territory, form Canada's most rugged mountain terrain. Agriculture is confined to certain narrow river valleys or flood plains, and the urban population is concentrated into one small area in the southwestern corner of British Columbia where seventy-five per cent of the population live. Most of the remaining settlements in the region derive their livelihood from the exploitation of natural resources, especially forests and minerals.

Finally, the sparsely populated Northwest Territories may be regarded as a distinct region despite the diversity of the natural environment. Within the large area of the Territories are two principal subregions: the subarctic Mackenzie River Valley in the west and the Arctic area of the islands and north-central mainland. In the Arctic area trees do not grow and crops cannot be cultivated. The somewhat warmer climate and better soil conditions in the subarctic Mackenzie Valley permit limited agriculture.

History

Within this vast and varied geographical domain, an equally varied population has taken root. The first occupants of what is now Canada are thought to have arrived during the last Ice Age, which began about 80,000 years ago and ended about 12,000 years ago. During this period a land bridge joined Siberia to Alaska across what is now the Bering Sea. Across this land bridge human hunters pursuing caribou, bison and other animals came from Asia into North America. Over thousands of years, these prehistoric inhabitants migrated and adapted to a variety of environments throughout the Americas.

The date when Europeans first landed and settled in Canada has been a matter for debate. Archaeological excavations at L'Anse Aux Meadows near the northern tip of Newfoundland suggest landings by Norse adventurers as early as 985 or 986. The first permanent settlement by Europeans was established by the French explorer, Samuel de Champlain, at Quebec (now Quebec City) in 1608. The

French were drawn to the New World by the search for natural products, notably fish and furs. The English also had an economic interest in these resources, and an intense competition for supremacy began. Ultimately the British were triumphant, the decisive battle being fought at the Plains of Abraham in Quebec in 1759.

The new imperial rulers now had to deal with the perplexing problem of governing a population with a different language and religion. The conquerors were Protestant and spoke English; the conquered were Roman Catholic and spoke French. Eventually, the British concluded that the colony was governable only if civil and religious rights were conceded to the francophones. The Quebec Act of 1774 was a constitutional document of great significance because it guaranteed the legal status of the Roman Catholic Church, the French system of seigneurial landholding, and French civil law. It became the key document for the defence of French rights.

During the time of the American Revolution, Canada remained in British hands. Thousands of United Empire loyalists, residents of the Thirteen Colonies who opposed the revolution, moved northward. In the years that followed, the British government encouraged the flow of immigrants into British North America. Although a substantial number of these people moved on to the United States, sufficient numbers of them stayed to allow English speakers to form a majority of the population. In Lower Canada (which Quebec was then called) francophones still constituted the majority. In that jurisdiction, an agricultural crisis, caused by a rapid population increase, a shortage of arable land, and declining agricultural productivity, formed the background of an agitation for more powers of self-government. Bloody uprisings broke out in 1837 and 1838, resulting in harsh suppression by British troops. The violence in Quebec had fainter echoes in what was Upper Canada (now Ontario) where a relatively small group of rebels took up arms against the ruling élite.

The rebellions caused the British government to re-evaluate its colonial policies. It concluded that long-term peace could be achieved only through assimilating the francophones to the language and culture of the British majority. To that end, Upper and Lower Canada were united into one colony with a legislative assembly having equal numbers of elected representatives from the two sections. The idea was that the anglophone majority in Upper Canada would combine with the anglophone minority in Lower Canada to dominate and, in the long run, assimilate the French Canadians. The plan failed. French Canadian nationalism, fired by the ill-fated rebellion, survived and even prospered under the new régime.

Meanwhile, external events began to exert powerful influences

Introduction

upon British North America. Great Britain adopted free trade in the 1840s, robbing the Canadian wheat and timber trade of its privileged position in the British economy. To make matters worse, Britain sided with the South in the American Civil War, creating fears in Canada that when the war was over, the Northern armies would turn north and take over the British colonies. These were some of the circumstances that led to serious discussions in the 1860s of a projected union of the colonies of British North America. A united country would be better able not only to defend itself, but also to promote internal trade, thereby compensating for fading British and American markets.

The Dominion of Canada was born on 1 July 1867 when the British North American Act, passed by the British parliament, became law. The four original provinces joining in federal union at that time were Nova Scotia, New Brunswick, Ontario (formerly Upper Canada) and Quebec (formerly Lower Canada). From the outset, the Fathers of Confederation had in mind the acquisition of additional territories and the building of a nation *ad mare usque ad mare*. Canada's first and formative prime minister, the Conservative leader, Sir John A. Macdonald, clung stubbornly to that goal. Macdonald was a supremely gifted politician who, despite his weakness for the bottle, managed to keep the federation together during its initial, troubled and uncertain decades.

As the basis for westward expansion, the Dominion of Canada in 1869 purchased the vast expanse of land controlled by the Hudson's Bay Company. This sparked an uprising by the Métis, a people created by the mingling of Indians and Europeans in the fur trade. Led by a French-speaking, Catholic Métis, Louis Riel, the protest was successful to the extent that it forced the federal government to grant provincial status to Manitoba in 1870 and to guarantee certain religious, linguistic and land rights. In 1871 British Columbia, attracted by the promise of a transcontinental railway to the Pacific Ocean within ten years, joined the Confederation. The Canadian Pacific Railway was completed in 1885 and can be considered one of Macdonald's major nation-building accomplishments. However, trouble in the West erupted again that same year. Louis Riel, supported by many Métis and Indians, spearheaded a second violent uprising in defence of the rights of the native people, who justifiably felt that the Canadian government was ignoring them. Troops rushed out to the West on the newly built railway and quickly suppressed the revolt. Louis Riel was hanged for treason. Macdonald's refusal to commute the death sentence caused an uproar in Quebec where many people regarded Riel as a defender of French rights. To this day, he is regarded as a hero and martyr of the Métis people and a victim of Anglo-Protestant prejudice.

Apart from the development of the West, Prime Minister Macdonald's major economic initiative was the national policy of protective tariffs introduced in 1879. Prior to the middle of the nineteenth century, Canada's wealth was based primarily upon the export of natural products such as furs, fish, wheat and lumber. From the 1840s onward, manufacturing became an ever more important part of the economy, especially in southern Ontario and Quebec. Railways were built and factories established. When industrial capitalists clamoured for protection from foreign competition, the Conservative government was happy to respond. In 1879 Macdonald raised the duties on imported goods to an unprecedented level. The process of industrialization, which was already underway, accelerated significantly.

Macdonald died in 1891 while still in office. He left an impressive legacy: a transcontinental nation with a substantial industrial base. His leadership enabled the Conservative party to dominate the first thirty years of Canada's history. The fortunes of Canada's other major political force, the Liberal party, improved dramatically in 1896 when Wilfrid Laurier won the election. Laurier, the first French Canadian to be prime minister, had a remarkable facility for compromise and conciliation. His 'middle of the road' approach was designed to keep the peace at a time when French-English tensions in Canada were running high.

Laurier had the luck of being in power during an era of rapid economic growth. From the late 1890s to 1914, hundreds of thousands of immigrants flocked to Canada from the United States, Britain, and Central and Eastern Europe. They crowded into cities, taking up industrial jobs, and built homesteads on millions of acres of new land on the western prairies.

Laurier's political downfall came in 1911 when his government negotiated a free trade agreement with the United States providing for the elimination of all tariffs on natural products and the reduction of tariffs on manufactured goods. The Conservatives, now led by Robert Borden, declared the deal to be a sell-out. It would lead to the severance of the cherished ties to the British Empire and, eventually, to the absorption of Canada into the United States. Laurier vainly protested that Canada could retain her distinct identity while trading with the Americans. In Quebec, Laurier fell victim to a backlash by French-Canadian *nationalistes* who accused him of giving in to English-Canadian opinion on such controversial issues as whether Canada should make a contribution to the British imperial navy. The result was a Conservative victory and the end of the Laurier era.

Introduction

The greatest challenge faced by Laurier's successor, Sir Robert Borden, was the management of Canada's participation in the First World War. Borden was a staunch imperialist to the point that he scarcely saw a difference between the interests of Canada and the interests of the British Empire. Since, for Borden, victory in the war meant everything, he did not hesitate in 1917 to introduce compulsory military service. French Canadians were outraged. They would fight for Canada, they said, but not for Britain or France. Riots broke out in Quebec City, but in the end the French-Canadians had to submit to the will of the English majority.

Canada emerged from the First World War a bitterly divided country: French against English, labour against capital, and rural Canada against urban Canada.

The victor in the 1921 election was William Lyon Mackenzie King, the successor to Laurier as the leader of the Liberal party. Mackenzie King's bland, unprepossessing exterior masked a genius for politics. He was cunning, calculating, ruthless, opportunistic, self-righteous, and eminently successful. It fell to King to apply 'the healing hand of the physician' to the badly divided and internally torn Canada of 1921. King's watchword was always 'national unity'.

One of Mackenzie King's major accomplishments was his gradual advancement of Canada's independence from Britain. Canada evolved from colony to nation and became an autonomous member of the British Commonwealth. King finally retired from politics in 1948, after first arranging for the continued electoral success of the Liberal Party under his hand-picked successor Louis St. Laurent.

The post-war years were prosperous ones for Canada. The average standard of living of Canadians doubled between 1944 and 1978. Economic growth was accompanied by large amounts of American investment and a shift in trading patterns from the British to the American market. Whereas in 1946 twenty-six per cent of Canadian exports had gone to Britain and thirty-eight to the United States, by 1978 the figures were respectively 3.8 per cent and seventy per cent. By 1980 forty-two per cent of the capital employed in the petroleum and natural gas industry, and forty-one per cent of the capital employed in mining and smelting was controlled in the United States.

Canadians enjoyed the prosperity and wealth, but many were troubled by the increasingly large American presence in the Canadian economy. Dependence on the United States also extended to the military sphere. The turning point was the Ogdensburg Declaration of 1940 when Canada and the United States agreed to establish a Permanent Joint Board on Defence for the defence of North America. Britain was a fading power and hence could no longer be relied upon to ensure Canada's security. A new ally had to be found.

In 1949 Canada joined NATO and then in 1957 entered the North American Air Defence (NORAD) agreement with the United States. Although NORAD was in theory an equal partnership, overpowering US military superiority meant that the United States was effectively responsible for the defence of the continent.

Another development of Canada's post-war era was the continued expansion of the welfare state. In 1962 the social democratic government in the province of Saskatchewan pioneered the first state medical insurance plan in North America. The federal government later extended the plan to all of Canada. Medicare, together with old age pensions, unemployment insurance, and social assistance plans, constituted a social safety net that became a basic feature of modern Canada.

The 1960s also saw dramatic social, economic, and political changes in the province of Quebec. The Québécois profoundly resented the fact that the commanding heights of the economy were still controlled by anglophones. This period of hectic modernization and surging Québécois nationalism was dubbed the Quiet Revolution. Unfortunately, it was not always quiet. A terrorist group resorted to bombing, kidnapping and assassination to achieve its goal of an independent Quebec. While the methods of the terrorists were almost universally condemned by the people of Quebec, the dream of a sovereign state was widely shared.

The burden of dealing with this national unity crisis fell to Prime Minister Pierre Elliott Trudeau. First elected in 1968 on a wave of 'Trudeaumania', Trudeau was a staunch believer in the preservation of a united Canada. His basic strategy to defeat the separatists was to establish and give meaning to the principle of bilingualism from coast to coast. The Official Languages Act of 1969 stipulated that 'the English and French languages are the official languages of Canada'. This provision was later entrenched in the Canadian Charter of Rights and Freedoms in the Constitution Act of 1982. The new Constitution confirmed that the Canadian public has the right to communicate with and to receive services from the federal government and its agencies in French or English. The principle of bilingualism has extended also to the school system so that increasing numbers of primary and secondary school children whose mother tongue is English are receiving instruction in French.

The Quebec government held a referendum in May 1980 in which they asked for a mandate to negotiate 'sovereignty-association' with the rest of Canada. The proposal was rejected by a vote of 59.8 per cent against 40.5 per cent for sovereignty-association. However, language and separatist issues are far from dead. The Canadian Government tried to reconcile Quebec to Confederation through the

Introduction

Meech Lake Accord, a set of amendments to the Constitution that would have given Quebec status as a 'distinct society' within Canada. When the Accord failed in 1990 to obtain the unanimous consent of the provinces, it collapsed, putting constitutional discussions in limbo.

Population

Canada's population in June 1986 was 25,354,064. This represents a modest growth rate of 4.2 per cent over the 1981-86 period. Although the nation's population has more than doubled since the Second World War, the growth rate has fluctuated from the high levels of the late 1940s and the 1950s to a low ebb in recent years. At the present time, natural increase (the excess of births over deaths) accounts for approximately seventy-five per cent of Canada's population growth.

The remainder of the increase results from immigration. Canada's immigration policy, at the present time, is based on the principle of non-discrimination and favours immigrants who are likely to adapt to the Canadian way of life and make a positive contribution to the culture and economy of the country. Immigrant arrivals for 1985 numbered 84,302, of whom 45.8 per cent came from Asia, 22.4 per cent from Europe, and 21.1 per cent from North and Central America.

Canada's population is distributed very unevenly across the country. Ontario, where 35.9 per cent of Canadians live, is the most heavily populated province, followed by Quebec with 25.8 per cent and British Columbia with 11.4 per cent. The four Atlantic provinces have only 9.0 per cent of the people, while the three prairie provinces have 17.6 per cent. Canada's population is preponderantly urbanized. In fact, the three largest metropolitan areas, Toronto, Montreal, and Vancouver together comprised 7.7 million people or 30.5 per cent of the total population in 1986.

Canada has become an ethnically diverse country, and both federal and provincial governments have given support to multiculturalism. Today, the largest ethnic group in Canada is British (forty per cent), followed by French (twenty-seven per cent), German (five per cent), Italian (three per cent) and Ukrainian (two per cent). British is the most common ethnic origin in every province, except, of course, in the province of Quebec.

The 491,460 individuals who identified themselves as native people in the 1981 census made up just two per cent of the total population. However, they constituted fifty-eight per cent of the people in the Northwest Territories and 17.5 per cent of Yukon territory inhabitants. In socio-economic terms, native people do not fare well in Canada.

Their average incomes in 1980 were approximately two-thirds of the non-native average. Nonetheless, the future prospects for native people appear to be brightening. After a hard-fought battle, aboriginal and treaty rights were firmly established in the Canadian Constitution in 1982.

Economy

The Canadian economy generated a total wealth in terms of Gross Domestic Product of US $363.9 billion (approximately £191.5 billion) in 1986. By way of comparison, the United States economy produced US $4,185.5 billion (approximately £2,202.9 billion) in GDP in the same year.

Agriculture, which has always been a significant component of the Canadian economy, made up ten per cent of Canada's total exports in 1985, and, when the processing, wholesale, and retail sectors are taken into account, was responsible for approximately ten per cent of Canada's economic activity. Nevertheless, today only three or four Canadian families out of every 100 is a farming family. The number of farms has dropped steeply as average farm size continues to grow. Meanwhile, the volume of agricultural production increased by 175 per cent during that forty-year period. Agriculture has become highly capital-intensive, making it very hard for the small producer to survive.

The tradition of the family-owned and operated farm in Canada is a strong one, reflected in the homestead and other land settlement policies established by the government over the years. Every rural politician has a set speech in praise of the 'family farm'. In 1986, family-controlled farms in Canada contributed 94.6 per cent, and farms controlled by non-family corporations contributed 4.4 per cent, of aggregate gross sales. However, over one-third of farm land was rented in 1986.

Canada's agriculture is very export-oriented. In 1985, fifty-one per cent of all agricultural products were exported, and seventy per cent of those exports were grains and oilseeds. Wheat alone accounted for approximately one-half of all agricultural exports. The mid 1980s have been characterized by declining world grain prices, which, when combined with a tremendous debt burden, skyrocketing interest rates in the early 1980s, and draught and grasshoppers in the prairie provinces, have produced great financial and psychological stress for farmers. Canadian agriculture has been a victim of the farm subsidy wars waged by the European Economic Community and the United States. Reduction of international subsidies which lead to excess production and depressed prices is a major objective of Canadian agricultural policy.

Introduction

As with agriculture, the importance of forests, furs, and fish to the Canadian economy has a long history. Canada is now the world's leading exporter of forest products. In 1985 such exports were valued at $16.2 billion (£8.12 billion) (all dollar references are Canadian dollars unless otherwise specified) and constituted twenty-two per cent of the world's total. Fur exports totalled $97.1 million (£48.7 million), while Canada maintained its status as the world's leading exporter of fish products with 1985 sales worth $1.86 billion (£0.93 billion).

Concern has been growing in recent years about the threat to Canada's natural resources caused by 'acid' rain. Sulphur dioxide and nitrogen oxide emissions from industrial plants are transformed in the atmosphere to sulphuric and nitric acids and fall on vegetation, soil, and surface waters. Plant life has been destroyed and fish taken from lakes affected by acid rain show high concentrations of mercury and other heavy metals. Toxic trace metals have reached such high levels in surface and ground waters that the water is sometimes unfit for human consumption.

To solve the problem, total sulphur dioxide emissions from industries in Canada must be reduced, and the federal government and the seven eastern provinces have agreed to cut emissions by fifty per cent by 1994. Securing the cooperation of the United States government has not been as easy, but some progress is being made.

Another natural resource of immense value to the Canadian economy is minerals. In 1986 Canada led the world in mineral exports and ranked third among mineral producers, trailing only the United States and the Soviet Union. On a volume basis, Canada is first in the world in uranium, zinc, and nickel; second in asbestos, potash, sulphur, and gypsum; third in gold, aluminum, and platinum group metals; fourth in molybdenum, copper, cadmium, and lead; and fifth in silver. Petroleum and natural gas production and refining are the largest components in the mineral industry. Although domestic production and exports are small in the world industry context, they are of considerable significance to Canada. Most of the crude oil comes from Alberta, with Saskatchewan second, and only minor production elsewhere. In terms of energy use, Canada is not merely self-sufficient but enjoyed a surplus worth $10.7 billion (£5.37 billion) in 1985. In the same year, 37.3 per cent of the primary energy consumed in Canada was from oil, 30.6 per cent from natural gas and by-products, 14.4 per cent from hydro and nuclear, 13.6 per cent from coal, and 4.2 per cent from wood.

Manufacturing in 1984 accounted for 21.1 per cent of Canada's gross domestic product or $230.1 billion (£115.4 billion). Manufacturing activity is far from being evenly distributed across the country.

Nearly eighty per cent is concentrated in the provinces of Ontario and Quebec, including all of the motor vehicle industry, which is Canada's largest manufacturing industry. Financial institutions and business service industries are also based primarily in the central provinces. In the eastern and western regions, by contrast, primary industries dominate the scene. Fishing, forestry, and mining are especially important to the Atlantic provinces, while agriculture and mineral fuels hold sway in the prairie economy. British Columbia's primary industries are dependent in large measure on forestry, mining, and fishing.

The regional diversity of the economy means that one area can be experiencing a boom while another goes through hard times. Shifts in economic activity from one region to another are often tied to the ups and downs in the international demand for primary commodities. Led by high oil prices, many commodity prices rose sharply during the 1970s. This led to an upsurge in the economy of Western Canada. The Atlantic provinces fared less well during this period, partly because markets for fish remained relatively weak and partly because major discoveries of offshore oil and gas were not made until the late 1970s. The decline in many commodity prices since 1981 has caused a relative weakening in the regional economies of Atlantic and Western Canada in the mid 1980s. Weak oil demand and low grain prices boosted unemployment rates to nearly ten per cent in the prairies and even higher in British Columbia and the Atlantic provinces. Ontario and Quebec, on the other hand, have done exceedingly well, with boom-time conditions in the housing and motor industries.

If the wealth generated by the Canadian economy is not equally distributed by regions, nor is it equally distributed by social class. The families who in 1987 comprised the top one-fifth of income earners received 39.4 per cent of the total income earned. The bottom fifth earned only 6.5 per cent of total income.

The inequalities of wealth in Canada have been mitigated to some extent by the efforts of organized labour to win higher wages and benefits for their members and by the establishment of social welfare programmes. At the beginning of 1986, there were 3,730,000 union members in Canada, representing 37.7 per cent of the non-agricultural paid work force. This compares with thirty-nine per cent of the work force belonging to unions in 1984. The decline in union membership is partly attributable to the implementation of 'privatization' policies by the federal and some provincial governments. The sale of Crown corporations to private owners and the transfer of government services to the private sector has contributed to the de-unionization of workers. Canada has a fairly well-developed social security system designed to ensure that all Canadians have at least a minimum of resources available to meet their basic needs and essential services to maintain their well-being. Almost forty-seven per cent of the 1986/87 federal budget was devoted to health and social welfare.

International trade is of major importance to the strength of the Canadian economy. Exports in 1986 equalled 23.9 per cent of the Gross Domestic Product, as compared with 5.2 per cent for the United States. Canada's major trading partner, by a wide margin, is the republic to the south. Geography, history, military strategy, economics, and social connections have created a very close relationship. In 1985 Canada sold seventy-eight per cent of its exports to the United States and bought twenty-two per cent of US global exports.

The Asia–Pacific region is also emerging as an area of notable economic significance and interest for Canada. In 1982, for the first time, Canada's two-way trade with countries of the Pacific Rim exceeded its trade with traditional Atlantic trading partners. Asian-Pacific countries have also supplanted Europe as the primary source of new immigrants to Canada. Japan is Canada's second largest trading partner as well as a source of capital and technological innovation. The third main focus of Canada's international trade is Western Europe, with which Canada has longstanding cultural and social ties as well as a shared commitment to security through membership in NATO.

By far the most important recent trade initiative is the Free Trade Agreement with the United States. The issue dominated the federal election campaign in November 1988 in which the Conservatives led by Brian Mulroney, who supported the deal, won a majority of seats in the House of Commons. In the course of the ten-year period beginning 1 January 1989, the Agreement will remove all tariffs between the two countries. This in itself would not be very significant in view of the steep decline in tariff rates that occurred in the 1960s and 1970s. The automobile trade – Canada's main export industry – has long been liberalized under the US-Canada Auto Pact. Of greater consequence is the reduction under the Free Trade Agreement of some non-tariff barriers to trade, the establishment of impartial procedures for the resolution of trade disputes, the elimination of some barriers to trade in services, and the liberalization of cross-border investment flows.

One of the main benefits to the United States from the Agreement is the guarantee of assured access to Canadian energy supplies. Restrictions on exports of Canadian oil and gas can be imposed, but any reduction in exports to the United States must be proportional to the total supply of oil and gas available in Canada. Nor can Canada charge the United States a higher price for oil and gas than that paid by Canadian consumers. In addition, the United States gains significantly from the removal of almost all barriers to American investment in Canada.

The Free Trade Agreement aroused a furore of debate in Canada not only because of the economic provisions, but also the political, social and cultural implications. On previous occasions in Canadian history, for example, in 1891, 1911 and 1948, free trade was rejected due to a belief that economic integration with the United States would lead to political and cultural integration. Opponents of the deal used the 'harmonization' argument; that is, the pressures of competing with the United States in a free trade environment would necessitate a harmonizing of tax structures, regional development initiatives, social programmes and industrial relations. Gradually Canada would have to conform to the more market-driven US model of society, a society characterized by relatively poor social security benefits, no universal medicare, comparatively low taxation of the wealthy, and antipathy to organized labour.

Culture

There were also many concerns expressed about the fate of Canadian culture under free trade with the United States, even though cultural industries were explicitly exempted from the deal. On the other hand, the cultural argument against free trade was undercut by the perceived vitality and strength of Canadian culture in recent decades, even as economic ties have drawn Canada closer to the United States. For example, the outburst of national pride accompanying the celebration of the centennial of Confederation in 1967 fostered increased awareness of Canadian literature and the expansion of Canadian literature courses. At the same time that Canadians became more conscious of their own literary tradition, the international audience became more attentive. Canadian studies organizations were established in the 1970s in Europe, the United States, Japan, the South Pacific, and elsewhere.

The list of Canadian writers who have emerged on the scene in recent years is a long and distinguished one. Margaret Laurence's novels, *The stone angel* (1981), *The fire-dwellers* (1969) and *The diviners* (1974) were major literary events, imprinting the prairie town of Manawaka on the national consciousness. Margaret Atwood's *The handmaid's tale* (1986) and *Cat's eye* (1988) among many other works of fiction, made her one of Canada's dominant literary personalities, while Robertson Davies won acclaim with *Fifth business* (1977) and *What's bred in the·bone* (1985), to name but two of his titles. Other Canadians who made their mark in the last three decades include: Mordecai Richler, Alice Munro, Timothy Findley, Mavis Gallant, Michael Ondaatje, Hugh Hood, Marie-Claire Blais, Victor-Levy Beaulieu, and Michel Tremblay.

Canada has evolved a number of institutions for the nourishment of Canadian culture. In 1985-86, the Canada Council, which was established by an Act of Parliament in 1957, disbursed $68.4 million (£34.3 million) in grants and services mainly to professional artists and arts organizations in the fields of dance, music, theatre, writing and publishing, visual arts and media arts.

The performing arts, generally speaking, do not earn enough money from ticket sales to be self-sustaining and depend upon large transfusions in grants and subsidies. On the average, grants represented forty-eight per cent of the total revenues of performing arts organizations in 1984. Of these grants seventy-six per cent came from the public purse and twenty-four per cent from the private sector. The public funds flowed from all levels of government: forty-three per cent federal, twenty-five per cent provincial, and eight per cent municipal.

The dependence on grants does not imply a lack of vitality in the performing arts. In 1984 Canada had 139 theatre companies, fifty-eight music organizations, thirty-two dance companies, and eleven opera companies. Most major cities support a symphony orchestra, those in Montreal, Toronto, and at the National Arts Centre, having achieved distinction. Three major dance companies, the National Ballet, the Royal Winnipeg Ballet, and Les Grands Ballets Canadiens, have solid international reputations.

Another institution, at least as important to the welfare of Canadian culture as the Canada Council, is the Canadian Broadcasting Corporation. It was created in response to a federal Royal Commission on broadcasting in 1929, which recommended a public corporation to foster a national spirit and interpret national citizenship. The CBC, with a total budget of $1.1 billion (£0.55 billion) in 1986-87, has a mandate to offer the whole range of programming in English and French, serve the special needs of geographical regions, contribute to the flow and exchange of cultural and regional information and entertainment, and provide an expression of Canadian identity. Other cultural institutions of lesser, but still considerable, importance are the National Museums of Canada, the National Archives of Canada, the National Library of Canada, the National Film Board of Canada and Telefilm Canada. The NFB goes back to 1939 and has over the years produced more than 6,000 films interpreting Canada to Canadians and to other nations. Telefilm Canada, formerly known as the Canadian Film

Development Corporation, was established by the federal government in 1967. It aims to foster the feature-film industry and an independent television production industry in Canada.

*Information cited in this essay has been drawn from, among other sources, *Canada Year Book*, 1988; *Canada Handbook*, 1989; *OECD Economic Surveys, Canada*, 1987-88; *The Canadian Encyclopedia*; and *Encyclopedia Canadiana*.

James Pitsula
August 1990

The bibliography

As is consistent with the objectives of the *World Bibliographical Series*, the purpose of this bibliography is to reflect, by way of a highly selective listing of available or easily accessible publications, the geography, history, demography, economy, culture, and general society of Canada. In keeping with the guidelines of the *Series*, the publications have been chosen and categorized so as to provide to a general and diverse audience, 'an interpretation of the country such as expresses its place in the world, and the qualities and background that make it unique'.

Writing and publishing have increasingly flourished over the past thirty years in Canada, with a high proportion of the resultant output devoted to works on Canadian topics. Since it was first published in 1951 and to the end of 1989, *Canadiana: Canada's national bibliography* (Ottawa: National Library of Canada/Bibliothèque nationale du Canada, 1951-. eleven times a year), has listed approximately 360,000 monographic titles issued by non-government publishers (an additional 300,000 titles are attributed to this latter source). In addition, there are countless pre-1950 titles represented in the many retrospective bibliographical compilations. Only 2,067 titles have been extracted from this vast store and are included here, contained in 1,316 annotated entries.

Certain criteria have been applied in the selection of these works. Primarily works of a monographic nature are included. Articles are omitted as Canada's periodical literature is simply too large, too varied and too rich to permit a judicious selection. Instead, key journals and magazines have been listed or referenced in their appropriate thematic categories, and the key indexing and abstracting publications, such as the *Canadian Magazine Index* (Toronto: Micromedia, 1985- . annual), the *Canadian News Index* (Toronto: Micromedia, 1977- . monthly) and the *Canadian Periodical Index*

(Toronto: Info Globe, 1986- . monthly) are identified in the reference section. Emphasis has been placed on the inclusion of books published in the last thirty years, with particular emphasis on the 1970s and 1980s. A factor in the listing of each work was its accessibility. Recognizing the international readership of the *Series* these criteria were considered of some importance in the inclusion decision. Works had to be readily available to the non-Canadian reader through the book trade or from public or academic libraries by way of the interlibrary loan network. Even given these considerations, readers will find entries for some scarce classic works of scholarship.

Canada prides itself on being a bilingual nation, French and English being the two official languages. But, given that this *Series* is intended for an English-speaking audience, the majority of titles included are in English, although there are some notable exceptions, particularly in those sections broadly categorized as 'the arts'. The reader must be mindful that the available literature on French-Canada and that relating to Canada in French, is as rich and diverse as that of English-Canada and the literature on Canada in English. Given the attention paid by Quebec to its cultural industries, and in particular to writing and publishing, a *Series* volume on this province alone could encompass as many entries as are represented here. Given the editorial parameters of the present project, however, the compiler makes no apology for the inclusion of some French titles, nor for the paucity of the numbers overall.

When selecting works for inclusion within the specified subject areas, a certain degree of subjectivity based on judgement and knowledge is inevitable. Given the aforementioned plethora of publications on which to draw, it was axiomatic that only a limited number in each area would be selected. In some areas the extent of available publications necessitated the application of compiler's licence in the selection process. For example, in the field of literature, only literary criticism is included. Readers are encouraged from these works and from the reference tools listed to identify creative writers whose works they may wish to sample. Also, with regard to reference tools (particularly bibliographies) only those of a general nature have been identified. The reader is encouraged to consult such tools as *Canadian reference sources* (Dorothy E. Ryder. Ottawa: Canadian Library Association, 1981) and the *Bibliography of Canadian bibliographies* (Douglas Lochhead. Toronto: University of Toronto, 1972) – revised and enlarged editions are soon to be published for both – to satisfy specialized thematic needs. Moreover, the reader or the developing library wishing to identify more titles than could be listed is directed to such collection development and reference tools as *Canadian selection: books and periodicals for libraries* (Mavis Cariou, Sandra J. Cox, Alvan Bregman. Toronto: University of Toronto Press, 1985).

Undoubtedly, there will be differences of opinion as to the appropriateness of included titles. In certain areas, notably the social sciences, the selections may rapidly become dated. (The effective cut-off date for consideration was early 1989, although some relevant imprints published in the latter part of the year were incorporated.) For Canada, as for most nations, change is the constant – particularly socio-economic and socio-political change. The inquirer must be mindful of the limitations inherent within a compilation of this nature. In the end, some titles included here might not have been the choice of a different compiler; some titles not included, similarly, might have found their way into the compilation. Given all elements of the selection criteria this list is justifiable and a representative selection of worthwhile, available publications.

Bibliographic elements are formatted in a manner consistent with the *Series* style with entries arranged thematically. The reader familiar with the arrangement of other volumes will note some adaptation of the standard classification scheme. Changes were made when unique Canadian circumstances warranted such differentiation. Within each of the subject areas, entries are in alphabetical order by author, editor, compiler or corporate author; if this is not available, they are listed by the first non-article word in the title. Descriptive and evaluative annotations will assist the reader in making personal judgements as to the usefulness of a title. The annotations attempt to summarize the content of the work and often give some sense as to level of readership, for example the informed *versus* the general reader. Occasionally, when it was judged suitable in order to describe contents more fully, quotations from the text or from an available abstract have been inserted. Frequently, to further assist the reader in pursuit of information, alternative titles of value are recommended. The three indexes (author/editor, title, and subject) at the end of the volume provide additional access support to the entries.

Acknowledgements

The compiler is indebted to a number of individuals for their assistance in the preparation of this bibliography. I owe a special debt to my colleague at the University of Regina, Jim Pitsula, who agreed to bring his considerable expertise in the field of Canadian studies to the task of preparing the introductory essay. Similarly, I am especially grateful to my research assistant, Agnes Bray, for her

Introduction

energy and dedication to the project. Her contribution was immeasurable in identifying, locating and retrieving the thousands of works from which the final selection for inclusion was made. My sincere thanks are extended also to the following colleagues who at various points provided assistance in identifying relevant titles: Bob Bryce, Gary Dean, Pat Fleming, Allison Hayford, Alex Kelly, Nick Russell, Adrian Seaborne, Dianne Secoy and Dan de Vlieger. I am grateful also to my friend and colleague, Jim Tomkins, for the many patient hours he listened, over coffee, to my interminable rambling about the project.

Within the international library community there is an army of often unrecognized but extremely dedicated librarians and library workers who perform yeoman's service on behalf of researchers. I refer to those individuals who comprise the international interlibrary loan network. My contact with this group was through Marion Lake, Head of Interlibrary Loan and Document Delivery at the University of Regina. Her dedication to the research enterprise demands special recognition. But through her, also, I would thank her staff, and her colleagues at the numerous libraries within and outside Canada who supplied materials for review.

Financial assistance for research support was provided through the University of Regina's President's Fund, those resources having been made available by the Social Sciences and Humanities Research Council of Canada. In addition, I thank my host institutions, the University of Regina and the University of Alberta for those many infrastructure supports which contribute to the successful execution of any research initiative.

To Dr. Robert Neville and the staff of Clio Press I express sincerest thanks for their assistance and patience. Various editors of the Press were involved in the preparation of the manuscript. Especially deserving of recognition are Katrina McClintock and her colleague Milica Djuradjević. Their keen insights, meticulous editing, helpful critiques, stylistic improvements and constant encouragement were much appreciated in seeing the manuscript through to completion.

Finally, I owe my greatest debt to my wife Claire and my daughter Erin for their understanding and forbearance in living with an absentee husband and father for periods longer than any family should abide.

Ernest Ingles
August 1990

The Country and its People

1 **Between friends=Entre amis.**
   Toronto: McClelland & Stewart Limited, 1976. [n.p.]
   A magnificent volume, produced by the Still Photography Division of the National
   Film Board of Canada to celebrate the US bicentennial. On the eve of that celebration
   a team of photographers was dispatched and instructed to interpret the border
   photographically; that is, to document places in both countries where the border plays
   a part in the daily lives of the people. Though the work has American content, it
   depicts as much about Canada and Canadians as it does Americans.

2 **Canada a portrait: the official handbook of present conditions and recent
   progress.**
   Ottawa: Communications Division, Statistics Canada, 1989. 247p.
   Previously entitled *Canada handbook*, this glossy, beautifully illustrated volume, issued
   yearly since 1930, provides a succinct and popular account of Canada's annual progress
   and the facts of its current economic, social and cultural situation.

3 **Canada: coast to coast.**
   Roger Boulton.   Toronto: Oxford University Press, 1982. 186p.
   (Regional Portraits of Canada).
   This volume presents a selection of photographs taken from other works in the
   commercially successful, and aesthetically pleasing Regional Portraits of Canada series.
   The volume portrays Canada's magnificence and variety, showing the diversity in
   scenery of her various regions from Newfoundland to the Pacific, from the Arctic to
   Southern Ontario. Other titles which visually portray Canada's landscape are: J. A.
   Kraulis' *Canada: a landscape portrait* (Edmonton, Alberta: Hurtig, 1982); *Canada:
   pictures of a great land* (Agincourt, Ontario: Gage, 1982); *Scenic wonders of Canada*
   (Montreal: Reader's Digest, 1977); and, *Canada across the land* (Toronto: Collins,
   n.d.).

1

The Country and its People

4 **A day in the life of Canada.**
David Cohen, Rick Smolan.   Toronto: Collins, 1984. 221p.

On 8 June 1984 one hundred of the world's leading photojournalists congregated in Canada to work on the assignment of capturing the life of a nation in one twenty-four hour period – a visual time capsule for future generations. The hundreds of photographs in this volume were chosen from well over 100,000 shot that day, and provide a unique view of the country and its people.

5 **Canada: a celebration.**
Robert Fulford.   Toronto: Key Porter, 1983. 240p.

The history of Canada is encapsulated by Fulford, whose text is complemented with photographs of scenic views by John de Visser, one of Canada's leading photographers.

6 **Canada with love=Canada avec amour.**
Lorraine Monk.   Toronto: McClelland & Stewart, 1982. [n.p.]

Produced as a special tribute to the country in honour of the patriation of the Constitution of Canada. Photographs were selected from a nationwide competition sponsored by McClelland and Stewart publishers. This is a beautiful work with text by Harold Town and Louis Gareau-Des Bois.

7 **Treasures of Canada=Trésors du Canada.**
Toronto: Samuel-Stevens, 1981. 415p.

A photographic record of the treasures of Canada – art objects, artifacts, architecture, historical sites, natural features, technical achievements, etc. Taken together, these represent the people, land and culture of Canada, and encapsulate the individuality and richness of Canadian cultural life of the past and present.

2

Geography

General

8 **The natural landscapes of Canada: a study in regional earth science.**
J. Brian Bird. Toronto: John Wiley, 1980. 2nd ed. 260p.
Describes the major landforms in Canada in terms of both the underlying geology, and
contemporary views as to their geomorphological evolution. Though directed at the
informed reader, the text is sufficiently non-technical to be useful and informative to
the general observer – particularly those interested in, and conscious of, the diversity
of landscape and ecology in Canada.

9 **The industrial geography of Canada.**
Anthony Blackbourn, Robert G. Putnam. London: Croom Helm, 1984.
201p. (Croom Helm Industrial Geography Series).
The main purpose of this book is to explore the complex patterns of industrial
development and the intricate problems of individual industries and regions within
Canada. In doing so, it avoids the oversimplified analysis of Canada's industrial
economy which simply argues that Canada is a land with abundant natural resources, a
high cost processing and fabricating sector and a dispersed market which is expensive
to serve because of high transport costs.

10 **Canadian Geographic.**
Vanier, Ontario: Royal Canadian Geographical Society, 1930- . bi-
monthly.
The journal of the Royal Canadian Geographical Society, a non-profit educational
organization whose purpose is to advance geographical knowledge, and, in particular,
stimulate awareness of the significance of geography in Canada's development, well-
being and culture. The periodical is profusely illustrated. Readers interested in the
geography of Canada may also wish to consult *The Canadian Geographer=Le
Géographe Canadien* (Montreal: Canadian Association of Geographers, 1951-).

11 **Physical geography: the Canadian context.**
Allan Falconer, Barry D. Fahey, Russell D. Thompson.   Toronto:
McGraw-Hill Ryerson, 1974. 314p. bibliog.
Not only does this volume present a generalized picture of the physical geography of
the country, it goes beyond the introductory to provide surveys of Canadian research
in a number of subject areas, such as geomorphology, weather and climate, soils and
vegetation, etc. Each section is supported by a comprehensive bibliography. A
valuable but now somewhat dated textbook.

12 **Canada: a natural history.**
Tim Fitzharris, John Livingston.   Markham, Ontario: Viking Studio,
1988. 199p.
A volume published in association with, and on the occasion of, the 60th anniversary
of the Royal Canadian Geographical Society of Canada. This is a stunningly beautiful
work depicting in prose and photograph the country's landscape, flora and fauna.

13 **Gazetteer of Canada=Répertoire géographique du Canada.**
Ottawa: Canadian Permanent Committee on Geographical Names, 1952-.

In 1897 the Geographic Board of Canada was established to advise and decide on all
questions relating to geographical nomenclature in Canada. This Board was later
renamed the Canadian Board on Geographical Names, and later still reorganized (in
1961) as the Canadian Permanent Committee on Geographical Names which publishes
the official Gazetteer of Canada Series. Primary compilations for each of the provinces
are supplemented (usually annually) with new information, as well as additions or
corrections. Standard information includes name, feature (i.e. town, lake, river,
mountain, etc.), location and position.

14 **The Macmillan book of Canadian place names.**
William B. Hamilton.   Toronto: Macmillan, 1978. 340p.
Provides a selection of some 2,500 names from over 300,000 recorded place names in
the country. Selection was made on the basis of: size of place; the importance of the
place in terms of physical features; significance of place in terms of the history of the
country; and the general human interest of particular places in terms of the author's
personal judgement. The work is organized by province with each place name enjoying
a brief entry. Also of interest, though dated, is George Armstrong's *The origin and
meaning of place names in Canada* (Toronto: Macmillan, 1972).

15 **Across Canada: resources and regions.**
Christine Hammell, Robert Harshman.   Toronto: John Wiley, 1987.
2nd ed. 332p.
This is one of a large number of texts, suitable for the secondary or undergraduate
student as well as the general reader, which provide an overview of the discipline of
Canadian geography. Other, more recent, examples of such texts are: Gaston Giroux
and Gaston Joyal's *Geographie du Québec et du Canada* (Outremont, Quebec: Lidec,
1984 – an English edition is also available); J. H. Paterson's *North America: a
geography of Canada and the United States* (New York: Oxford University Press,
1984); Bruce W. Clark and John K. Wallace's *Canada: land of diversity* (Scarborough,

Ontario: Prentice-Hall, 1983); and Ralph Krueger and Ray Corder's *Canada: a new geography* (Toronto: Holt, Rinehart & Winston, 1982).

16 **Climate Canada.**
F. Kenneth Hare, Morley K. Thomas. Toronto: John Wiley, 1979. 230p.
Written for the general reader, this work provides a descriptive account of Canada's climates.

17 **Canada's natural environment: essays in applied geography.**
Edited by G. R. McBoyle, E. Sommerville. Toronto: Methuen, 1976. 264p.
Presents ten essays directed at the informed reader. Taken together the collection 'is concerned with the definition of the nature and scope of problems stemming from man-nature interactions within the contemporary Canadian ecumene, but its focus is upon actual and/or potential applications of the concepts, methods, tools and techniques developed by the family of academic specialties which may be grouped under the broad umbrella of environmental studies'. The topics discussed include environmental research, climate and weather, water resources, soil management, ecological planning, and environmental policies and planning.

18 **Heartland and hinterland: a geography of Canada.**
Edited by L. D. McCann. Scarborough, Ontario: Prentice-Hall, 1987. 2nd ed. 587p.
A readable text for the general observer or the student, which introduces Canadian regional geography, at a level beyond mere descriptive analysis. Each contributor in this collection examines the economic and social development of a region, explaining growth and change, the settlement of the area, and its urbanization. The essays also explore the ways in which regions interact with each other economically, socially, culturally, and politically.

19 **The boundaries of the Canadian Confederation.**
Norman Nicholson. Toronto: Macmillan in association with the Institute of Canadian Studies, Carleton University, 1979. 252p. bibliog. (The Carleton Library, vol. 115).
This book examines the evolution and location of boundaries within Canada, with reference to historical, political and economic factors which have played a rôle in determining these boundaries. The final emphasis, however, is upon the geographical reasons for Canadian boundaries and the results thereof. The volume includes a bibliography.

20 **Concepts and themes in the regional geography of Canada.**
J. Lewis Robinson. Vancouver: Talonbooks, 1983. 342p.
The author considers the regional geography of Canada from the viewpoint of geeographical concepts and principles in order to help examine many Canadian problems arising from the environment, resources and people. The work is divided first by various themes and then by the six regions of the country. A selection of references supports each division of the book.

21 **Studies in Canadian geography= Études sur la géographie du Canada.**
Edited by Louis Trotier. Toronto: University of Toronto Press, 1972. 6
vols.
Prepared for, and created by, the organizers of the 22nd International Geographical
Congress held in Montreal in 1972, this series was designed to present an overview of
the geographical research then current with regard to the regions of the country.
Volumes in the series are entitled: *The Atlantic provinces*; *Québec*; *Ontario*; *The
prairie provinces*; *British Columbia*; and *The north*.

22 **Canada: a geographical interpretation.**
Edited by John Warkentin. Toronto: Methuen, 1970. 608p.
An anthology of essays compiled and published as a centennial project by the
Canadian Association of Geographers. Twenty-two authorities contributed pieces
intended to record collectively the geographical change that has occurred in Canada
from 1867 to 1967. The overall purpose of the book was to provide a comprehensive,
balanced, geographical interpretation of the country.

Regional

British Columbia

23 **1001 British Columbia place names.**
G. P. V. Akrigg, Helen B. Akrigg. Vancouver: Discovery Press, 1973.
195p.
A selection of place names, their origins and history for Canada's westernmost
province. Though out of print, the interested toponymist should also consult John T.
Walbran's *British Columbia coast names 1592–1906* (Ottawa: Government Printing
Bureau, 1909).

24 **British Columbia: its resources and people.**
Edited by Charles N. Forward. Victoria, British Columbia:
Department of Geography, University of Victoria, 1987. 433p. (Western
Geographical Series, vol. 22).
By any measure the geographical features of the province of British Columbia are as
diverse, interesting and beautiful as any in the world. This anthology provides a
balanced coverage of the geography of the province, embracing themes ranging from
physical to human geography. The interested general reader can gain a sense of the
grandeur of this landscape from the following titles: Sherman Hines' *British Columbia*
(Toronto: McClelland & Stewart, 1982); Ian Smith's *The unknown island* (West
Vancouver: Douglas & McIntyre, 1982); Liz Bryan's *British Columbia: this favoured
land* (West Vancouver: Douglas & McIntyre, 1982); Menno Fieguth's *Vancouver
Island and the gulf islands* (Toronto: Oxford University Press, 1981); Bill Brooks'
British Columbia (Willowdale, Ontario: Hounslow, 1980); Carol Baker's *British
Columbia, the Pacific province* (Vancouver: Whitecap, 1980); Ulli Steltzer and
Catherine Kerr's *Coast of many faces* (Seattle, Washington: University of Washington
Press, 1979); and Liz Bryan's *Backroads of British Columbia* (Vancouver: Sunflower,
1975).

Northwest Territories

25 **The magnetic north.**
Mike Beedell. Toronto: Oxford University Press, 1983. [n.p.]
The north has shaped the Canadian identity. This work is a magnificent collection of images which reinforces the grandeur of that landscape. Other works of interest are: Sherman Hines' *The north* (Montreal: Four Seasons, 1984); *Kluane pinnacle of the Yukon* (Toronto: Doubleday, 1980); Peter Buerschaper's *Arctic journey: paintings, sketches, and reminiscences of a vanishing world* (Toronto: Pagurian, 1977); and *Canada's changing north* (Toronto: McClelland & Stewart, 1971). The more informed reader might wish to consult J. Brian Bird's *The physiography of Arctic Canada* (Baltimore, Maryland: Johns Hopkins Press, 1967).

26 **Yukon: places & names.**
R. C. Coutts. Sidney, British Columbia: Gray's Publishing, 1980.
294p.
An alphabetical listing of Yukon place names, providing information regarding the places, sites or features to which they apply, their locations and some historical background.

27 **Canadian nordicity: it's your north, too.**
Louis-Edmond Hamelin. Montreal: Harvest House, 1979. 373p.
This award winning study deals with the entirety of the Canadian north, not only the Territories but the northern areas of seven provinces. The author introduces the concept of 'nordicity'; that is, the 'state or level of being polar in the Northern Hemisphere'. Hamelin deftly develops his thesis weaving geography, ethnology, industry, settlement and communications, as well as corporate and governmental policies into a fabric which portrays contemporary life and development in the Canadian north.

Prairie provinces

28 **A region of the mind: interpreting the western Canadian plains.**
Edited by Richard Allen. Regina, Saskatchewan: Canadian Plains Research Center, University of Regina, 1977. 209p. (Canadian Plains Studies, vol. 1).
A number of works, directed at the informed as well as the general reader, treat the three prairie provinces as a region. This work, by way of a series of essays, surveys the course of research in the geography of the region. Though dated it serves to provide background for the interested reader. Other anthologies of a similar nature are: Nigel M. Waters' *Contemporary geography in western Canada* (Vancouver: Tantalus Research, 1980); and Benton M. Barr's *New themes in western Canadian geography: the Langara papers* (Vancouver: Tantalus Research, 1975). More popular titles with illustrations include: Courtney Milne's *Prairie light* (Saskatoon, Saskatchewan: Western Producer Prairie Books, 1985); and R. H. Macdonald's *Four seasons west* (Saskatoon, Saskatchewan: Western Producer Prairie Books, 1975).

29 **Place names of Manitoba.**
Penny Ham.   Saskatoon, Saskatchewan: Western Producer Prairie
Books, 1980. 155p.
'Manitoba's place names portray the music of her multilanguages, the melodies of her
ancient sagas, the rhythm of her Indian legends, and the stories of her pioneers'.
Almost 1,800 place names are listed and arranged in alphabetical order, providing
background detail on the origin and history of the place.

30 **Over 2000 place names of Alberta.**
Eric J. Holmgren, Patricia M. Holmgren.   Saskatoon, Saskatchewan:
Western Producer Prairie Books, 1976. 3rd ed. 309p.
This is a comprehensive source providing standard information as to location, name
origin and historical context.

31 **Saskatchewan landscapes.**
Rusty Macdonald.   Saskatoon, Saskatchewan: Western Producer
Prairie Books, 1980. 91p.
Popularly viewed as dominated by a flat, prairie landscape, much of the beauty of the
province is overlooked. Two-thirds of the area is heavily forested, with many lakes
dotting the Canadian Shield terrain of rock and hill. The prairie landscape itself is
extremely varied, encompassing ranges of hills and long-stretching valleys as opposed
to the prevailing view of a flat and uninteresting region. Other informative works
include: J. E. Jones' *Saskatchewan* (North Vancouver: Whitecap, 1983); and Menno
Fieguth's *Saskatchewan* (Toronto: Oxford University Press, 1980).

32 **The best of Alberta.**
Tom Radford, Harry Savage.   Edmonton, Alberta: Hurtig, 1987. 224p.
Without any doubt the landscape of Alberta is the most diverse in Canada. From the
grandeur of the Rocky Mountains to the desert of the badlands, from the forest, lakes
and rock formations of the Canadian Shield to the cosmopolitan urban centres,
Alberta claims special attention. Further relevant information may be found in: Robin
Savage's *Alberta* (North Vancouver: Whitecap, 1987); Sherman Hines' *Alberta*
(Toronto: McClelland & Stewart, 1981); and Bill Simpkins' *Chinook country: Alberta
south* (Toronto: Oxford University Press, 1979).

33 **What's in a name: the story behind Saskatchewan place names.**
E. T. Russell.   Saskatoon, Saskatchewan: Western Producer Prairie
Books, 1973. rev. ed. 350p.
Nearly 2,000 place names, with their origins, are identified. Entries contain text
outlining the derivation of the name, the location of the community and a short
historical sketch.

34 **Manitoba.**
Robert Taylor.   Toronto: Oxford University Press, 1981. [n.p.]
The life and landscape of Manitoba are portrayed in this volume. Another source is
Earl Johnson's *Manitoba montage* (Winnipeg, Manitoba: Panther, 1985).

Central Canada

35 Quebec.
Sherman Hines. Toronto: McClelland & Stewart, 1983. [n.p.]

The flavour of Quebec's rural and urban landscape is captured in photographs by this award winning photographer. Other similar works in English of interest to the reader would be: *Québec: an illustrated tour of 80 scenic sites* (Montreal: Reader's Digest, 1984); J. A. Kraulis' *Québec* (North Vancouver: Whitecap, 1982); John de Visser and Paul von Baich's *Quebec and the St. Lawrence* (Toronto: Oxford University Press, 1980); *Québec* (Toronto: Hounslow, 1973); Jean-Charles Harvey's *The many faces of Quebec* (Toronto: Macmillan, 1966).

36 Places in Ontario: their name origins and history.
Nick Mika, Helma Mika. Belleville, Ontario: Mika Publishing, 1977.
3 vols. bibliog. (Encyclopedia of Ontario).

Contains condensed histories of over 5,000 places in Ontario. Each brief article includes the origin of the name, location and topographical features, date of first settlement and names of settlers, historical highlights and population growth, important persons, events and industries. Also included are bibliographical sources. Complementing this work, and by the same authors, is *Historic sites of Ontario* (Belleville, Ontario: Mika Publishing, 1974). Floreen Ellen Carter's *Place names of Ontario* (London, Ontario: Phelps Publishing, 1984) may also be of interest.

37 Ontario: a bicentennial tribute.
Toronto: Key Porter, 1983. 160p.

This title is one of a multitude of volumes which record the diversity and beauty of the Ontario landscape, as well as the more academic aspects of that province's geography. Some of additional interest are: L. J. Chapman and D. F. Putnam's *The physiography of southern Ontario* (Toronto: Ontario Geological Survey, 1984); J. A. Kraulis' *Ontario* (North Vancouver: Whitecap, 1982); John de Visser's *Southwestern Ontario* (Toronto: Oxford University Press, 1982); Paul von Baich's *Northern Ontario* (Toronto: Oxford University Press, 1981); Peter Fowler's *Niagara* (Toronto: Oxford University Press, 1981); and William Gillard and Thomas Tooke's *The Niagara escarpment: from Tobermory to Niagara Falls* (Toronto: University of Toronto Press, 1975).

38 Répertoire toponymique du Québec. (Index of Quebec place names.)
Quebec: Editeur officiel, 1979. 1,199p.

Lists and locates some 75,000 place names (cites, towns, hamlets, municipalities, rivers, lakes, etc.) in Quebec.

Atlantic provinces

39 **Prince Edward Island.**
Wayne Barrett, Edith Robinson. Toronto: Oxford University Press,
1977. [n.p.]
Beauty and tranquillity characterize the landscape of Canada's smallest province. This
work, and the others listed, provide the reader with unforgettable images. Other works
of interest include: *Spirit of place* (Toronto: Oxford University Press, 1982); and
Lionel Stevenson's *The island* (Charlottetown, Prince Edward Island: Ragweed Press,
1982).

40 **Image of Acadia.**
Roméo Courmier. Toronto: Oxford University Press, 1980. 86p.
The introduction to this book explains: 'The place-name Acadia comes from the word
arcady or arcadia, a term of Greek mythology that denotes the ideal land of rural
peace and happiness'. The history of New Brunswick has been anything but tranquil,
and has seen considerable turbulence. The landscape, however, does not reflect this
troubled past. This visual representation portrays the diverse nature of the province.
Other works of interest are: Stuart Trueman's *The colour of New Brunswick=La
couleur du Nouveau-Brunswick* (Willowdale, Ontario: Hounslow, 1981); and John
Porteous' *New Brunswick images/Images Nouveau-Brunswick* (Fredericton, New
Brunswick: Brunswick Press, 1977).

41 **Atlantic Canada.**
Sherman Hines. Toronto, Vancouver: Clarke, Irwin & Company,
1979. [n.p.]
This is one of a number of visual portraits of the landscape of Atlantic Canada. One
other such work is: Anne Brooks' *Atlantic Canada* (Don Mills, Ontario: Collins, 1984).

42 **Nova Scotia.**
Sherman Hines. Halifax, Nova Scotia: Nimbus, 1986. 158p.
Although Nova Scotia is peninsular, it has many of the characteristics of an island, and
various physical features add to its uniqueness. The bays and inlets of its coastline, and
its inland valleys, provide the observer with natural landscapes of interest and beauty.
The ruggedness of Cape Breton provides yet another dimension to the region's
geographical diversity. Books of interest include: David Street's *The Cabot trail*
(Toronto: Gage, 1979); Owen Fitzgerald's *Cape Breton* (Toronto: Oxford University
Press, 1978); Harry Bruce's *Nova Scotia* (Toronto: Hownslow, 1975); and Ernest
Buckler's *Nova Scotia: window on the sea* (Toronto: McClelland & Stewart, 1974).

43 **The peopling of Newfoundland: essays in historical geography.**
Edited by John J. Mannion. St. John's, Newfoundland: Institute of
Social and Economic Research, Memorial University of Newfoundland,
1977. 289p. (Social and Economic Papers, vol. 8).
The primary purpose of this volume is to analyse the population process of
Newfoundland. Not only does the work focus on the inflow of migrants and settlers, its
essays consider many questions relating to economic geography, as well as the cultural

landscape. Readers of this book will quickly realize that sense of place is particularly strong in Newfoundland and Labrador, and in consequence a number of other works focus on 'place' in terms of descriptions of the landscape, accompanied by illustrations. Some examples of these are: *Newfoundland and Labrador* (Toronto: Oxford University Press, 1979); Ben Hanson's *Newfoundland portfolio* (St. John's, Newfoundland: Breakwater, 1977); Harold Horwood's *Newfoundland* (Toronto: Macmillan, 1977); Farley Mowat's *This rock within the sea: a heritage lost* (Toronto: McClelland & Stewart, 1976); and Harold Horwood and Stephen Taylor's *Beyond the road: portraits & visions of Newfoundlanders* (Toronto: Van Nostrand Reinhold, 1976).

44 **Place-names and places of Nova Scotia.**
Belleville, Ontario: Mika, 1982. 2nd ed. 751p.
More than 2,300 Nova Scotia names are included in this volume. Entries provide name derivation, topographical distribution, and a short local history.

45 **Geographical names of New Brunswick.**
Alan Rayburn. Ottawa: Surveys and Mapping Branch, Department of Energy, Mines and Resources, 1975. 304p. (Toponymy Study, 2).
This study includes some 4,000 place names which have interesting anecdotes connected with them – whether historical, geographical or concerned with folklore. Information is recorded in point form following an alphabetical arrangement.

46 **Geographical names of Prince Edward Island.**
Alan Rayburn. Ottawa: Surveys and Mapping Branch, Department of Energy, Mines and Resources. 135p. (Toponymy Study, 1).
The location, name origin and general historical information on nearly 1,700 place names are provided in this study.

47 **Place names of the Avalon Peninsula of the island of Newfoundland.**
E. R. Seary. Toronto: University of Toronto Press, 1971. 383p. bibliog. (Memorial University Series, 2).
History, as reflected in the systematic study of place names, is the focus of this book. It is composed of an historical and analytical introduction as well as two bibliographies – one of maps, the other of texts, and is essential for geography studies, history and cartography.

Maps, atlases and gazetteers

48 **Canada gazetteer atlas.**
Ottawa: Macmillan in cooperation with Department of Energy, Mines and Resources Canada and the Canadian Government Publishing Centre, Department of Supply and Services Canada, 1980. 164p.
As a companion to the *National atlas of Canada* (q.v.), this work is comprised of two main components: the maps themselves, providing physical features, roads, railways,

and places; and a gazetteer to the places and their physical features. It is intended that the work be revised and reissued following each national census.

49 The northpart of America.
Verner Coolie, Basil Stuart-Stubbs   Toronto: Academic Press Canada, 1979. 292p. bibliog.

The volume is a magnificent collection of map reproductions (many in colour) selected and arranged so as to illustrate the development and dissemination of knowledge about the north part of America. Accompanying textual material provides information to enhance the interest of the reader in the maps and their historical context. The maps provided span the period beginning in 1562 and ending in 1875. A carto-bibliography and a bibliography are provided.

50 Historical atlas of Canada: from the beginning to 1800.
Edited by R. Cole Harris.   Toronto: University of Toronto Press, 1987. 198p.

This is the first volume in what is intended to be a three volume atlas – in its preparation the work is the largest cartographic project ever undertaken in Canada. The other two volumes in preparation will be entitled *The nineteenth century* and *Addressing the twentieth century* respectively. Volume 1 is unprecedented in its scholarship and its physical production. It deals with the prehistory of Canada and ends about 1800, when the principal exports were still fish and furs. Taken together it is expected that the three volumes will provide for the general reader a history of the processes of social and economic change within Canada, and the political responses to such changes. This is a reference set of lasting value, made available also in a French edition. Supported by numerous bibliographical notes, and with cartography by Geoffrey J. Matthews.

51 Hydrological atlas of Canada=Atlas hydrologique du Canada.
Ottawa: Minister of Supply and Services Canada, 1978. [n.p.]

Water resources are an important part of Canada's physical geography and this work, compiled by the Canadian National Committee for the International Hydrological Decade, serves as a source of information for water management and as a general reference document on water resources in Canada.

52 The national atlas of Canada.
Ottawa: Macmillan in association with the Department of Energy, Mines and Resources and Information Canada, 1974. 4th ed. 254p.

This national atlas is intended to give 'the extent of the national domain, the variety of its natural resources and climatic conditions'. Though somewhat dated, this work remains useful. The reader should note that a new edition has recently been promised. Also useful as a general atlas is the *Atlas of Canada* (Montreal: Reader's Digest in conjunction with the Canadian Automobile Association, 1981).

53 **The maps of Canada: a guide to official Canadian maps, charts, atlases and gazetteers.**
N. L. Nicholson, L. M. Sebert.   Hamden, Connecticut: Archon, 1981. 251p.

A survey of official maps and chart series produced on Canada which includes an instructive essay on the history and development of the mapping of Canada.

Special features

54 **The Arctic world.**
Fred Bruemmer.   Toronto: Key Porter, 1985. 256p.

A visually beautiful and informative book. The Arctic encompasses some twenty-eight million square miles incorporating parts of seven countries. Although it is partitioned by geo-political boundaries, it is one natural realm, where plants, animals and humans have learned to exist in natural balance. This work concentrates on Canadian territory, while looking at the Arctic as a whole.

55 **Canada's national parks.**
R. D. Lawrence.   Toronto: Collins, 1983. 288p.

One of the most beautiful and one of the best overviews of Canadian national parks – those areas representative of the natural wilderness and rich variety of landscape, animals and plants that make up Canada.

56 **Hotsprings of western Canada: a complete guide.**
Jim McDonald, Donna Pollock, Bob McDermot.   Vancouver: Labrador Tea Company, 1978. 162p.

Ninety-four hotsprings, accessible to the public (either directly by car or by foot along hiking paths) have been identified. Information provided includes location, rating, volume and flow, temperature, character of water, access and other descriptive or historical information.

57 **Canada/the mountains.**
Randy Morse.   Toronto: McClelland & Stewart, 1980. 126p.

Perhaps the most significant feature of the Canadian landscape – and this is a landscape with more than its share of special features – are the mountains of the western region, primarily those in the provinces of Alberta and British Columbia, as well as the Yukon territory. Innumerable books have been produced over the years in order to quench Canadians' insatiable thirst for material on this subject. Some other titles of interest are: Randy Morse's *The mountains of Canada* (Edmonton, Alberta: Hurtig, 1978); Shin Sugino's *The Rockies: high where the wind is lonely* (Toronto: Gage, 1978); and Andy Russell's *The Rockies* (Edmonton, Alberta: Hurtig, 1975).

58 **Columbia Icefield: a solitude of ice.**
Bart Robinson. Banff, Alberta: Altitude Publishing, 1981. 103p.
bibliog.
An account for the general reader of the natural and human history of the Columbia Icefield, an immense slab of shifting blue ice spanning the border of Banff and Jasper National Parks. The Icefield forms the geographic and hydrographic apex of North America, as well as characterizing the surrounding peaks of the Rocky Mountains. With photography by Don Harmon.

59 **Forest regions of Canada.**
J. S. Rowe. Ottawa: Canadian Forestry Service Department of the Environment, 1972. 172p.
Forest regions of Canada provides a general description of the forest geography of Canada, from the east to west coasts and from the USA borders to the Arctic and alpine tundra. Text on the soil, geology and climate, and maps indicating climate and physiography, have been included.

60 **The forests of British Columbia.**
Cameron Young. North Vancouver: Whitecap, 1985. 192p.
Canada is particularly fortunate in the size and quality of its forests. The forest as a staple resource was fundamental in the economic development of the country and today forests continue to support a large and lucrative industry. However, the forest landscape is equally important for its value as habitat for wildlife and for its cultural and recreational properties. Nowhere in Canada is this more true than in the diverse terrain of the province of British Columbia. This work is a particularly handsome and informative book which introduces the reader to these forests.

Travel guides

61 **Canadian book of the road.**
Montreal: Reader's Digest in conjunction with the Canadian Automobile Association, 1980. rev. ed. [n.p.]
A motoring guide to every part of Canada which can be reached by road. It presents such attractions as recreational locations, scenic wonders, historical sites, etc. Organized by 'road units', each in turn providing information which includes: maps; a description of the region; photographs, illustrations and descriptions of attractions; and special features. Colour plates throughout.

62 **Travel in Canada: a guide to information sources.**
Nora Teresa Corley. Detroit, Michigan: Gale Research Company, 1983. 294p. (Geography and Travel Information Guide Series, vol. 4).
Aimed at the traveller who has no personal knowledge of the country, region, or city in question, this information guide looks at Canada as a whole, then Canada by regions. Each section has then been further sub-divided by subject, including: guidebooks; periodicals; atlases and maps; parks; accommodations; attractions and events; recreation and sport; and, cities.

63 **Where to Eat in Canada.**
Anne Hardy.   Ottawa: Oberon, 1971- . annual.
This guide is considered the standard for the country, the restaurant-goer's 'who's who'.

64 **First-class Canada: the discriminating traveller's guide to the country's best hotels, restaurants, shops and entertainment.**
Mechtild Hoppenrath, Charles Oberdorf.   Toronto: Collins, 1987. 256p.
As admitted by the authors in the book's introduction, '[this] is not a comprehensive guidebook, but a highly selective, personal and opinionated one'. Hotels, restaurants, entertainments and shops in eight Canadian cities are selected and commented upon according to how the authors perceived their respective merits.

65 **Canada: a travel survival kit.**
Mark Lightbody.   Victoria, Australia: Lonely Planet Publications, 1989. 3rd ed. 476p.
The traveller in and to Canada is served by the standard host of travel guides, of which this is a good example. Those which are commonplace include: *Birnbaum's Canada 1989* (Boston, Massachusetts: Houghton Mifflin, 1989); *Fodor's 89: Canada* (New York, London: Fodor's Publications, 1989); *Frommer's dollarwise guide to Canada* (New York: Simon & Schuster, 1987); *The Penguin guide to Canada: 1989* (New York: Penguin, 1989); and Ted Kosoy's *Kosoy's travel guide to Canada* (Toronto: Kosoy Travel Guides, 1987). There is also an extensive literature of guides for various regions, provinces, cities and parks of the country. The traveller is encouraged to write to the appropriate agencies to acquire the requisite publications.

66 **Tourism in Canada: selected issues and options.**
Edited by Peter E. Murphy.   Victoria, British Columbia: Department of Geography, University of Victoria, 1983. 334p. (Western Geographical Series, vol. 21).
Tourism is one of Canada's largest industries, involving over 100,000 businesses and countless people. With the direct and indirect spending resulting from tourism exceeding $32 billion (£16 billion) in 1982 one would expect that the industry itself should demand considerable study. This volume, however, is one of few on the industry. The essays included identify and comment upon key issues which will influence this sector in the years to come. Topics discussed include: the nature of the industry; trends for the 1980s; tourism and the resource base; tourism and the aging population; tourism in the various regions; and tourism and park management.

67 **The Canadian bed & breakfast guide.**
Gerda Pantel.   Toronto: Fitzhenry & Whiteside, 1988. 4th ed. 337p.
Considered the best guide for those travellers who are looking for an alternative to hotel accommodation.

68 **Railway country: across Canada by train.**
Dudley Witney, Brian D. Johnson. Toronto: Key Porter, 1985. 200p.

A fascinating as well as handsome book, documenting one of the more romantic, scenic and possibly disappearing methods of crossing Canada; that is via the 'Canadian', the 'glamour train of the Canadian Pacific'. The 'Canadian' covers some three thousand miles in four and a half days, travelling a greater distance than any passenger train in the world with the exception of the Soviet Trans-Siberian Express. Alas, it will be missed! See also George Galt's *Whistlestop: a journey across Canada* (Toronto: Methuen, 1987); Bill Coo's *Scenic rail guide to western Canada* (Toronto: Greey de Pencier, 1982) and *Scenic rail guide to central & Atlantic Canada* (Toronto: Greey de Pencier, 1983).

Flora and Fauna

General

69 **Wildlife of Canada.**
Bill Brooks. Toronto: Hounslow, 1976. [n.p.]
Canadians have always had an interest in animals and in their wilderness homes. In consequence, wildlife books, like those dealing with the natural landscape itself, have been, and are today, popular with Canadians. Typically, this genre of publishing has produced works combining prose and photography in a way which yields books of both interest and beauty. The main title is but one of many such titles. Others representative of the genre include: Fred Bruemmer's *Arctic animals: a celebration of survival* (Toronto: McClelland & Stewart, 1986); Doug Gilroy's *Prairie wildlife: the best of Doug Gilroy's nature photography* (Saskatoon, Saskatchewan: Western Producer Prairie Books, 1985); Monte Hummel's *Arctic wildlife* (Toronto: Key Porter, 1984); Dennis and Esther Schmidt's *Western wildlife* (Toronto: Oxford University Press, 1983); Tim Fitzharris' *The wild prairie: a natural history of the western plains* (Toronto: Oxford University Press, 1983); and Don Blood and Tom W. Hall's *Rocky mountain wildlife* (Saanichton, British Columbia: Hancock House, 1976).

70 **On the brink: endangered species in Canada.**
J. A. Burnett (et al.). Saskatoon, Saskatchewan: Western Producer Prairie Books, 1989. 192p.
Within Canada approximately one in forty species of vertebrates are endangered or threatened, and this book is an attempt to inform the public about this serious loss. In general the authors call upon Canadians to change attitudes and habits, as well as to act politically with regard to this problem. Endangered species are identified and organized by habitat, i.e. marine coastal areas, prairies, Arctic regions, etc. Essays are illustrated, with a map showing the location of each species. Extensive references are also included.

Flora and Fauna. General

71 **Canadian wildlife and man.**
Anne Innis Dagg. Toronto: McClelland & Stewart, 1974. 192p.
A general work dealing with the interrelationship between wildlife and man, outlining Canadian problems concerning wildlife, as well as proposing solutions. The author provides a history of wildlife in Canada and discusses the relationship of wildlife with three main geographical areas (forests, agricultural lands and urban areas). She examines the failure of management programmes which have resulted in the extinction of species and looks at the effects of pollution and of man-made structures on the wildlife habitat in general.

72 **Equinox: the Magazine of Canadian Discovery.**
Camden East, Ontario: Telemedia Publishing, 1981- . bi-monthly.
Equinox contains photo essays on topics relating to nature, natural history, the environment and Canadian flora and fauna. Of interest also to the reader are: *Seasons* (Don Mills, Ontario: Federation of Ontario Naturalists, 1960-); and, *Nature Canada* (Ottawa: Canadian Nature Federation, 1972-).

73 **Working for wildlife: the beginning of preservation in Canada.**
Janet Foster. Toronto: University of Toronto Press, 1978. 283p. bibliog.
Over a period of thirty-four years, a small group of remarkably dedicated civil servants managed to turn their own goals of wildlife preservation into a declared government policy. The contribution they made to Canadian wildlife preservation – and the determination, understanding and foresight they showed in pursuit of this aim – forms the subject of this book.

74 **Endangered spaces: the future for Canada's wilderness.**
Edited by Monte Hummel. Toronto: Key Porter, 1989. 288p. bibliog.
In a series of essays, noted and respected conservationists discuss questions relating to what has happened to our wilderness areas, what is happening today, and what must happen in the future in order to preserve these important natural resources. Places are broadly divided into sections dealing with: legacies from the past; current issues and perspectives; the state of wilderness across Canada today; and strategies for the future. This contains a number of useful appendices, plus a listing of conservation organizations, and a selected bibliography. A handsome book in its own right.

75 **The illustrated natural history of Canada.**
Toronto: NSL Natural Science of Canada, 1970-74. 12 vols.
This series, designed with a visual format and directed to the general reader, was devoted to explaining and illustrating the natural formation and development of Canada. The first nine volumes of the series dealt with the formation of the mountains, plains, forests and lakes, and the development and evolution of the plants and animals. The initial series was augmented by three additional volumes which dealt with the fauna of the country. In addition to the introductory volume, the initial series was comprised of: Franklin Russell's *The Atlantic coast*; Ken Lefolii's *The St. Lawrence valley*; Robert Thomas Allen's *The Great Lakes*; Barbara Moon's *The Canadian Shield*; Max Braithwaite's *The western plains*; R. Yorke Edwards' *The mountain barrier*; Fred Bodsworth's *The Pacific coast*; and Douglas Wilkinson's *The Arctic coast*. The subsequent volumes were: *The nature of fish*; *The nature of mammals*; and *The nature of birds*.

76   **The natural history of Canada.**
      R. D. Lawrence.   Toronto: Key Porter, 1988. 304p.
An absolutely first-rate work, directed to the general reader, characterizing the nature
of Canada. This sumptuously illustrated volume relates the story of the vast Canadian
landscape, its geography, climate, topography, plant life, and wildlife. The best general
guide on the topic available. Its only shortfall is its lack of further readings or a
bibliography.

77   **Sea of slaughter.**
      Farley Mowat.   Toronto: McClelland & Stewart, 1984. 438p.
Many Canadian writers of the past and present have written eloquently and
persuasively about the country's natural habitat – its wonders and also the problems
brought about through man's use and abuse of the environment. Mowat is one of the
more recent and articulate of these writers sounding the alarm with regard to wildlife
preservation issues and the interested reader is directed to his many books on natural
life. This work, arguably his best, is a forceful call to cease the devastation occurring to
animate life. It is a book 'about a massive diminution of the entire body corporate of
animate creation . . . this record of our outrageous behaviour in and around the Sea of
Slaughter will help us comprehend the consequences of unbridled greed'.

78   **The worlds of Ernest Thompson Seton.**
      Ernest Thompson Seton, edited by John G. Samson.   New York:
      Alfred A. Knopf, 1976. 204p.
Few would argue that Ernest Thompson Seton is ranked as Canada's premier
naturalist. Certainly he was the country's most prolific writer of nature books and
animal stories. Seton also was an artist, credited with nearly 8,000 paintings and
drawings, most of which depict creatures in the wild. This work provides a convenient
introduction both to the stories and the drawings of this remarkable author and
naturalist. Represented here are fifty-seven paintings, reproduced in full colour,
complemented by sketches and selections from his books, journals, articles and notes
on nature.

79   **From the edge of extinction: the fight to save endangered species.**
      Darryl Stewart.   Toronto: McClelland & Stewart, 1978. 191p. bibliog.
As the book's frontispiece comments: 'Man's population explosion increasingly
threatens the environments of many animals with whom he shares the earth. He traps,
shoots, and poisons indiscriminately. He logs the forests and drains the wetlands. His
pollution of land, water, and air, and his destruction of wildlife habitats, endanger
scores of species. By these means he reduces some of the rarest, most beautiful, most
superbly adapted species of our wildlife heritage to the brink of extinction'. A
thoughtful work for the general reader, which includes a bibliography. A similar title
of interest is David Grainger's *Animals in peril: a guide to the endangered animals of
Canada and the United States* (Toronto: Pagurian Press, 1978).

80   **Sciencescape: the nature of Canada.**
      David T. Suzuki, Hans Blohm, Marjorie Harris.   Toronto: Oxford
      University Press, 1986. [n.p.]
Canadians take great pride, indeed revel, in the beauty and majesty of the landscape
and of nature. These feelings have manifested themselves in the publication of many,
many books which combine text and photography to celebrate the Canadian landscape

19

and its natural wonders. Other works representative of this genre are: John and Janet Foster's *Adventures in wild Canada* (Toronto: McClelland & Stewart, 1984); Tim Fitzharris' *The island: a natural history of Vancouver Island* (Toronto: Oxford University Press, 1983); Doug Gilroy's *Parkland portraits: some natural history of the prairie parklands* (Saskatoon, Saskatchewan: Western Producer Prairie Books, 1979); Andy Russell's *Alpine Canada* (Edmonton, Alberta: Hurtig, 1979).

Fauna

Mammals

81 The mammals of Canada.
A. W. F. Banfield. Toronto: University of Toronto Press for the National Museum of Natural Sciences, National Museums of Canada, 1977. 438p.

There are a number of good, general books on mammals in Canada. This work is highly regarded, as it provides a popular account of the mammals of Canada at a level which is useful for students, lay readers and professional biologists. To this end less emphasis has been placed on the descriptions and distributions of the subspecies. Listed here are 196 species of recent mammals known to have occurred since historic times in Canada or in the coastal waters. Information provided includes habits, environment, distribution, reproduction and economic value. The introduction to the work provides a valuable guide to other works and references. Other titles of interest to the general reader are: Adrian Forsyth's *Mammals of the Canadian wild* (Camden East, Ontario: Camden House, 1985); and, Frederick H. Wooding's *Wild mammals of Canada* (Toronto: McGraw-Hill Ryerson, 1982).

82 Marine mammals of eastern north Pacific and Arctic waters.
Edited by Delphine Haley. Seattle, Washington: Pacific Search Press, 1978. 256p.

An introduction to the whales and dolphins common to west coast Canadian waters. See also Erich Hoyt's *The whales of Canada* (Camden East, Ontario: Camden House, 1984).

83 The mammals of eastern Canada.
Randolph L. Peterson. Toronto: Oxford University Press, 1966. 465p. bibliog.

This standard work combines essential scientific details on 122 species of mammal from eastern Canada with descriptive information in a manner that should be easily understood by the general reader. An extensive bibliography, although somewhat dated, is included. An additional related reference would be Anne Innis Dagg's *Mammals of Ontario* (Waterloo, Ontario: Otter Press, 1974).

84   **The North American buffalo: a critical study of the species in its wild
state.**
Frank Gilbert Roe.   Toronto: University of Toronto Press, 1970.
2nd ed. 991p.

The prehistory and early history of western Canada was inextricably linked to the
buffalo. As stated in the introduction: 'The presence of this animal has deeply affected
the civilization of the North American continent – perhaps more vitally than has ever
been the case with any other single species – in its indigenous environment in any
portion of the globe'. For this reason this classic work, telling the story of the buffalo,
deserves a special place in any listing of Canadian fauna.

85   **Wild mammals of western Canada.**
Arthur Savage, Candace Savage.   Saskatoon, Saskatchewan: Western
Producer Prairie Books, 1981. 209p.

Western Canada is home to 160 different species of wild mammals. This work
describes and illustrates seventy representative species. Aimed at the general reader,
the text presents the natural history, behaviour, habitat and ecology of the species
included. A reasonable list of references is provided.

86   **Handbook of Canadian mammals: 1 marsupials and insectivores.**
C. G. van Zyll de Jong.   Ottawa: National Museum of Natural
Sciences, National Museums of Canada, 1983. 210p. bibliog.

The first in a series of works which promise to contribute to a wider appreciation and
understanding of Canadian mammal fauna. This volume is intended as a basic
reference for students, professional biologists and naturalists. It aims to provide an up-
to-date summary of the systematics, distribution and life history of all free-living
species of mammals, other than man, that occur or that have occurred, in Canada in
the past. Useful primarily for the informed reader. A bibliography is included. Volume
2 of the *Handbook* is entitled *Bats* (Ottawa: National Museum of Natural Sciences,
1985).

Birds

87   **The birds of Canada.**
W. Earl Godfrey.   Ottawa: National Museum of Natural Sciences,
National Museums of Canada, 1979. 428p.

Canadians are fascinated by birds – scores of books have been devoted to the subject.
This standard work includes descriptions of 518 species, 431 of which are depicted in
colour. A substantial list of references is provided. Other general books of interest
include, but are not limited to: Candace Savage's *The wonder of Canadian birds*
(Saskatoon, Saskatchewan: Western Producer Prairie Books, 1985); J. C. Finlay's *A
bird-finding guide to Canada* (Edmonton, Alberta: Hurtig, 1984); John P. S.
Mackenzie's *The complete outdoorsman's guide to birds of Canada and eastern North
America* (Toronto: McGraw Hill Ryerson, 1976); and Terence Michael Shortt's *Wild
birds of Canada and the Americas* (Toronto: Pagurian Press, 1977).

88 **Birds of North America.**
David A. Hancock.   Don Mills, Ontario: General Publishing, 1973.
4 vols.
Four volumes of this series are of interest to Canadians: *Birds of the Atlantic provinces*; *Birds of Ontario and Quebec*; *Birds of Alberta, Saskatchewan and Manitoba*; and, *Birds of British Columbia*. These works are for the general reader, perhaps even the secondary school student. Each volume supplies general information about the birds of the region, identifying the bird groups and providing information on birdwatching.

89 **Glen Loates birds of North America.**
Ross James.   Scarborough, Ontario: Cerebrus Publishing/Prentice-Hall, 1979. [n.p.].
The beautiful paintings of Glen Loates, accompanied by the profiles prepared by the author, provide not only a handsome portfolio for the coffee-table, but contribute to the reader's understanding of birds and their various rôles in nature.

90 **Birds of the West Coast.**
J. F. Lansdowne.   Boston, Massachusetts: Houghton Mifflin, 1976-1980. 2 vols.
Based on their beauty alone, each of Lansdowne's works demands a separate entry. Alas, this is not possible. Interested readers are encouraged, however, to treat themselves to these exquisite works of art. The text of these volumes is interesting and informative, but perhaps even greater enjoyment comes from one's appreciation of the paintings and drawings. Other titles include: *Birds of the northern forest* (Toronto, Montreal: McClelland & Stewart, 1966); and *Birds of the eastern forest* (Toronto, Montreal: McClelland & Stewart, 1968).

91 **North American birds of prey.**
William Mansell.   Toronto: Gage, 1980. 176p. bibliog.
This work describes sixteen diurnal birds of prey, illustrated by colour plates. Introductory essays provide background information on these fascinating birds. A bibliography is included.

92 **Canadian songbirds and their ways.**
Trudy Rising, Jim Rising.   Montreal: Tundra Books, 1982. 176p. bibliog.
A work best classified as an authoritative, coffee-table book. This description, however, should take nothing away from what is a readable, interesting and handsome publication. The book is divided into three sections: Part I is a general survey of the biology of birds; Part II follows the cycle of the birds and describes the varied ways they court, mate, build nests, defend themselves, etc.; Part III covers the individual families of perching birds that are represented in Canada, and describes the characteristics of each. Includes a number of maps, a glossary and a bibliography.

93 **Arctic birds of Canada.**
L. L. Snyder.   Toronto: University of Toronto Press, 1957. 310p.
Detailed information with regard to birds common to the more northerly region of the country. Text provides information on: status; habitat; characteristics; and general

commentary, i.e. additional names, etc. Richly illustrated with line drawings by T.M. Shortt.

94   **Birds of Ontario.**
     J. Murray Speirs.   Toronto: Natural Heritage/Natural History Inc.,
     1985. 2 vols.
Bird books, either identification guides or more authoritative catalogues, either directed at the layperson or the expert, have been produced for most regions of the country. *Birds of Ontario* is one of the more attractive and authoritative of these publications, produced to encompass a geo-political region. Other good examples of this style might be: Robie W. Tufts' *Birds of Nova Scotia* (Halifax, Nova Scotia: Nimbus, 1986); W. Ray Salt and Jim R. Salt's *The birds of Alberta* (Edmonton, Alberta: Hurtig, 1976); or Doug Gilroy's *Prairie birds in color* (Saskatoon, Saskatchewan: Western Producer Prairie Books, 1976).

Fish

95   **Pacific fishes of Canada.**
     J. L. Hart.   Ottawa: Fisheries Research Board of Canada, 1973. 740p.
     bibliog. (Bulletin no. 180).
Includes the fishes found in salt water off the Canadian Pacific coast, thus containing descriptions of 325 kinds of fish. Each account of a species is headed by the common name followed by the scientific name and comments. The description deals with shape and other characteristics, including size, life history, range and distribution. Includes an extensive bibliography. Books of interest to the more general reader are: Andy Lamb and Phil Edgell's *Coastal fishes of the Pacific northwest* (Madeira Park, British Columbia: Harbour, 1986); and Stefani Hewlett and K. Gilbey Hewlett's *Sea life of the Pacific northwest* (Toronto: McGraw-Hill Ryerson, 1976).

96   **Freshwater fishes of Canada.**
     W. B. Scott, E. J. Crossman.   Ottawa: Fisheries Research Board of
     Canada, 1973. 966p. (Bulletin no. 184).
A thoroughly researched, meticulously documented compendium on the identification, distribution, biology, and economic importance of the freshwater fishes of Canada. Provided here are facts and figures on all species. Descriptions are based on examinations of specimens carried out expressly for the work. Numerous maps graphically present the range of species, including world distribution if relevant. Drawings and colour photographs provide the user with a high level of accuracy and realism in terms of identification. There are over 1,400 references scattered through the work as well as 'Suggested Reading' sections. Other recommended works are: M. C. Healey and R. R. Wallace's *Canadian aquatic resources* (Ottawa: Department of Fisheries and Oceans, 1987); J. D. McPhail and C. C. Lindsey's *Freshwater fishes of northwestern Canada and Alaska* (Ottawa: Fisheries Research Board of Canada, 1970); and W. B. Scott's *Freshwater fishes of eastern Canada* (Toronto: University of Toronto Press, 1967).

97 **Atlantic fishes of Canada.**
W. B. Scott, M. G. Scott.   Toronto: University of Toronto Press in
cooperation with the Minister of Fisheries and Oceans and the Canadian
Government Publishing Centre, Supply and Services Canada, 1988.
731p. (Canadian Bulletin of Fisheries and Aquatic Sciences, no. 219).
An authoritative reference book on the fishes off the 21,000 miles of the Canadian
Atlantic coastline from the Georges Bank to Cape Chidley. An introductory essay
provides an overview of the oceanography of the Canadian Atlantic and neighbouring
waters. In addition, there is an extensive list of references.

Miscellaneous

98 **Introduction to Canadian amphibians and reptiles.**
Francis R. Cook.   Ottawa: National Museum of Natural Sciences,
National Museums of Canada, 1984. 200p.
A handbook of Canadian herpetology which treats all species of amphibians and
reptiles recorded in Canada. This authoritative guide provides information relating to
identification as well as general information on natural history. More popular
treatments can be found in two works by Barbara Froom, entitled: *Amphibians of
Canada* (Toronto: McClelland & Stewart, 1982); and *The snakes of Canada* (Toronto:
McClelland & Stewart, 1972).

99 **Canada and its insect fauna.**
Edited by H. V. Danks.   Ottawa: Entomological Society of Canada,
1978. 573p. (Memoirs of the Entomological Society of Canada, vol.
108).
Brings together diverse materials for an understanding of the insect fauna of the
country. The papers included herein explore the physical environment and distribution
of insects in Canada, with further details of general problems encountered by this
fauna in relation to Canadian conditions.

Flora

100 **Budd's flora of the Canadian prairie provinces.**
Archibald C. Budd, edited by J. Looman, K.F. Looman.   Ottawa:
Research Branch, Agriculture Canada, 1987. rev. ed. 863p.
Previously published with the title *Wild plants of the Canadian prairies*, the work is
directed at the amateur botanist, the farmer and rancher, as well as the researcher. It
aims to include all native species presently known to occur in the prairie provinces, as
well as species, native or introduced, which are likely to be found along roads,
railroads, rivers, and lakeshores. See also such titles as: Jan Looman's *Prairie grasses:
identified and described by vegetative characters* (Ottawa: Minister of Supply and
Services Canada, 1982); H. J. Scoggan's *Flora of Manitoba* (Ottawa: Minister of
Northern Affairs and Natural Resources, 1957); and P. A. Rydberg's *Flora of the
Rocky Mountains and adjacent plains* (New York: Hafner, 1954).

101 **Wild flowers of British Columbia.**
Lewis J. Clark.   Sidney, British Columbia: Gray's Publishing, 1973.
591p.
Some 900 species of flowering plants are described, and illustrated by 640 coloured
plates. The arrangement of contents is alphabetical, genera within each family, species
within each genera.

102 **Wildflowers of Canada.**
Tim Fitzharris.   Toronto: Oxford University Press, 1986. 156p.
This is one of a number of excellent books for the general reader which highlight some
of the wildflowers of Canada. It contains 116 representative species, classed according
to habitat, i.e. woodlands, wetlands, prairies and meadows, and alpine tundra. Each
flower is presented: by a full-colour photograph; by a description of the plant's
characteristics and functions, its growing conditions, and range; and by a detailed
drawing of the entire plant. A recommended kindred work is Mary Ferguson and
Richard M. Saunder's *Canadian wildflowers through the seasons* (Toronto: Van
Nostrand Reinhold, 1982).

103 **Atlantic wildflowers.**
Diane Griffin.   Toronto: Oxford University Press, 1984. 136p.
Atlantic wildflowers examines a representative sample of plants that grow in Atlantic
Canada in a variety of habitats. A colour photograph accompanies each flower
described.

104 **The flora of New Brunswick.**
Harold Hinds.   Fredericton, New Brunswick: Primrose Press, 1986.
460p. bibliog.
A guide to all the vascular plants, i.e. trees and shrubs, wildflowers, grasses and
sedges, ferns, horsetails and clubmosses, to be found in New Brunswick. Included is an
extensive bibliography concerning the flora of the province. Of equal interest would
be: D.S. Erskine's *The plants of Prince Edward Island* (Ottawa: Research Branch,
Agriculture Canada, 1985); and, A .E. Roland and E. C. Smith's *The flora of Nova
Scotia* (Halifax, Nova Scotia: Nova Scotia Museum, 1983).

105 **Native trees of Canada.**
R. C. Hosie.   Toronto: Fitzhenry & Whiteside in cooperation with the
Canadian Forestry Service (Environment Canada) and the Canadian
Government Publishing Centre, Supply & Services, Canada, 1979.
380p.
This standard work provides a guide to more than 140 species of trees indigenous to
Canada, as well as telling the history of Canadian forests.

106 **Flore laurentienne.** (Flora of the Laurentian valley.)
Frère Marie-Victorin.   Montreal: Les Presses de L'Université de
Montréal, 1964. 2nd ed. 925p.
Identifies and describes the flora native to that portion of the valley of the St.
Lawrence river which is in Quebec.

107 **Illustrated flora of the Canadian Arctic archipeligo.**
A. E. Porsild. Ottawa: National Museums of Natural Sciences,
National Museums of Canada, 1973. 209p. (Bulletin, vol. 146).

Intended as a guide to the 340 species and major geographical races of flowering plants
and ferns that comprise the vascular flora as it is known at present of the Canadian
Arctic archipelago. Besides conventional keys to families, genera, and species, it
contains brief descriptions, line drawings, and maps showing the North American
ranges of all species.

108 **Rocky Mountain wild flowers.**
A. E. Porsild. Ottawa: National Museum of Natural Sciences,
National Museums of Canada and Parks Canada, Department of Indian
and Northern Affairs, 1974. 454p. (Natural History Series, vol. 2).

Primarily intended for those visiting Jasper, Banff and Waterton Lakes National Parks,
Alberta, this guide will familiarize the visitor both with the commoner and the more
spectacular wild flowers within the alpine and subalpine zones. The plants described
and illustrated (in delicate and exquisite colour drawings) are grouped in the
conventional manner of floristic manuals, beginning with the most primitive. Plants are
grouped first within their plant family and then within their proper genus. Of the 1,250
plants known in the parks some 250 are illustrated in this book. Notes and descriptions
for an additional 180 are provided but without illustration. A more recent publication
by George W. Scotter and Hälle Flygare entitled *Wildflowers of the Canadian Rockies*
(Edmonton, Alberta: Hurtig, 1986), provides a photographic field guide to some 200
plant species in the same region, written in non-technical language for the non-
specialist reader. Ben Gadd's *Handbook of the Canadian Rockies* (Jasper, Alberta:
Corax Press, 1987) serves as a convenient guide to both flora and fauna of the region.

109 **The flora of Canada.**
H. J. Scoggan. Ottawa: National Museum of Natural Sciences,
National Museums of Canada, 1978. 4 vols. (Publications in Botany,
vol. 7(1)).

This is a text for the well-informed researcher, consisting of a survey of some 4,153
species of the ferns and flowering plants of Canada. Similar information, in a more
concise and readable format, can be found in F. H. Montgomery's *Plants from sea to
sea* (Toronto: Ryerson, 1966). Here over 1,500 species are identified, and over 870 of
these are illustrated with line drawings.

110 **More than meets the eye: the life and lore of western wildflowers.**
J. Ward-Harris. Toronto: Oxford University Press, 1983. 242p.

This very handsome work provides a comprehensive and practical handbook picturing
and describing some of the wildflowers of the four western provinces of Canada. The
text includes details of species, family, distribution, habitat, season and appearance, as
well as behavioural information on how the plants interrelate with other forms of life;
and how their sexual relations are specialized and selective. The work is greatly
enhanced by beautiful, coloured illustrations of the plants represented. Recommended
also is F. R. Vance, J. R. Jowsey and J. S. McLean's *Wildflowers across the prairies*
(Saskatoon, Saskatchewan: Western Producer Prairie Books, 1984).

111 **Flowers of the wild: Ontario and the Great Lakes region.**
Zile Zichmanis, James Hodgins. Toronto: Oxford University Press,
1982. 272p.

A beautifully produced book featuring 127 species of wild flowering plants found in Ontario. Text for each of the species represented includes information about etymology, habitat, ecology, uses and horticulture, as well as selected references for further reading. The strength of the work, however, is in its superb line-drawings which reveal the characteristics of each plant and the vivid colour photographs which capture the plants in their natural surroundings. A glossary of botanical terms is included, as is an appendix of French and Ojibway (regional Indian) plant names.

Prehistory

112 **The Eskimos and Aleuts.**
Don E. Drummond.   London: Thames & Hudson, 1977. 180p.
(Ancient Peoples and Places, vol. 87).
Though the geographical focus of this work is not strictly Canadian, there is sufficient direct relevance to the Canadian experience to include the work here. This book presents the prehistory of the Eskaleut peoples, focusing, but not exclusively, on the area between the Bering Strait in the north and the Aleutian Islands and Alaska Peninsula in the south.

113 **Tracking ancient hunters: prehistoric archaeology in Saskatchewan.**
Edited by Henry T. Epp, Ian Dyck.   Regina, Saskatchewan:
Saskatchewan Archaeology Society, 1983. 260p.
Details the prehistoric archaeology and cultural history of Saskatchewan.

114 **British Columbia prehistory.**
Knut R. Fladmark.   Ottawa: Archaeological Survey of Canada,
National Museum of Man, National Museums of Canada, 1986. 150p.
(Canadian Prehistory Series).
This volume in the series introduces the reader to the prehistory of Canada's westernmost province. This history is discussed within the context of two broad regions, the coast and the interior.

115 **The Norse discovery of America.**
Anne Stine Ingstad, Helge Ingstad.   Oslo: Norwegian University
Press, 1985. 2nd ed. 2 vols.
The volumes are respectively subtitled: *Excavations of a Norse settlement at L'Anse aux Meadows, Newfoundland 1961-1968*; and *The historical background and the evidence of the Norse settlement discovered in Newfoundland*. This scholarly work outlines the

archaeological investigation, and the historical interpretation of its findings which led to the discovery of the fabled first European settlement in North America, the Norse site of Vinland. Volume One provides analysis of the archaeological work and is directed at the informed reader; Volume Two, more readable, deals with the historical aspects and other matters of significance to an assessment of the Norse discovery of America, including the background to the Vinland voyages. Investigations concerning geographical matters, navigation, climatic conditions and natural environment are also included in this volume.

116 **Introducing Manitoba prehistory.**
Winnipeg, Manitoba: Manitoba Department of Cultural Affairs and Historical Resources, 1983. 225p. (Papers in Manitoba Archaeology, vol. 4).
Attempts to convey the development of man's prehistoric past in the province of Manitoba.

117 **The owners of Eden: the life and past of the native people.**
Robert MacDonald. Calgary, Alberta: Ballantrae Foundation, 1974. 232p. (Romance of Canadian History, vol. 2).
Designed for the general reader, this is the story of the first Canadians: it is both history and prehistory. Profusely illustrated, it includes a list of selected references.

118 **Years & years ago: a prehistory.**
Robert MacDonald. Calgary, Alberta: Ballantrae Foundation, 1971. 208p. (Romance of Canadian History, vol. 1).
A chronicle of Canadian prehistory, beginning with the origin of the land, continuing through the millennia of geologic time and documenting in text and illustration the Great Ice Ages, the prehistoric flora and fauna and early inhabitants of the land. Enhanced by over twenty maps and some 150 illustrations.

119 **Prehistory of the eastern Arctic.**
Moreau S. Maxwell. Orlando, Florida: Academic Press, 1985. 327p. (New World Archaeological Record).
Outlines the strategies and technologies of prehistoric Eastern Arctic Eskimos over 4,000 years, as they responded to major changes in climate and food availability with little modification of their technology. Above all it is the story of a people living in a state of equilibrium with their ecosystem for four millennia.

120 **Canadian Arctic prehistory.**
Robert McGhee. Toronto: Van Nostrand Reinhold, 1978. 128p. (Canadian Prehistory Series).
Prepared under the auspices of the National Museum of Man in Ottawa, this volume traces the ancestors of the Inuit, the native inhabitants of the Canadian Arctic. The work draws not only from the science of archaeology but also from the domain of myth and legend.

Prehistory

121 **Early voyages and northern approaches 1000-1632.**
Tryggvi J. Oleson.   Toronto: McClelland & Stewart, 1963. 211p.
(Canadian Centenary Series, vol. 1).

This is primarily a study of the earliest European contacts with Canada beginning with the Vikings, but including also chapters on other documented and mythical pre-Columbian European voyages of exploration, as well as the early English voyages of exploration to Canada and the Canadian Arctic. Much of the work deals with the relations of the early Viking and Icelandic explorers, settlers and hunters with the aboriginal peoples of the region. See also Gwyn Jones' *The Norse Atlantic saga* (Oxford: Oxford University Press, 1986) and Helge Ingstad's *Westward to Vinland* (Toronto: Macmillan, 1969).

122 **Cartier's Hochelaga and the Dawson site.**
James F. Pendergast, Bruce G. Trigger.   Montreal: McGill-Queen's University Press, 1972. 388p.

The disciplines of archaeology or prehistory and ethnohistory continue to develop in Canada shedding light on the origins and identity of the first inhabitants of Canada. Many works could be listed as sound examples of these developments. This study is one of the better examples of the confluence of the various branches of anthropological inquiry, as it serves to explain the disappearance of the Iroquoian-speaking peoples in the St. Lawrence valley.

123 **A vanished world: the dinosaurs of western Canada.**
Dale A. Russell.   Ottawa: National Museum of Natural Sciences, National Museums of Canada, 1977. 142p. (Natural History Series, vol. 4).

Beautiful illustration and photography as well as interesting text mark this examination of the giant reptiles which inhabited western Canada millions of years ago. Of related interest is Renie Gross' *Dinosaur country: unearthing the badlands' prehistoric past* (Saskatoon, Saskatchewan: Western Producer Prairie Books, 1985).

124 **The children of Aataentsic: a history of the Huron people to 1660.**
Bruce G. Trigger.   Kingston; Montreal: McGill-Queen's University Press, 1987. 913p.

This monumental ethnohistory attempts to trace the development of the Huron people from the earliest hunting and gathering economies in southern Ontario through European contact to their rôle in the fur trade in eastern Canada in the first half of the seventeenth century. The author uses techniques from archaeology, history, ethnology, linguistics and geography to show that 'far from being a static prehistoric society quickly torn apart by European contact and the fur trade, almost every facet of Iroquoian culture had undergone significant change in the centuries preceding European contact'. See also Conrad Heidenreich's *Huronia: a history and geography of the Huron Indians 1600-1650* (Toronto: McClelland & Stewart, 1971).

125   Natives and newcomers: Canada's "heroic age" reconsidered.
Bruce G. Trigger.   Kingston; Montreal: McGill-Queen's University
Press, 1985. 430p. bibliog.
Using archaeology and social anthropology the author endeavours to examine and
recount the rôle played by native peoples in the shaping of Canada in the earliest
period of European colonization. Though some of the period under study (the work
ends in 1663 with the reorganization of the administration of New France) is in the
'historical period', the work is better classified as prehistory. Suitable for the general
reader, the work contains a bibliographical essay and a lengthy bibliography.

126   **Maritime provinces prehistory.**
James A. Tuck.   Ottawa: Archaeological Survey of Canada, National
Museum of Man, National Museums of Canada, 1984. 102p. (Canadian
Prehistory Series).
This volume reconstructs the appearance and ways of life of the prehistoric Micmacs
and Malecites. The work provides a tentative outline for the general reader of the
cultural history of the Maritime provinces over the period beginning some 10,000 years
ago and ending at the time of European contact.

127   **Newfoundland and Labrador prehistory.**
James A. Tuck.   Toronto: Van Nostrand Reinhold, 1976. 126p.
(Canadian Prehistory Series).
Prepared under the auspices of the National Museum of Man in Ottawa, this work
introduces the general reader to the Indian and Inuit cultures of prehistoric
Newfoundland and Labrador.

128   **Ontario prehistory: an eleven-thousand-year archaeological outline.**
J. V. Wright.   Toronto: Van Nostrand Reinhold, 120p. (Canadian
Prehistory Series).
Prepared under the auspices of the National Museum of Man in Ottawa, this work
introduces the general reader to the prehistoric Indian cultures that existed in the
region defined today as Ontario, before the arrival of the first Europeans.

129   **Quebec prehistory.**
J.V. Wright.   Toronto: Van Nostrand Reinhold, 1979. 128p.
(Canadian Prehistory Series).
Prepared under the auspices of the National Museum of Man in Ottawa, this volume in
the series introduces the prehistory of Quebec to the general reader. Some 11,000
years of man's occupation of the area is discussed, particularly as it relates to two
distinct populations – the Indians and the Inuit (Eskimos).

130 **Six chapters of Canada's prehistory.**
J. V. Wright.   Toronto: Van Nostrand Reinhold, 1976. 118p.
(Canadian Prehistory Series).

Prepared under the auspices of the National Museum of Man in Ottawa, this volume introduces the general reader to the native people and cultures that existed in Canada before European contact. The six chapters are: 'The Prehistoric Hunter'; 'The Prehistoric Farmer'; 'The Prehistoric Fisherman'; 'The Prehistoric Toolmaker'; 'The Prehistoric Trader'; and, 'Prehistoric Houses'.

History

Reference

131 **America: History and Life.**
Santa Barbara, California: ABC-Clio, 1964- . quarterly.
Abstracts and bibliographical citations of articles on the history and culture of the United States and Canada from prehistoric times to the present. Citations reflect work from approximately 2,000 serial publications in more than forty languages. Of these some 700 are published in the United States and Canada, including journals of provincial, state and local historical societies, the social sciences and the humanities generally, and leading journals in other fields of knowledge.

132 **Bibliographie de l'histoire du Québec et du Canada=Bibliography of the history of Quebec and Canada 1976-1980.**
Paul Aubin, Louis-Marie Côté. Quebec: Institut Québécois de recherche sur la culture, 1985. 2 vols.
A monumental work of bibliographic compilation. This work, together with its companion volumes *Bibliographie de l'histoire du Québec et du Canada 1966-1975* and *Bibliographie de l'histoire du Québec et du Canada 1946-1965*, provide unequalled access to the literature of Canadian history. To date this set provides access to over 70,000 items representing books, pamphlets, periodical articles, theses, etc., relating to the history of Canada published during the period 1945 to 1980. The work is inclusive, the compiler deliberately avoiding judgements based on any criteria with regard to importance or scientific value. The citations are extracted from the database HISCABEQ – Base de données bibliographiques ordinolingue sur l'histoire du Québec et du Canada (Bibliographic database on the history of Quebec and Canada). Entries are grouped into three divisions: a systematic classification by broad subject grouping; an analytic classification using key-words not already used in the subject groupings; and an author index.

133 A reader's guide to Canadian history, [vol.] 2: Confederation to the
present.
Edited by J. L. Granatstein, Paul Stevens. Toronto: University of
Toronto Press, 1982. 329p.
This revised and expanded edition of the guide supersedes two earlier editions entitled
Canada since 1867: a bibliographical guide (1974, 1977). Its purpose remains the same;
that is, to identify the best works and focus on the most recent research and writing,
available at the time of publication, in the area of Canadian history. The
bibliographical essays by noted historians are presented within thematic chapters (i.e.
national politics) and chapters with a regional focus (i.e. the prairie provinces).

134 True daughters of the north: Canadian women's history: an annotated
bibliography.
Beth Light, Veronica Strong-Boag. Toronto: OISE Press/Ontario
Institute for Studies in Education, 1980. 210p.
The 1960s and 1970s saw an emergence of a heightened consciousness of women and
their unique situation. This consciousness prompted an energetic search for critical
information about modern women and their predecessors in order to search out and
focus on the published and unpublished material of women's history. The purpose of
this bibliography is to present the published sources 'by which Canadians may continue
to improve their understanding of women's experience and rôle in the creation of the
modern community'. Entries are annotated and are arranged first by traditional
periods of Canadian history, i.e. New France, British North America, etc., and then
under broad subject headings, i.e. education, law, marriage and family, etc. See also
Carol Mazur and Sheila Pepper's *Women in Canada: a bibliography, 1965-1982*
(Toronto: OISE/Ontario Institute for Studies in Education, 1984).

135 A reader's guide to Canadian history, [vol.] 1: beginnings to
Confederation.
Edited by D. A. Muise. Toronto: University of Toronto Press, 1982.
253p.
These bibliographical essays by seven noted Canadian historians act as guides to the
study of pre-Confederation Canadian history (i.e. pre-1867). The guide is useful as a
tool which integrates and comments on the most recent writings, at the time of
publication, on a variety of subjects relating to the study of Canadian history. The
work emphasizes more recent material over older works, at least in cases where
previous treatments have been clearly superseded. This collection also favours the
work of professional historians over that of amateurs. Chapters are structured
thematically and presented within the context of regional perspectives.

136 The history of Canada: an annotated bibliography.
Edited by Dwight L. Smith. Santa Barbara, California: ABC-Clio,
1983. 327p. (Clio Bibliography Series, vol. 10).
An annotated bibliography of periodical literature relating to Canadian history and life
with entries drawn from the database of *America: history and life*. The volume focuses
on articles published from 1973 up until the end of 1978. Material is organized in order
to highlight the history of Canada on a chronological basis or by geographical location.
The work is supported by a comprehensive subject profile index employing generic and
specific index terms.

137 **Bibliographia Canadiana.**
Claude Thibault. Don Mills, Ontario: Longman, 1973. 795p.
An impressive bibliographical guide of some 26,600 entries to Canadian (French and English) printed historical literature. It includes both monographs (published to 1970) and periodical articles (to the end of 1969). Included are books and articles which are historiographical rather than historical. The volume is divided into five parts: 'Tools of Research'; 'French Colonial Regime'; 'British North America 1713-1867'; 'Dominion of Canada 1867-1967'; and, 'Addenda'. It includes an extensive table of contents which outlines the daunting chronological arrangement of the entries, as well as a less useful combined name as subject and subject index.

General

138 **The writing of Canadian history: aspects of English-Canadian historical writing since 1900.**
Carl Berger. Toronto: University of Toronto Press, 1986. 2nd ed. 364p.
Acclaimed as a classic study in Canadian historiography, this work examines aspects of English-Canadian historical thought and literature since the turn of the century. It deals with major figures such as George Wrong, Adam Shortt, Chester Martin, Harold Innis, Arthur Lower, Frank Underhill, Donald Creighton and William Morton. The final chapter of the revised edition is devoted to contemporary scholars, and the work as a whole is useful also as a bibliographic guide to significant Canadian historical writing. A must for readers at all levels. See also the book of readings edited by Berger and entitled *Contemporary approaches to Canadian history* (Toronto: Copp Clark Pitman, 1987).

139 **Canada since 1945: power, politics, and provincialism.**
Robert Bothwell, Ian Drummond, John English. Toronto: University of Toronto Press, 1981. 489p.
This work, together with its predecessor *Canada, 1900-1945* (Toronto: University of Toronto Press, 1987) provide an excellent overview of post-war Canadian political, economic, social and cultural history. The sections dealing with Canadian economic development are particularly good. These two works should be required reading for anyone wishing to understand present day Canada, its problems, its successes and its future.

140 **The illustrated history of Canada.**
Edited by Craig Brown. Toronto: Lester & Orpen Dennys, 1987. 574p.
A richly illustrated, highly readable general history of Canada, in which respected Canadian scholars – historians and historical geographers – provide a sweeping chronicle of the Canadian people. The work is impressive in scope and magnitude, taking the reader from vivid description of early native peoples through to the political and social ferment of the late twentieth century. The reader will take away not only a sense of historical panorama but also a reasonably detailed portrait of the Canadian

scene, including such issues as: the growth of urban Canada, the diversification of Canadian industry, the nature of Canada's multicultural character, the background to immigration policy, continental relationships, the impact of environment, Canada's rôle within the international community and many other themes.

141 **Canada 1896-1921: a nation transformed.**
Robert Craig Brown, Ramsay Cook. Toronto: McClelland & Stewart, 1974. 412p. (Canadian Centenary Series, vol. 14).
The period studied here was one of transformation. Two new provinces were created and the northern regions were opened up revealing vast new sources of mineral wealth and energy. Foreign trade and foreign investment rose to unprecedented levels. Two completely new transcontinental railways were chartered, with the influx of new Canadians adding a fresh ethnic dimension to Canadian life. At the same time, the altering balance between city and rural dweller struck a significant note. All of these factors and more (for example the turbulence of European politics) contributed to fundamental social, economic and political change over the period.

142 **Historical booklets.**
Canadian Historical Association. Ottawa: Canadian Historical Association, 1960- .
The Association produces a series of short booklets for the purpose of providing the general reader, the educator and, in some instances, the specialists, with concise accounts of special historical problems or events.

143 **The Canadian Historical Review.**
Toronto: University of Toronto Press, 1920- . quarterly.
The Canadian Historical Review is considered to be the premier journal of Canadian history, including articles on all aspects of the subject. It reviews current historical writing, and regularly publishes relevant bibliographical listings. Canadian history is also well served by numerous regional or thematic historical journals. Standard sources such as the *Canadian serials directory* will provide the researcher with title listings. For scholarship on French Canada, in French, the reader is directed to the *Revue l'histoire de l'Amérique française* (Historical Review of French America. Outremont, Quebec: L'Institut d'histoire de l'Amérique française, 1947-).

144 **The union of the Canadas: the growth of Canadian institutions 1841-1857.**
J. M. S. Careless. Toronto: McClelland & Stewart, 1967. 256p. bibliog. (Canadian Centenary Series, vol. 10).
With the union of Upper and Lower Canada came a new set of challenges for the maturing colony. The period under study was one of developing institutions. Under a single constitution the system of responsible government took shape, underpinned by the party mechanism to make it work. Central administrative departments were created, as well as those at the municipal level. Systems of public and separate school education were developed. It was a time of economic change, including the opening of continental markets, the coming of railways, and of developing business and industry. However, running through the period was the theme of French and English relations within the United Province. Includes a bibliography.

145 **Prophecy and protest: social movements in twentieth-century Canada.**
Edited by Samuel D. Clark, J. Paul Grayson and Linda M. Grayson.
Toronto: Gage, 1975. 437p.

Collectively this volume of readings provides a convenient overview of significant social moments in Canadian history. Essays encompass such movements as the social gospel (a Christian movement to deal with the problems of an industrializing society), western protest, union unrest, labour radicalism, nationalism, etc.

146 **Upper Canada: the formative years 1784-1841.**
Gerald M. Craig. Toronto: McClelland & Stewart, 1963. 315p.
bibliog. (Canadian Centenary Series, vol. 7).

The years following the American Revolution saw a considerable influx of settlers into Canada. They settled, in large measure, in Upper Canada, or the province of Ontario as it is known today. The development of this frontier community is the subject of this work. It recounts the economic, political and social development of the community, examining the divisions and rivalries which marked a turbulent era. The volume, in the words of its author, is also a story about people; people who 'not only endured the hardships of a primitive pioneer life, but faced war and invasion in 1812 and rebellion and confusion in 1837. Out of the clashing and blending of British and American views and customs there gradually emerged a people who were neither British nor American, but a people with a distinctive personality of their own'. Includes a bibliography.

147 **Canada's first century 1867-1967.**
Donald Creighton. Toronto: Macmillan, 1982. 378p. (Laurentian Library, vol. 43).

A readable and important perspective, by a distinguished historian, on Canada's first century of nationhood.

148 **The empire of the St. Lawrence.**
Donald Creighton. Toronto: Macmillan, 1956. 2nd ed. 441p.

Originally published as *The commercial empire of the St. Lawrence, 1760-1850* (Toronto: Ryerson, 1937), this work has proved a classic interpretation of Canada's historical development based on the thesis that the St. Lawrence was the inspiration and the basis of the transcontinental, east-west character of the country.

149 **The forked road: Canada 1939-1957.**
Donald Creighton. Toronto: McClelland & Stewart, 1976. 319p.
(Canadian Centenary Series, vol. 18).

This history begins with Canada's declaration of war against Germany in 1939 and ends with the general election in 1957. It encompasses the experience of the Second World War, the Korean War, the Cold War, as well as the consequential growth and development of the country. It chronicles political issues and events and the personalities of the period. Further, it provides analyses of Canadian-American relations, economic trends, social reforms and the cultural maturing of a nation.

150 **The road to Confederation: the emergence of Canada: 1863-1867.**
Donald Creighton. Toronto: Macmillan, 1964. 489p.
A presentation of the forces and events leading to the federation of the various colonies. Equally useful is P. B. Waite's *The life and times of Confederation 1864-1867: politics, newspapers, and the union of British North America* (Toronto: University of Toronto Press, 1967).

151 **Canada under Louis XIV 1663-1701.**
W. J. Eccles. Toronto: McClelland & Stewart, 1964. 275p. bibliog. (Canadian Centenary Series, vol. 3).
This study deals with but thirty-eight years of Canadian history, yet it might well be argued that much of the fabric of today's Canada, and in particular French Canada, was woven in this period. The year 1663 marked the year the administration of New France was taken from the hands of the commercial organization, The Company of New France, and placed directly under the control of the King of France. The end of the period, 1701, was the eve of the War of the Spanish Succession, and a date when French policy in relation to the colony was radically altered. These were years of expansion into the interior of the continent, under the leadership of able colonial administrators. In this period the institutions, basic values and concepts of society were also established in the colony. Includes a bibliography.

152 **The Canadian frontier 1534-1760.**
W. J. Eccles. Albuquerque, New Mexico: University of New Mexico Press, 1983. rev. ed. 238p. (Histories of the American Frontier).
When first published this work was an important revisionist version of the forces which shaped the French era of Canadian history. Particularly notable is the rôle assigned and documented by Eccles to the merchants of the colony, as well as the rôle cast for the Indian peoples. Includes a lengthy section of bibliographical notes.

153 **The structure of Canadian history.**
J. L. Finlay, D. N. Sprague. Scarborough, Ontario: Prentice-Hall, 1989. 3rd ed. 605p.
Canadian scholars have produced numerous historical surveys of the country. This work is of the pre-Confederation and post-Confederation periods of Canadian history and focuses on the political perspective. Other classic survey works include: Edgar McInnis' *Canada: a political & social history* (Toronto: Holt, Rinehart & Winston, 1982); Arthur R. M. Lower's *Colony to nation: a history of Canada* (Toronto: McClelland & Stewart, 1977); W. L. Morton's *The kingdom of Canada: a general history from earliest times* (Toronto: McClelland & Stewart, 1969); and Donald Creighton's *Dominion of the north: a history of Canada* (Toronto: Macmillan, 1962). J. M. S. Careless's general history, originally published in 1953 is available in a convenient pocketbook format, entitled *Canada: a story of challenge* (Toronto: Macmillan, 1970). Similarly, Kenneth McNaught provides a handy pocketbook history in *The Pelican history of Canada* (Markham, Ontario: Penguin, 1982).

154 **Canada 1957-1967: the years of uncertainty and innovation.**
J. L. Granatstein. Toronto: McClelland & Stewart, 1986. 375p.
(Canadian Centenary Series, vol. 19).

This book is chronologically the last volume in the Canadian Centenary Series. It deals with a tumultuous decade, that was punctuated by the centennial celebrations of 1967. The period was marked simultaneously by political instability and developing strained federal-provincial relations, but also by innovative social policies, an enhanced cultural awareness and a growing national identity.

155 **Canada before Confederation: a study in historical geography.**
R. Cole Harris, John Warkentin. Toronto: Oxford University Press, 1974. 338p. bibliog. (Historical Geography of North America Series).

This historical geography treats the area that became Canada from the time of modern European contact to 1867. It focuses on European rather than aboriginal inhabitants, arguing that the major developments of the period were triggered by Europeans. Bibliographies punctuate the end of each chapter.

156 **New France 1701-1744: "a supplement to Europe".**
Dale Miquelon. Toronto: McClelland & Stewart, 1987. 345p.
(Canadian Centenary Series, vol. 4).

The period 1713 to 1744, included within this study, has been called Canada's golden age. The author ably captures the flavour of the period under study; that is, the eve of the War of the Spanish Succession, which saw the introduction of a new imperial policy in relation to New France as France prepared herself for that conflict, to the end of the thirty years' peace which followed this conflict. And, although New France was stripped of some of its territory (Acadia, Hudson Bay, Newfoundland) with the Treaty of Utrecht in 1713, the years following were ones of development within the colony. These years were marked by the expansion of the fur trade, and the development of trade in general, not only with Europe, but also with the West Indies and other markets as well. This economic development, it is argued, related to the fashioning of a truly Canadian society over the course of the period.

157 **A military history of Canada.**
Desmond Morton. Edmonton, Alberta: Hurtig, 1985. 305p.

The introduction states that 'War has shaped Canadians more than most of them realize'. The author synthesizes here the rich and diverse work done by many historians in this historical military overview which spans the period from the *ancien régime* to the 1980s. Contains a lengthy and valuable bibliographic essay.

158 **The critical years: the union of British North America 1857-1873.**
W. L. Morton. Toronto: McClelland & Stewart, 1964. 322p. bibliog.
(Canadian Centenary Series, vol. 12).

An account of the forces at work which led to the Confederation of the provinces of British North America in 1867 as well as the consequences which followed from this union. The narrative exposes the complicated events orchestrated by men of vision and determination which ultimately produced the Dominion. The author makes clear the parts played by both founding nations, examining the unique and particular concerns of these nationalities which fostered unity and common purpose. Includes a bibliography.

159 **Quebec: the revolutionary age 1760-1791.**
Hilda Neatby. Toronto: McClelland & Stewart, 1966. 300p. bibliog.
(Canadian Centenary Series, vol. 6).

After 1760 what remained of the French colonies in America came under the control of the British. This study examines the responses made by the British government to the question of developing workable systems of law and government in Quebec. Of the thirty-one years covered, Britain was at war for eleven. During much of this time Quebec was under military occupation or was threatened by armed invasion. It was a period which encompassed the American War of Revolution and the French Revolution, both of which profoundly affected the social, religious and political life of the colony. Within this context the study at the same time chronicles the continued growth of the fur trade and examines the factors which ultimately would lead to bitter competition and rivalry between the merchants working out of the St. Lawrence basin and those accessing the interior from the Hudson Bay.

160 **Lower Canada 1791-1840: social change and nationalism.**
Fernand Ouellet. Toronto: McClelland & Stewart, 1980. 427p.
(Canadian Centenary Series, vol. 8).

In 1791, the people of the St. Lawrence Valley were granted a new constitution which gave them representative government and divided their territory into two distinct entities. This volume examines the development of one of those entities, Lower Canada, today's province of Quebec, with an emphasis on the social and political changes influencing the development of the community. The work examines the factors which contributed to the rebellion in the colony in 1837-38, as well as providing an examination of the interrelations among political movements, socio-ethnic change and economic and demographic problems. This work derives from the author's *Histoire économique et sociale du Québec: 1760-1850: structures et conjoncture* (Economic and social history of Quebec: 1760-1850: structure and circumstances) (q.v.) and is an adaptation of his *Le Bas-Canada: 1791-1840: changements structuraux et crise* (Lower Canada: 1791-1840: structural changes and crisis).

161 **The fur trade and the northwest to 1857.**
E. E. Rich. Toronto: McClelland & Stewart, 1967. 336p. bibliog.
(Canadian Centenary Series, vol. 11).

This is the history of a territory, and of the part played by the fur-traders in opening and developing that territory. The fur trade was inextricably linked to the fortunes of the Dominion, as those fortunes influenced the development of the eastern communities. It was linked also to the exploration of the interior of the continent as the fur trade, and the commercial organizations active within this trade, pushed the boundaries of known land to the West Coast, paving the way for agricultural settlement by the end of the nineteenth century. In this way, the great names of continental exploration are the same names associated with the fur trade.

162 **New France: the last phase 1744-1760.**
George F. G. Stanley. Toronto: McClelland & Stewart, 1968. 319p.
bibliog. (Canadian Centenary Series, vol. 5).

The turbulent period leading to the end of the French colonies in Canada is chronicled here. The American colonies, and New France in particular, were pawns in the economic and military rivalries of Britain and France. The War of the Austrian Succession marked the beginning of the period under study, and although the conflict revolved around European issues, it was inevitable that once hostilities escalated, the colonies would be involved. Ultimately the war raised and resolved the question of supremacy in North America.

163 **Canada 1922-1939: decades of discord.**
John Herd Thompson, Allen Seager. Toronto: McClelland & Stewart, 1985. 438p. (Canadian Centenary Series, vol. 15).
The subtitle of the work effectively describes two decades popularly termed the 'roaring' twenties and the 'dirty' thirties. It is both a political history and a story of individual Canadians who struggled with the respective problems of both decades. Revealed here are some of the fundamental 'cracks of Confederation' as well as domestic political turmoil and social and economic policy failure. The work also makes clear, however, the indisputable achievements of the country in the international arena.

164 **The beginnings of New France 1524-1663.**
Marcel Trudel. Toronto: McClelland & Stewart, 1973. 323p. bibliog. (Canadian Centenary Series, vol. 2).
The book is primarily a synthesis of three other works by this author on the early period of New France: *Les vaines tentatives, 1524-1603* (Futile efforts, 1524-1603); *Le comptoir, 1604-1627* (The settlement, 1604-1627); *La seigneurie des Cent-Associés, 1627-1663* (The seignory of the 100 Associates, 1627-1663). The history begins with the year 1524, the year the Italian, Giovanni da Verrazano, discovered the Atlantic Coast between Florida and Newfoundland. He named the region Nova Gallia or New France. The study traces the struggle of the French to establish a foothold on the continent in various locations. The history of the region is tied to that of the fur trade and the development of the colony for the purpose of exploiting the natural resources of America. The work concludes when responsibility for New France was taken from commercial organizations and was brought under the direct control of the King.

165 **Canada 1874-1896: arduous destiny.**
Peter B. Waite. Toronto: McClelland & Stewart, 1971. 340p. bibliog. (Canadian Centenary Series, vol. 13).
An historical survey of the new Dominion. The study gives primary attention to the political history of the country, tying all regions into the balanced narrative. On a grand scale the work engages politics, poetry and personalities to tell its story. Fortunately, the period was rich in all three, encompassing such important events and issues as the entry into Confederation of British Columbia, the building of the Canadian Pacific Railway across the country, the National Policy, the second Riel rebellion, and generally, the excitement of post-Confederation politics, replete with its colourful players.

Regional

British Columbia

166 **British Columbia: a history.**
Margaret Ormsby. Toronto: Macmillan, 1971. 566p.
Remains the best historical survey of the province. Though focused on political history, the work contains much of interest in areas of economic and social history. Additional useful historical information of the province can be found in books of readings, such as: Dickson M. Falconer's *British Columbia: patterns in economic, political and cultural development: selected readings* (Victoria, British Columbia: Camosun College, 1982); W. Peter Ward and Robert A. J. McDonald's *British Columbia: historical readings* (Vancouver: Douglas & McIntyre, 1981); or J. Friesen and H. K. Ralston's *Historical essays on British Columbia* (Toronto: Gage, 1980).

167 **The rush for spoils: the company province 1871-1933.**
Martin Robin. Toronto: McClelland & Stewart, 1972. 318p.
To be read together with a companion volume entitled *Pillars of profit: the company province 1934-1972* (Toronto: McClelland & Stewart, 1973). This is a political history which examines class conflict over shares in the wealth, disputes between political parties over the course of development, [and] the ways and means used by politicians to purchase allegiance. It is to the task of illuminating the political side of British Columbia history that these two volumes address themselves.

Northwest Territories

168 **Land of the midnight sun: a history of the Yukon.**
Ken S. Coates, William R. Morrison. Edmonton, Alberta: Hurtig, 1988. 336p.
A general history of the Yukon Territory, including both Indians and settlers in the area, which illuminates the major themes of Yukon history: native persistence, the transiency of the white population, formal and informal processes of racial segregation, the boom-and-bust cycles of the economy, the debilitating effects of colonial status, and the Yukon's inability to control its own destiny. See also the author's *Canada's Colonies: a history of the Yukon and Northwest Territories* (Toronto: James Lorimer, 1985); and, Allen A. Wright's *Prelude to bonanza: the discovery and exploration of the Yukon* (Sidney, British Columbia: Gray's Publishing, 1976).

169 **The exploration of northern Canada: 500 to 1920: a chronology.**
Alan Cooke, Clive Holland. Toronto: Arctic History Press, 1978. 549p. bibliog.
Chronologically arranged entries of varying length provide information on expeditions which led to geographical discoveries, to the collection of scientific information and to some form of publication. Also included are 'events' such as political actions, dates of trading posts, establishment of settlements, epidemics, disasters, etc. Entries include details of the expedition's date, its nature and national, commercial or other

association, its leader, ship, etc. There is a statement of the expedition's points of departure and return, as well as the dates of its duration. A lengthy bibliography is included.

170 **The political economy of the Canadian north: an interpretation of the course of development in the northern territories of Canada to the early 1960s.**
K. J. Rea.   Toronto: University of Toronto Press, 1968. 453p.
An overview of the economic history of the Northwest Territories, focusing on the rôle of government in the development process. Another reference for the reader is the author's *The political economy of northern development* (Ottawa: Science Council of Canada, 1976) which is a survey of policy-making in relation to the north.

171 **The northward expansion of Canada 1914-1967.**
Morris Zaslow.   Toronto: McClelland & Stewart, 1988. 421p.
(Canadian Centenary Series, vol. 17).
This volume is a continuation of the author's *The opening of the Canadian north, 1870-1914* (q.v.), Volume 16 in The Canadian Centenary Series. The first volume concentrated on the discovery and expansion phase of northern development, while this work analyses the more powerful surge of development into the north which brought it more firmly into the Canadian orbit. It outlines the expansion of transportation and communications, the exploitation of natural resources, and the slow growth of European settlement. The author focuses his study on three main themes: the sweep of the industrial frontiers across Subarctic Canada; the changing situations of the native population and the wildlife industries, and the economic, social, and political maturation of the Northwest Territories and Yukon.

172 **The opening of the Canadian north 1870-1914.**
Morris Zaslow.   Toronto: McClelland & Stewart, 1971. 339p. bibliog.
(Canadian Centenary Series, vol. 16).
The book deals with the opening of the Canadian north. Beginning with a general overview of the westerly and northwesterly development of the country, the study then concentrates on the region north of the St. Lawrence lowlands and the prairie region, and on the treeless tundra farther north. This latter region is most often identified as the Arctic. It is a study, on the one hand, of organizations such as the Geological Survey, the North-West Mounted Police, and various government departments instrumental in the opening of the north. But it also is the story of the fur-trader, the missionary and the gold-seeker all of whom made their contribution to the development of the region. Includes a bibliography.

Prairie provinces

173 **Saskatchewan: a history.**
John H. Archer.   Saskatoon, Saskatchewan: Western Producer Prairie Books, 1981. 422p.
A general history of the province. Companion to this work is D. H. Bocking's *Saskatchewan: a pictorial history* (Saskatoon, Saskatchewan: Western Producer Prairie

Books, 1979). Saskatchewan's political history is presented in any number of works. Also of interest to the reader are: S. M. Lipset's *Agrarian socialism: the cooperative commonwealth federation in Saskatchewan: a study in political sociology* (Berkeley, California: University of California Press, 1971); and Norman Ward and Duff Spafford's *Politics in Saskatchewan* (Toronto: Longman, 1968).

174 Prairie fire: the 1885 north-west rebellion.
Bob Beal, Rod Macleod. Edmonton, Alberta: Hurtig, 1984. 384p.

The two Riel rebellions, the first in the Red River colony (now Manitoba) in 1870, the second in the present province of Saskatchewan in 1885, were turning points in western Canadian political history, as well as the cultural and social development of the Métis people. This work deals extensively with the latter. An historical summary of both events can be found in George F. G. Stanley's *The birth of western Canada: a history of the Riel rebellions* (Toronto: University of Toronto Press, 1978).

175 The Canadian prairies: a history.
Gerald Friesen. Toronto: University of Toronto Press, 1984. 524p.

A scholarly synthesis of the history and development of the prairie region. The story is told from the early days of Indian-European contact to the present, discussing such issues as the adaptation of natives and Europeans to changing diplomatic and economic circumstances, the transition of the region to an industrial capitalist economy, and the political tensions of the region. The author also introduces the reader to the literature of the region, political ideology, geography and class structure. The text is readable and is directed to the general reader and the student. Of interest also is Arthur S. Morton's classic *A history of the Canadian West to 1870-71* (Toronto: University of Toronto Press, 1973).

176 A history of Alberta.
James G. MacGregor. Edmonton, Alberta: Hurtig, 1981. 2nd ed. 335p.

Though not a scholarly study, this remains the best historical overview of the province.

177 Manitoba: a history.
W. L. Morton. Toronto: University of Toronto Press, 1970. 2nd ed. 547p.

Morton's classic history remains the best narrative and analysis of Manitoba's political, economic, social and cultural development. Of interest also is James A. Jackson's *The centennial history of Manitoba* (Toronto: McClelland & Stewart, 1970).

178 Promise of Eden: the Canadian expansionist movement and the idea of the West, 1856-1900.
Doug Owram. Toronto: University of Toronto Press, 1980. 264p.

A superb piece of historical research which examines the changing perception of the West during the latter half of the nineteenth century. Considered at first a 'far and distant corner of the Empire' the West went on to become a frontier of great importance to the new nation. Encouraged by the findings of a new generation of explorers, many Canadians began to regard the West as a land of ideal opportunity for large-scale agricultural settlement, rather than as an inhospitable wilderness suited only for the fur trade. This change of attitude resulted also in a change in economic relationship and cultural interest by central Canada.

179 Wolf willow: a history, a story, and a memory of the last plains frontier.
Wallace Stegner. Toronto: Macmillan, 1977. 2nd ed. 306p.

Undoubtedly one of the most beautifully written books about western Canada ever published. At one and the same time this is a memoir, a history and a work of fiction – a combination which provides the best evocation available to the reader of the West; its history, the people and the landscape.

Ontario

180 A short history of Ontario.
Robert Bothwell. Edmonton, Alberta: Hurtig, 1986. 222p.

A succinct history of the province, ranging from prehistory to the present, written for the general reader. Similar in nature and in audience is Randall White's *Ontario: a political and economic history* (Toronto, London: Dundurn Press, 1985).

181 Ontario since 1867.
Joseph Schull. Toronto: McClelland & Stewart, 1978. 400p.

This is a narrative account of the development of the province from Confederation to 1961, directed at the general reader. Roger Hall and Gordon Dodds provide an introduction to the visual heritage of the province in their *A picture history of Ontario* (Edmonton, Alberta: Hurtig, 1978).

Quebec

182 Québec and Canada: past, present and future.
John Fitzmaurice. New York: St. Martin's Press, 1985. 343p.

An overview of Quebec economic, social and political history, designed to acquaint the general reader with the antecedents and current affairs of the province. Particularly useful as a synthesis of the major social and economic change which preceded the upheavals of the 1960s, termed collectively the 'Quiet Revolution', as well as a survey of events relating to the sovereignty-association movement.

183 Histoire du Québec. (History of Quebec.)
Edited by Jean Hamelin (et al.). Montreal: Éditions France-Amérique, 1977. 538p.

Considered one of the better overview textbook histories of the province.

184 **Quebec: a history 1867-1929.**
Paul-André Linteau, René Durocher, Jean-Claude Robert. Toronto: James Lorimer, 1983. 602p. bibliog.

Originally published as *Histoire du Québec contemporain: de la confédération à la crise (1867-1929)* (Contemporary history of Quebec: from Confederation to crisis [1867-1929]. Montreal: Boréal Express, 1979). An acclaimed synthesis of a period of profound change in the development of Quebec; that is, the period from Confederation to the Great Depression. The work itself is divided into two sub-periods – 1867-1896 and 1896-1929. For each section the authors deal thematically with their material, looking at economic, social, political, cultural and ideological history in turn. Readers are advised to look for a second volume from the same authors which will deal with the history of modern Quebec. Includes a bibliography.

185 **Quebec: social change and political crisis.**
Kenneth McRoberts. Toronto: McClelland & Stewart, 1988. 3rd ed. 530p.

This political scientist identifies, describes and analyses the processes of economic, social and political change in Quebec, from the Second World War to the late 1980s, focusing on the neo-nationalism of the 1960s, the independence movement of the 1970s, and the post-referendum events of the 1980s. He provides perceptive insight into the 'Quiet Revolution', the rise of the Parti Québécois, and the events leading to the referendum on sovereignty-association. He concludes by assessing the future prospects of Quebec nationalism.

186 **The French-Canadian idea of Confederation 1864-1900.**
A. I. Silver. Toronto: University of Toronto Press, 1982. 257p.

Bilingualism in Canada, and the spectre of Quebec separatism have been issues of considerable debate over the past twenty years. This study examines how the desire to maintain the French character and autonomy of Quebec at Conferation gradually evolved into the issue of French-Canadian rights throughout the whole of Canada.

187 **The dream of nation: a social and intellectual history of Quebec.**
Susan Mann Trofimenkoff. Toronto: Macmillan, 1982. 344p.

This is perhaps the best interpretive synthesis in English of the history of Quebec.

188 **The French Canadians 1760-1967.**
Mason Wade. Toronto: Macmillan, 1975-76. 2 vols. (Laurentian Library, vol. 44).

Essentially an attempt to explain why the French Canadians live, think, act, and react differently from English-speaking North Americans, this work traces the intellectual and cultural history of French Canada from its beginnings to modern-day Quebec. In doing so, the author examines these events in the context of the struggle of a minority group to maintain its cultural identity in the face of pressure to conform to a dominant civilization and another culture.

Atlantic provinces

189 **The government of Nova Scotia.**
J. Murray Beck. Toronto: University of Toronto Press, 1957. 372p.
(Canadian Government Series, vol. 8).
This is the classic political history of the province. For a detailed examination of the all-important Confederation years, readers could refer to Kenneth G. Pryke's *Nova Scotia and Confederation 1864-74* (Toronto: University of Toronto Press, 1979).

190 **Canada's smallest province: a history of P. E. I.**
Edited by Francis W. P. Bolger. Charlottetown, Prince Edward Island: The Prince Edward Island 1973 Centennial Commission, 1973. 403p.
Collectively these essays provide an outline history of the province. Similarly the volume of essays entitled *The garden transformed: Prince Edward Island, 1945-1980* (Charlottetown, Prince Edward Island: Ragweed Press, 1982) provides insights into present day Prince Edward Island. In terms of an historical overview, the general reader would find useful Lorne C. Callbeck's *The cradle of Confederation: a brief history of Prince Edward Island from its discovery in 1534 to the present time* (Fredericton, New Brunswick: Brunswick Press, 1964). For historical geography the reader is referred to Andrew Hill Clark's *Three centuries and the island: a historical geography of settlement and agriculture in Prince Edward Island, Canada* (Toronto: University of Toronto Press, 1975). The best political history remains Frank MacKinnon's *The government of Prince Edward Island* (Toronto: University of Toronto Press, 1951).

191 **Acadia: the geography of early Nova Scotia to 1760.**
Andrew Hill Clark. Madison, Wisconsin: University of Wisconsin Press, 1968. 450p.
The early history of settlement in Nova Scotia is treated by this pre-eminent historical geographer. Another classic work, covering a relatively short but nonetheless vitally important period in the colony's history, is John Bartlet Brebner's *The neutral yankees of Nova Scotia: a marginal colony during the revolutionary years* (New York: Columbia University Press, 1937). Also of importance is D. Campbell and R. A. MacLean's *Beyond the Atlantic roar: a study of the Nova Scotia Scots* (Toronto: McClelland & Stewart, 1974).

192 **The Acadians of the Maritimes: thematic studies.**
Edited by Jean Daigle. Moncton, New Brunswick: Centre d'études acadiennes, 1982. 637p.
Solid scholarship is the hallmark of this anthology of essays which cover almost every aspect of the life and history of the Acadians. The topics covered here include an historical overview 1604-1978, geography and population growth, and the political, economic and religious life of the region. Culture and the arts are also explored in this collection. Of further interest are two works by Jean-Claude Dupont on the folklore and material culture of the Acadians, entitled: *Histoire populaire de l'Acadie* (Popular history of Acadia. Montreal: Lémeac, 1979); and *Héritage d'Acadie* (Heritage of Acadia. Montreal: Lémeac, 1977).

47

193 **The Atlantic provinces: the emergence of colonial society 1712-1857.**
W. S. MacNutt.   Toronto: McClelland & Stewart, 1965. 305p. bibliog.
(Canadian Centenary Series, vol. 9).
This volume is a survey of the political, economic and social development of five colonies over a period of a century and a half. The colonies in question comprise today's four provinces of New Brunswick, Nova Scotia, Prince Edward Island, and Newfoundland.

194 **New Brunswick: a history: 1784-1867.**
W. S. MacNutt.   Toronto: Macmillan, 1984. 2nd ed. 496p.
Remains the best historical synthesis for the pre-Confederation period. Hugh G. Thorburn's *Politics in New Brunswick* (Toronto: University of Toronto Press, 1961) should be consulted for an outline of the political development of the province.

195 **A history of Newfoundland and Labrador.**
Frederick W. Rowe.   Toronto: McGraw-Hill Ryerson, 1980. 563p.
An historical overview suitable for the general reader. This level of readership might also find interesting Peter Neary and Patrick O'Flaherty's *Part of the main: an illustrated history of Newfoundland and Labrador* (St. John's, Newfoundland: Breakwater Books, 1983). The political history of the province is developed in S. J. R. Noel's *Politics in Newfoundland* (Toronto: University of Toronto Press, 1971), and Gertrude E. Gunn's *The political history of Newfoundland 1832-1964* (Toronto: University of Toronto Press, 1966). Other works of interest include: David MacKenzie's *Inside the Atlantic triangle: Canada and the entrance of Newfoundland into Confederation, 1939-1949* (Toronto: University of Toronto Press, 1986); and James Hiller and Peter Neary's *Newfoundland in the nineteenth and twentieth centuries: essays in interpretation* (Toronto: University of Toronto Press, 1980).

Population

196 **Growth and dualism: the demographic development of Canadian society.**
Roderic Beaujot, Kevin McQuillan.   Toronto: Gage, 1982. 249p.
bibliog.

A good overview of the population of Canada and the rôle of demographic questions in the development of the country. The authors place the study within an historical context covering rather summarily the period before Confederation but giving more attention to the course of mortality, fertility and international migration after Confederation – the baby boom generation is highlighted. The work deals at length with the most distinctive characteristic of the Canadian population: that is, its English-French dualism. A lengthy bibliography is included.

197 **Canadian Studies in Population.**
Edmonton, Alberta: Department of Sociology, Population Research Laboratory, University of Alberta, 1973- . quarterly.

This periodical publishes scholarly articles on population studies, with an emphasis on Canada.

198 **Canada's population outlook: demographic futures and economic challenges.**
David K. Foot.   Toronto: James Lorimer, 1982. 268p.

The author considers all the factors that affect the size and composition of Canada, and makes demographic projections up to the year 2051. The projections provide information concerning the future economic and social needs of the country.

Population

199 **Population projections for Canada, provinces and territories 1984-2006=Projections démographiques pour le Canada, les provinces et les territoires 1984-2006.**

M. V. George, J. Perreault. Ottawa: Statistics Canada, Demography Division, Population Projections Section, 1985. 346p.

This report presents revised population projections for the provinces and territories from 1984 to 2006 and up to 2031 for Canada as a whole. It shows how the demographic scene of Canada is changing rapidly. While the birth-rate has declined to an all-time low, mortality, especially among the elderly, has likewise decreased. Another radical change, also documented here, concerns migration within Canada itself as the westward trend goes into reverse.

200 **The demographic bases of Canadian society.**

Warren E. Kalbach, Wayne W. McVey. Toronto: McGraw-Hill Ryerson, 1979. 2nd ed. 402p.

Through the presentation and analysis of basic information about the origins, geographical factors and other characteristics of Canada's population the interrelationships of population processes and social change are examined. An excellent overview of Canada's population which will provide the reader with a sense of its character and the changes which are occurring.

201 **The big generation.**

John Kettle. Toronto: McClelland & Stewart, 1980. 264p.

As outlined in Chapter 1, the Big Generation consists of the 6,715,000 people born between mid-1951 and mid-1966, plus the 260,000 people of the same age who emigrated to Canada during this period. This futurist attempts to describe and interpret the phenomenon of the baby boom of the 1950s and 1960s in Canada. He also attempts to predict the impact of this generation on such factors as potential markets for goods, housing, education, travel, etc., as the bulge passes through various stages of life. The potential problems of manpower shortages, competition for jobs and the problems to be expected as the group reaches old age are also speculated upon here. Much generalization but on the whole a fascinating book.

202 **A statistical profile of Canadian society.**

Daniel Kubat, David Thornton. Toronto: McGraw-Hill Ryerson, 1974. 200p. (McGraw-Hill Ryerson Series in Canadian Sociology).

Described in the preface as a pocketbook of numerical documentation of Canadian society, this provides numerical data on Canadian population in terms of births, deaths, and migrations, and with regard to basic social institutions like families, schools, and work. Sections are prefaced with interpretive essays. Bibliographical references throughout. Somewhat dated but provides good background information for the interested researcher.

203 **Canadian population trends and public policy through the 1980s.**

Claude Marceau, Leroy O. Stone. Montreal, London: McGill-Queen's University Press, 1977. 109p. bibliog.

The authors were commissioned to identify problem areas and implications for Canadian public policy through the study of demographic trends and developments in

Canada to the year 2000. This resulting report introduces a variety of social and economic problems that are connected to trends in size, geographic distribution and composition of Canada's population. Issues identified relate to the need for improvements in the quality of urban life and services and the need for policies to guide metropolitan growth. The question of the deterioration of social services in inner city areas and the topics of education and the welfare of the elderly are also dealt with. Includes a substantial bibliography.

204 **Population probe.**
Lorna R. Marsden.   Toronto: Copp Clark, 1972. 179p. bibliog.

Though dated, the author articulates various key population issues as they apply to Canada and reinforces the need for a public debate on population questions in the country, including the relation between population growth and environmental considerations, educational and health services and employment. The work's popular qualities do not lessen its academic qualities. An annotated bibliography is included.

205 **Population and Canadian society.**
Johannes Overbeek.   Toronto: Butterworths, 1980. 178p.

Through population study the author examines the relationships between population changes and social, economic, political, geographical and psychological factors in Canadian society.

Nationalities and Minorities

206 **Ethnicity in Canada: theoretical perspectives.**
Alan B. Anderson, James S. Frideres.   Toronto: Butterworths, 1981.
334p.

The authors attempt to synthesize the writings on Canadian ethnic minorities and develop a theoretical generalization of ethnicity in Canada. With regard to the latter, ethnicity is explored together with the emergence of government policies focusing on multiculturalism. The reader is also introduced to the theoretical perspectives of ethnic relations in Canada; here the authors apply conflict theory and various theories relating to social control mechanisms against their thesis. A work of interest to the informed reader.

207 **Canadese: a portrait of the Italian Canadians.**
Kenneth Bagnell.   Toronto: Macmillan, 1989. 287p.

The Italian community is Canada's fourth largest ethnic group, after the British, French and German populations. In certain major centres, i.e. Toronto, the communities are large and crucial in terms of local society and history. This journalist skilfully outlines the history of Italians in Canada, and weaves this into the broader Canadian story, focusing on the twentieth century.

208 **Racial oppression in Canada.**
B. Singh Bolaria, Peter S. Li.   Toronto: Garamond, 1985. 232p.

Race relations in Canada are re-examined working from a paradigm that race problems begin as labour problems; that is, racial antagonism is a product of an economic problem not a matter merely of cultural misunderstanding. This work first presents the thesis of the authors within the theoretical context of the political economy of race; then they present a number of case studies, involving Indians, Métis, Chinese, Japanese, East Indians, blacks and migrant workers, which illustrate the exploitation of groups based on superimposed precepts of racial superiority.

209 **Coming Canadians: an introduction to a history of Canada's peoples.**
Jean Burnet and Howard Palmer.   Ottawa: McClelland & Stewart, in
association with the Multiculturalism Directorate, Department of the
Secretary of State and the Canadian Government Publishing Centre,
Supply and Services, Canada, 1988. 209p. (Generations: a History of
Canada's Peoples.)

There are few projects where the energies of the scholarly, government and trade
publishing sectors have come together in a more productive enterprise than is the case
with this series, introduced by the series' editors in the above volume. Presented are
objective, readable histories of the ethnic groups contributing to Canadian society and
identity. Titles to date include (authors have been excluded for the sake of brevity): *A
member of a distinguished family: the Polish group in Canada* (1976); *A future to
inherit: Portuguese communities in Canada* (1976); *The Scottish tradition in Canada*
(1976); *An olive branch on the family tree: the Arabs in Canada* (1980); *From fjord to
frontier: a history of the Norwegians in Canada* (1980); *The Canadian odyssey: the
Greek experience in Canada* (1980); *Struggle and hope: the Hungarian-Canadian
experience* (1982); *From China to Canada: a history of the Chinese communities in
Canada* (1982); *A heritage in transition: essays in the history of Ukrainians in Canada*
(1982); *For a better life: a history of the Croatians in Canada* (1982); *The political
refugees: a history of the Estonians in Canada* (1985); *Continuous journey: a social
history of south Asians in Canada* (1985); and *A bittersweet land: the Dutch experience
in Canada, 1890-1980 (1988).*

210 **Canada Ethica Series.**
Ottawa, Ontario; Winnipeg, Manitoba: National Publishers, 1967-69. 8
vols.

This early series of histories provides generally scholarly introductions to various ethnic
groups in Canada. Complements the *Generations* series (q.v.) published a decade later.
Titles included are: *The Indians and Eskimos in Canada*; W. J. Lindal's *The Icelanders
in Canada*; H. W. Debor's *The Germans in Canada*; Ol'Ha Woycenko's *The
Ukrainians in Canada*; *Lithuanians in Canada*; A. V. Spada's *The Italians in Canada*;
L. K. R. Zubkowski's *The Poles in Canada*; and E. Ide's *The Japanese in Canada*.

211 **Canadian Ethnic Studies = Études ethniques au Canada.**
Halifax, Nova Scotia: Dalhousie University, 1969- . tri-annually.

An interdisciplinary journal devoted to the study of ethnicity, immigration, inter-group
relations and the history and cultural life of ethnic groups in Canada.

212 **The other Canadians: profiles of six minorities.**
Morris Davis, Joseph F. Krauter.   Toronto: Methuen, 1971. 132p.

The social conditions and political problems of six Canadian groups are examined: they
include native Indians, Eskimos, blacks, Asians, Doukhobors and Hutterites.

213 **Ethnic Canada: identities and inequalities.**
Compiled by Leo Driedger.   Toronto: Copp Clark Pitman, 1987.
442p.

The compiler of this collection here draws together twenty-one writings on ethnic
relations. Perspectives include ethnic change, demography, identity, social stratification and inequalities. Many such collections of readings have been produced, either

of commissioned essays or of conference proceedings. Other useful examples include: Neil Nevitte and Allan Kornberg's *Minorities and the Canadian state* (Oakville, Ontario: Mosaic Press, 1985); Jean Leonard Elliott's *Two nations, many cultures: ethnic groups in Canada* (Scarborough, Ontario: Prentice-Hall, 1983); Jay E. Goldstein and Rita M. Bienvenue's *Ethnicity and ethnic relations in Canada: a book of readings* (Toronto: Butterworths, 1980); and Martin L. Kovacs *Ethnic Canadians: culture and education* (Regina, Saskatchewan: Canadian Plains Research Center, University of Regina, 1978). The researcher is also directed to the superb work published as the annual conference proceedings of the Canadian Ethnic Studies Association.

214 Irish migrants in the Canadas: a new approach.
Bruce S. Elliott.   Kingston, Ontario; Montreal: McGill-Queen's University Press, 1988. 371p. (McGill-Queen's Studies in Ethnic History, vol. 1).

The author looks at one of the major groups which has contributed to the cultural complexity of the country. The Irish were the largest non-French ethnic group in nineteenth-century Canada. By way of meticulous research on the life paths of hundreds of migrants the author is able to generalize on the migration process for this group as well as the economic and social consequences of that migration. This study is complemented by Donald Harman Akenson's *The Irish in Ontario: a study in rural history* (Kingston, Ontario; Montreal: McGill-Queen's University Press, 1984). Akenson presents background of the settlement characteristics in Ontario of the Irish migrants.

215 When cultures clash: case studies in multiculturalism.
John W. Friesen.   Calgary, Alberta: Detselig, 1985. 171p.

Designed to assist the secondary school teacher in presenting the concept of ethnicity in Canada, this work sketches the growth of multiculturalism in Canada and suggests a variety of theoretical models for its study. Five case studies are included to illustrate various concepts. These include the French in western Canada, the plains Indians, the Métis, the Hutterites and the Mennonites.

216 The Czechs and Slovaks in Canada.
John Gellner, John Smerek.   Toronto: University of Toronto Press, 1968. 172p.

This study provides an historical survey of these two closely related groups in Canada.

217 Ethnicity and human rights in Canada.
Evelyn Kallen.   Toronto: Gage, 1982. 268p.

The social scientific theories of racism and ethnicity and the biological concept of race are discussed here for the purpose of understanding questions relating to the protection of fundamental human rights and freedoms in Canada. The author's message is that the 'essential biological unity of the human species and our high degree of adaptability to changing social and geographic contexts override all of the arbitrary and ever-shifting racial subdivisions'. The interested reader is also advised to consult the author's previous book *Anatomy of racism: Canadian dimensions* (Montreal: Harvest House, 1974).

218 **Minority Canadians: ethnic groups.**
Joseph F. Krauter, Morris Davis. Toronto: Methuen, 1978. 120p.

A discussion of the treatment experienced by ethnic groups in specific areas such as immigration and citizenship, franchise, education, employment, health care, and housing. The work focuses upon such groups as the native Indians, Inuit, Métis, blacks, Asians, Italians, Ukrainians, Mexicans and more recent European refugees.

219 **The Icelandic people in Manitoba: a Manitoba saga.**
W. Kristjanson. Winnipeg, Manitoba: Wallingford, 1965. 557p.

The Icelandic people have made a significant contribution to Canada in any number of areas. Most Icelanders arrived in western Canada during the settlement period of the late nineteenth and early twentieth centuries. Victims of oppression at home, they realized their independence in Canada. The resulting spirit of renaissance, coupled with a determination to succeed, led to a history of collective and individual achievement.

220 **The Chinese in Canada.**
Peter S. Li. Toronto: Oxford University Press, 1988. 164p.

Dealing with the oppression, the survival, and the triumph of the Chinese in Canada, the subject matter of this book includes the history of Chinese immigration to Canada, the impact of racism on the Chinese community, and also focuses on the achievements of Chinese-Canadians.

221 **The Ukrainian Canadians: a history=L'histoire des Ukrainiens-Canadiens.**
Michael H. Marunchak. Winnipeg, Manitoba: Ukrainian Academy of Arts and Sciences in Canada, 1982. 970p.

A work of encyclopaedic proportions which provides a comprehensive history of the Ukrainians in Canada. From history, to culture, to various social issues, every aspect of the Ukrainian experience in Canada is covered in this work. For those interested in the nature of multiculturalism in Canada no better case study can be found than that of this group. Other works which deal with various aspects of Ukrainian-Canadian history and culture include: Jaroslav Petryshyn's *Peasants in the promised land: Canada and the Ukrainians 1891-1914* (Toronto: James Lorimer, 1985); Jaroslav Rozumnyj's *New soil – old roots: the Ukrainian experience in Canada* (Winnipeg, Manitoba: Ukrainian Academy of Arts and Sciences in Canada, 1983); Michael Czuboka's *Ukrainian Canadian, eh?: the Ukrainians of Canada and elsewhere as perceived by themselves and others* (Winnipeg, Manitoba: Communigraphics Printers Aid Group, 1983); William A. Czumer's *Recollections about the life of the first Ukrainian settlers in Canada* (Edmonton, Alberta: Canadian Institute of Ukrainian Studies, 1981); Zonia Keywan's *Greater than kings* (Montreal: Harvest House, 1977); and Vladimir J. Kaye's *Early Ukrainian settlements in Canada 1895-1900* (Toronto: University of Toronto Press, 1964).

222 **The Canadian family tree: Canada's peoples.**
Multiculturalism Directorate, Department of the Secretary of State.
Don Mills, Ontario: Corpus, 1979. 250p. bibliog.
An overview which profiles seventy-eight ethno-cultural groups which are a part of the multicultural mosaic of Canada. Short essays provide information about language, geographic origin, historical continuity and religion of each group. Provided also are brief outlines of the contributions each group has made to the social, cultural, physical and economic development of the country. Every effort was made by the Department to include all the groups and countries which have played a part in Canadian immigration. A good introduction to multiculturalism in Canada. Includes a short bibliography.

223 **Non-official languages: a study in Canadian multiculturalism.**
K. G. O'Bryan, J. G. Reitz, O. M. Kuplowska. Ottawa: Supply and Services Canada, 1976. 274p.
'To what degree have Canadians whose origin is neither French nor British integrated with anglophone or francophone society? To what degree have they remained attached to their original cultures and languages?' These questions, as quoted in the book's introduction, were posed by the Royal Commission on Bilingualism and Biculturalism. This study attempts to answer these questions; that is, it examines the issues of language retention. Ten ethnic groups in five metropolitan areas were systematically interviewed for the study. The groups interviewed were the Chinese, Dutch, Germans, Greeks, Hungarians, Italians, Polish, Portuguese, Scandinavians and Ukrainians, from locations as widespread as Montreal, Toronto, Winnipeg, Edmonton and Vancouver.

224 **Immigration and the rise of multiculturalism.**
Edited by Howard Palmer. Toronto: Copp Clark, 1975. 216p. (Issues in Canadian History).
The Issues series seeks to compile relevant, contemporary documents on historical crises, problems and personalities, supplemented by open-ended editorial comment. This volume examines the impact of immigrants on the country's social, economic, political and religious life, as well as immigration policy and the differing attitudes in Canadian society toward immigration. Reprinted documents date from the late nineteenth century to the early 1970s. A 'Suggested Reading' list is provided.

225 **The dynamics of Hutterite society: an analytical approach.**
Karl A. Peter. Edmonton, Alberta: University of Alberta Press, 1987. 232p.
The author explores the social and economic life of the Hutterites, a pacifist communal-living Christian sect that immigrated to Canada early in the century. In this analysis, he presents the Hutterite phenomenon as an ongoing sociocultural unit continually adapting to environmental, political, and social circumstances while at the same time realizing the opportunities which their social grouping offers. Another solid work is that by David Flint entitled *The Hutterites: a study in prejudice* (Toronto. Oxford University Press, 1975). Flint examines his subjects from another perspective attempting to give a sociological, anthropological, and historical understanding of the Hutterite Brethren. Another work of interest is Victor Peters' *All things common: the Hutterian way of life* (Minneapolis, Minnesota: University of Minnesota Press, 1965).

226 **The politics of gender, ethnicity and language in Canada.**
Toronto: University of Toronto Press in cooperation with the Royal
Commission on the Economic Union and Development Prospects for
Canada, and the Canadian Government Publishing Centre, Supply and
Services Canada, 1986. 245p. bibliog.

The mandate of the Royal Commission on the Economic Union and Development
Prospects for Canada, which commissioned the work in hand, was directed to report
on the 'appropriate institutional and constitutional arrangements to promote the liberty
and well-being of individual Canadians'. The essays in this volume focus on various
groups and their attempts to shape the distribution of status and power in Canada.
Areas of examination include the general changes to Canadian values, multiculturalism
and nation-building, the French language in Quebec and in Canada, women's issues
and women's movements, and the impact of aboriginal self-government in Canada.
Appended to each essay is a substantive bibliography.

227 **The survival of ethnic groups.**
Jeffrey G. Reitz. Toronto: McGraw-Hill Ryerson, 1980. 292p.
bibliog. (McGraw-Hill Ryerson Series in Canadian Sociology).

Ethnic group survival in large Canadian cities is the focus of this work. The author
examines here the strength of ethnic solidarity in Canada's largest cities through ethnic
group histories and contemporary survey data, relating community solidarity both to
economic and to cultural human needs. He starts by showing how the various ethnic
communities first developed, identifying conditions conducive to strong ethnic
cohesion. Within this historical context, he then studies a set of current findings to
explain why such communities are slow to disappear, whatever changes may occur in
the conditions which first led to their establishment.

228 **The politics of racism: the uprooting of Japanese Canadians during the
Second World War.**
Ann Gomer Sunahara. Toronto: James Lorimer, 1981. 222p.

Any number of works record, document, and analyse that tragic and shameful chapter
of Canadian history which saw the expulsion from homes on the west coast of over
20,000 Japanese Canadians – Canadian citizens who were uprooted from their homes,
confined in detention camps, stripped of property, and forcibly dispersed across the
country or deported. Other works to be consulted are: Toyo Takata's *Nikkei legacy:
the story of Japanese Canadians from settlement to today* (Toronto: NC Press, 1983);
Barry Broadfoot's *Years of sorrow, years of shame: the story of the Japanese Canadians
in World War II* (Toronto: Doubleday, 1977); and Ken Adachi's *The enemy that never
was: a history of the Japanese Canadians* (Toronto: McClelland & Stewart, 1976).

229 **Issues in cultural diversity.**
Harold Troper, Lee Palmer. Toronto: The Ontario Institute for
Studies in Education, 1976. 130p. (Canadian Critical Issues Series).

This series focuses on issues of contemporary interest and by way of case studies,
followed by questions and analogy situations, provides a vehicle for reflection and
discussion. This volume details cases which concern minority groups, individuals and

the wider Canadian community. Particular emphasis is given to the nature of the Hutterite experience, the problems in black neighbourhoods in Halifax and Toronto, as well as the issues surrounding immigrants and various urban experiences.

230 **Visible minorities and multiculturalism: Asians in Canada.**
Edited by K. Victor Ujimoto, Gordon Hirabayashi. Toronto: Butterworths, 1980. 388p.

This consists of papers presented at a meeting of the Learned Societies of Canada in 1977 and 1978. Drawn from a number of disciplines, collectively these essays provide a useful overview of the experiences and perspectives of Asians in Canada. The subjects under discussion here include settlement experience, inter-group relations, assimilation, and contributions to the creative arts. A more concentrated study of Asians in Canada can be found in W. Peter Ward's *White Canada forever: popular attitudes and public policy toward orientals in British Columbia* (Montreal: McGill-Queen's University Press, 1978).

231 **Language & nationhood: the Canadian experience.**
Ronald Wardhaugh. Vancouver: New Star, 1983. 269p. bibliog.

Government policies relating to bilingualism and multiculturalism are examined, and the result is not an optimistic outlook. This academic fears multiculturalism is empty rhetoric and urges the 'charter' groups, i.e. the English and the French, to 'forego certain aspects of their distinctiveness, language being the crucial one'. He urges accommodation not confrontation in moving toward cultural pluralism. A well written, readable and thought-provoking work.

232 **The Canadian Jewish mosaic.**
Edited by M. Weinfeld, W. Shaffir, I. Cotler. Toronto: John Wiley, 1981. 511p.

A collection of commissioned essays which provide description and analysis of Canadian Jewry at the beginning of the 1980s. Many of the essays deal with issues currently facing the Jewish community. In addition to this fine work, other titles are recommended, including: the pioneering work of B. G. Sack's *The history of Jews in Canada* (Montreal: Harvest House, 1965); Simon Belkin's *Through narrow gates . . .* (Montreal: Canadian Jewish Congress and the Jewish Colonization Association, 1966); Stuart E. Rosenberg's handsome *The Jewish community in Canada* (Toronto: McClelland & Stewart, 1970); Evelyn Kallen's *Spanning the generations: a study in Jewish identity* (Toronto: Longman, 1977); Aron Horowitz's *Striking roots: reflections on five decades of Jewish life* (Oakville, Ontario: Mosaic, 1979); and Erna Paris' *Jews: an account of their experience in Canada* (Toronto: Macmillan, 1980).

233 **The blacks in Canada: a history.**
Robin W. Winks. Montreal: McGill-Queen's University Press; New Haven, Connecticut; London: Yale University Press, 1971. 546p.

This book outlines the history of blacks in Canada from 1628 to the 1960s, and by so doing explores something of the nature of prejudice in Canada. The author also uses this story as a means of examining some of the ways in which Canadian attitudes toward immigration and ethnic identity differ from the American. The black community in Canada, never very large in terms of percentage of population, divide themselves between those who came, or descended from those who came, from the United States, and those whose origins were in the West Indies. In addition to Winks' exhaustive history, the interested general reader may wish to examine Daniel G. Hill's *The freedom-seekers: blacks in early Canada* (Agincourt, Ontario: Book Society of Canada, 1981) or the partisan work by Headley Tulloch entitled *Black Canadians: a long line of fighters* (Toronto: NC Press, 1975).

Aboriginal Peoples

Reference

234 **About Indians: a listing of books.**
Indian and Eskimo Affairs Program, Education and Cultural Support
Branch. Ottawa: Minister of Indian and Northern Affairs, 1977. 4th
ed. [n.p.]. bibliog.
A bibliography of books written about Indians, organized according to school level,
i.e. kindergarten to grade 3 (ages 5-8), grade 3 to grade 6 (ages 8-11), grade 6 and
beyond (age 11 upwards), and including books available in the French language. It
includes critical annotations, and is indexed by author, title and subject. This is a
useful compilation for the general reader, the researcher and the teacher.

235 **Aboriginal self-government in Canada: a bibliography 1986.**
Evelyn J. Peters. Kingston, Ontario: Institute of Intergovernmental
Relations, Queen's University, 1986. 112p.
The question of self-government for the aboriginal peoples is possibly one of the most
pressing, controversial and topical issues in Canada today. This book provides access
to the considerable and varied literature on this topic.

236 **Indians of the United States and Canada: a bibliography.**
Edited by Dwight L. Smith. Santa Barbara, California: ABC-Clio,
1974. 453p. (Clio Bibliography Series, vol. 3).
The 1,687 entries in this work are extracted from the database of *America: History and
Life* (ABC-Clio, published five times a year). They represent scholarship taken from
the historical and social sciences periodical literature from 1954 to 1972. Entries are
annotated and organized by region and cultural grouping. There is a combined index of
author, biographical, geographical and subject entries.

237 **Indians of the United States and Canada: a bibliography. Volume II.**
Edited by Dwight L. Smith. Santa Barbara, California: ABC-Clio,
1983. 345p. (Clio Bibliography Series, vol. 10).
Because of the period of time between the publication of the two volumes in this set
and the nature of the publications, this work is considered more than a supplement or
continuation of Volume 1. Some 3,218 citations are listed with annotations and
consecutively numbered following on from Volume 1. As with Volume 1 (q.v.), entries
are taken from the database of *America: History and Life*, and represent the history
and social science periodical literature from 1973 to 1983. The work is supported by a
comprehensive Subject Profile Index employing generic and specific index terms.

238 **Canadian Indian policy: a critical bibliography.**
Robert J. Surtees. Bloomington, Indiana: Indiana University Press,
1982. 107p.
A listing of 293 items on Indian policy, prefaced by a most useful and lengthy
bibliographic, evaluative essay.

239 **Aboriginal people: a selected bibliography concerning Canada's first
people.**
Don Whiteside. Ottawa: National Indian Brotherhood, 1973. 345p.
This is one of the early contemporary bibliographies relating to Canada's aboriginal
people. It represents a wide range of the major published works, but with particular
emphasis on unpublished speeches, reports, and proceedings of various conferences as
well as relevant newspaper articles. Works by the aboriginal people themselves are also
covered, including a section on the philosophy of Indian resistance. Entries are
arranged under topical headings, and there is an author and subject index. Another
bibliography of this subject is Thomas Abler and Sally Weaver's *A Canadian Indian
bibliography 1960-1970* (Toronto: University of Toronto Press, 1974).

General

240 **Prison of grass: Canada from the native point of view.**
Howard Adams. Toronto: General Publishing, 1975. 238p. (Trent
Native Series, vol. 1).
An historical discussion from a native viewpoint. As expressed in the introduction it is
the author's intention to 'unmask the white-supremacist and the white-liberal view that
the natives were warring savages without any government, who craved white
civilization. Three hundred years of white supremacy, imperialism, colonization, and
capitalism are discussed in terms of their effect on the native people and their nation.
Racism and colonization are analyzed as both subjective and objective conditions in
order to show how imperialism operates to conquer and colonize Indians and Métis,
while seizing their land and resources at the same time'.

241 **The quest for justice: aboriginal peoples and aboriginal rights.**
Edited by Menno Boldt, J. Anthony Long, Leroy Little Bear.
Toronto: University of Toronto Press, 1985. 406p.

This book develops further the issues raised in the editors' earlier volume, *Pathways to self-determination: Canadian Indians and the Canadian state* (Toronto: University of Toronto Press, 1984). Based on some twenty-three papers from representatives of the aboriginal people's organizations, of governments, and of a variety of academic disciplines, as well as constitutional documents from 1763, it addresses issues such as land rights; Métis, non-status Indians, the Inuit; and the rights of aboriginal peoples in general.

242 **Never in anger: portrait of an Eskimo family.**
Jean L. Briggs. Cambridge, Massachusetts: Harvard University Press, 1970. 379p.

Beginning in the summer of 1963 the author spent seventeen months living with a group of Eskimos who lived at the mouth of the Back River, northwest of Hudson Bay. This resultant work forms a picture of Eskimo life as seen by the researcher, who describes the geographical and historical setting of her subjects, as well as the seasonal, nomadic cycle which they follow. Social relationships are discussed, as is family life. The work is, at one and the same time, a scholarly treatise and a personal diary.

243 **The people's land: Eskimos and whites in the eastern Arctic.**
Hugh Brody. Toronto: Penguin, 1975. 240p. bibliog.

The nature and consequences of white-Eskimo interaction are the focus of this work. It is the author's view that 'the predicament of the contemporary Canadian Eskimo is deeply troubling. It embodies – within its very short history – the destructive processes and social deformations that colonialism everywhere entails'. The author concentrates not on traditional Eskimo society nor on the Eskimo people's early responses to the southerners, he focuses instead on the present situation of both Eskimos and whites in the north as deserving of attention. A bibliography is included.

244 **Seasons of the Eskimo: a vanishing way of life.**
Fred Bruemmer. Toronto: McClelland & Stewart, 1971. [n.p.]

This fascinating chronicle presents a photographic portrayal of the life of the Canadian Eskimos. Brief commentaries accompany the images.

245 **The Canadian Journal of Native Studies.**
Brandon, Manitoba: Society for the Advancement of Native Studies, 1981- . bi-annual.

This journal publishes papers, discussions, comments, reviews and other contributions relating to all areas of native studies, with emphasis on Canadian materials. *Abstracts of Native Studies* (Brandon, Manitoba: Abstracts of Native Studies Press, 1986-) provides further reading in this area of study.

246 **The rebirth of Canada's Indians.**
Harold Cardinal. Edmonton, Alberta: Hurtig, 1977. 222p.

An important polemic by one of the country's leading native spokespersons, who relates, from personal experience, the story of the Indian peoples and their fight for 'justice through the tunnels and mazes of bureaucracy'. He documents the 'reawakening of the Indian consciousness, the rebirth of the Indian pride, and the rediscovery of importance in Indian culture and traditions'. The interested reader should also consult the author's earlier controversial work entitled *The unjust society: the tragedy of Canada's Indians* (Edmonton, Alberta: M. G. Hurtig, 1969).

247 **A history of the original peoples of northern Canada.**
Keith J. Crowe. Kingston, Ontario; Montreal: McGill-Queen's University Press, 1974. 226p.

This text, written for native teenage students, is just as valuable for the general reader. The author attempts to record the history of the Indian and Inuit peoples of northern Canada, from a native standpoint. He moves from prehistory to the emergence of the major groups of hunting peoples (the Algonkian, the Athapaskan and the Inuit). He describes their lifestyles and characteristics, as well as various phases of their development, particularly as affected by European influences. This interesting work also contains a list of supplementary reading.

248 **Native people in Canada: contemporary conflicts.**
James S. Frideres. Scarborough, Ontario: Prentice-Hall Canada, 1983. 2nd ed. 344p. bibliog.

A reasonably comprehensive survey of the state of native affairs in the country. Divided into three major parts the work provides an historical context essential to the understanding of such contemporary issues as treaties, native claims and the Indian Act, profiles the native peoples of today in an attempt to illustrate their overall position within Canadian society, and introduces a theoretical perspective by which native-white relations can be explained. A bibliography is included.

249 **As long as the sun shines and water flows: a reader in Canadian native studies.**
Edited by Ian A. L. Getty, Antoine S. Lussier. Vancouver: University of British Columbia Press, 1983. 363p. (Nakoda Institute Occasional Paper, vol. 1).

The literature in the area of native studies is rich with collections of essays and compilations of papers published as proceedings of conferences. This volume is one of the better anthologies, including contributions which focus upon Canadian native history since 1763. The papers represent varied approaches to native studies, and reflect upon a number of issues, such as colonial Indian policy, constitutional and legislative developments, Indian treaties, policy and government decision-making, native responses to change; and aboriginal and treaty rights.

250 **The Métis in the Canadian West.**
Marcel Giraud, translated by George Woodcock. Edmonton, Alberta: University of Alberta Press, 1986. 2nd ed. 2 vols.

The term 'Métis' has had several historical definitions; in the broadest terms it is used to describe people of mixed North American Indian/European descent. While such bi-racial interaction was common throughout Canadian history, it was in the Canadian West that the Métis became recognized as a people – particularly in Manitoba and Saskatchewan and notably through the person of Louis Riel. Giraud's study, though written over forty years ago, remains the most thorough ethnographic and historical study of these people. Other works, perhaps more readable, and more current, have been published and include: D. N. Sprague's *Canada and the Métis, 1869-1885* (Waterloo, Ontario: Wilfred Laurier University Press, 1988); Donald Purich's *The Métis* (Toronto: James Lorimer & Company, 1988); Don McLean's *Home from the hill: a history of the Métis in western Canada* (Regina, Saskatchewan: Gabriel Dumont Institute, 1987); F. Laurie Barron and James B. Waldram's *1885 and after: native society in transition* (Regina, Saskatchewan: Canadian Plains Research Center, 1986); Jacqueline Peterson and Jennifer Brown's *The new peoples: being and becoming Métis in North America* (Winnipeg, Manitoba: The University of Manitoba Press, 1985); and D. Bruce Sealey and Antoine S. Lussier's *The Métis: Canada's forgotten people* (Winnipeg, Manitoba: Manitoba Métis Federation Press, 1975).

251 The Inuit: life as it was.
Richard Harrington. Edmonton, Alberta: Hurtig, 1981. 143p.

Prose and photography document the life of the Inuit peoples between 1947 and 1953. This is a beautiful as well as informative work which portrays an existence which is simultaneously simple, harsh and precarious.

252 Eskimo administration.
Diamond Jenness. Montreal: Arctic Institute of North America, 1962-68. 5 vols.

This investigation and the scholarship of Jenness admirably stand the test of time. These five volumes in turn deal with the diverse histories of the Eskimo administration in Alaska, Canada, Greenland and Labrador, with a lengthy concluding essay appraising the merits and weaknesses of the different methods of administration adopted by each country in turn.

253 The Indians of Canada.
Diamond Jenness. Toronto: University of Toronto Press, 1977. 7th ed. 432p. (Canadian University Paperbacks, vol. 203).

With its initial publication this work provided the first comprehensive presentation of Canadian aborigines. It lays claim today, not only to the status of a classic, but also as a continuously useful reference tool. It includes chapters on languages, economic conditions, food resources, hunting and fishing, dress and adornment, dwellings, travel and transportation, trade and commerce, social and political organization, social life, religion, folklore and traditions, and drama, music and art. Jenness describes the various tribes within different groupings, i.e. woodlands, plains, Pacific coast, Cordillera, Mackenzie and Yukon River basins, and the Eskimo.

254 Urban Indians: the strangers in Canada's cities.
Larry Krotz. Edmonton, Alberta: Hurtig, 1980. 157p.

In the jails and penitentiaries west of Sudbury, Ontario the proportion of Indian inmates does not reflect their numbers in the population in general. In Manitoba, where twelve per cent of the population is native, the proportion of Indian inmates of the Portage la Prairie Correctional Centre for Women forms an astonishing eighty per cent of the total. The author attempts to account for these facts and to answer related questions. He looks at the migration of Indian people to three urban centres, Edmonton, Regina and Winnipeg. He considers the way Indians live and the way they are treated by bureaucracies, in schools, in business and in the law. A further discussion of this subject can be found in Edgar J. Dosman's *Indians: the urban dilemma* (Toronto: McClelland & Stewart, 1972).

255 **Governments in conflict?: provinces and Indian nations in Canada.**
Edited by J. Anthony Long, Menno Boldt, Leroy Little Bear.
Toronto: University of Toronto Press, 1988. 296p.
Presents a selection of papers by Indian leaders, government officials, and legal and academic scholars, which addresses the issues surrounding the relations between the Indians and provincial governments. The moves to include Indians in social and economic programmes by the provincial governments, and their implications for the Indians are discussed.

256 **The uncharted nations: a reference history of the Canadian tribes.**
Robert MacDonald.   Calgary, Alberta: Ballantrae Foundation, 1978.
280p. (Romance of Canadian History, vol. 3).
This is a popular, profusely illustrated account of the native peoples of Canada, and is organized into sections which include: the Algonkian; the Athapascans of the north and west; the Inuit of the Arctic Maritimes; the Iroquoians of the eastern woodlands; the coast and interior Salish; the Siouan tribes of Canada; and the Waukeshans of the Pacific coast.

257 **Native peoples and cultures of Canada: an anthropological overview.**
Alan D. McMillan.   Vancouver; Toronto: Douglas & McIntyre, 1988.
340p.
A contemporary overview of Canadian natives, past and present. It is a readable, though scholarly synthesis of the anthropological, archaeological, ethnohistorical, linguistic, ethnographic research of the past several decades. The results of work in these disciplines is woven into a broad historical narrative which deals with native Canadian life from prehistory to modern issues.

258 **Native peoples: the Canadian experience.**
Edited by R. Bruce Morrison, C. Roderick Wilson.   Toronto:
McClelland & Stewart, 1988. 542p.
An excellent collection of essays, written from an anthropological perspective, which serves as a primer for the general reader. Taken together the essays provide an understanding of native peoples, through an appreciation of aboriginal society, as it existed and continues to exist, and outline the history of relationships between Indians and Canadian society. The reader is given a firm grounding in the complexity of native life.

259 **Aboriginal peoples and the law: Indian, Métis and Inuit rights in Canada.**
Edited by Bradford W. Morse.   Ottawa: Carleton University Press,
1985. 800p. (Carleton Library Series, vol. 131).
Presents cases and legal materials relating to the law and aboriginal peoples. The book begins with a chapter describing the general position of the indigenous population, and then focuses on several themes: aboriginal rights in international law; aboriginal land

claims; pre- and post-Confederation treaties; constitutional issues in native law; the application of provincial laws; reserve lands; taxation; the resolution of land claims; and, the north and native rights. Other texts on this subject include Derek G. Smith's *Canadian Indians and the law: selected documents, 1663-1972* (Toronto: McClelland & Stewart, 1975); and *Native rights in Canada* (Toronto: The Indian-Eskimo Association of Canada, 1972).

260 **The white Arctic: anthropological essays on tutelage and ethnicity.**
Edited by Robert Paine. St John's, Newfoundland: Institute of Social and Economic Research, Memorial University of Newfoundland, 1977. 418p. (Newfoundland Social and Economic Papers, vol. 7).

Inuit-white relations are discussed within the context of the learning process. The work examines government programmes of development and administration in the north, the concept of colonialism (that is a colonialism based on welfare), and the colonial encounter as it is reflected in the tutelage by whites of native peoples.

261 **The Canadian Indian: a history since 1500.**
E. Palmer Patterson. Toronto: Collier-Macmillan Canada, 1972. 210p.

An historical overview, and thus of limited usefulness, of the Indian in Canada. In addition to such very general works as this, there continues to emerge a rich, scholarly historical literature on Canada's native peoples. The interested reader is directed to the following which is far from an exhaustive list: Olive P. Dickason's *The myth of the savage: and the beginnings of French colonialism in the Americas* (Edmonton, Alberta: University of Alberta Press, 1984); Leslie F. S. Upton's *Micmacs and colonists: Indian-white relations in the Maritimes, 1713-1867* (Vancouver: University of British Columbia Press, 1979); Robin Fisher's *Contact and conflict: Indian-European relations in British Columbia, 1774-1890* (Vancouver: University of British Columbia Press, 1977); Cornelius J. Jaenen's *Friend and foe: aspects of French-Amerindian cultural contact in the sixteenth and seventeenth centuries* (Toronto: McClelland & Stewart, 1976); Arthur J. Ray's *Indians in the fur trade: their role as trappers, hunters, and middlemen in the lands southwest of Hudson Bay 1660-1870* (Toronto: University of Toronto Press, 1974); and Alfred G. Bailey's *The Conflict of European and eastern Algonkian cultures 1504-1700: a study in Canadian civilization* (Toronto: University of Toronto Press, 1969).

262 **Arduous journey: Canadian Indians and decolonization.**
Edited by J. Rick Ponting. Toronto: McClelland & Stewart, 1986. 413p.

For Indians the 1970s and the first half of the 1980s was a period of enormous change marked by a 'social, political, cultural, and to a lesser extent economic revolution [which] was triggered by events surrounding the federal government's 1969 white paper on Indian policy'. This interesting collection of essays provides an historical overview and socio-demographic background to the discussion, then deals in turn with such topics as economic and community development, aboriginal rights and claims, and Indian self-government. Another book on this subject is Ponting and Roger Gibbins' *Out of irrelevance: a socio-political introduction to Indian affairs in Canada* (Toronto: Butterworths, 1980).

263 **Indians of Canada: cultural dynamics.**
John A. Price.   Scarborough, Ontario: Prentice-Hall, 1979. 261p.
bibliog.

A survey of the dynamics of Indian life in Canada, this book 'looks at ecological adaptations, historical persistence and acculturation, cultural evolution, and the background to current Indian-White relationships'. Individual chapters deal with such topics as racial characteristics, native languages and cultural patterns. It is organized according to region.

264 **Our land: native rights in Canada.**
Donald Purich.   Toronto: James Lorimer & Company, 1986. 252p.
(Canadian Issues Series).

A succinct account of the various issues confronting the native peoples in Canada. The author considers social issues, economic issues, native rights, government policies, as well as other issues. Although somewhat biased, it can be recommended for its treatment of a series of complex and interrelated social problems.

265 **Reservations are for Indians.**
Heather Robertson.   Toronto: James Lorimer & Company, 1970.
303p.

Though dated, this exposé by a respected investigative journalist focuses attention on Canada's native peoples. Robertson writes, 'I was shocked by the reserves and Métis communities, shocked by the destitution, the squalor, the chaos, the brutality, the apathy. Worse, however, was the people's fear, servility and hatred, and the knowledge that these feelings were based on the color of my skin . . . I could no longer believe . . . society to be benevolent, nor could I believe the government to be just'. Much has changed since Robertson's investigation (for example, native peoples have become more politically active), regrettably, much also remains the same.

266 **Handbook of North American Indians.**
William C. Sturtevant, general ed.   Washington: Smithsonian
Institution, 1978- . [20] vols.

To date all volumes of this set are not yet published, although twenty volumes are planned. The intent of this encyclopaedic work is to supply information on the prehistory, history, and cultures of the aboriginal peoples of North America who lived north of the urban civilizations of central Mexico. This monumental work of scholarship is destined to become the authoritative reference work on North American Indians.

267 **The Canadian Indian: the illustrated history of the great tribes of Canada.**
Fraser Symington.   Toronto: McClelland & Stewart, 1969. 272p.

This richly illustrated volume is a somewhat stereotypical portrayal of the first Indian nations, yet it is useful for the general reader or the student. On the same topic, the author's similar, but abbreviated version may also be of interest, *The first Canadians* (Toronto: Natural Science of Canada, 1978. Canada's Illustrated Heritage series).

268 **The politics of Indianness: case studies of native ethnopolitics in Canada.**
Edited by Adrian Tanner. St. John's, Newfoundland: Institute of
Social and Economic Research, Memorial University of Newfoundland,
1983. 321p. (Social and Economic Papers, vol. 12).

Three investigators examine three groups of Indians, one in the Northwest Territories,
another in Nova Scotia, and the third in an unidentified western province, in terms of
political attempts by regional and local groups of Indians 'to improve their social and
economic conditions'. All three groups 'share a common background in the upsurge of
national-level native issues and political activities of the time'.

269 **Eskimo of the Canadian Arctic.**
Victor Valentine, Frank G. Vallee. Toronto: McClelland & Stewart,
1968. 241p. (Carleton Library, vol. 41).

Presents a useful collection of articles for the general reader, the subjects of which
extend from Shamanism to Eskimo language, and from the Eskimo economy to
Eskimo art. —

270 **Dene nation – the colony within.**
Edited by Mel Watkins. Toronto: University of Toronto Press, 1977.
189p.

This collection of papers has been selected from presentations made to the Berger
Inquiry into the Mackenzie Valley Pipeline, and reflects the efforts of the Dene people
to block the construction of the pipeline. However, they also 'reflect the Dene nation's
fundamental perception that their struggle is for the most universal of human rights,
the right to be a self-determining people, living with their land as they have always
done . . . the Dene nation will continue to assert this right and continue to strive for
decolonization in matters of economics, politics, education, law, and culture'.

271 **Making Canadian Indian policy: the hidden agenda 1968-70.**
Sally M. Weaver. Toronto: University of Toronto Press, 1981. 236p.
(Studies in the Structure of Power: Decision-Making in Canada, vol. 9).

This study attempts to look inside the decision making process which led to the 'white
paper' on Indian policy issued by the Trudeau government in 1969, which proposed the
termination of all special rights and went against the expectations of the Indian
community who were led to believe that 'their rights would be honoured and that they
would participate in shaping the policies that determined their future'. This policy was
finally abandoned but left in its wake a legacy of mistrust between the federal
government and the Indian community.

272 **In the middle: the Inuit today.**
Stephen Guion Williams. Toronto: Fitzhenry & Whiteside, 1983.
[n.p.]

An anthropological, photographic essay of a culture in a state of change, describing the
dilemma in which the Inuit find themselves – they cannot return to their old ways yet
they have no wish to adopt the ways of modern society. The result of this is 'an almost
schizophrenic way of life. The Inuit live, in a sense, directly in between their two
worlds'.

273 **The dispossessed: life and death in native Canada.**
Geoffrey York.   Toronto: Lester & Orpen Dennys, 1989. 283p.

An articulate and moving account of the issues and of the tragedies which have faced and continue to face native peoples in Canada. The author is able to provide a disturbing account, documented with examples, of the social attitudes and government policies which have reinforced racism and sought to assimilate the native peoples – policies which were designed to dispossess these people of their culture, their language, their families and their rights to self-determination.

Emigration and
Immigration

274 **None is too many: Canada and the Jews of Europe 1933-1948.**
Irving Abella, Harold Troper.   Toronto: Lester & Orpen Dennys,
1982. 336p.

A disturbing work dealing with a black chapter in Canadian history. For the Jews of
Europe during the period under discussion Canada was 'a paradise, enormous,
wealthy, overflowing and full of life; but out of bounds, a haven totally inaccessible'.
Why Canada, traditionally a country which provided sanctuary for refugees, was closed
to the Jews of Europe is the focus of this work. Of all the nations of the world Canada
documented the worst record in providing sanctuary to Jews fleeing Nazi terror. Of
related interest is Simon Belkin's *Through narrow gates: a review of Jewish
immigration, colonization and immigrant aid work in Canada (1840-1940)* (Montreal:
Canadian Jewish Congress and the Jewish Colonization Association, 1966).

275 **'Dangerous foreigners': European immigrant workers and labour
radicalism in Canada 1896-1932.**
Donald Avery.   Toronto: McClelland & Stewart, 1979. 204p.
(Canadian Social History Series).

This well documented study examines the rôle of European immigrant workers in the
economic and social life of Canada during that period of high immigration ending with
the Great Depression. The authors record the back-breaking nature of their industry,
the poor working conditions, low wages and often violent treatment at the hands of
employers and authorities. Little wonder that the inevitable recourse of such
circumstances was the development of radical ethnic and political organizations of
redress.

276 **The immigrant years: from Europe to Canada 1945-1967.**
Barry Broadfoot. Vancouver; Toronto: Douglas & McIntyre, 1986.
255p.

An historical treatment for the general reader of the influx of some 2,500,000 immigrants during the post-war period. Broadfoot deals with the nature of post-war Canada, the circumstances of the immigrant population, focusing on those coming from Europe, the obstacles and discrimination faced upon their arrival in Canada, and the legacy of cultural enrichment which they brought to the country.

277 **After the war.**
Jean Bruce. Toronto: Fitzhenry & Whiteside in cooperation with the Multiculturalism Directorate, Secretary of State and the Canadian Government Publishing Centre, Supply and Services Canada, 1982. 192p.

Over 1,000,000 immigrants came to Canada during the ten years which followed the Second World War. This is a popular, illustrated account of the people who came to Canada in the aftermath of the war including 'the warbrides, the British, the Dutch farm families, the Americans; the refugees and displaced persons from central and eastern Europe and the Baltic states; . . . the former "enemy aliens"'. This is an entertaining introduction to the subject but contains little analysis or critical examination of policy issues.

278 **Canada's refugee policy: indifference or opportunism?**
Gerald E. Dirks. Montreal; London, Ontario: McGill-Queen's University Press, 1977. 316p.

At the present time Canada's policy in relation to refugees is in the process of change, although some might argue it is in a state of confusion. Nonetheless, in the past Canada has had a reasonable record in terms of offering sanctuary to individuals escaping intolerable political or social conditions, such as those compelled to leave their homelands. This work analyses Canada's policies and programmes in relation to refugees and, although it discusses refugee matters during the nineteenth century, it concentrates on the period immediately preceding the Second World War up until 1973.

279 **Boomtime: peopling the Canadian prairies.**
James H. Gray. Saskatoon, Saskatchewan: Western Producer Prairie Books, 1979. 148p.

A popular, profusely illustrated account of the settlement of the Canadian prairies. As noted by the author 'never before had any government embarked so deliberately on a project of comparable magnitude to populate so vast an area of empty wilderness, nor embarked on so grandiose a scheme to persuade people . . . to travel half way round the world or across half a continent, to pioneer the establishment of . . . a new nation'.

280 **Immigration and the postwar Canadian economy.**
Alan G. Green. Toronto: Macmillan; Maclean-Hunter Press, 1976. 312p. bibliog.

The author examines Canada's liberal and expansionary post-war immigration policy in some depth during the period 1946-69. He looks at the economic determinants underpinning this policy and comments on the influences which determined the timing and composition of immigrant arrivals. A section is devoted to the movement of highly trained manpower, a movement often referred to as the 'brain-drain' or 'brain-gain' problem. The methodology of the study is econometric and thus is directed at the informed reader. A modest bibliography is included.

281 **Immigration law in Canada.**
Julius H. Grey. Toronto: Butterworths, 1984. 237p.

A practical summary of Canadian immigration law and jurisprudence.

282 **The great migration: the Atlantic crossing by sailing-ship since 1770.**
Edwin C. Guillet. Toronto: University of Toronto Press, 1963. 2nd ed. 284p.

This classic study records the migration of over 11,000,000 people who left the British Isles in order to settle in North America. Attention is given to the conditions under which these emigrants left their homeland, as well as to the trying conditions of the Atlantic crossing and their early experiences in their new home. This is a very readable, entertaining and still relevant account in the grand style of historical scholarship.

283 **Immigrants: a portrait of the urban experience 1890-1930.**
Robert F. Harney, Harold Troper. Toronto: Van Nostrand Reinhold, 1975. 212p.

Using photographs, and brief commentaries, this work provides an album of immigrant life in the city of Toronto for the period which encompassed the great migration from southern and eastern Europe to the west and to the industrial centres of Canada. The photographs have particular impact as a visual representation of the experiences of these people.

284 **Canada and immigration: public policy and public concern.**
Freda Hawkins. Kingston, Ontario; Montreal: McGill-Queen's University Press, 1988. 2nd ed. 476p. (Canadian Public Administration Series).

An examination of immigration policy since the Second World War to the early 1970s, with a sequel bringing it up to 1986. The author advocates that the policy of the period, driven by manpower needs, was inappropriate and narrow within the context of world overcrowding; consideration should be given to policies related to future political, social and environmental needs. Also of interest as an historical commentary is David Corbett's *Canada's immigration policy: a critique* (Toronto: University of Toronto Press, 1957).

285 The Scots to Canada.
Douglas Hill. London: Gentry, 1972. 136p. (Great Emigrations).
A chronicle, written in a popular style, of the Scottish immigration to Canada with emphasis on the Maritimes, Ontario and Quebec, and the experiences of the Selkirk settlers in the early nineteenth century. A more scholarly work, which focuses on a narrow time scale, is J. M. Bumsted's *The people's clearance: Highland emigration to British North America 1770-1815* (Edinburgh; Winnipeg, Manitoba: Edinburgh University Press; University of Manitoba Press, 1982).

286 The immigrant's handbook: a critical guide.
Law Union of Ontario. Montreal: Black Rose, 1981. 263p.
Canada's immigration laws, regulations and procedures are changing rapidly. As such the potential immigrant is encouraged to seek advice and guidance from appropriate authorities. The work in hand, although now somewhat dated, does provide assistance to the interested reader leading to an understanding of the law and relevant procedures as they existed in June, 1981. Much of the information continues to be useful.

287 The annotated Immigration Act of Canada.
Edited and annotated by Frank N. Marrocco, Henry M. Goslett.
Toronto: Carswell, 1988. 446p.
Includes all the relevant decisions reported to November 30, 1987 which interpret the various sections of the Immigration Act and Regulations. This volume is useful for the person involved in the application of Canadian Immigration Law. Those interested should seek out the most recent future edition of the work in order to ensure accuracy of information.

288 The immigrants.
Gloria Montero. Toronto: James Lorimer & Company, 1977. 222p.
By way of interviews Montero presents the stories of a number of immigrants who chose Canada as their home. These vignettes provide a view of the personal side of the immigration process; the perceptions, the hopes, the humiliations, the disappointments, the achievements and the inevitable problems with the immigration bureaucracy. The work is divided into two parts: the first is made up of personal histories; the second is comprised of thematic chapters which bring together the experiences of a number of people on topics such as job search, cultural assimilation and relationships.

289 **A report of the Canadian immigration and population study.**
Ottawa: Manpower and Immigration, 1974. 4 vols.

Comprises a 'green paper' issued for the purposes of discussion as part of a comprehensive government review of immigration policy. The four component parts of the paper, published as separate volumes, were: *Immigration policy perspectives*, which examined the immigration programme from the viewpoint of broad policy issues; *The immigration program*, which provided a history of legislation and procedures (selection procedures, refugee programme, etc.); *Immigration and population statistics* which brought together a comprehensive set of immigration statistics; and *Three years in Canada* which examined the experiences of a group of immigrants over a three year period.

290 **Post-war immigrants in Canada.**
Anthony H. Richmond. Toronto: University of Toronto Press, 1967. 320p. (Canadian Studies in Sociology, vol. 2).

This is a sociological study of the absorption of post-war immigrants into Canadian society. Specifically the work develops an overall picture of the economic and social aspects of the absorption, it compares the experiences of British immigrants with those from other countries, it examines the reasons why immigrants chose to become Canadian citizens, and it explores the factors associated with a return of British immigrants to the United Kingdom. Although dated, the work does provide an understanding of the development of post-war Canada.

291 **Immigrating to Canada: who is allowed? what is required? how to do it!**
Gary L. Segal. Vancouver: International Self-Counsel Press, 1987. 7th ed. 170p.

A straightforward explanation of the intricacies of Canadian immigration law and a step-by-step explanation of the processes involved if a person wishes to immigrate, visit, or set up business in Canada.

292 **Double standard: the secret history of Canadian immigration.**
Reg Whitaker. Toronto: Lester & Orpen Dennys, 1987. 348p.

A polemic on recent immigration policy in Canada, focusing on a perceived political bias in the system. The author is critical of Canadian immigration policy and the misleading rhetoric surrounding the implementation of that policy, citing racism and other policies which reflect a discriminatory self-interest. In his introduction he describes Canada as 'a country that, out of an extreme fear of totalitarianism, enacts what must be termed quasi-totalitarian controls'.

293 **Strangers within our gates or coming Canadians.**
James S. Woodsworth, introduction by Marilyn Barber. Toronto: University of Toronto Press, 1972. 279p. (Social History of Canada).

First published in 1909, *Strangers within our gates* is a classic within the literature of immigration in Canada. At the time of its writing Woodsworth was Superintendent of the All People's Mission in Winnipeg, a post he held from 1904-13. He later went on to be a major figure in the labour movement and reform politics, being the first leader of the Cooperative Commonwealth Federation (CCF). This book was intended to provide an introduction for Canadians to the newly arrived immigrant groups; it also documented the social problems, particularly in the urban areas, encountered by these peoples as well as the difficulties they faced in assimilating into the Canadian, Anglo-Saxon mould and adopting Canadian standards.

Languages

Dictionaries

294 **Dictionary of Canadian English: the senior dictionary.**
Edited by W. S. Avis, P. D. Drysdale, R. J. Gregg, M. H. Scargill.
Toronto: W. J. Gage, 1967. 1284p.
This is the last of a three volume set which includes *The beginning dictionary*, designed for children in Grades 3, 4, and 5 (ages 9-11), and *The intermediate dictionary*, directed at students in senior elementary and junior high schools. This *Senior dictionary* is intended for high school users and beyond. Many of the entries are based on material collected for the *Dictionary of Canadianisms*.

295 **Dictionary of Canadianisms on historical principles.**
Edited by Walter S. Avis. Toronto: W. J. Gage, 1967. 927p.
An illustrated dictionary documenting the history, usage, etymology and other aspects of Canadianisms – language 'which is native to Canada or which is distinctively characteristic of Canadian usage though not necessarily exclusive to Canada.' Attention is drawn also to a companion volume, entitled *A Concise dictionary of Canadianisms* (Toronto: Gage Educational Publishing, 1973) which provides a generous sampling of the words and expressions found in the primary work. Similar works both in terms of intent, and in terms of scholarship are: T. K. Pratt's *Dictionary of Prince Edward Island English* (Toronto: University of Toronto, 1988); and, G. M. Story, W. J. Kirwin, and J. D. A. Widdowson's *Dictionary of Newfoundland English* (Toronto: University of Toronto Press, 1982). Of interest also, but more as a curiosity, is John Sandilands' *Western Canadian dictionary and phrase book* (Edmonton, Alberta: University of Alberta Press, 1977).

296 **Dictionnaire de la langue québécoise.** (Dictionary of Québécois French.)
Léandre Bergeron. Montreal: VLB Éditeur, 1980. 575p.
There is a language particular to the Québécois, which is very much alive. It is used not only in the day-to-day lives of the Quebec people, but it is the language of Quebec

culture, literature, politics and business. It is, like Canadian English, more than a dialect of another European mother country. The *Dictionnaire* contains over 17,500 words and over 5,500 expressions (a *Supplément* published in 1981 contains an additional 2,300 words and 500 expressions) unique to Quebec French. A condensed and adapted English version of the *Dictionnaire* was published entitled *The Québécois dictionary* (Toronto: James Lorimer & Company, 1982). Its purpose was to serve as a 'handbook to explore Quebec, to understand the Québécois in all their living processes'. Other dictionaries include Louis-Alexandre's Bélisle's *Dictionnaire nord-américain de la langue française* (Dictionary of North American French. Montreal: Librairie Beauchemin Limitée, 1979).

297 **Practical handbook of Quebec and Acadian French=Manuel pratique du français québécois et acadien.**
Sinclair Robinson, Donald Smith. Toronto: Anansi, 1984. 302p.

This handbook is a reworking, expansion and revision of the *Practical handbook of Canadian French* published in 1973. It provides a convenient guide to the usages of words in Canada, as compared with those of mainland France and of standard English. Word lists are grouped under broad headings, and then broken into three columns, headed Quebec, France and [blank]. Under the first column are words or expressions used in Quebec which are unknown or have a limited usage in France; and the middle column gives the equivalent word or expression used in France. The last column gives the equivalent English usage. This work is not to be taken as a scholarly socio-linguistic study; it is as its title portrays, a ready guide for the communicator.

298 **The Canadian dictionary: French-English: English-French=Dictionnaire canadien: français-anglais: anglais-français.**
Edited by Jean-Paul Vinay, Pierre Daviault, Henry Alexander.
Toronto: McClelland & Stewart, 1962. 862p.

Although this dictionary is somewhat dated, it still represents one of the best bilingual desk dictionaries available which provides a Canadian standard for precise translation. The work was prepared at the Lexicographic Research Centre of the University of Montreal.

General

299 **Le choc de patois en Nouvelle-France: essai sur l'histoire de la francisation au Canada.** (The impact of patois in New France: essay on the history of Gallicization in Canada.)
Philippe Barbaud. Sillery, Quebec: Presses de l'Université du Québec, 1984. 204p.

A technical and scholarly study of the origins of, and influences on, the French language in New France (a region including at one time most of eastern North America) by emigrants from the various regions of France primarily during the colonization period of the seventeenth century. The study incorporates various demolinguistic techniques to analyse the linguistic assimilation of idioms which resulted ultimately in the unique form of the language in Canada.

300 **Conflict and language planning in Quebec.**
Edited by Richard Y. Bourhis. Clevedon, England: Multilingual
Matters, 1984. 304p. (Multilingual Matters, vol. 5).
This multidisciplinary book aims to provide a description of the moves in Quebec
towards making French the only official language in Quebec society. The implementation of Bill 101 by the Quebec government, which enforced French in state and
commercial matters, and its implications for the province's independence are
discussed.

301 **Official-language populations in Canada: patterns and contacts.**
Donald G. Cartwright. Montreal: Institute for Research on Public
Policy/L'Institut de recherches politiques, 1980. 160p. (Occasional
Paper, No. 16).
An examination of some of the processes and patterns that are associated with the
contact and interaction of Canada's two official language populations.

302 **Canadian English: origins and structures.**
Edited by J. K. Chambers. Toronto: Methuen, 1975. 144p.
Presents a number of articles about the English language as it is spoken in Canada. A
number of the essays have been reprinted from other sources, while several were
prepared for this compilation. The individual studies have been balanced both by
region and by linguistic methodology, and are organized in three sections: 'Origins'
discusses the history of English speakers in Canada; and 'Linguistic Enclaves' and
'Heartland Canadian English' deal with aspects of pronunciation and vocabulary of the
English spoken in the various regions of the country.

303 **The languages of Canada.**
Edited by J. K. Chambers. Montreal: Didier, 1979. 259p.
Canada has indeed a cultural diversity as varied as its geographic and climatic diversity.
This collection of scholarly articles reflects this fact in that it encompasses a section on
native languages (including the Algonquian languages, the Central Indian languages,
the languages of British Columbia, and Eskimo), with a chapter on the 'Maintenance
of the native languages'. The second section deals with the 'Official languages', while
the final section reflects on the 'Other languages in Canada', particularly the languages
of immigrants coming to the country. There is an index which references each language
discussed, or referred to in the body of the text.

304 **Les anglicisms au Québéc: répertoire classifié.** (Quebec anglicisms: a
categorized list.)
Gilles Colpron. Montreal: Librairie Beauchemin Limitée, 1970. 247p.
Anglicisms which have found common usage in Quebec are listed here, together with
notes of explanation and the correct French form.

305 **Languages in conflict: the Canadian experience.**
Richard J. Joy. Toronto: McClelland & Stewart, 1972. 2nd ed. 149p.
(Carleton Library, vol. 61).
This is an interesting book with a curious publishing history, which is chronicled in the
preface to the Carleton Library edition. The author presents a linguistic history of

Canada, primarily as revealed and interpreted by census records. The work can be said to have been prophetic in the sense that the conclusions drawn were of a type which ultimately saw some of the most vigorous debates on language which were to follow in the 1970s and 1980s. The book itself had little contemporary impact.

306　**The demolinguistic situation in Canada: past trends and future prospects.**
Réjean Lachapelle, Jacques Henripin.　Montreal: Institute for Research on Public Policy/L'Institut de recherches politiques, 1982. 387p. bibliog.

An objective demolinguistic examination which describes and projects future linguistic trends. The work deals primarily with French and English, describing the evolution of the current demolinguistic situation, with attention on the period 1951-76. It analyses the effects of mortality, fertility, linguistic mobility and migration on regional linguistic composition. This work may be of some interest to the student of the Canadian identity. A bibliography is included.

307　**Our own voice: Canadian English and how it came to be.**
R. E. McConnell.　Toronto: Gage, 1978. 276p. bibliog.

A well-researched, very readable examination of the characteristics of Canadian English, and the varieties of English used in the country. The author explores the origins of Canadian English, the forces at work in the creation of new words, the language and dialects of the country, and the regional variations to be found from the Atlantic provinces through to the west coast. The book is well designed, illustrated and contains a 'General Bibliography on Canadian English and Dialectology' and a 'Bibliography of Literary and Historical Sources Quoted'. This is a work for the academic and non-specialist alike.

308　**Speaking Canadian English: an informal account of the English language in Canada.**
Mark M. Orkin.　New York: David McKay, 1970. 276p. bibliog.

Yes, there is a Canadian English which is distinct from that of Great Britain and that of the United States, although clearly its origins are from the former and many influences come from the latter. This is a most readable and informative book on the subject, written in the popular style, although it is well documented and contains an impressive bibliography. The various sections set out the 'ingredients' or influences on the language, discuss pronunciation, spelling and syntax and the origins of names (this latter section not wholly appropriate within such a study), and finally, examine Canadian slang and the future of the language.

309　**Speaking Canadian French: an informal account of the French language in Canada.**
Mark M. Orkin.　New York: David McKay, 1971. rev. ed. 132p. bibliog.

While this is a companion volume to the author's *Speaking Canadian English: an informal account of the English language in Canada* (q.v.), clearly the author's expertise is in the English language. Nevertheless, this text provides an interesting, if not definitive, account as to the nature and origins of Canadian French. It includes a 'List of Words and Phrases' as well as a lengthy bibliography.

310 **A preliminary report of the Royal Commission on Bilingualism and Biculturalism = Rapport préliminaire de la Commission royale d'enquête sur le bilinguisme et le biculturalisme: Preliminary report and Books I & II.**
New York: Arno Press, 1978. (Bilingual-Bicultural Education in the United States).
This is a more recent, and thus perhaps more available, reprint of the original reports published in 1965-68 by the Queen's Printer of Canada. This Commission was charged with the examination of existing bilingualism and biculturalism in Canada and was instructed to make recommendations ensuring the wider recognition of the cultural dualism of Canada. In part the Commission was established in response to the growing concerns among the French Canadian population in Quebec. Its mandate was wide-ranging but focused on areas such as the bilingual nature of the federal government, the rôle of various agencies and institutions in the promotion of cultural relations, and also the structures required to promote bilingualism for individual Canadians. In a great many ways the present nature of the Canadian identity, whether related to culture, language, education or other areas, is a product of the Commission's recommendations. A significant document for the understanding of Canada.

311 **A short history of Canadian English.**
M. H. Scargill. Victoria, British Columbia: Sono Nis, 1977. 70p.
The author was the Director of the Lexicographical Centre at the University of Victoria. This respected academic provides the general reader with a history of Canadian English which traces the forces that shaped the language. He shows how the language continues to grow and change, and wittily and concisely, reveals the fascinating origins of many of our most common words as well as some of the more exotic ones.

Religion

312 **The social passion: religion and social reform in Canada 1914-28.**
Richard Allen.   Toronto: University of Toronto Press, 1973. 385p.
This is a landmark work of scholarship which studies the history of ideas, specifically
the conjunction of the movements of religion and social reform in Canada during the
period when the influence of the phenomenon was at its height. The technical term for
the movement under study is the 'social gospel'. Other titles of interest include: *The
social gospel in Canada: papers of the interdisciplinary conference on the social gospel in
Canada, March 21-24, 1973* (Ottawa: National Museums of Canada, 1975); and Salem
Bland's *The new Christianity: or the religion of the new age* (Toronto: University of
Toronto Press, 1973).

313 **Prairie spirit: perspectives on the heritage of the United Church of
Canada in the West.**
Edited by Dennis Butcher (et al.).   Winnipeg, Manitoba: University of
Manitoba Press, 1985. 388p.
Written in celebration of the sixtieth anniversary of the United Church of Canada, this
collection of articles explores the issues and concerns of the prairie congregations of
the Presbyterian, Methodist and Congregational Churches that combined in 1925 to
form the United Church of Canada. The volume also includes essays about individual
congregations, two bibliographic guides and a photo essay on historic churches.

314 **Canadian churches & social justice.**
Toronto: Anglican Book Centre and James Lorimer, 1984. 293p.
Increasingly Canadian churches are taking an active rôle in a wide range of
contemporary public issues broadly categorized as issues of social justice. This is a
collection of twenty-one documents, (issued either with the authority of a national
church, by regional sectors of a church, by inter-church organizations, or by
knowledgeable and respected church leaders) which deal with such issues as poverty in
Canada, capitalism and corporations, nuclear energy, northern development and

Religion

native rights, Canada, Quebec and the Constitution, population, immigration and refugees, and Canada and the Third World.

315 The Anglican Church in Canada: a history.
Philip Carrington. Toronto: Collins, 1963. 320p.

Although dated, this remains one of the best histories of the Anglican Church in Canada. Also of interest is Spencer Ervin's *The political and ecclesiastical history of the Anglican church of Canada* (Ambler, Pennsylvania: Trinity Press, 1967). Complementing this study is T. C. Boon's *The Anglican church from the bay to the Rockies: a history of the Ecclesiastical Province of Rupert's Land and its dioceses from 1820 to 1950* (Toronto: Ryerson Press, 1962) and Thomas R. Millman and A. R. Kelley's *Atlantic Canada to 1900: a history of the Anglican church* (Toronto: Anglican Book Centre, 1983). Recently, Brian Cuthbertson published *The first bishop: a biography of Charles Inglis* (Halifax, Nova Scotia: Waegwoltic Press, 1987) which adds greatly to the understanding of the foundations of the Anglican Church of Canada.

316 Language and religion: a history of English-French conflict in Ontario.
Robert Choquette. Ottawa: University of Ottawa Press, 1975. 264p. (Cahiers d'Histoire de l'Université d'Ottawa, vol. 5).

The fascinating story of English-French conflict within the Catholic Church in Ontario which peaked in intensity during the first quarter of the twentieth century. This conflict was primarily between Catholics of Irish and French-Canadian descent, and it manifested itself through such issues as the University of Ottawa Question (which related to its secularization), denominational/bilingual schools, and conscription during the First World War. Particular attention is given to the rôle of Bishop M. F. Fallon as a key leader of the Irish Catholic faction.

317 Church and sect in Canada.
S. D. Clark. Toronto: University of Toronto Press, 1948. 458p.

A classic work of scholarship in the field of Canadian church history. Working from a sociological perspective, the author examines the conflict between church and sect forms of religious organization in relation to Canada. It is Clark's thesis that 'the church has been dependent upon a condition of social stability and when such a condition has not been present it has given way to the sect form of religious organization . . . The church has grown out of the conditions of a mature society; the sect has been a product of what might be called frontier conditions of social life'. Clark's analysis and conclusions wear well even today. A work similar in nature, is that of W. E. Mann, entitled *Sect, cult and church in Alberta* (Toronto: University of Toronto Press, 1972). This study is a sociological and historical report of the growth of sects and cults in Alberta from 1887 to 1947.

318 The regenerators: social criticism in late Victorian English Canada.
Ramsay Cook. Toronto: University of Toronto Press, 1985. 291p.

An important work for those interested in the growth of social criticism and social reform in Canada, the author explores the nature of social criticism and its relationship to the religious beliefs of late nineteenth-century Canadian society. He notes the crisis of faith faced by Canadian Protestants, whose beliefs were challenged by developments in the natural sciences and historical criticism of the bible.

319 **Religion in Canadian society.**
Edited by Stewart Crysdale, Les Wheatcroft. Toronto:
Macmillan/Maclean-Hunter, 1976. 498p.
Thirty-three papers, primarily within the disciplines of sociology and anthropology, deal with various areas of interaction between religion and Canadian society. The adaptation of religion to social change is examined from cultures as diverse as those of the native peoples to the French of Quebec and the English-speaking Protestants of central Canada and the west. The largest section of the work deals with religion in contemporary life. Within all of these papers three general themes recur: secularization, urbanization and economic and scientific rationalism. This work would be of great value to the reader interested in Canadian religious studies. Also of interest is Peter Slater's *Religion and culture in Canada/Religion et culture au Canada* (Toronto: Canadian Corporation for Studies in Religion, 1977).

320 **Mennonites in Canada, 1786-1920: the history of a separate people.**
Frank H. Epp. Toronto: Macmillan, 1974. 480p.
The first volume of a two volume history, the companion being *Mennonites in Canada, 1920-1940: a people's struggle for survival* (Toronto: Macmillan, 1982). Both volumes are scholarly treatments of a group of people, defined by religion, and their place and problems in Canadian society. In this regard, the first volume has as its dominant theme the Mennonite search for a 'measure of separation from Canadian and other secular societies'. The second volume deals with their 'struggle to survive despite the failure to maintain the traditional physical or geographic separation'. Another recommended work is Lawrence Klippenstein and Julius G. Toews' *Mennonite memories: settling in western Canada* (Winnipeg, Manitoba: Centennial, 1977).

321 **Parsons & politics: the rôle of the Wesleyan Methodists in Upper Canada and the Maritimes from 1780 to 1855.**
Goldwin French. Toronto: Ryerson Press, 1962. 303p.
The Methodists of Upper Canada and Nova Scotia were always viewed suspiciously by the conservative and Anglican ruling circles of British North America. In the former region, however, the Methodists early gained the esteem of the political reformers, and the growing reform movement. Indeed, the Methodist church, through leaders such as Egerton Ryerson, were vocal advocates of reform. This work examines the important place of Methodism in Canadian history. It concentrates on the political and educational policies of Methodists; for the period under study Methodist politics were the politics of education. This is an important work in so far as education in Canada was much influenced by Methodist ideas, particularly those of Ryerson.

322 **A history of the Christian Church in Canada.**
Edited by John Webster Grant. Toronto: McGraw-Hill Ryerson, 1966-72. 3 vols.
This set of books was commissioned as a centennial project and was intended to serve as a definitive historical overview of the Christian Church in Canada. The studies are ecumenically focused. Volume One, by H. H. Walsh, is entitled *The Church in the French era: from colonization to the British conquest* (1966); volume Two, by John S. Moir, is entitled *The Church in the British era: from the British conquest to Confederation* (1972); and volume Three, by John Webster Grant, is entitled *The Church in the Canadian era: the first century of Confederation* (1972).

Religion

323 **Moon of wintertime: missionaries and the Indians of Canada in encounter since 1534.**
John Webster Grant. Toronto: University of Toronto Press, 1984. 315p.

Grant describes the introduction and ongoing pattern of missionary activity which influenced the relationship between the Christian churches and the native peoples of Canada. He 'tells the story of the encounter between Christianity and the Indian peoples over a span of 450 years, from 1534, when Jacques Cartier first erected a cross before the Indians of the Gaspé, to the present. Grant examines both the aims and activities of missionaries of all denominations and the varying responses of Indians at different times and under different circumstances'.

324 **A profusion of spires: religion in nineteenth-century Ontario.**
John Webster Grant. Toronto: University of Toronto Press, 1988. 291p. (Ontario Historical Studies Series).

An account of the development of religious traditions and institutions in Ontario, beginning with a description of the religion of native peoples and ending in 1900 when the Christian churches had achieved a dominant position in the community.

325 **Histoire du catholicisme québécois: le XXe siècle.** (History of Quebecois Catholicism: the 20th century.)
Jean Hamelin, Nicole Gagnon. Montreal: Boréal Express, 1984. 2 vols.

While Catholicism in Canada is by no means limited to the Province of Quebec, the vast majority of Catholics are found in that province. This work by distinguished scholars looks at the Church in the twentieth century. A broader chronological perspective is provided in Nive Voisine's more popular *Histoire de l'Église catholique au Québec (1608-1970)* (History of the Catholic Church in Quebec, Montreal: Éditions Fides, 1971), this work is itself a volume within a larger multi-volume report on the Church in Quebec, sponsored by the Commission d'étude sur les laïcs et l'Église. Abbé Hermann Plante's work is also useful, entitled *L'Église catholique au Canada (1604-1886)* (The Catholic Church in Canada, Trois-Rivières, Quebec: Éditions du Bien Public, 1970). Other regional works have also been produced, for example J. Brian Hanington's *Every popish person: the story of Roman Catholicism in Nova Scotia and the Church in Halifax (1604-1984)* (Halifax, Nova Scotia: Archdiocese of Halifax, 1984). An interesting work of a contemporary nature is Michael Higgins and Douglas Letson's *Portraits of Canadian Catholicism* (Toronto: Griffin House, 1986).

326 **A history of the churches in the United States and Canada.**
Robert T. Handy. New York: Oxford University Press, 1977. 471p.

A scholarly treatment of church history in North America, with an emphasis on the United States. The author recognizes the similarities and differences of religious patterns in the two countries, particularly with regard to the Catholic presence in French Canada. Acknowledgement, rather than analysis, of the differences however, lessens the usefulness of the text. Nevertheless, the similarities of the situations of the two countries, combined with a considerable sensitivity to the Canadian situation, is reason enough to recommend this work as a valuable overview. It contains a very good bibliographical essay.

327 **The role of the Church in New France.**
Cornelius J. Jaenen.   Toronto: McGraw-Hill Ryerson, 1976. 182p.
(Frontenac Library, vol. 7).

A penetrating overview of the rôle of the Catholic Church during the French régime. The author assesses the two principal functions of that institution: the conversion of the native Indians and the maintenance of the Catholic faith in the French colony. He discusses the interrelationship between religion and commerce, with reference to the indigenous population, commenting also on the effects of intercultural contacts as they affected the development of the Church. He also examines the part played by the Church in the political, social and economic life of the colony.

328 **Religion in Canada: the spiritual development of a nation.**
Edited by William Kilbourn.   Toronto: McClelland & Stewart, 1968.
128p. (Canadian Illustrated Library).

A popular, profusely illustrated, overview of religion in Canada prepared for Canada's centennial year. A leading historian, Kilbourn, outlines past history, a noted church journalist, A. C. Forrest, describes the then contemporary religious scene in Canada, and a broadcast journalist, Patrick Watson, speculates on the future place and rôle of religion and the Church in Canadian society. An excellent work for the general and informed reader alike.

329 **Church and State in Canada West: three studies in the relation of**
denominationalism and nationalism, 1841-1867.
John S. Moir.   Toronto: University of Toronto Press, 1959. 223p.
(Canadian Studies in History and Government, vol. 1).

The author examines the question of relations between Church and State as they sought clarification in Canada West, the geographical portion of the United Province of Canada which today approximates Ontario. Three areas of conflict are studied in detail: the secularization of the Clergy Reserves; the reform of higher education, known as the University Question; and the question of religion and elementary education, i.e. the demand for denominational schools. Solutions, in the form of compromises, were found in all three areas which were nominally favourable to the forces of separation of Church and State. These compromises, particularly in the areas of education, are reflected in the nature of the institutions of today. Consult also John S. Moir's *Church and State in Canada 1627-1867: basic documents* (Toronto: McClelland & Stewart, 1967).

330 **The cross in Canada.**
Edited by John S. Moir.   Toronto: Ryerson Press, 1966. 247p.

Reproduced are documents which reflect episodes from the past which collectively provide a view of the church as it influenced, and was influenced by, the Canadian story. The documents range from an account of the erection of a cross on the banks of the Gulf of the St. Lawrence river by Jacques Cartier in 1534, to the description of the Christian Pavilion built by seven of Canada's Christian churches for Expo '67, Canada's centennial celebrations. Taken together the documents, with editorial comment, provide a readable version of the history of the Canadian Church.

Religion

331 **Enduring witness: a history of the Presbyterian Church in Canada.**
John S. Moir. Toronto: Presbyterian Church in Canada, 1987. 2nd ed. 326p.

A history authorized by the Presbyterian Church as part of its centenary celebrations in 1975. This respected church historian presents in readable fashion the denominational history of the Church, placing it in the context of secular and other religious trends which surrounded and influenced its development. Also of some interest is the photographic record by Thomas Melville Bailey entitled *The covenant in Canada: four hundred years history of the Presbyterian Church in Canada* (Hamilton, Ontario: Macnab Circle, 1975).

332 **The blood and fire in Canada: a history of the Salvation Army in the Dominion 1882-1976.**
R. G. Moyles. Toronto: Peter Martin Associates, 1977. 312p.

The Salvation Army, an institution dedicated to worship and social outreach, began as the Christian Mission in London, founded by William Booth, a dissident Methodist preacher. Today operations are world-wide. Moyles provides a scholarly, yet very readable, chronicle of the historical events, the successes, the setbacks and the social forces which marked the Army's Canadian story. In addition, he has attempted, successfully, to 'recapture the essential characteristics and peculiarities of Salvationism as expressed in the songs, the meetings, the literature and the social concerns of the Salvationists themselves'. Of interest also is Robert Collins' *The holy war of Sally Ann: the Salvation Army in Canada* (Saskatoon, Saskatchewan: Western Producer Prairie Books, 1984).

333 **Jehovah's Witness in Canada: champions of freedom of speech and worship.**
M. James Penton. Toronto: Macmillan/Maclean-Hunter, 1976. 388p.

A scholarly, sympathetic treatment of a minority faith which might well be considered Canada's most controversial religion. Particular attention is given to such issues as the treatment of conscientious objectors during both World Wars, to questions of freedom of speech and generally to the conflicts with Canadian federal and provincial governments with regard to religious freedoms.

334 **Heritage & horizon: the Baptist story in Canada.**
Harry A. Renfree. Mississauga, Ontario: Canadian Bapist Federation, Fédération Baptiste Canadienne, 1988. 380p.

Provides an overview of Baptist history in Canada. Other works of interest include: G. A. Rawlyk's *Ravished by the spirit: religious revivals, Baptists, and Henry Alline* (Kingston, Ontario; Montreal: McGill-Queen's University Press, 1984); Murray J. S. Ford's *Canadian Baptist history and polity: papers from the McMaster Divinity College, Baptist history conference, October 1982* (Hamilton, Ontario: McMaster University Divinity College, 1983); Barry M. Moody's *Repent and believe: the Baptist experience in Maritime Canada* (Hantsport, Nova Scotia: Lancelot, 1980); Jarold K. Zeman's *Baptists in Canada: search for identity amidst diversity* (Burlington, Ontario: G. R. Welch, 1980); Margaret E. Thompson's *The Baptist story in western Canada* (Calgary, Alberta: The Baptist Union of Western Canada, 1974); and J. M. Bumsted's *Henry Alline 1748-1784* (Toronto: University of Toronto Press, 1971).

335 **The Christian Church in Canada.**

H. H. Walsh. Toronto: Ryerson Press, 1956. 355p.

Although dated, this early overview of religious development in Canada remains of
interest to the present day reader. The author, a noted churchman and academic,
avoids denominational suppositions, and surveys the regions of the country and a
variety of the religious movements which flourished over the course of the country's
history. Throughout he is sensitive to the interaction between Church and State and
relates the development of Canadian churches to the political history of Canada.

336 **Two worlds: the Protestant culture of nineteenth-century Ontario.**

William Westfall. Kingston, Ontario; Montreal: McGill-Queen's
University Press, 1989. 273p. (McGill-Queen's Studies in the History of
Religion, vol. 2).

The author examines the development of a Protestant culture growing out of an
informal alliance between the Anglicans and Methodists on a large number of social
and moral issues during the nineteenth century. Within this context Westfall examines
the whole of the social system, social change, the process of secularization, and
generally the effect of religion on Canadian life during this period.

337 **The Doukhobors.**

George Woodcock, Ivan Avakumovic. Toronto: McClelland &
Stewart, 1977. 382p. (Carleton Library, vol. 108).

These noted academics chronicle the history of this communal sect of Russian
dissenters from their original homes in southern Russia to their settlement in western
Canada. The Doukhobors emigrated to Canada in 1898-99, under the leadership of
Peter Verigin, settling initially in Saskatchewan, then moving to southern British
Columbia a decade later. From that time until the 1960s this group was constantly in
dispute with governments on issues ranging from education to military service; splinter
groups, like the Sons of Freedom, engaged in fanatical activism. Today, most members
and descendants of members have integrated into Canadian society. Also of interest is
Koozma J. Tarasoff's *A pictorial history of the Doukhobors* (Saskatoon, Saskatchewan:
Prairie Books Department, Western Producer, 1969).

338 **The Ukrainian Greek Orthodox Church of Canada, 1918-1951.**

Paul Yuzyk. Ottawa: University of Ottawa Press, 1981. 210p. bibliog.

The first study of its kind in Canada, the author provides background by introducing
the reader to the Orthodox Church in the Ukraine. He examines the roots of
Ukrainian immigration to Canada, and the forces which led to the establishment of the
Orthodox Church in Canada, and the place and significance of the Church in the lives
of Ukrainian-Canadians. It is clear from the story that this group's desire (in part
through the Church) is to maintain their identity within Canadian multicultural society.
An extensive bibliography is included.

Social Conditions, Problems and Change

339 **Feminist organizing for change: the contemporary women's movement in Canada.**
Nancy Adamson, Linda Briskin, Margaret McPhail.   Toronto: Oxford University Press, 1988. 332p. bibliog.
Documents and examines the struggle of the contemporary Canadian women's movement. The authors begin with an historical treatment of the post-1960 feminist movement, emphasizing grass-roots rather than institutionalized feminism. From this base the work outlines a conceptual framework for the understanding of current feminist practice and the ideology of the women's movement. Includes an extensive bibliography. See also: Betty Steele's *The feminist takeover: patriarchy to matriarchy in two decades* (Willowdale, Ontario: Tercet, 1987); *Still ain't satisfied: Canadian feminism today* (Toronto: Women's Press, 1982); Marylee Stephenson's *Women in Canada* (Don Mills, Ontario: General Publishing Co., 1977); and, Gail Cook's *Opportunity for choice: a goal for women in Canada* (Ottawa: Statistics Canada, 1976).

340 **Approaches to economic well-being.**
Toronto: University of Toronto Press in cooperation with the Royal Commission on the Economic Union and Development Prospects for Canada and the Canadian Government Publishing Centre, Supply and Services Canada, 1985. 249p.
This is the first of two volumes dealing with economic ideas and social issues in Canada included as part of the collected research of the Royal Commission on the Economic Union and Development Prospects for Canada. These volumes deal with the theory of economic policy; the nature of economic well-being and the rôle of the State in promoting it; the rôle of markets and government in ensuring that environmental resources are well utilized; and the ability of the economic and political system to generate and cope with change. The other title in the set is entitled *Responses to economic change*.

341 **Social welfare in Canada: ideals, realities and future paths.**
Andrew Armitage. Toronto: McClelland & Stewart, 1988. 2nd ed.
294p. bibliog.
The author examines all aspects of social welfare in Canada within the context of
demographic changes, economic changes, political trends, social service effectiveness,
service organizations, the de-institutionalization of service delivery, and professional
diversification. This is a standard text in the field.

342 **The welfare state and Canadian federalism.**
Keith G. Banting. Kingston, Ontario; Montreal: McGill-Queen's
University Press, 1987. 2nd ed. 263p.
Documents the rôle of the federal and provincial governments in Canada in setting up
the modern welfare state, paying particular attention to income security. The author
examines the origins, operation and consequences of programmes designed to protect
living standards of lower-income citizens. Policies and programmes are compared with
those of other industrialized countries. Also of interest is David P. Ross's *The working
poor: wage earners and the failure of income security policies* (Toronto: James Lorimer
& Company, 1981).

343 **Models & myths in Canadian sociology.**
Edited by S. D. Berkowitz. Toronto: Butterworths, 1984. 295p.
Excellent introductions to Canadian sociology and books of readings on aspects of
Canadian society abound. This book is but one of the more recent publications which,
in a collection of essays, provides readers with a summary of important social and
economic factors and issues which shape the lives of Canadians. Many other works can
be located through standard bibliographical sources.

344 **Report of the Royal Commission on the Status of Women in Canada.**
Royal Commission on the Status of Women in Canada. Ottawa:
Information Canada, 1970. 488p.
Presents the report of a key enquiry which launched fundamental changes in Canadian
society. The Commission was charged 'to inquire into and report upon the status of
women in Canada, and to recommend what steps might be taken by the Federal
Government to ensure for women equal opportunities with men in all aspects of
Canadian society'.

345 **Pornography and prostitution in Canada: report of the Special
Committee on Pornography and Prostitution.**
Special Committee on Pornography and Prostitution. Ottawa:
Minister of Supply and Services Canada, 1985. 2 vols.
These issues are subject of an ongoing debate in Canada. The Special Committee was
empowered in 1983 to consider the problems of access to pornography, its effects and
its definition; to consider prostitution in Canada with particular reference to loitering
and street soliciting, the operation of bawdy houses, living off the avails and the
exploitation of prostitutes and the laws relating to these matters; to ascertain public
views on ways and means to deal with these problems; to consider the experiences and
attempts to deal with these problems in other countries; and, to consider alternatives
and report the findings and recommendations.

Social Conditions, Problems and Change

346 **The Canadian Journal of Sociology=Cahiers Canadiens de Sociologie.**
Edmonton, Alberta: Department of Sociology, University of Alberta,
1975- . quarterly.
This is a journal of current research on topics of relevance to Canadian society.
Another journal of interest is the *Canadian Review of Sociology and Anthropology =
La Revue Canadienne de Sociologie et d'Anthropologie* (Toronto: University of
Toronto Press, 1964-).

347 **Capital punishment in Canada: a sociological study of repressive law.**
David B. Chandler. Toronto: McClelland & Stewart, 1976. 224p.
(Carleton Library, vol. 94).
Examines the Canadian context of capital punishment, from the point of view of a
sociologist, bringing together an impressive amount of empirical evidence with regard
to public opinion and the consequent legislative results emerging from the capital
punishment debates of 1967 and 1973.

348 **The social development of Canada: an introductory study with select
documents.**
S. D. Clark. New York: AMS Press, 1976. 2nd ed. 484p.
A classic work which provides insight into the development of Canadian society. This
noted author examines aspects of Canada's frontier economic expansion (such as the
fur trade, the timber trade, fisheries, mining, and the transcontinental railways), and
within each sector looks at questions of social welfare, crime and moral order, cultural
organization and education, and the rôle of the church. See also the author's *Canadian
society in historical perspective* (Toronto: McGraw-Hill Ryerson, 1976); and, *The
developing Canadian community* (Toronto: University of Toronto Press, 1968). For a
discussion of Clark's contribution to the study of Canadian society see Harry H.
Hiller's *Society and change: S. D. Clark and the development of Canadian sociology*
(Toronto: University of Toronto Press, 1982).

349 **The Canadian corporate elite: an analysis of economic power.**
Wallace Clement. Toronto: McClelland & Stewart, 1975. 479p.
(Carleton Library, vol. 89).
Clement, an important commentator and contributor to the literature concerning
concentrated power, has written a number of works relating to social stratification in
Canada. This work focuses on the concentration and perpetuation of economic power
in Canadian society. Other works by this author include *Class, power and property:
essays on Canadian society* (Toronto: Methuen, 1983). William K. Carroll's *Corporate
power and Canadian capitalism* (Vancouver: University of British Columbia Press,
1986) is also of interest.

350 **Social policy in the 1990s: agenda for reform.**
Thomas J. Courchene. Toronto: C. D. Howe Institute, 1987. 184p.
(Policy Study, vol. 3).
The author discusses the changing social and demographic patterns in Canada and
notes that the challenges of the 1990s demand a restructuring of the present social
policy system, which was designed to meet the needs of the 1960s. Books which deal
with Canada's social policy include Jacqueline S. Ismael's *Canadian social welfare*

policy: federal and provincial dimensions (Kingston, Ontario; Montreal: McGill-Queen's University Press, 1985); and Shankar A. Yelaja's *Canadian social policy* (Waterloo, Ontario: Wilfred Laurier University Press, 1987).

351 Professional child and youth care: the Canadian perspective.
Edited by Carey Denholm, Roy Ferguson, Alan Pence. Vancouver: University of British Columbia Press, 1987. 221p.

'In this book, the first of its kind, the contributors illustrate the broad scope of child care in Canada and note some of the similarities, differences, and critical issues within selected practice areas'. Topics under discussion include residential child care, child care and the Canadian youth justice system, school-based child care, day care, infant programmes, community-based child care, and the future of child care in Canada.

352 The Canadian class structure.
Dennis Forcese. Toronto: McGraw-Hill Ryerson, 1986. 3rd ed. 202p. (McGraw-Hill Ryerson Series in Canadian Sociology).

Introduces the reader to the complexity, and the issues of controversy relating to social stratification in Canada. Issues discussed include social class and opportunity, class as it relates to lifestyle and behaviour and class conflict.

353 Social issues: sociological views of Canada.
Edited by Dennis Forcese and Stephen Richer. Scarborough, Ontario: Prentice-Hall Canada, 1982. 506p.

Readings in Canadian sociology. Essays by noted academics focus on various types of inequality in Canadian society, i.e. regional, gender based, ethnic, the aged, etc. Other papers focus on education, the criminal justice system, social class,.the mass media, and, corporations and corporate power. Similar collections of essays can be found in *Social inequality in Canada: patterns, problems, policies* (Scarborough, Ontario: Prentice-Hall Canada, 1988); and John Harp and John R. Hofley's *Structured inequality in Canada* (Scarborough, Ontario: Prentice-Hall of Canada, 1980). See also Alfred Hunter's *Class tells: on social inequality in Canada* (Toronto: Butterworths, 1981).

354 The emergence of social security in Canada.
Dennis Guest. Vancouver: University of British Columbia Press, 1980. 257p.

Chronicles the evolution of the social security system from the pre-Confederation era to the present day, with a primary focus on the events between 1914 and the closing years of the Second World War. Major topics include the establishment of a social minimum standard of living, the redefinition of the causes of dependency, the growth of public participation in welfare programmes, and the constitutional questions involved in such programmes.

355 The disreputable pleasures: crime and deviance in Canada.
John Hagan. Toronto: McGraw-Hill Ryerson, 1984. 2nd ed. 275p. bibliog. (McGraw-Hill Ryerson Series in Canadian Sociology).

This very readable volume reviews the various theories of crime and deviance and compares deviance in Canada with deviance in other countries. A full bibliography is included. Further reading on this topic includes Thomas Fleming and L. A. Visano's *Deviant designations: crime, law and deviance in Canada* (Toronto: Butterworths, 1983), Edmund W. Vaz and Abdul Q. Lodhi's *Crime and delinquency in Canada* (Scarborough, Ontario: Prentice-Hall, 1979), Edmund W. Vaz's *Aspects of deviance* (Scarborough, Ontario: Prentice-Hall, 1976); and W. E. Mann's *Social deviance in Canada* (Toronto: Copp Clark, 1971).

356 **Sociology for Canadians: images of society.**
Alexander Himelfarb, C. James Richardson. Toronto: McGraw-Hill Ryerson, 1982. 471p.
An introductory text, with some Marxist bias, which gives a sociological perspective on Canada. The authors provide commentary on and treatment of such basic concepts as culture, social structure, crime and deviance, population and demography, political culture, capitalism and industrialism, social inequality, educational inequality, ethnic inequality, and the changing family. It is complemented by a collection of readings by the same editors and entitled *Sociology for Canadians: a reader* (Toronto: McGraw-Hill Ryerson, 1984).

357 **The Canadian family.**
Edited by K. Ishwaran. Toronto: Gage, 1983. 380p. bibliog.
Two earlier editions of this work include articles relevant to this subject. This collection is comprised of new articles, organized under seven prominent themes: demographics; family structures; family and society; family, ethnicity and identity; husbands and wives; courtship, marriage and divorce; and families in crises. It also includes an extensive bibliography. Other excellent works on the subject include: *The family: changing trends in Canada* (Toronto: McGraw-Hill Ryerson, 1984); Margrit Eichler's *Families in Canada today: recent changes and their policy consequences* (Toronto: Gage, 1983); Benjamin Schlesinger's *Families: Canada* (Toronto: McGraw-Hill Ryerson, 1979) and his *Family planning in Canada: a sourcebook* (Toronto: University of Toronto Press, 1974); Lyle E. Larson's *The Canadian family in comparative perspective* (Scarborough, Ontario: Prentice-Hall, 1976); and S. Parvez Wakil's *Marriage, family and society: Canadian perspectives* (Toronto: Butterworths, 1975).

358 **The Canadian welfare state: evolution and transition.**
Edited by Jacqueline S. Ismael. Edmonton, Alberta: University of Alberta Press, 1987. 390p.
Presents an exploration into 'the evolution and transition of the Canadian welfare state from a variety of perspectives'. The changing relationship between the welfare state and employment related issues is discussed and an 'insight into the dynamics of change and the direction of transition' is provided.

359 **Canada's aging population.**
Susan A. McDaniel. Toronto: Butterworths, 1986. 136p.
(Perspectives on Individual and Population Aging).
Presents a comprehensive and unique analysis of the causes and consequences of population aging in Canada. The author introduces the links between demographic processes and biological, psychological and sociological processes. The reader is introduced to such issues as: housing; institutionalization; the family; women;

ethnicity; migration; health care; crime; retirement; and widowhood. For further study see: Alan Roadburg's *Aging: retirement, leisure and work in Canada* (Toronto: Methuen, 1985); Mark Novak's *Successful aging: the myths, realities and future of aging in Canada* (Markham, Ontario: Penguin, 1985); Victor W. Marshall's *Aging in Canada: social perspectives* (Toronto: Fitzhenry & Whiteside, 1980); Leroy O. Stone and Susan Fletcher's *A profile of Canada's older population* (Montreal: Institute for Research on Public Policy, 1980); and Kenneth Bryden's *Old age pensions and policy-making in Canada* (Montreal: McGill-Queen's University Press, 1974).

360 **Crime and its treatment in Canada.**
Edited by W. T. McGrath. Toronto: Gage, 1980. 2nd ed. 610p.

One of the best overviews of crime and correction in Canada, appropriate for the general, as well as the informed reader. The reader may also like to consult Robert A. Silverman and James J. Teevan's *Crime in Canadian society* (Toronto: Butterworths, 1986), Augustine Brannigan's *Crimes, courts and corrections: an introduction to crime and social control in Canada* (Toronto: Holt, Rinehart & Winston, 1984), Daniel Jay Baum's *Discount justice: the Canadian criminal justice system* (Toronto: Burns & MacEachern, 1979), and Alice Parizeau and Denis Szabo's *The Canadian criminal-justice system* (Toronto: Lexington, 1977).

361 **The police function in Canada.**
Edited by William T. McGrath, Michael P. Mitchell. Toronto: Methuen, 1981. 278p.

This anthology provides an overview of the varied dimensions of the contemporary police function in Canada, including an historical perspective and in-depth studies of specific issues confronting private and public police. Those interested readers should also consult William and Nora Kelly's *Policing in Canada* (Toronto: Macmillan; MacLean-Hunter, 1976).

362 **The bedroom and the State: the changing practices and politics of contraception and abortion in Canada, 1880-1980.**
Angus McLaren, Arlene Tigar McLaren. Toronto: McClelland & Stewart, 1986. 186p. (Canadian Social History Series).

An objective account of how Canadian men and women have sought to limit births, and 'how public figures have attempted to turn such private concerns to political purposes'. The authors discuss the forms of contraception available prior to the Pill, the distribution and dangers involved in abortion, the initial opposition to birth control by many feminists, socialists, ministers, and doctors, the first proponents of birth control, the fact that contraception was not made legal until 1969, and the reasons for the drop in the birth rate in Quebec in the 1960s. This work is essential reading for those wishing to understand the volatile nature of the issue as it is currently being debated today. Anne Collins's *The big evasion: abortion, the issue that won't go away* (Toronto: Lester & Orphen Dennys, 1985) also provides an interesting discussion of the issues.

363 **Changing residence: the geographic mobility of elderly Canadians.**
Herbert C. Northcott. Toronto: Butterworths, 1988. 135p.
(Perspectives On Individual and Population Aging).
This volume 'focuses on the patterns of migration by older adults, on the consequences of this movement for both the individual and the communities which gain or lose elderly residents, on the implications of Canadian policies for elderly migration, and on the impact of later life migration for Canadian policies'. Within this context the author examines the relationship between public policy and mobility, particularly in such areas as health care, housing, and immigration.

364 **Childhood and family in Canadian history.**
Edited by Joy Parr. Toronto: McClelland & Stewart, 1982. 221p.
(Canadian Social History Series).
Drawing from an array of sources, the contributions in this volume portray the lives of children in Canada from the seventeenth century to the present. Various issues are dealt with, including: child labour practices; the modes of child-rearing; the family structure and economy; and the lives of children in and outside of institutions. Discussions of related topics include Patricia T. Rooke and R. L. Schnell's *Studies in childhood history: a Canadian perspective* (Calgary, Alberta: Detselig Enterprises, 1982); J. J. Kelso's *In the children's aid: child welfare in Ontario* (Toronto: University of Toronto Press, 1981); and Neil Sutherland's *Children in English-Canadian society: framing the twentieth-century consensus* (Toronto: University of Toronto Press, 1976).

365 **Women at work: discrimination and response.**
Stephen G. Peitchinis. Toronto: McClelland & Stewart, 1989. 176p.
Examines the issues that concern working women, covering the explanations justifying discriminatory practices; the myths and perceptions which feed those practices; the changes in occupational distribution; the threats to the employment of women in the labour market; and the ways in which women have responded to discriminatory employment practices.

366 **The vertical mosaic: an analysis of social class and power in Canada.**
John Porter. Toronto: University of Toronto Press, 1968. 626p.
(Studies in the Structure of Power: Decision-Making in Canada).
Porter is credited by many as developing a distinctive Canadian sociology. This book, a classic work of scholarship and monumental in its scope and import of theme, deals with social class and power in Canadian society. Other of Porter's 'reflective pieces' can be found in the anthology entitled *The measure of Canadian society: education, equality and opportunity* (Ottawa: Carleton University Press, 1987).

367 **Canadian women: a history.**
Alison Prentice (et al.). Toronto: Harcourt Brace Jovanovich, 1988. 496p.
Although the authors admit a feminist orientation, this is a generally objective, historical overview of women in Canada. Other books on this subject include *Quebec women: a history* (Toronto: Women's Press, 1987); Veronica Strong-Boag and Anita Clair Fellman's *Rethinking Canada: the promise of women's history* (Toronto: Copp Clark Pitman, 1986); Susan Mann Trofimenkoff and Alison Prentice's *The neglected*

majority: essays in Canadian women's history, vols. 1 and 2 (Toronto: McClelland & Stewart, 1977, 1985) as well as Ramsay Cook and Wendy Mitchinson's *The proper sphere: woman's place in Canadian society* (Toronto: Oxford University Press, 1976).

368 Prostitution in Canada.
Ottawa: Canadian Advisory Council on the Status of Women, 1984. 139p.
Examines the nature of prostitution within a Canadian context and the factors that concentrate the social, physical and legal risks and consequences of prostitution upon the woman, rather than upon the others who patronize her or otherwise profit from her activities.

369 Social mobility in Canada.
Lorne Tepperman.   Toronto: McGraw-Hill Ryerson, 1975. 220p. (McGraw-Hill Ryerson Series in Canadian Sociology).
This study is described in the introduction as containing 'a mélange of observations on formal and informal organization, demography, and the Canadian stratification system as thrown into perspective by the central question: what determines who succeeds and who fails in Canada? The book is both about Canada and about social mobility but, on balance, more about the latter than the former'.

370 Public violence in Canada, 1867-1982.
Judy M. Torrance.   Kingston, Ontario; Montreal: McGill-Queen's University Press, 1986. 270p. bibliog.
The author introduces the concept of public violence as acts widely considered to be violent and of importance to society. She attempts to place Canadian violence within its proper social context, and at the same time brings to the reader's attention the major theories of violence which are applicable to Canada. A somewhat different, but nevertheless recommended work on this topic, is Mary Gammon's *Violence in Canada* (Toronto: Methuen, 1978). Here the issue is examined as a statistical trend, as a qualitative act, as stereotyped behaviour, as originating from many causes, as a subcultural behaviour, and as a function of mass media influence.

371 Canadian social welfare.
Edited by Joanne Turner, Francis J. Turner.   Don Mills, Ontario: Collier Macmillan Canada, 1986. 2nd ed. 484p.
A textbook intended to inform about social welfare policies, this book is directed at students, voluntary members of boards of institutions, agencies, clinics, and other similar organizations involved in the social welfare system, as well as the general public. Further discussion of this topic can be found in Allan Moscovitch and Glenn Drover's *Inequality: essays on the political economy of social welfare* (Toronto: University of Toronto Press, 1981).

Health and Welfare

Reference

372 **The welfare state in Canada: a selected bibliography, 1840 to 1978.**
Allan Moscovitch.   Waterloo, Ontario: Wilfred Laurier University
Press, 1983. 246p.
This is a selected bibliography of literature on Canadian social welfare policy which is divided into two sections. The first part deals with general aspects of the origins, development, organization, and administration of the welfare state in Canada, while the second part focuses on particular areas of policy such as unemployment, disabled persons, prisons, child and family welfare, health care, and day care. There is also an introductory essay which reviews the literature on Canadian social welfare policy.

General

373 **Canadian hospitals, 1920 to 1970: a dramatic half century.**
G. Harvey Agnew.   Toronto: University of Toronto Press, 1974. 276p.
Presents the story of the evolution and development in the hospital field in Canada. As well as being of interest to the student or general reader interested in this dimension of medical history, the health care policy analyst, the professional hospital administrator, and the physician will gain much from this work.

374 **Who speaks for the patient?: the crisis in Canadian health care.**
Andrew Allentuck.   Don Mills, Ontario: Burns & MacEachern, 1978.
111p.
Though dated, this work remains relevant in relation to problems facing the Canadian health care system today. This economist exposes inefficiencies in the system. He states in the preface that 'Government health insurance bodies have failed to come to terms

with the inefficiencies of fee-for-service medicine and have, in fact, adopted the worst of its features in an effort to avoid political conflict with the health industry. Medical equipment and pharmaceutical manufacturers sell wares which are sometimes ineffective, inefficient, and dangerous. Hospital administrators and physicians may be ignorant of the implications of and alternatives to the goods they think they need. Medical schools pass along the shibboleths of technological medicine and thus lay the groundwork for new generations of doctors oblivious of the costs, while patients are left to form grass-roots movements to demand rights and a voice in how they are treated'.

375   National health insurance: can we learn from Canada?

Edited by Spyros Andreopoulos.   New York: John Wiley, 1975. 273p.

The 1974 symposium of the Sun Valley Forum on National Health focused on the Canadian experience with national health insurance, which 'was felt to represent the foreign model most relevant to the United States'. It provides retrospective and statistical information with regard to Canadian health care.

376   Warehouses for death: the nursing home industry.

Daniel Jay Baum.   Don Mills, Ontario: Burns & MacEachern, 1977. 191p.

A disturbing work which deals with the pressures and circumstances that force elderly Canadians into nursing homes. It examines their regimented existence in these institutions and asks the question: Can we not develop policies and attitudes that would allow the elderly to keep their place in the community and maintain a degree of independence?

377   Medicare: Canada's right to health.

Monique Begin.   Montreal: Optimum Publishing International, 1988. 215p.

A previous Minister of Health, Begin relates the history, evolution and challenges of health and medical care services in Canada. She concentrates upon the years of her involvement, which themselves comprised a key (and turbulent) period in the development of health care.

378   A darkened house: cholera in nineteenth-century Canada.

Geoffrey Bilson.   Toronto: University of Toronto Press, 1980. 222p. (Social History of Canada, vol. 31).

Bilson presents an account of the cholera epidemics 'as they ravaged the Canadas and the Atlantic colonies', noting the physical and psychological consequences of the diesease. Cholera claimed the lives of 20,000 people and 'unsettled governments, undermined the medical profession, exposed inadequacies in public health, and widened the division between rich and poor'.

379   The discovery of insulin.

Michael Bliss.   Toronto: McClelland & Stewart, 1982. 304p.

One of Canada's best historians traces the dramatic events, the crises, the climaxes and the absurdities of the breakthrough discovery of insulin by Sir Frederick Banting.

380 **The secret plague: venereal disease in Canada 1838-1939.**
Jay Cassel.   Toronto: University of Toronto Press, 1987. 340p. (Social History of Canada, vol. 41).

The author explores the development of medical treatment for syphilis and gonorrhoea, and public efforts to cope with the spread of infection, from the dawn of the Victorian era, through to the mid-twentieth century. Woven into this study is a discussion of the responses to the VD crisis made from within the health care system in Canada, such as state funded medical facilities, drug manufacturing and clinics for diagnosis and treatment.

381 **The Canadian health care system.**
Anne Crichton, Jean Lawrence, Susan Lee.   Ottawa: Canadian Hospital Association, 1984. 5 vols. bibliog.

This set of books provides an introduction to Canadian health services; volume 1 sets the scene, reprinting readings from various sources in order to present a picture of the health service and the organizations charged with the delivery of that service; volume 2 presents case studies relating to the theory in volume 1; volume 3 presents cases on the management of health-related institutions, while volume 4 looks at the top management of these institutions; volume 5 is a guide to the use of the other volumes and also contains a bibliography. Although it is designed for a teaching environment, this set is also useful for the lay inquirer.

382 **A history of dentistry in Canada.**
D. W. Gullett.   Toronto: University of Toronto Press, 1971. 308p.

Chronicles the development of the art and science of dentistry in Canada from the early settlement era to the mid-twentieth century.

383 **Health and Canadian society.**
Toronto: Fitzhenry & Whiteside, 1981. 496p.

Essays on the sociology of health, focusing on illness as a social as well as a biological phenomenon. Essays divide themselves into such broad topic groupings as health status and the health care system, social contingencies of health and illness, the healing occupations, health institutions, society, health and health care, and trends, issues and prospects in Canadian health care. An extensive list of references is included.

384 **Rogues, rebels, and geniuses: the story of Canadian medicine.**
Donald Jack.   Toronto: Doubleday, 1981. 662p.

Written for the general reader, this work is a fascinating examination of the place of doctors in Canadian history. A remarkable number of these men and women have gained international renown for many achievements, including the discovery of insulin, discoveries relating to the cellular determination of sex, contributions to anaesthesia, among others. However, this story is as much about the daily routine of the frontier doctors as it is about those exceptional men and women. The reader may also like to consult H. E. MacDermot's *One hundred years of medicine in Canada* (Toronto: McClelland & Stewart, 1967).

385 **Community mental health action: primary prevention programming in Canada.**
Edited by D. Lumsden. Ottawa: Canadian Public Health Association, 1984. 374p.

The essays in this handbook focus on mental health action in Canada. Topics under discussion range from child abuse to problems of retirement and widowhood, from occupational stress among policemen to the health and social impacts of unemployment, from social factors in depression to programming for the needs of Canadian Indians. A discussion of the national rôle of the Canadian Mental Health Association is also included.

386 **Madness: an indictment of the mental health care system in Ontario.**
John Marshall. Toronto: Ontario Public Service Employees Union, 1982. 224p.

Presents a condemnation of mental health care in Canada's largest and most affluent province.

387 **Perspectives on Canadian health and social services policy: history and emerging trends.**
Edited by Carl A. Meilicke, Janet L. Storch. Ann Arbor, Michigan: Health Administration Press, 1980. 520p.

Presents a number of readings which provide an introduction to the historical development of Canadian social security policy and programmes. Social security is defined as health and social services, for example, public health, hospital and medical services, personal social services, and income security programmes. Although some essays begin with the earliest days of settlement in Canada, the majority of papers emphasize the period from the early 1940s until the 1970s.

388 **Essays in the history of Canadian medicine.**
Edited by Wendy Mitchinson, Janice Dickin McGinnis. Toronto: McClelland & Stewart, 1988. 218p. bibliog.

An anthology of original essays which explore various subjects in the field of medical history in Canada. Essays cover the nineteenth and twentieth centuries and deal with such topics as urban mortality, the development of public health care, the nature of medical research, hospitalization of pregnant women, and the treatment of the insane and those with venereal disease. Includes an extensive bibliography. Of interest also is the anthology of essays edited by S. E. D. Shortt entitled *Medicine in Canadian society: historical perspectives* (Montreal: McGill-Queen's University Press, 1981); and Charles G. Roland's *Health, disease and medicine: essays in Canadian history* (Toronto: Hannah Institute for the History of Medicine, 1982).

389 **Private practice, public payment: Canadian medicine and the politics of health insurance 1911-1966.**
C. David Naylor. Kingston, Ontario; Montreal: McGill-Queen's University Press, 1986. 324p.

Public health insurance has been and remains one of Canada's most contentious policy subjects. The author here follows the evolution of Canadian health insurance from 1911, when attention was focused on the issues by developments in Britain, to the enactment of the Medical Care Act in 1966. He chronicles the developments in medical politics and policies, noting the nature and extent of opposition by the medical profession to government-administered systems of health insurance. He shows that physicians generally regarded medical insurance schemes over which they had little administrative control, as threats to professional incomes and autonomy. Other books on this subject include C. Howard Shillington's *The road to medicare in Canada* (Toronto: Del Graphics Publishing, 1972). The views of the medical profession on medical care insurance are captured and examined by Bernard R. Blishen in his work entitled *Doctors & doctrines* (Toronto: University of Toronto Press, 1969). Of additional interest is E. A. Tollefson's *Bitter medicine: the Saskatchewan medicare feud* (Saskatoon, Saskatchewan: Modern Press, 1964).

390 **Second opinion: what's wrong with Canada's health-care system and how to fix it.**
Michael Rachlis, Carol Kushner. Toronto: Collins, 1989. 371p. bibliog.

As described in the introduction, 'This is a controversial book on at least two fronts. It challenges conventional wisdom about the importance of health care to our health and it exposes the awesome extent of waste and inefficiency within our beloved Medicare . . . The topics . . . are far ranging – from C-T scanners to affordable housing, from cancer treatment to violence against women, from prescription drugs to poverty'. The work includes extensive bibliographical references.

391 **A brief history of pharmacy in Canada.**
Edited by Arnold V. Raison. Canadian Pharmaceutical Association, 1967. 113p.

An anthology of articles originally published in the Canadian Pharmaceutical Journal as a centennial project. The essays depict the progress of pharmacy in Canada.

392 **Condition critical.**
Nicholas Regush. Toronto: Macmillan, 1987. 316p.

An investigative journalist uncovers deficiencies in the Canadian health-care system, noting the long waiting lists for hospital admission, which shocked patients who 'couldn't understand why a health-care system often hailed by politicians as the best in the world couldn't provide them with care when they needed it'.

393 **The Canadian health system.**
Lee Soderstrom. London: Croom Helm, 1978. 271p. bibliog.

The author describes this book as 'an introduction to the health services system in Canada. Its primary purpose is to describe the system: important public and private institutions and programs are identified, and their functions and organization described; key terms and concepts are defined; considerable descriptive data are provided; and a short bibliography is also included'.

394 **Health insurance and Canadian public policy: the seven decisions that created the Canadian health insurance system and their outcomes.**
Malcolm G. Taylor. Kingston, Ontario; Montreal: McGill-Queen's University Press, 1987. 2nd ed. 563p. (Canadian Public Administration Series).
A study of the development of the Canadian health insurance system, incorporating both hospital insurance and medical care insurance. The author focuses on seven key decisions taken by federal or provincial governments over a thirty year period. These decisions are analysed in terms of their significance to the overall development of the system and for the contribution they have made to that system. Within the analysis the author examines the impact of ideas, public opinion, interest groups and political forces as they came to bear on the problems.

395 **The miracle of the empty beds: a history of tuberculosis in Canada.**
George Jasper Wherrett. Toronto: University of Toronto Press, 1977. 299p.
It is stated in the preface that, 'Tuberculosis was the leading cause of illness and death during the first fifty years covered in the study. The astounding achievements realized through the combination of medical and social measures demonstrated among other things the benefits derived from public health departments, without which the needed services could not have been provided'. The author presents a story full of harrowing tales; an account of the dedicated and unselfish work done by scores of professionals and an army of lay workers.

Constitution and Legal System

Reference

396 **A bibliography of Canadian law = Bibliographie du droit Canadien.**
Reynald Boult.   Ottawa: Canadian Law Information Council, 1977.
2nd ed. 658p.

This book provides an access tool to over 11,000 treatises, articles, reviews and periodicals relevant to legal research. Included are both primary and secondary materials, in both French and English, from all legal jurisdictions in the country. Entries are grouped by general subject heading. The *First Supplement* (Ottawa: Canadian Law Information Council, 1982), adds over 3,300 entries to the listing, utilizing the same terms of reference for inclusion and principles for arrangement. Of related interest is *Canadian criminal justice history: an annotated bibliography* (Toronto: University of Toronto Press, 1987).

397 **Index to Canadian Legal Literature = Index à la Documentation Juridique au Canada.**
Toronto: Carswell, 1969- . quarterly.

This periodical is published in three quarterly cumulations and one bound annual cumulation. Between cumulations, updates are published in the twenty annual issues of *Canadian Current Law*. The *Index* is both a periodical index and a bibliography of Canadian secondary legal literature – covering articles, case comments and annotations, monographs, individual essays from edited collections, federal and provincial government documents, theses, and fugitive literature. Collectively it provides comprehensive access to all the secondary literature of interest to the Canadian legal community and the general reader. Related fields such as criminology, taxation and finance are covered.

General

398 **Home and native land: aboriginal rights and the Canadian Constitution.**
Michael Asch. Toronto: Methuen, 1984. 156p.
Section 35 of the Constitution Act for the first time expressly acknowledges that there are aboriginal people and aboriginal rights in Canada. This work discusses aboriginal self-determination and self-government within this context. The author defines and provides a detailed account of the meaning of the phrase 'aboriginal rights' and discusses the question of political rights and the means by which the current constitutional impasse might be resolved. Another treatment of this subject is Bryan Schwartz's *First principles, second thoughts: aboriginal peoples, constitutional reform and Canadian statecraft* (Montreal: Institute for Research on Public Policy/L'Institut de recherches politiques, 1986).

399 **And no one cheered: federalism, democracy and the Constitution Act.**
Edited by Keith Banting, Richard Simeon. Toronto: Methuen, 1983. 376p.
'In this book, seventeen Canadian scholars of varying backgrounds, disciplines and languages seek to come to terms with the nature and significance of the recent struggle over constitutional reform and its results as embodied in the Constitution Act, 1982'. The authors consider the processes which led to the results, their implications and what they reveal about the character of Canadian democracy.

400 **Canada and the new Constitution: the unfinished agenda.**
Edited by Stanley M. Beck, Ivan Bernier. Montreal: Institute for Research on Public Policy/L'Institut de recherches politiques, 1983. 2 vols.
Presents a number of essays which review the issues which were, and continue to be, of significance with regard to constitutional change. As the subtitle reflects, many critical items of the constitutional agenda remain to be resolved. The essays discuss the justice system, reform of the Supreme Court, the Constitution and aboriginal peoples, economic issues, energy issues and foreign policy issues. It was published prior to the Meech Lake Agreement, which was a constitutional accord devised to facilitate the signing of the Constitution by Quebec.

401 **The Canadian criminal justice system.**
Edited by Craig L. Boydell, Ingrid Arnet Connidis. Toronto: Holt, Rinehart & Winston of Canada, 1982. 311p.
An anthology of essays which provides a perspective on the criminal justice system as an evolving, complex, social process. Broad topics of inclusion are criminal law and criminal justice, policing, the courts, and alternatives to the present system. There are bibliographical references throughout.

402 **Political rights: the legal framework of elections in Canada.**
J. Patrick Boyer. Toronto: Butterworths, 1981. 348p. (Canadian
Election Law Series).

This work is the first of a series which outlines the legal framework, rights and obligations of life under a system of representative government. It brings together an outline of the fundamental laws which provide the framework for Canadian elections, and also comments on the political rights which allow for the right to criticize governments at all levels. Other volumes in the series deal with such topics as referendums and plebiscites, election financing, advertising and campaigning, and the law of elections at all levels.

403 **The Canadian Bar Review=La Revue du Barreau Canadien.**
Vancouver: Faculty of Law, University of British Columbia, 1923- .
quarterly.

Contains articles on topics of contemporary relevance in law, jurisprudence and law reform and includes reviews. Similarly, see *Canadian Current Law* (Agincourt, Ontario: Carswell, 1982-). More popular articles on recent developments in Canadian law, interviews with lawyers, etc., can be found in *Canadian Lawyer* (Aurora, Ontario: Canadian Lawyer Magazine, 1977-).

404 **The revised Canadian Constitution: politics as law.**
Ronald I. Cheffins, Patricia A. Johnson. Toronto: McGraw-Hill
Ryerson, 1986. 244p. (McGraw-Hill Ryerson Series in Canadian
Politics).

One of the better overviews of the new Canadian Constitution. The authors begin by outlining the inheritance of responsible government, which was reinforced by the British North America Act of 1867, tracing constitutional development through to 1982. They look at the Constitution in some detail, and also devote space to various related topics such as the amending formula, executive authority, legislative authority, judicial authority, the division of powers, and the Charter of Rights and Freedoms. Particularly interesting, and important, is the question of judicial authority and the transfer of power from the elected representatives to an appointed court. Important also is Ronald Cheffin's earlier work entitled *The constitutional process in Canada* (Toronto: McGraw-Hill Ryerson, 1976).

405 **The Constitution Acts 1867 to 1982.**
Ottawa: Department of Justice, 1986. 84p.

A convenient reproduction of the significant Constitution acts of Canada, including: the Constitution Act, 1867 (formerly the British North America Act, 1867), with amendments; the Constitution Act, 1982, as amended by the Constitution Amendment Proclamation, 1983; as well as the Canadian Charter of Rights and Freedoms. The informed reader will find the critical edition by Peter W. Hogg, entitled *Canada act 1982: annotated* (Toronto: Carswell, 1982) to be of interest.

406   **Constitutionalism, citizenship and society in Canada.**
Toronto: University of Toronto Press in cooperation with the Royal
Commission on the Economic Union and Development Prospects for
Canada and the Canadian Publishing Centre, Supply and Services
Canada, 1985. 231p.
This is the first of two volumes dealing with the Constitution and the Canadian people,
included as part of the collected research of the Royal Commission on the Economic
Union and Development Prospects for Canada. These volumes look at the concept of
citizenship within the framework of the Charter of Rights and Freedoms. The essays
consider the ties between citizenship and community, and citizenship as it relates to
various groups within Canadian society. The other title is *The politics of gender,
ethnicity and language in Canada*.

407   **Essays in the history of Canadian law.**
Edited by David H. Flaherty.   Toronto: University of Toronto Press,
1981. 2 vols.
This two-volume anthology illustrates the wide range of research and writing in
Canadian legal history. Collectively the essays provide the reader with an overview of
the development and issues of that history, and essays cover such topics as the history
of company law, the law and the economy, legal reform, custody law, the law of
master and servant, the law of nuisance, origins of the Criminal Code, women's rights,
legal education, political corruption, rape law, the police, and labour law.

408   **The Canadian legal system.**
Gerald L. Gall.   Toronto: Carswell Legal Publications, 1983. 2nd ed.
348p.   .
This introduction to the Canadian legal system, although intended for a university
readership, is appropriate for the general reader. A similar work, which is more
concise, is Patrick Fitzgerald and King McShane's *Looking at law: Canada's legal
system* (Ottawa: Bybooks, 1982).

409   **All about law: exploring the Canadian legal system.**
Dwight L. Gibson, Terry G. Murphy, Frederick E. Jarman.   Toronto:
John Wiley, 1984. 2nd ed. 706p.
This is one of several excellent texts, designed for the secondary school student or the
general reader, which introduces Canadian law and the Canadian legal system. Other
works of a similar nature are W. A. Jennings and Thomas G. Zuber's *Canadian law*
(Toronto: McGraw-Hill Ryerson, 1986), and Steven N. Spetz and Glenda S. Spetz's
Take notice: an introduction to Canadian law (Toronto: Copp Clark Pitman, 1984).

410   **Meech Lake Constitutional Accord: annotated.**
Peter W. Hogg.   Toronto: Carswell, 1988. 85p.
The Meech Lake Constitutional Accord, which was signed on 3 June 1987 between the
federal government and the provincial governments, was heralded by many as the
mechanism to deal with a number of the issues which remained unresolved with regard
to constitutional reform – most notably facilitating constitutional reconciliation with
Quebec. Since the signing of the Accord the factions for and against have taken
entrenched positions, and despite all attempt at conciliation, the Accord was ultimately

not ratified by all provincial legislatures. Canada's constitutional crisis thus remains ongoing. Also of interest are Roger Gibbins (et al.) *Meech Lake and Canada: perspectives from the West* (Edmonton, Alberta: Academic Print & Publishing, 1988); Katherine Swinton & Carol J. Rogerson's *Competing constitutional visions: the Meech Lake Accord* (Toronto, Carswell, 1988), Clive Thomson's *Nagivating Meech Lake: the 1987 constitutional accord* (Kingston, Ontario: Institute of Intergovernmental Relations, Queen's University, 1988) and Bryan Schwartz' *Fathoming Meech Lake* (Winnipeg, Manitoba: Legal Research Institute, University of Manitoba, 1987).

411 **The law of your land: a practical guide to the new Canadian Constitution.**

J. Stuart Langford. Toronto: Canadian Broadcasting Corporation, 1982. 112p.

A journalist reviews the events which led to the passing of the Constitution Act in 1982. He leads the reader through the Act and the Charter of Rights and Freedoms explaining, as best as is possible, the nature of the provisions of the Act and the guarantees of basic human rights and fundamental freedoms entrenched in the Charter. He also speculates on the problem areas which, in 1982, remained to be resolved. Little has changed to this date.

412 **Laskin's Canadian constitutional law.**

Bora Laskin, edited by Neil Finkelstein. Toronto: Carswell, 1986. 5th ed. 2 vols.

There are a number of texts on constitutional law, or aspects thereof, prepared for the legal practitioner, the academic, the student of law or the well-informed reader. Since its first publication in 1951 this text has come to be the classic in the field of jurisprudence. Other titles of note include Peter H. Russell's *Federalism and the charter: leading constitutional decisions* (Ottawa: Carleton University Press, 1989), Joseph Eliot Magnet's *Constitutional law of Canada: cases, notes and materials* (Toronto: Carswell, 1985), W. H. McConnell's *Commentary on the British North America Act* (Toronto: Macmillan, 1977), and Peter W. Hogg's *Constitutional law of Canada* (Toronto: Carswell, 1977).

413 **Law, society and the economy.**

Toronto: University of Toronto Press in cooperation with the Royal Commission on the Economic Union and Development Prospects for Canada and the Canadian Publishing Centre, Supply and Services Canada, 1986. 230p.

This is the first in a series of six volumes dealing with law, society and the economy in Canada, included as part of the collected research of the Royal Commission on the Economic Union and Development Prospects for Canada. This series deals with the complexity of the legal system and its apparent inability to respond to the needs of Canadians, the rôle of the Supreme Court in our legal system, administrative law, family law and social-welfare legislation, legal values, interest groups and political considerations, labour law, and urban law. Other titles in the series include *The Supreme Court of Canada as an instrument of political change*; *Regulations, crown corporations and administrative tribunals*; *Family law and social welfare legislation in Canada*; *Consumer protection, environmental law, and corporate power*; and *Labour law and urban law in Canada*. Also within the collected research of the Commission are series on *The international legal environment* and the *Harmonization of law in Canada.*

414 **Continuing Canadian constitutional dilemmas: essays on the constitutional history, public law and federal system of Canada.**
W. R. Lederman. Toronto: Butterworths, 1981. 442p.
Essays on constitutional law written over a period of twenty-five years by one of Canada's leading constitutional experts. The author ranges over the entire field of constitutional history. This is of particular interest to the informed reader.

415 **Canada and the Constitution 1979-1982: patriation and the Charter of Rights.**
Edward McWhinney. Toronto: University of Toronto Press, 1982. 227p.
This volume follows on from the author's *Quebec and the Constitution 1960-1978* in which he describes 'the players and the events in this last, complex chapter in the patriation drama'. He shows how Quebec's special claims have given way to a regional approach; how the prime minister sacrificed the possibility of a genuine Canadian-made Constitution by trying the old 'made-in-Britain' amending route one last time; how the British government properly and firmly resisted the meddling in Canadian matters . . .; how the Supreme Court has taken an increasingly activist role in interpreting constitutional law . . .'. For an analysis of Quebec's demands for social, economic, linguistic and political self-determination, and the implications thereof, see the aforementioned *Quebec and the Constitution 1960-1978* (Toronto: University of Toronto Press, 1979). For a more personal assessment of the process during the same period see *Canada . . . notwithstanding: the making of the Constitution 1976-1982* (Toronto: Carswell/Methuen, 1984). Noted journalists Robert Sheppard and Michael Valpy chronicle the events of the Constitution debate in *The national deal: the fight for a Canadian constitution* (Toronto: Fleet, 1982).

416 **Politics and the Constitution: the charter, federalism and the Supreme Court of Canada.**
Patrick Monahan. Toronto: Carswell, 1987. 260p.
The theme of this work 'relates to the nature of the Supreme Court's role in Canadian politics', which deals with constitutional issues that are 'fundamentally and inescapably political'. The author abandons the traditional paradigm that the Supreme Court is a forum for a specialized and technical form of reasoning, and substitutes a view which recognizes the essential continuity between 'the constitutional analysis of the Supreme Court and more generalized forms of political argument'.

417 **Recurring issues in Canadian federalism.**
Toronto: University of Toronto Press in cooperation with the Royal Commission on the Economic Union and Development Prospects for Canada and the Canadian Publishing Centre, Supply and Services Canada, 1986. 187p.
This is the first of two volumes dealing with institutional and constitutional arrangements in Canada, included as part of the collected research of the Royal Commission on the Economic Union and Development Prospects for Canada. These

volumes deal with Quebec's status in the Confederation and the rôle of the courts in Canada's social system, particularly since the advent of the Charter of Rights. The second title is *The courts and the charter.*

418 **Le choix d'un pays: le débat constitutionnel Québec-Canada 1960-1976.** (A country's choice: the constitutional debate Quebec–Canada 1960-76.)
Jean-Louis Roy. Montreal: Leméac, 1978. 366p

A compilation and summary of Quebec's constitutional positions up to the date of publication.

419 **Essays on the Constitution: aspects of Canadian law and politics.**
Frank R. Scott. Toronto: University of Toronto Press, 1977. 422p.

Contains essays and occasional pieces spanning five decades of the career of Frank Scott, one of Canada's most prominent constitutional lawyers, teachers and poets. The essays range from those of strict legal analysis to others which demonstrate the author's partisan preferences. This anthology provides background for the student of constitutional processes and Canadian history.

420 **The Supreme Court of Canada: history of the institution.**
James G. Snell, Frederick Vaughan. Toronto: University of Toronto Press, 1985. 319p.

This book is described as tracing 'the development of the Supreme Court of Canada from its establishment in the earliest days following Confederation, through its attainment of independence from the Judicial Committee of the Privy Council in 1949, to the adoption of the Constitution Act, 1982. The authors describe the politics of the judicial appointments and document the internal struggles and tensions between the justices . . .'

421 **The Canadian Constitution and the courts: the function and scope of judicial review.**
Barry L. Strayer. Toronto: Butterworths, 1983. 2nd ed. 310p.

With the passage of the Constitution Act (1982), the courts face both new and important challenges in that their mandate has been significantly expanded and a 'new burden of value judgments' imposed on their judgements. This work attempts to outline, within an ever changing environment, the rôle of the courts with regard to constitutional litigation.

422 **The Canadian Charter of Rights and Freedoms: commentary.**
Walter S. Tarnopolsky, Gerald-A. Beaudoin. Toronto: Carswell, 1982. 590p.

The Charter of Rights and Freedoms, entrenched in the Constitution Act of 1982, 'will influence both federal and provincial legislation. It will affect both those who have a rôle in the administration of justice, as well as the ordinary citizen and public interest groups . . .' This work includes sixteen individual studies focusing on the impact of the Charter on federal laws, with some reference to provincial laws. Other works of related interest include: Dale Gibson's *The law of the Charter: general principles* (Toronto: Carswell, 1986); Anne F. Bayefsky and Mary Eberts' *Equality rights and the*

Canadian Charter of Rights and Freedoms (Toronto: Carswell, 1985); Morris Manning's *Rights, freedoms and the courts: a practical analysis of the Constitution Act, 1982* (Toronto: Emond-Montgomery, 1983); and David C. McDonald's *Legal rights in the Canadian Charter of Rights and Freedoms: a manual of issues and sources* (Toronto: Carswell, 1982).

423 You and the law: a practical family guide to Canadian law.

Westmount, Quebec: Reader's Digest Association, 1985. 3rd ed. 911p.

Considered one of the best, and most thorough, general guides to Canadian law prepared for the lay reader. A more abbreviated work on Canada's legal system can be found in Jack Battin and Marjorie Harris' *Everyday law: a survival guide for Canadians* (Toronto: Key Porter/Lorraine Greey, 1987) or Patrick Fitzgerald and King McShane's *Looking at law: Canada's legal system* (Ottawa: Bybooks, 1985). In addition, the Reader's Guide Association has also produced a handbook for the consumer entitled *You and your rights: a practical guide for all Canadians* (Montreal: Reader's Guide Association, 1980). In Canada, nine out of the ten provinces have legal systems based on common law, inherited from England and adapted over the years. Quebec, however, has a system derived from that of France, whose *Code Napoleon* formed the basis of civil law in Quebec. Those interested in the latter should consult Martin Franklin and David Franklin's *Introduction to Quebec law* (Toronto: Copp Clark Pitman, 1984), or Sheilah Martin's *Quebec laws* (Montreal: Guerin, 1983).

Politics

Reference

424 Canadian political facts 1945-1976.
Colin Campbell. Toronto: Methuen, 1977. 151p.
Though somewhat dated, this volume is a useful compendium of political information, including sections on such subjects as the executive, parliament, elections, political parties and pressure groups, judiciary, federal–provincial relations, economy, and population and language.

425 Canadian annual review of politics and public affairs.
Toronto: University of Toronto Press, 1960- .
This series of books, which is revised and updated annually, provides a record of the year's events and an appraisal of important political and governmental developments. Essays are solicited from noted scholars and deal with the political scene at both the federal and the provincial level. It is indispensable to the reader interested in political and public affairs, either on a current basis or retrospectively.

426 Canadian political parties, 1867-1968: a historical bibliography.
Compiled by Grace F. Heggie. Toronto: Macmillan, 1977. 603p.
Approximately 8,850 items are listed in this exceptional bibliography devoted to federal Canadian politics. The entries represent books, articles, essays, and theses published up to 1970. The work is divided into two parts: the first is concerned with the general theme, and follows events and issues that constitute national political history; the second is based on a topical arrangement, with the works tending towards constitutional history and political science.

427 **Contemporary Canadian politics: an annotated bibliography, 1970-1987.**
Gregory Mahler.   New York: Greenwood, 1988. 400p. (Bibliographies
and Indexes in Law and Political Science, vol. 10).
Presents some 3,738 bibliographic entries, with short annotations thematically arranged
under headings which include: the Constitution and legal system; federalism, finance
and public policy; regionalism and local politics; English Canada and political culture;
French Canada and Quebec; public opinion; political parties, ideology, and elections;
the executive; the legislature; the administrative process; and foreign policy.

428 **The language of Canadian politics: a guide to important terms and
concepts.**
John McMenemy.   Toronto: John Wiley & Sons, 1980. 294p.
An extraordinarily useful work for the reader who may be unfamiliar with government
and the political system in Canada. The terms and concepts in standard usage are
summarized here by commentators, academics, journalists, and others.

General

429 **The Communist Party in Canada: a history.**
Ivan Avakumovic.   Toronto: McClelland & Stewart, 1975. 309p.
The author provides a history covering over five decades of the Communist Party of
Canada. Other works of interest include: *Canada's party of socialism: history of the
Communist Party of Canada 1921-1976* (Toronto: Progress Books, 1982); and Ian
Angus' *Canadian bolsheviks: the early years of the Communist Party of Canada*
(Montreal: Vanguard, 1981).

430 **The roots of disunity: a look at Canadian political culture.**
David Bell, Lorne Tepperman.   Toronto: McClelland & Stewart,
1979. 262p. (Canada in Transition Series).
The authors attempt to contribute to an understanding of the crisis of national unity
then facing Canadians. Of paramount interest was the challenge of Quebec separation,
although other federal-provincial issues were also important. Within this context the
authors explore the cultural diversity of Canada.

431 **Divided loyalties: Canadian concepts of federalism.**
Edwin R. Black.   Montreal: McGill-Queen's University Press, 1975.
272p.
This work explores and analyses five major concepts of federalism which competed
(and continue to compete to some degree) for adoption in Canada. These are the
centralist concept, administrative federalism, coordinate federalism, the compact
theory of federalism, and the theory of a dual alliance framework. This work is
intended for the informed reader.

432 **Women and politics in Canada.**
Janine Brodie. Toronto: McGraw-Hill Ryerson, 1985. 145p. bibliog.
(McGraw-Hill Ryerson Series in Canadian Politics).

Employing a quantitative, analytical methodology, drawing on questionnaires, published reminiscences, the literature of the popular press and other scholarly studies, the author surveys the position of women in politics in Canada between 1945 and 1975. She 'documents the experiences of 327 Canadian women who, as candidates for public office, ventured into the male-dominated world of politics'. The conclusions she draws are not encouraging.

433 **Crisis, challenge and change: party and class in Canada revisited.**
M. Janine Brodie, Jane Jenson. Ottawa: Carleton University Press, 1988. 341p. (Carleton Library Series, vol. 148).

This revised version of the authors' *Crisis, challenge and change: party and class in Canada* (Toronto: Methuen, 1980) provides an examination of the links between the evolution of the federal party system to changes in the Canadian political economy, class structure and political movements from Confederation to the present. They incorporate a history of the Canadian political economy and party system.

434 **Canadian Journal of Political Science = Revue Canadienne de Science Politique.**
Waterloo, Ontario: Wilfrid Laurier University Press, 1934- . quarterly.

This journal contains articles and reviews of a scholarly nature on a wide range of political science topics, with a particular emphasis on Canada. This subject is also dealt with in the *Canadian Journal of Political and Social Theory = Revue Canadienne de Théorie Politique et Sociale* (Montreal: Concordia University, 1977-); and *Canadian Public Policy = Analyse de politiques* (Guelph, Ontario: University of Guelph, 1975-).

435 **Political parties and ideologies in Canada: Liberals, Conservatives, Socialists, Nationalists.**
William Christian, Colin Campbell. Toronto: McGraw-Hill Ryerson, 1983. 2nd ed. 247p. (McGraw-Hill Ryerson Series in Canadian Politics).

The authors go beyond the opportunistic practices associated with the game of politics and attempt to analyse the values and principles inherent in the intellectual thought and positions taken by the mainstream political parties in Canada.

436 **Political choice in Canada.**
Harold D. Clarke (et al.). Toronto: McGraw-Hill Ryerson, 1979. 445p.

Political choice as manifested in voting decisions is examined from three main perspectives. Firstly, the authors focus on the citizens' attitudes toward Canadian politics; how they are formulated and whether they are determined or affected by regional orientations. Secondly, the authors look at the voters' perceptions of and attitudes toward the elements of electoral politics and the nature of partisan attachments. Finally, they consider the significance of the images of party leaders and the issues of the day when it comes to electoral choice.

437 **The selection of national party leaders in Canada.**
John C. Courtney. Toronto: Macmillan, 1973. 278p.
The issues under discussion in this study focus on the contradictory nature of Canada's parliamentary system, which is based on the British model and yet adopts the US convention system for the selection of party leaders. The author examines why the earlier, more traditional processes of selection used by Canadian parties were abandoned and notes the effects of this change on Canadian politics.

438 **A choice of futures: politics in the Canadian north.**
Gurston Dacks. Toronto: Methuen, 1981. 226p.
The author presents a variety of issues affecting the north of Canada (i.e. native claims, political development, economic development), in an integrated political analysis and provides the reader with some sense of the magnitude of change engulfing this area. This is a highly recommended book. See also the volume on the north entitled *The north* (Toronto: University of Toronto Press, 1985), which includes essays commissioned as part of the research programme by the Royal Commission on the Economic Union and Development Prospects for Canada.

439 **Provincial politics in Canada.**
Rand Dyck. Scarborough, Ontario: Prentice-Hall, 1986. 626p. bibliog.
An overview of party politics in Canada at the provincial level, examining each of the provinces as if it were a separate political entity. The treatment of each province includes a political history and an account of recent political developments. A bibliography is provided. See also Martin Robin's *Canadian provincial politics: the party systems of the ten provinces* (Scarborough, Ontario: Prentice-Hall, 1978). Other useful works relating the political processes of the provinces are *Small worlds: provinces and parties in Canadian political life* (Toronto: Methuen, 1980); Marsha Chandler and William Chandler's *Public policy and provincial politics* (Toronto: McGraw-Hill Ryerson, 1979); and *The provincial political systems: comparative essays* (Toronto: Methuen, 1976). Also of interest is the work *Representative democracy in the Canadian provinces* (Scarborough, Ontario: Prentice-Hall, 1982). The reader should be aware that a large and diverse body of literature is available with regard to the provincial political parties, the history and development of those parties and the current and expected issues which will affect the provincial political systems in Canada. Examples of this literature have not been reproduced in this compilation due to space restrictions. However, some of the more interesting and colourful developments in Canadian political history, whether it is the history of the Social Credit in Alberta, the Union Nationale in Quebec or the birth of Canadian socialism in Saskatchewan, occurred within the provincial sectors.

440 **Canadian political thought.**
Edited by H. D. Forbes. Toronto: Oxford University Press, 1985. 471p.
An interesting and useful anthology of materials brought together to introduce and chronicle the development of political thought in Canada. The items reproduced range from party platforms to philosophical essays and span the period from 1799 to 1979. Taken together the collection provides many of the key documents upon which our political history rests.

441 **Politics: Canada.**
Edited by Paul W. Fox, Graham White. Toronto: McGraw-Hill
Ryerson, 1987. 6th ed. 670p. bibliog. (McGraw-Hill Ryerson Series in
Canadian Politics).
This anthology, taken as a whole, provides one of the best overviews of Canadian
politics available to the general reader. It includes a general bibliography of the field as
a separate contribution.

442 **PQ: Réné Lévesque & the Parti Québécois in power.**
Graham Fraser. Toronto: Macmillan, 1984. 434p.
A very readable, journalistic account of the Lévesque government and the rise and fall
of the Parti Québécois. A number of additional accounts are available, including such
works as Marcel Leger's *Le Parti Québécois: ce n'était qu'un début* . . . (The Parti
Québécois: only a beginning) (Montreal: Québec/Amérique, 1986) and John Saywell's
The rise of the Parti Québécoise 1967-76 (Toronto: University of Toronto Press, 1977).

443 **Conflict and unity: an introduction to Canadian political life.**
Roger Gibbins. Toronto: Methuen, 1985. 388p.
As described by the author in the first chapter, 'This text provides an introduction to
the complex and often tumultuous world of Canadian politics. Its focus is on what
might be termed the dynamics of politics, the issues and conflicts which drive the
political process. Woven into this analysis is a discussion of the institutional arenas
within which political conflict takes place and the parties, leaders, and groups through
which conflicting interests are mobilized'.

444 **Local and urban politics in Canada.**
Donald J. H. Higgins. Toronto: Gage, 1986. 417p.
Higgins provides a comprehensive framework within which local politics can be
analysed, compared and assessed. Within this context both current and historical
situations are explored. Of equal interest is Warren Magnusson and Andrew Sancton's
City politics in Canada, (Toronto: University of Toronto Press, 1983) in which
informative essays provide 'a new perspective on Canadian municipal politics. Its
concern is not with the mechanics of government, but with the practice of politics at
the local level'. Also recommended is Harold Kaplan's *Reform, planning, and city
politics: Montreal, Winnipeg, Toronto* (Toronto: University of Toronto Press, 1982).

445 **Apex of power: the Prime Minister and political leadership in Canada.**
Edited by Thomas A. Hockin. Scarborough, Ontario: Prentice-Hall,
1977. 2nd ed. 359p.
A landmark collection of essays which explore various facets of the relationships
between the Prime Minister of Canada, and the Canadian political and governmental
system. See also R. M. Punnett's *The Prime Minister in Canadian government and
politics* (Toronto: Macmillan; Maclean-Hunter Press, 1977).

446 **Public policies and political development in Canada.**
Ronald Manzer. Toronto: University of Toronto Press, 1985. 240p.
Provides an 'historical analysis of how Canadian governments have used public power
to promote economic development, relieve poverty, regulate markets, control crime,

build school systems, and protect human rights'. The author concludes that 'Canadian principles of policy-making have been drawn overwhelmingly from the tenets of liberalism'.

447 **Ideological perspectives on Canada.**
M. Patricia Marchak. Toronto: McGraw-Hill Ryerson, 1988. 3rd ed. 267p. (McGraw-Hill Ryerson Series in Canadian Sociology).
A sociologist discusses ideologies within the context of contemporary Canadian society, and comments on the relationships between the positions of various adherents to the major philosophies. She discusses such beliefs as Liberalism, Conservatism, Marxism and Socialism. The author concludes by examining the present class structure of Canada and the ideological themes which are emerging today.

448 **Canadian federalism: myth or reality.**
Edited by J. Peter Meekison. Toronto: Methuen, 1977. 3rd ed. 525p. (Canadian Politics and Government).
Presents a number of essays which reflect the strains and tensions of Canadian federalism. The pieces are organized into sections dealing with the dimensions of Canadian federalism, the Constitution and Canadian federalism, intergovernmental relations, regionalism and Canadian federalism, policy making and Canadian federalism, and Quebec and Confederation.

449 **The new democrats, 1961-1986: the politics of change.**
Desmond Morton. Toronto: Copp Clark Pitman, 1986. 3rd ed. 253p. (Canadiana Reprint Series).
This edition updates Morton's ongoing chronicle of the New Democratic Party (NDP) of Canada. Previous editions were entitled: *NDP: the dream of power* (Toronto: A. M. Hakkert, 1974), and *NDP: social democracy in Canada* (Toronto: Samuel Stevens Hakkert, 1977). Other works of interest, which deal also with the forerunner of the NDP, the Co-operative Commonwealth Federation, include: Lynn McDonald's *The party that changed Canada: the New Democratic Party, then and now* (Toronto: Macmillan, 1987); Michael Bradley's *Crisis of clarity: the New Democratic Party and the quest for the holy grail* (Toronto: Summerhill Press, 1985); *"Building the co-operative commonwealth": essays on the democratic socialist tradition in Canada* (Regina, Saskatchewan: Canadian Plains Research Center, University of Regina, 1984); Ivan Avakumovic's *Socialism in Canada: a study of the CCF-NDP in federal and provincial politics* (Toronto: McClelland & Stewart, 1978); Walter D. Young's *The anatomy of a party: the national CCF 1932-61* (Toronto: University of Toronto Press, 1969); and Gad Horowitz's *Canadian labour in politics* (Toronto: University of Toronto Press, 1968).

450 **The Canadian state: political economy and political power.**
Leo Panitch. Toronto: University of Toronto Press, 1977. 475p.
A number of Marxist scholars look at various aspects of the federal state in Canada. Topics include: the aspirations of Alberta and Quebec within the federation; relations between government élites and Canada's various socio-economic classes and ethnic groups; the management of the economy through budgets and welfare state policies; and the management of culture through education, the arts and citizen participation.

451 **Party government and regional representation in Canada.**
Toronto: University of Toronto Press in cooperation with the Royal
Commission on the Economic Union and Development Prospects for
Canada and the Canadian Government Publishing Centre, Supply and
Services Canada, 1985. 161p.

This is the first in a series of four volumes dealing with representative institutions in
Canada, included as part of the collected research of the Royal Commission on the
Economic Union and Development Prospects for Canada. This series deals with the
ineffectiveness of Canada's original constitutional design with regard to regional
interests, the party system and integration of the regions, the interaction of politics and
the administration of government, reforms to the system or representative government,
and reforms to the structures and institutions of government in our federal system.
Other titles in the series are: *Regional responsiveness and the national administrative
state*; *Institutional reforms for representative government*; and *Intrastate federalism in
Canada*.

452 **The Canadian Left: a critical analysis.**
Norman Penner. Scarborough, Ontario: Prentice-Hall, 1977. 287p.

Penner integrates the history of socialist movements and looks at the evolution of
socialist ideas and traditions and their impact on Canadian political thought.

453 **The Tory syndrome: leadership politics in the progressive Conservative
Party.**
George C. Perlin. Montreal: McGill-Queen's University Press, 1980.
250p.

The author examines the electoral weakness of the Conservative Party up to the late
1970s in the light of persistent internal conflict – particularly in the areas of values and
social composition. These problems, speculates Perlin, have created a mutually
reinforcing cycle of conflict and defeat in the party. Works also of interest include:
Sacred trust?: Brian Mulroney and the Conservative Party in power (Toronto:
Doubleday Canada, 1986); Charles Taylor's *Radical Tories: the Conservative tradition
in Canada* (Toronto: Anansi, 1982); John English's *The decline of politics: the
Conservatives and the party system 1901-1920* (Toronto: University of Toronto Press,
1977); Marc La Terreur's *Les tribulations des concervateurs au Québec* (Quebec: Les
Presses de L'Université Laval, 1973); J. L. Granatstein's *The politics of survival: the
Conservative Party in Canada 1939-1945* (Toronto: University of Toronto Press, 1970);
and John R. Willams' *The Conservative Party of Canada: 1920-1949* (Durham, North
Carolina: Duke University Press, 1956).

454 **Group politics and public policy.**
A. Paul Pross. Toronto: Oxford University Press, 1986. 343p. bibliog.

The author surveys the historical development, structure and political behaviour of
pressure groups as well as their increasingly important rôle within the framework of
Canadian political institutions and culture. An extensive bibliography is included.

455　**Pressure group behaviour in Canadian politics.**
Edited by A. Paul Pross.　Toronto: McGraw-Hill Ryerson, 1975.
196p. bibliog. (McGraw-Hill Ryerson Series in Canadian Politics).

Discusses the rôle of Canadian pressure groups whose functions are often not recognized and are not completely understood. The author notes that, although these groups are often thought of as not entirely respectable and are regarded with suspicion, they do form an 'essential part of Canadian politics'. A bibliography is provided.

456　**Regionalism in Canada: flexible federalism or fractured nation?**
Edited by George A. Rawlyk, Bruce W. Hodgins,
Richard P. Bowles.　Scarborough, Ontario: Prentice-Hall, 1979. 244p.
(Canada: Issues & Options).

A collection of secondary source materials including speeches, newspaper reports, magazine articles and the like, are brought together here for the purpose of providing viewpoints on the issues surrounding regionalism in Canada. In compiling the materials the editors have addressed the following questions: 'What is regionalism?' 'Why does it exist?' 'Can regionalism be a unifying force in Canada?' 'What can be done to counteract regional protest?' 'What alternatives face Canada if regionalism becomes a dividing force?'

457　**Federal-provincial diplomacy: the making of recent policy in Canada.**
Richard Simeon.　Toronto: University of Toronto Press, 1972. 324p.
(Studies in the Structure of Power: Decision-Making in Canada, vol. 5).

Much of Canada's political/governmental life is influenced and determined by the interplay of two or more levels of government. This work provides a most useful context for the informed and general reader in terms of how eleven governments interact and respond to the pressing issues of policy. The work also sheds light on the relationships between politicians and civil servants, between political party leaders and their backbenchers, and between the government and various public interest groups and élites.

458　**Canada in question: federalism in the eighties.**
Donald V. Smiley.　Toronto: McGraw-Hill Ryerson, 1980. 3rd ed.
346p. bibliog. (McGraw-Hill Ryerson Series in Canadian Politics).

One of Canada's premier political scientists provides his assessment of Canadian federalism in the 1980s. In this comprehensive work the author describes and provides an historical backdrop to Canada's constitutional system of parliamentary and federal government; he discusses regionalism and interprovincial relations, including the complicated issues associated with federal-provincial financial relations and provides one of the best overviews of the sometimes cohesive, sometimes divisive actions of political parties within the Canadian federal system. He also deals with the issue of cultural duality and language policies. A selective bibliography is provided.

459　**The federal condition in Canada.**
Donald V. Smiley.　Toronto: McGraw-Hill Ryerson, 1987. 202p.
(McGraw-Hill Ryerson Series in Canadian Politics).

Smiley's assessment as to the future of Canadian federalism is significantly more optimistic than in his previous work. In this volume he brings the reader to the present, taking into account the constitutional developments of the 1980s. He does recognize that the constitutional agenda remains incomplete and that issues such as aboriginal rights, the status of the Territories, the rôle of the provinces in international relations, remain to be resolved. A valuable work for the general reader wishing to understand present-day Canada.

460 **Party politics in Canada.**
Edited by Hugh G. Thorburn. Scarborough, Ontario: Prentice-Hall, 1985. 5th ed. 349p.

A collection of twenty-eight essays by knowledgeable academic commentators who analyse the party political scene in Canada. Essays explore such topics as the development of the Canadian party system, the effects of regionalism on Canadian politics, the changing fortunes of the two major parties, and the rôle of third parties in Canada.

461 **The Canadian political system: environment, structure and process.**
Richard J. Van Loon, Michael S. Whittington. Toronto: McGraw-Hill Ryerson, 1987. 4th ed. 879p. bibliog.

Because the political landscape of the country changes from day to day, it is difficult to recommend texts on the Canadian political scene which remain true to the patterns of the political environment for any length of time. Van Loon's text is one of the better ones, and although designed as a text for the post-secondary student, it stands on its own as an excellent introduction for the general reader to Canada's political system. It includes an extensive and particularly well-produced bibliography. Also recommended is *Politics in Canada: culture, institutions, behaviour and public policy* (Scarborough, Ontario: Prentice-Hall, 1986). Of a somewhat different nature, but also useful, is John Redekop's *Approaches to Canadian politics* (Scarborough, Ontario: Prentice-Hall, 1983).

462 **The L-shaped party: the Liberal Party of Canada 1958-1980.**
Joseph Wearing. Toronto: McGraw-Hill Ryerson, 1981. 260p.
(McGraw-Hill Ryerson Series in Canadian Politics).

A book about the organization and political fortunes of the Liberal Party of Canada from the period of its decline and electoral defeat in the late 1950s through its revival and electoral successes in the 1960s and 1970s. The work follows and is somewhat of a sequel to Reginald Whitaker's *The government party: organizing and financing the Liberal Party of Canada 1930-1958* (Toronto: University of Toronto Press, 1977). See also Christina McCall-Newman's *Grits: an intimate portrait of the Liberal Party* (Toronto: Macmillan, 1982), David Smith's *The regional decline of a national party: Liberals on the prairies* (Toronto: University of Toronto Press, 1981), James and Robert Laxer's *The liberal idea of Canada: Pierre Trudeau and the question of Canada's survival* (Toronto: James Lorimer & Company, 1977), and J. W. Pickersgill's *The Liberal Party* (Toronto: McClelland & Stewart, 1962).

463 **Political parties in Canada.**
Conrad Winn, John McMenemy.   Toronto: McGraw-Hill Ryerson,
1976. 291p. (McGraw-Hill Ryerson Series in Canadian Politics).
The authors scan the spectrum of political party activity in Canada. They provide a readable historical description of the major parties and some of the minor parties in the federal arena; but, of more importance, the work focuses on the place of parties in the political system. Generally speaking, this study explodes many of the myths and conventional wisdoms surrounding Canadian political parties. See also Frederick C. Engelmann and Mildred A. Schwartz's *Canadian political parties: origin, character, impact* (Scarborough, Ontario: Prentice-Hall, 1975).

National Identity

464 **The English fact in Quebec.**
Sheila McLeod Arnopoulas, Dominique Clift. Kingston, Ontario; Montreal: McGill-Queen's University Press, 1984. 2nd ed. 247p.
The authors consider the effects of a variety of English-French encounters on the political and economic growth of Canada. They comment on the reasons behind the recent 'resurgence of English-French animosity' and examine the opposing views of the English and French on a number of topics. The French edition of this book won the Governor-General's Award for non-fiction in 1979.

465 **Canada and the burden of unity.**
Edited by David Jay Bercuson. Toronto: Macmillan, 1977. 191p.
'What emerges from this book is a picture of the power of Central Canada, manifest through the federal government and other "national" institutions, which has created regional disparity and imposed its own version of national character and ambitions on Westerners and Maritimers'. Knowledgeable commentators point to the problems experienced by the West and the Maritimes within the Canadian federal system, advocating recognition by Central Canada, and federal institutions of the need for regional equality.

466 **Nationalism, self-determination and the Quebec question.**
David Cameron. Toronto: Macmillan, 1974. 177p.
Directed to the English-Canadian reader who wishes to be better informed, and from that information to formulate an opinion with regard to relations between Quebec and the rest of Canada. Though somewhat dated this work remains true to its intention and is recommended. The author attempts also to place his discussion within a broader historical and theoretical context.

467 **Quebec nationalism in crisis.**
Dominique Clift. Kingston, Ontario; Montreal: McGill-Queen's
University Press, 1982. 155p.

A perceptive, and award-winning journalist traces, in a series of essays, the trends of
recent Quebec history. In these essays she identifies the dominant traits of nationalism
in Quebec over the past twenty years.

468 **The independence movement in Quebec 1945-1980.**
William D. Coleman. Toronto: University of Toronto Press, 1984.
274p. (Studies in the Structure of Power: Decision-Making in Canada,
vol. 11).

A study of the independence coalition which united organized labour, the francophone
business class, and other segments of Quebec society in the aftermath of the 'Quiet
Revolution'. The author examines post-war Quebec in terms of what it meant to be
'québécois' and presents a distinct interpretation of the 'Quiet Revolution'. Coleman
systematically looks at the historical background, Quebec cultural institutions, federal-
provincial questions of autonomy, the economy and education, all to the end of
demonstrating that Quebec has fundamentally redefined itself in the period under
examination. Another excellent work which covers much of the same period is Michael
D. Behiels' *Prelude to Quebec's Quiet Revolution: liberalism versus neo-nationalism
1945-1960* (Kingston, Ontario; Montreal: McGill-Queen's University Press, 1985).

469 **Canada and the French-Canadian question.**
Ramsay Cook. Toronto: Copp Clark Pitman, 1986. 2nd ed. 219p.
(Canadiana Reprint Series).

Through the historical essays in this volume this eminent historian not only sheds light
on critical events in the country's history, he implicitly and explicitly suggests changes
in attitude by English Canadians which could 'go a little distance towards restoring the
equilibrium in French-English relations' (i.e. finding in our institutions ways of giving
expression to the cultural duality of Canada; or recognizing the need for English
Canadians to show willingness to examine constitutional change).

470 **Canada, Quebec and the uses of nationalism.**
Ramsay Cook. Toronto: McClelland & Stewart, 1986. 224p.

Cook continues to explore aspects of Canadian nationalism in a manner consistent with
his previous incisive works. He addresses questions concerning the identity of the 'first
Canadians', the validity of aboriginal peoples' 'historical claims', the rights of the
French Canadians in comparison with those of English Canadians. Quebec's right to
self-determination, immigration and the effects of US influence and capital on the
Canadian identity.

471 **French-Canadian nationalism: an anthology.**
Edited by Ramsay Cook. Toronto: Macmillan, 1969. 336p.

A valuable anthology of essays which, on the one hand attempts to 'interpret and
define the French Canadians' collective sense of identity', and on the other brings
together 'statements by individuals actively involved in the struggle for French-
Canadian survival'. The first section entitled 'Interpretations' includes work by Jean-C.
Bonenfant and Jean-C. Falardeau, Pierre Elliot Trudeau, and Fernand Ouellet. The

second section entitled 'The Exponents' includes the work of twenty-two commentators who collectively illustrate the development of the concept of nationalism in French Canada.

472 **The maple leaf forever: essays on nationalism and politics in Canada.**
Ramsay Cook. Toronto: Copp Clark Pitman, 1986. 2nd ed. 245p.
A variety of essays, (some historical, some which provide analysis of then recent events, and some which are critical of contemporary ideas about Canadian problems) that taken collectively explore the background, nature and currents of Canadian nationalism. Consistent with his other writing Cook believes, and demonstrates, that 'contrary to received and widely held Canadian opinion, our problem has long been one of too much nationalism rather than too little'.

473 **Quebec confronts Canada.**
Edward M. Corbett. Baltimore, Maryland: Johns Hopkins Press, 1967. 336p.
The 1960s and the 1970s produced a vast array of both popular and scholarly works which attempted to examine and comment on the nationalist sentiment in Quebec. This work, by a career bureaucrat, is one of the earliest, it is also one of the best. Other similar works are also available: Andre Bernard's *What does Quebec want?* (Toronto: James Lorimer & Company, 1978); *Canadian Confederation at the crossroads: the search for a federal-provincial balance* (Vancouver: Fraser Institute, 1978); Douglas H. Fullerton's *The dangerous delusion: Quebec's independence obsession* (Toronto: McClelland & Stewart, 1978); Richard Simeon's *Must Canada fail?* (Montreal; London, Ontario: McGill-Queen's University Press, 1977); Richard Jones' *Community in crisis: French-Canadian nationalism in perspective* (Toronto: McClelland & Stewart, 1972); Marcel Rioux' *Quebec in question* (Toronto: James Lewis & Samuel, 1971); R. M. Burns' *One country or two?* (Montreal: McGill-Queen's University Press, 1971); Thomas Sloan's *Quebec: the not-so-quiet revolution* (Toronto: Ryerson, 1965); Peter Desbarets' *The state of Quebec: a journalist's view of the quiet revolution* (Toronto: McClelland & Stewart, 1965); and Frank Scott and Michael Oliver's *Quebec states her case* (Toronto: Macmillan, 1964).

474 **Québec: the unfinished revolution.**
Léon Dion. Montreal: McGill-Queen's University Press, 1976. 218p.
A noted Quebec social scientist provides an important perspective on the nationalist movement in the province during a period of apparent calm in the mid-1970s (at least from the perspective of the uninformed observer). He analyses the problems of Quebec by tracing the changing values of French Canada (from the period of the church-centred, rural community, to the present day), and does so within the even broader context of the profound changes affecting the entire western world. This English version is expanded from the original work, entitled *La prochaine révolution* (The next revolution, Ottawa: Lemeac, 1973). Included is a lengthy chapter, entitled 'Politics and nationalism in Quebec' which contributes much to an understanding of 'the nature of Quebeckers' historical consciousness'. See also the author's *Nationalismes et politiques au Québec* (Nationalism and politics in Quebec. Montreal: Hurtubise HMH, 1975).

475 **Lament for a nation: the defeat of Canadian nationalism.**
George Grant. Ottawa: Carleton University Press, 1986. 97p.

This noted scholar makes an impassioned statement, which is now considered a classic, on the Canadian national identity, particularly with reference to his 'lament' or fear of continentalism; that is specifically, the gradual absorption of Canada into the United States – culturally, economically and finally politically. It is as relevant today as it was when first published in 1965.

476 **The sociology of contemporary Quebec nationalism: an annotated bibliography and review.**
Ronald D. Lambert. New York; London: Garland, 1981. 148p. (Garland Reference Library of Social Science, vol. 78).

The subject matter of this bibliography is Quebec nationalism, defined for the purpose as the 'personal sentiments, ideology and social movements which place a value on and seek to enhance the status of the French-Canadian community'. It provides standard enumerative entries, with annotations.

477 **Quebec versus Ottawa: the struggle for self-government 1960-72.**
Claude Morin. Toronto: University of Toronto Press, 1976. 164p.

During the period under study the author was the Deputy Minister of Intergovernmental Affairs in the Quebec provincial government. Here Morin provides an insider's viewpoint on the issues and conflicts between Quebec and the federal government in an attempt to 'help English-speaking Canadians to an understanding of the Québécois ideas of federalism during these years and of how people in Quebec can come to believe that sovereignty is essential'.

478 **Three scales of inequality: perspectives on French–English relations.**
Raymond N. Morris, C. Michael Lanphier. Toronto: Longman, 1977. 300p. bibliog. (Canadian Social Problems Series).

A sociological review of the relationships between the French and the English in Canada. The work is divided into three primary parts: 'French-English relations, the contemporary scene'; 'French-English relations, the historical background'; and 'French-English relations, some possible options'. This last section provides interesting perspectives on nationalist options, assimilationist options (economic and political), and Quebec independence. A bibliography is included.

479 **Québec-Canada: a new deal: the Québec government proposal for a new partnership between equals: sovereignty-association.**
Quebec: Éditeur officiel, 1979. 109p.

'For the Government of Québec has reached the conclusion that our government as a people requires the transformation of today's federalism into an association in which Québec, as part of an economic and monetary union, would have all the powers of a sovereign country, just like Canada. This new deal, between equals, is the only path leading from our past, through demands of the present, toward a future which belongs to us'. This text provides the official proposal on independence or 'sovereignty-association' put forward by the provincial government of Quebec.

480 **The Union Nationale: Quebec nationalism from Duplessis to Lévesque.**
Herbert F. Quinn. Toronto: University of Toronto Press, 1979. 2nd
ed. 342p.
'The increasing momentum of the separatist movement in Quebec under René
Lévesque and the Parti Québécois has focused renewed attention on the history of
French-Canadian nationalism'. The author provides an account of the period following
the First World War, and in this revised and expanded edition, continues up to the
emergence of the Parti Québécois and the victory of a more radical nationalism over
one of a more conservative nature.

481 **Federalism and the French Canadians.**
Pierre Elliott Trudeau. Toronto: Macmillan, 1977. 212p. (Laurentian
Library, vol. 48).
An anthology of political thought which has, arguably, become a classic in the
literature of Canada. Here can clearly be seen the genesis of Trudeau's views on
Canadian federalism, views that were destined to be reflected, and in many ways,
shaped Canada during his years as Prime Minister.

482 **Nationalism in Canada.**
University League for Social Reform, edited by Peter Russell.
Toronto: McGraw-Hill, 1966. 377p.
Twenty-two academic contributors provide a variety of perspectives and views with
regard to Canadian nationalism on the eve of the country's centennial year. Taken
collectively, the essays not only provide rich and diverse views, but offer both an
historical or descriptive dimension to nationalism in Canada, as well as providing some
sense as to the effect of nationalist attitudes on the development of the country, its
culture and its institutions. The work remains useful and widely cited today.

Administration and Government

Reference

483 **Canadian official publications.**
Olga B. Bishop. Toronto: Pergamon, 1981. 297p. (Guides to Official Publications, vol. 9).
Introduces the reader to the various types of publications issued by parliament and the various departments and agencies of the federal government, with a commentary on the kind of information which typically may be found in the different documents. The work is not intended as a bibliography of federal government publications. Includes short essays on the structure and make-up of the federal government and its bureaucracy.

484 **Canadian government programs and services.**
Don Mills, Ontario: CCH Canadian, 1970- .
Organizational and personnel information on federal government programmes and services, as well as an outline of federal assistance programmes. Includes such areas and agencies as: parliament, the executive, the judiciary, government departments, crown corporations, commissions, boards and councils, etc. Kept current.

485 **Government of Canada Publications = Publications du Governement du Canada: Quarterly Catalogue Trimestriel.**
Ottawa: Canadian Government Publishing Centre/Centre d'édition du governement du Canada, 1953- .
Supersedes the weekly checklists and any special lists issued on occasion, this periodical provides a comprehensive listing of official publications issued by the federal Government of Canada. Indexes to each quarterly *Catalogue* are cumulated annually.

486 **Bibliography Canadian public administration = Administration publique canadienne bibliographie.**
Compiled by W. E. Grasham. Toronto: Institute of Public Administration of Canada, 1972. 261p.
Though dated, this work is a starting point for information relating to public administration in Canada. Includes citations in related fields, including law, political science, economics, sociology, geography and history.

487 **Canadian Parliamentary Guide = Guide Parlementaire Canadien.**
Edited by Pierre G. Normandin. [Ottawa]: Normandin, 1862- . annual.
A source of information relating to the governments, federal and provincial, of Canada. The guide provides concise biographies of members of the Privy Council, the House of Commons, the Senate and the Assemblies of all the Provincial Governments and the Territories, as well as of the Supreme Court, the Federal Court and the Tax Court. It provides an historical chronology of sitting members in Parliament by constituency. Information is included on various federal boards and commissions and on senior public servants.

General

488 **Canadian regulatory agencies: quis custodiet ipsos custodes?**
C. Lloyd Brown-John. Toronto: Butterworths, 1981. 268p.
Regulatory activity is defined as a set of governmental constraints on freedom related to a specified policy area, and a regulatory agency is, therefore, a government body which administers that specified policy area. The author outlines the regulatory environment in Canada. Another useful reference is G. Bruce Doern's *The regulatory process in Canada* (Toronto: Macmillan, 1978).

489 **The Canadian Senate: a lobby from within.**
Colin Campbell. Toronto: Macmillan, 1978. 184p. (Canadian Controversies Series).
The debate with regard to Senate reform in Canada is ongoing and in recent years the discussion has intensified. This work, though dated, provides some background to the issue.

490 **The superbureaucrats: structure and behaviour in central agencies.**
Colin Campbell, George J. Szablowski. Toronto: Macmillan, 1979. 286p.
Key agencies within the Canadian government structure are examined in terms of function and operation. These agencies include the Prime Minister's Office, the Privy Council Office, the Federal-Provincial Relations Office, the Finance Department and the Treasury Board. An understanding of these agencies is necessary for a full general comprehension of Canadian government.

491 **Canadian Public Administration/Administration Publique du Canada.**
Toronto: Institute of Public Administration of Canada/L'Institut d'administration publique du Canada, 1958- . quarterly.

Dealing with aspects of public administration in Canada, this also includes book reviews. Another important source is *Policy options* = *Options politiques* (Halifax, Nova Scotia: Institute for Research on Public Policy, 1979-). The latter is published ten times a year and provides a forum for diverse views on Canadian public policy.

492 **Dawson's the government of Canada.**
R. MacGregor Dawson, revised by Norman Ward. Toronto: University of Toronto Press, 1987. 6th ed. 373p.

This work is considered the classic treatise on the structure and functioning of government in Canada, but some similar and equally important works include: J. R. Mallory's *The structure of Canadian government* (rev. ed.) (Toronto: Gage, 1984); and Thomas Hockin's *Government in Canada* (Toronto: McGraw-Hill Ryerson, 1976). More current works, and works directed more to the general reader are: *Introduction to Canadian politics and government* (Toronto: Holt, Rinehart & Winston, 1985); Allen S. Merritt and George W. Brown's *Canadians and their government* (Toronto: Fitzhenry & Whiteside, 1983).

493 **Canadian public policy: ideas, structure, process.**
G. Bruce Doern, Richard W. Phidd. Toronto: Methuen, 1983. 624p. bibliog.

Examining policy-making in Canada, this volume encompasses the broadest of historical, economic, social and institutional contexts. It describes and critically observes such structures and processes as the executive (Prime Minister, cabinet and the central agencies), as well as the rôle of departments, agencies and senior bureaucrats. In addition, it reviews selected policy fields both from an historical and a contemporary slant, and includes how policy is reviewed and evaluated. Throughout the work, particular attention is paid to the rôle of federal–provincial relations and foreign policy formation processes. Includes a lengthy bibliography.

494 **The machinery of government in Canada.**
Audrey D. Doerr. Toronto: Methuen, 1981. 223p.

Focuses on the practice of government in Canada. Here is an overview of the essential elements of the machinery of government and the processes of management and policy-making. Attention is paid to the structure of government, including the rôle of such institutions and agencies as cabinet, departments and non-departmental bodies. Issues such as accountability and control are discussed at length.

495 **The Parliament of Canada.**
C. E. S. Franks. Toronto: University of Toronto Press, 1987. 305p.

There is growing dissatisfaction with the way parliamentary government functions in Canada. Polls would suggest that parliament is considered neither important nor effective, and considerable discussion at various federal-provincial forums has reflected this fact. This work examines the successes and failures of parliamentary reform, focusing on three perspectives: the theoretical viewpoint, explaining the gap between Canadians' expectations of parliament and its reality; the effect of recent reforms, i.e. rules of debate, question period, rôle of MPs, etc., and their impact; and the potential of additional reforms, i.e. to the Senate, to the electoral system. See also John B. Stewart's *The Canadian House of Commons: procedure and reform* (Montreal: McGill-Queen's University Press, 1977).

496 **The Ottawa men: the civil service mandarins, 1935-1957.**
J. L. Granatstein. Toronto: Oxford University Press, 1982. 333p.

While constantly changing, like any institution of its kind, the civil service in Canada is generally viewed very positively, both within Canada and outside the country. In large measure this profile is attributed to the high standards which were set by senior civil servants in the formative years of departmental development and expansion. This highly readable work combines a biographical and a policy-oriented approach in its attempt to document the rôle of key individuals and trace the development of the government departments in which they served. Essential reading for those wishing to better understand the culture of the Canadian bureaucracy.

497 **The Canadian public service: a physiology of government 1867-1970.**
J. E. Hodgetts. Toronto: University of Toronto Press, 1973. 363p. (Studies in the Structure of Power: Decision-Making in Canada).

In analysis of the conditions under which the Canadian government makes its decisions, this knowledgeable academic provides a guidebook to the administrative forms and formations of Canadian government structure. The author comes to praise the public service as flexible, adaptable and innovative – a creative force in Canadian society. Canada has taken great pride in the competence, leadership and dedication of its public servants and the Civil Service Commission is in large measure the guardian of the public virtue. Hodgetts writes its story in *The biography of an institution: the Civil Service Commission of Canada, 1908-1967* (Montreal: McGill-Queen's University Press, 1972).

498 **The Canadian legislative system: politicians and policymaking.**
Robert J. Jackson, Michael M. Atkinson. Toronto: Gage, 1980. 2nd ed. 222p. (Canadian Controversies Series).

The authors proceed here to dissect major institutions and parliament in order to ascertain the rôle played by politicians in the policy-making process. From their assessment the authors conclude that major reforms are required to parliament if it is to continue to function appropriately. Also studied within this work are the parts played by the parliamentary committees, interest groups and political parties.

499 **Public administration in Canada: a text.**
Kenneth Kernaghan, David Siegel. Toronto: Methuen, 1987. 642p.

Although designed as a comprehensive text for the study of public administration in Canada, this work stands as an introduction for the knowledgeable general reader, to the subject – although given its size it might best be thematically sampled rather than read. A more manageable work, though dated, is T.J. Stevens' *The business of government: an introduction to Canadian public administration* (Toronto: McGraw-Hill Ryerson, 1978). Related works of interest include: Robert F. Adie and Paul G. Thomas' *Canadian public administration: problematical perspectives* (Scarborough, Ontario: Prentice-Hall, 1987); Kenneth Kernaghan's *Public administration in Canada: selected readings* (Toronto: Methuen, 1985); and, by the same author, *Canadian cases in public administration* (Toronto: Methuen, 1977).

500   The crown in Canada.
Frank MacKinnon.   Calgary, Alberta: Glenbow-Alberta
Institute/McClelland & Stewart West, 1976. 189p.

As the author sees it, 'the Crown is a fundamental source of power in the Canadian constitution' enabling political institutions to operate the way they do, reinforcing federalism and supporting democracy. At the same time, it is so unobtrusive that many citizens are unaware of its action, which in turn facilitates its successful operation. This book's aim is to examine the Crown in Canadian government today.

501   The Prime Minister and the cabinet.
W. A. Matheson.   Toronto: Methuen, 1976. 246p. (Canadian Politics and Government).

Examinging the rôle and status of the Prime Minister, the author describes the cabinet system of government in Canada. The cabinet is the source examining statements of policy and legislation, as well as administrative and quasi-judicial decisions, and its function as the mainspring of Canadian government is studied here.

502   The Canadian public sector.
Douglas J. McCready.   Toronto: Butterworths, 1984. 457p.

The Canadian public sector deals with traditional questions of public finance, with emphasis on fiscal policy, federalism and public institutional decision making. The author deals with a variety of topics under this heading, including: government and the economy; the nature of the Canadian public sector; Canadian fiscal federalism; the formulation of government policy; taxation policies in Canada; and, social security and welfare in Canada. For further information see also: D. A. L. Auld and F. C. Miller's *Principles of public finance* (Toronto: Methuen, 1982).

503   Tug of war: Ottawa and the provinces under Trudeau and Mulroney.
David Milne.   Toronto: James Lorimer & Company, 1986. 275p.

The author explores questions relating to federalism, and federal and provincial relations during the past two decades. This was a period of intense political conflict between Ottawa and the provinces, when questions such as the future of Quebec, constitutional revision, the National Energy Program, industrial policy, the Canada Health Act, and free trade with the United States were at issue. The author attempts to provide a critical commentary on the central themes and practices of the respective governments as each defined itself, as well as its relations with the provinces.

504   Federalism and economic union in Canada.
Kenneth Norrie, Richard Simeon, Mark Krasnick.   Toronto:
University of Toronto Press in cooperation with the Royal Commission on the Economic Union and Development Prospects for Canada and the Canadian Publishing Centre, Supply and Services Canada, 1986. 349p.

This is one of twelve volumes which deals with federalism and the economic union in Canada, included as part of the collected research of the Royal Commission on the Economic Union and Development Prospects for Canada. This series deals with the theoretical and practical complications of the Canadian condition, including such issues as: economic integration as relates to the federal system; national common-markets;

the political backdrop to the formulation of public policy; divisions of power; intergovernmental relations; regional disparity; financial institutions and federalism; interest groups in a federal system; and, the particular status of Quebec within Confederation.

505 **Party government and regional representation in Canada.**
Toronto: University of Toronto Press in cooperation with the Royal Commission on the Economic Union and Development Prospects for Canada and the Canadian Government Publishing Centre, Supply and Services Canada, 1985. 161p.

This is the first in a series of four volumes dealing with representative institutions in Canada, included as part of the collected research of the Royal Commission on the Economic Union and Development Prospects for Canada. This series tackles such subjects as the ineffectiveness of Canada's original constitutional design with regard to regional interests, while also examining the party system and integration of the regions. Some other themes include the interaction of politics and the administration of government, reforms to the system of representative government, and reforms to the structures and institutions of government in Canada's federal system. Other titles in the series are: *Regional responsiveness and the national administrative state*; *Institutional reforms for representative government*; and *Intrastate federalism in Canada*.

506 **The judiciary in Canada: the third branch of government.**
Peter H. Russell. Toronto: McGraw-Hill Ryerson, 1987. 388p. (McGraw-Hill Ryerson Series in Canadian Politics).

This noted political scientist breaks new ground by providing at one and the same time, a guide book to Canadian courts as part of the political and governmental system, and, an examination of the way in which the Canadian judiciary functions, as well as describing the structure and organization of the courts of which it is comprised.

507 **The office of Lieutenant-Governor: a study in Canadian government and politics.**
John T. Saywell. Toronto: University of Toronto Press, 1986. 279p. (Canadiana Reprint Series).

Though dated, this work provides the reader, particularly the uninformed reader, with an introduction to the history and the function of the Lieutenant-Governorship, an office common in all provinces and an office thought, inappropriately so, to be a parallel to that of the Monarchy or the Governor-General.

508 **Local government in Canada.**
C. R. Tindal, S. Nobes Tindal. Toronto: McGraw-Hill Ryerson, 1984. 2nd ed. 272p. bibliog. (McGraw-Hill Ryerson Series in Canadian Politics).

An examination of local government and municipal policy making in Canada. The authors trace the origins and evolution of the Canadian local government system; they analyse the machinery of municipal government and assess their adequacy; they look at the public dimension of government, that is the rôle played by citizen groups; and they discuss relations between local, provincial and federal governments. In addition, the authors outline the processes of municipal policy making, financial and personnel management, providing the reader with a summary text on public administration. A bibliography is included. The reader interested in municipal finance might wish to consult Richard M. Bird and N. Enid Slack's *Urban public finance in Canada* (Toronto: Butterworths, 1983). Of general interest also is Lionel D. Feldman's *Politics and government of urban Canada: selected readings* (Toronto: Methuen, 1981); and, John C. Weaver's *Shaping the Canadian city: essays on urban politics and policy, 1890-1920* (Toronto: The Institute of Public Administration of Canada, 1977).

509 **Canadian public policy and administration: theory and environment.**
V. Seymour Wilson. Toronto: McGraw-Hill Ryerson, 1981. 442p.

This is a textbook treatment of the subject, designed to introduce the reader to theoretical considerations in the field of public policy and administration, and particularly to punctuate that knowledge with concrete perspectives on such topics as ministerial responsibility, the rôle of central agencies, and the origins of the ministerial department. Thoroughly documented.

Foreign Relations

Reference

510 **A bibliography of works on Canadian foreign relations 1981-1985.**
Compiled by Jane R. Barrett, Jane Beaumont, Lee-Anne Broadhead.
Toronto: Canadian Institute of International Affairs, 1987. 157p.
This is the fourth in a series of bibliographies under the same title published by the Institute. Previous volumes cover the periods: 1945-70; 1971-75; and, 1976-80 respectively. Includes Canadian and foreign monographs, articles, theses, research papers, government documents, conference papers, and selected departmental press releases. Considered the standard in the field.

511 **Documents on Canadian external relations.**
Ottawa: Department of External Affairs, 1967- .
This ongoing series is by far the most valuable source of published documentation for the serious researcher in the field. The documents reproduced are official correspondence, memoranda, reports, etc. taken from the Department's files and archives. To date the project has covered the period from 1909 to 1946.

General

512 **Canadian–Soviet relations 1939-1980.**
Edited by Aloysius Balawyder. Oakville, Ontario: Mosaic, 1981. 222p.
This work is a companion to the editor's own *Canadian–Soviet relations between the World Wars* (Toronto: University of Toronto Press, 1972). Since the Second World War both Canada and Russia have matured and emerged on the international scene as a middle-power and super-power respectively. Over this period relations have grown

and diversified. From the Canadian point of view, the importance of relations with the Soviet Union is outranked only by those with the United States, the European Community, including Great Britain and Japan. In Soviet eyes, however, the relationship is of much less significance. The work contains an interesting appendix, entitled 'A Chronology of Canadian Soviet Relations'.

513 **The in-between time: Canadian external policy in the 1930s.**
Edited by Robert Bothwell, Norman Hillmer. Toronto: Copp Clark, 1975. 224p. (Issues in Canadian History).

Works in this series contain readings of selected Canadian historical crises, problems and personalities. The format combines relevant documents with open-ended editorial comment. This volume deals with years immediately following the passage of the Statute of Westminster of 1931, an act which provided for Canada's full constitutional independence under the monarchy, to the outbreak of the Second World War. A companion volume in the series, dealing also with foreign relations, is J. L. Granatstein's *Canadian foreign policy since 1945: middle power or satellite?* (Toronto: Copp Clark, 1973). This volume examines foreign policy from the war's end to the early 1970s, focusing on the distinctiveness of Canadian policy in the light of that followed by the United States.

514 **North Atlantic triangle: the interplay of Canada, the United States and Great Britain.**
John Bartlet Brebner. Toronto: McClelland & Stewart, 1968. 377p. (The Carleton Library, vol. 30).

A classic work of historiography in this convenient paperback reprint. 'My primary aim', wrote Brebner, 'was to get at, and to set forth, the interplay between the United States and Canada – the Siamese Twins of North America who cannot separate and live. By interplay I do not mean merely the manifestations in what are usually called international relations, but the various kinds of things which the peoples of the two countries did in common, or in complementary fashion, or in competition'. A must for anyone interested in Canadian foreign relations, and in particular Canadian–American relations.

515 **Canada and the international political/economic environment.**
Toronto: University of Toronto Press in cooperation with the Royal Commission on the Economic Union and Development Prospects for Canada and the Canadian Government Publishing Centre, Supply and Services Canada, 1985. 151p.

This is the first in a series of three volumes dealing with Canada and the international political economy, included as part of the collected research of the Royal Commission on the Economic Union and Development Prospects for Canada. This series deals with: the prospects for the expansion and diversification of Canadian exports; the issues surrounding Canada–United States free trade, including the topics of economic nationalism and continental integration; and the rôle of the foreign service and Canada's Department of External Affairs, particularly relating to such topics as security abroad, defence spending, etc. Other titles in the series are: *The politics of Canada's economic relationship with the United States*; and *Selected problems in formulating foreign economic policy*.

516 **Canada in world affairs.**
Toronto: Oxford University Press, under the auspices of the Canadian Institute of International Affairs, 1941-1968. 12 vols.
While out of print, this set continues to be highly regarded as a source for commentary on Canadian foreign relations, primarily for the 1940s and 1950s. (The first volume deals with the years prior to the Second World War, the last published covers the period 1961-63.) The Canadian Institute of International Affairs had as its object the promotion and encouragement in Canada of research and discussion in international affairs, and sought to give attention to Canada's position as a member of the international community and as a member of the Commonwealth. Each volume in the set is written by a noted academic and comments on a two year period of the nation's foreign relations.

517 **American dollars – Canadian prosperity: Canadian–American economic relations 1945-1950.**
R. D. Cuff, J. L. Granatstein. Toronto: Samuel-Stevens, 1978. 286p.
Increasingly the economic relations of Canada and the United States are being treated separately from other diplomatic/political issues. This work provides a valuable perspective for discussions of economic relations in the period after the Second World War. Here the authors conceptualize the relationship 'as a series of ongoing negotiations with developing American imperial power'.

518 **Ties that bind: Canadian–American relations in wartime: from the great war to the cold war.**
R. D. Cuff, J. L. Granatstein. Toronto: Samuel Stevens; Sarasota, Florida: Hakkert, 1977. 2nd ed. 205p.
The focus of the work is wartime relations between the countries, for the authors believe that the periods of war are even more important than peacetime in coming to understand the factors which affected present-day Canada. The war years played a significant part in the evolution of Canadian–American relationships, bringing about adjustments and readjustments which frequently predominated over the desires of political leaders.

519 **Canada as a principal power: a study in foreign policy and international relations.**
David B. Dewitt, John J. Kirton. Toronto: John Wiley, 1983. 478p.
Canada's place and influence within the international community of nations is seen by some observers and scholarly commentators as that of an internationalist middle power – a rôle to which it brings certain qualities; others view it as a dependent satellite operating within limits set by the United States. This work discusses these two positions and brings forward a new perspective termed 'complex neo-realism', which is propounded on the emergence of a new international order characterized by the decline in position of the principal powers, i.e. the United States, and the rise of the middle powers to assume the rôle of the great powers in an increasingly diffuse international system.

520 **Forgotten partnership: US–Canada relations today.**
Charles F. Doran. Baltimore, Maryland; London: Johns Hopkins
University Press, 1984. 294p.

Richard Gwyn, political journalist, wrote in his work *The 49th paradox: Canada in North America* (q.v.), that 'Library shelves buckle beneath the studies, tomes, reports on the subject [of US–Canada relations]'. Few statements are more correct – the literature is staggering, the present decade contributing greatly as various bilateral issues come to the fore. The work listed is one of many which could be recommended. Others include: *Canada and the United States: enduring friendship, persistent stress* (Englewood Cliffs, New Jersey: Prentice-Hall, 1985); Edelgard E. Mahant and Graeme S. Mount's *An introduction to Canadian–American relations* (Toronto: Methuen, 1984); Roger Frank Swanson's *Inter-governmental perspectives on the Canada–US relationship* (New York: New York University Press, 1978); H. Edward English's *Canada–United States relations* (New York: Academy of Political Science, 1976); *Canada and the United States: transnational and transgovernmental relations* (New York: Columbia University Press, 1976); and *Continental community: independence and integration in North America* (Toronto: McClelland & Stewart, 1974).

521 **Pacific challenge: Canada's future in the new Asia.**
Eric Downton. Toronto: Stoddart, 1986. 258p.

A journalist's critical assessment of Canada's past and present relations with the countries of the Pacific Rim, particularly concentrating on matters of trade, defence, diplomacy and culture.

522 **In defence of Canada.**
James Eayrs. Toronto: University of Toronto Press, 1964- . 5 vols.
(Studies in the Structure of Power: Decision-Making in Canada).

Eayrs' multi-volume work is considered to encompass the best study of post-war defence and foreign policy available. It is, at least, a major contribution to the literature and essential reading for the interested reader. Individual volumes are entitled: *From the Great War to the Great Depression* (1964); *Appeasement and rearmament* (1965); *Peacemaking and deterrence* (1972); *Growing up allied* (1980); and *Indochina: roots of complicity* (1983). On the general topic of foreign policy the reader should also consult the author's *The art of the possible: government and foreign policy in Canada* (Toronto: University of Toronto Press, 1961).

523 **Southern exposure: Canadian perspectives on the United States.**
Edited by David H. Flaherty, William R. McKercher. Toronto:
McGraw-Hill Ryerson, 1986. 246p. bibliog. (McGraw-Hill Ryerson
Series in Canadian Politics).

Canada–US relations are examined from the perspective of the Canadian view of the United States. Nineteen eminent Canadian authorities analyse here the major problematical issues experienced by Canada in dealings with the United States. In doing so, the authors range through topics such as politics, economics, culture, the environment and resources. The aim of the work is to provide the informed reader with a clearer understanding of the American impact on Canada, and it adds an interesting dimension to the existing literature. A bibliography of other relevant and up-to-date works is included.

524 **A history of Canadian external relations.**
G. P. de T. Glazebrook. Toronto: McClelland & Stewart, 1966. rev.
ed. 2 vols. (Carleton Library, vol. 27).
Though published in 1966, with scholarship predating even this date, this survey is still
highly regarded and provides a readable account of Canada's participation in
international affairs, first as a colony, then as a sovereign nation.

525 **Canadian foreign policy: historical readings.**
Edited by J. L. Granatstein. Toronto: Copp Clark Pitman, 1986.
263p. (New Canadian Readings).
An anthology of excerpts from official, public documents, speeches, etc. combined
with critical essays by noted academics. The package is intended to illustrate the
development and the complexity of the evolution of Canadian foreign policy.

526 **The 49th paradox: Canada in North America.**
Richard Gwyn. Toronto: McClelland & Stewart, 1985. 362p.
A prominent political journalist takes 'a stereoscopic view, peering at Canada–US
relations in all its dimensions, political, cultural, economic, commercial, and historic,
beginning with the Loyalists, who began it all'. While this is a popular treatment,
Gwyn provides a most worthwhile addition to the literature of relations between the
United States and Canada. This is a book for the general and informed reader.

527 **A foremost nation: Canadian foreign policy and a changing world.**
Edited by Norman Hillmer, Garth Stevenson. Toronto: McClelland
& Stewart, 1977. 296p. (Carleton Contemporaries).
A number of respected academics and commentators on Canadian foreign relations
present their views and opinions, their perceptions of the issues and challenges of
Canadian foreign policy. The views are indeed divergent, thus reflecting the complex
and diverse nature of policy. The essays are balanced, mainly focusing on economic
aspects of external relations and those dealing with the diplomatic, security-orientated
aspects.

528 **Canada: middle-aged power.**
John W. Holmes. Toronto: McClelland & Stewart in association with
the Institute of Canadian Studies, Carleton University, 1976. 293p.
(Carleton Library, vol. 98).
This collection is a companion to *The better part of valour: essays on Canadian
diplomacy* (Toronto: McClelland & Stewart, 1970). Both works contain essays which
examine Canada's international rôle as a 'middle power'. Essays concern themselves
with general foreign policy, international organizations, Canada–US relations,
Canadian involvement in Vietnam, and Canada's rôle within North America generally.

529 **The shaping of peace: Canada and the search for world order 1943-1957.**
John W. Holmes. Toronto: University of Toronto Press, 1979-1982. 2
vols.
Official policy and official perspectives, particularly those of the Department of
External Affairs, dominate this excellent study of Canadian foreign policy in the late

war years and the years following. The author, a career civil servant, diplomat and academic, chronicles the events of the time and establishes Canada's rôle in those events. With realism, he notes that Canada's part was played against the world panorama, and that her rôle was 'not in the proposing of grand designs but in the responses, in constructive amendments and imaginative formulas, in the exploiting of occasions, and in the insistence on certain basic principles'.

530 **An independent foreign policy for Canada?**
Stephen Clarkson. Toronto: McClelland & Stewart, 1968. 286p.

A polemical discussion, reflecting discussions and debates held under the auspices of the University League for Social Reform, an organization intended to provide a forum for academics and others to discuss public policy problems. This work is included here to reflect the debate, now long-standing, concerning the independent/dependent/interdependent nature of Canadian foreign policy, and the resultant utilitarian nature of the country's foreign relations policies. It also reflects on the domestic issues and problems which have placed restraints and conditions on those policies.

531 **International Journal.**
Toronto: Canadian Institute of International Affairs, 1946- . quarterly.

The mission of the Institute is to provide interested Canadians with a non-partisan, nationwide forum for informed discussion, analysis, and debate. The *Journal* is considered the best publication in the field of Canadian foreign relations. Another relevant publication is *International Perspectives: the Canadian Journal on World Affairs* (Toronto: Baxter, 1972- . bi-monthly).

532 **Canada and the Arab world.**
Edited by Tareq Y. Ismael. Edmonton, Alberta: University of Alberta Press, 1985. 206p.

Papers prepared for this anthology resulted from discussions and meetings which took place in 1981 at the Canadian–Arab Relations Conference at the University of Calgary. Collectively, the essays examine the issues which have arisen that involve Canada's dealings with, and understanding of, Middle Eastern countries. Canada's foreign policy, national interests, economic relations and peacekeeping rôle in the Middle East are examined. The material also covers the Palestinian question, religious perceptions of Arabs by Canadians and the influence of Zionist interest groups in Canada.

533 **Canada on the Pacific Rim.**
J. Arthur Lower. Toronto: McGraw-Hill Ryerson, 1975. 230p. bibliog.

This highly readable overview gives a contemporary as well as an historical perspective on Canada's relations with a variety of countries which share the coastline of the Pacific Ocean. An extensive bibliography is included.

534 **Canada and the Third World.**
Edited by Peyton V. Lyon, Tareq Y. Ismael. Toronto: Macmillan/Maclean-Hunter, 1976. 342p.

Though dated, this work remains useful by providing background to Canada's relations to those countries collectively termed 'the Third World'. This collection of essays provides an overview of Canadian policy to its date of publication. Areas discussed include: South Asia; Anglophone Africa; Francophone Africa; Latin America; the Caribbean; the Middle East; and, Southeast Asia. Also of interest is the title *Canada and the Third World: what are the choices?* (Toronto: Yorkminster Publishing, 1975).

535 **Canadian foreign policy 1945-1954: selected speeches and documents.**
Edited by R. A. Mackay. Toronto: McClelland & Stewart, 1971.
407p. (Carleton Library, vol. 51).
This work is the first in a subseries within the Carleton Library of selected speeches and documents relating to Canadian foreign policy. The other titles are: *Canadian foreign policy 1955-1965: selected speeches and documents* (1977); and, *Canadian foreign policy 1966-1976: selected speeches and documents* (1980). All works, selected from official sources, are intended to document the main course of Canadian foreign policy.

536 **The presidents and the prime ministers: Washington and Ottawa face to face: the myth of bilateral bliss 1867-1982.**
Lawrence Martin. Toronto: Doubleday, 1982. 300p.
The story of Canada–US relations is told within the context of the leaders of the countries. Focus is on personalities rather than issues. The work is written in journalistic style and is meant for the general reader. On the whole an interesting addition to the literature on this topic. Of a related nature, the interested reader is directed to Roger Frank Swanson's *Canadian–American summit diplomacy 1923-1973* (Toronto: McClelland & Stewart, 1975). This latter volume identifies and documents the summit meetings between Canadian prime ministers and US presidents for the period stated.

537 **The politics of Canadian foreign policy.**
Kim Richard Nossal. Scarborough, Ontario: Prentice-Hall, 1985.
232p.
This work deals not with the content of Canadian foreign policy, not with the process by which foreign policy decisions are arrived at, but with the politics of Canadian foreign policy. Who makes foreign policy and under what political constraints? – these are the questions considered by the author. In this regard both domestic and international politics are examined. In addition, considerable attention is directed towards governmental politics – the relations between the executive, the bureaucracy, the legislature and the provincial governments.

538 **Gringos from the far north: essays in the history of Canadian–Latin American relations, 1866-1968.**
J. C. M. Ogelsby. Toronto: Macmillan/Maclean-Hunter, 1976. 346p.
A Canadian academic attempts an initial exploration of the history of Canada's relations with Latin America since Confederation. These relations, in fact, were fragmented, in terms of time and place. Generally, they fell into three categories: official relations at the diplomatic and commercial levels; investment and trade ties and religious issues and interests. The essays in this work focus on these divisions.

539 **Three decades of decision: Canada and the world monetary system, 1944-75.**
A. F. W. Plumptre. Toronto: McClelland & Stewart, 1977. 335p.

'Over a period of some three decades, from the mid-forties to the mid-seventies, a love-hate relationship grew between Canadians on the one hand, and, on the other, the new world monetary system which they worked so hard to build, strove so tenaciously to keep alive, and yet found so difficult to live with'. This expert in international monetary developments attempts to set out the complex sequence of events which led to the aforementioned relationships. The work provides not only an historical perspective on Canada's international financial relations, but a review of domestic financial policy and its impact on these international forces.

540 **Neighbors across the Pacific: the development of economic and political relations between Canada and Japan.**
Klaus H. Pringsheim. Westport, Connecticut; London: Greenwood, 1983. 241p. (Contributions in Political Science: Global Perspectives in History and Politics, vol. 90).

In this thorough and well-researched work, the author traces general relations between Canada and Japan from 1877 to 1978. He defines the relationship which has developed as one of increasing understanding and cooperation. However, in the author's opinion much remains to be done. Japan sees Canada as little more than a resource hinterland of the United States. Canada, in turn, has much to learn about Japan and the Japanese if it is to compete for a part of their market in manufactured goods. Communication and genuine intimacy are essential if relations between the two countries are to grow to another productive level. For those interested more in the economic relations between the two countries the following works are recommended: Frank Langdon's *The politics of Canadian– Japanese economic relations, 1952-1983* (Vancouver: University of British Columbia, 1983); and, *Canadian perspectives on economic relations with Japan* (Montreal: The Institute of Research on Public Policy, 1980). For a more business-orientated approach the reader is directed to Richard W. Wright's *Japanese business in Canada: the elusive alliance* (Ottawa: Institute for Research on Public Policy/L'Institut de recherches politiques, 1984).

541 **Time of fear and hope: the making of the North Atlantic Treaty 1947-1949.**
Escott Reid. Toronto: McClelland & Stewart, 1977. 315p.

One of the best accounts of the forces leading to the signing of the North Atlantic Treaty in 1949, and thus the origins of the North Atlantic Treaty Organization (NATO), an organization which is key in foreign policy formulation today. At the time of signing of the Treaty Lester Pearson said it had been 'born out of fear and frustration: fear of the aggressive and subversive policies of Communism and the effect of those policies on our own peace and security and well-being; frustration over the obstinate obstruction by Communist states of our efforts to make the United Nations function'. He went on to speculate, however, that the resulting alliance must 'lead to positive social, economic, and political achievements if it is to live – achievements which will extend beyond the time of emergency which gave it birth'.

542 **Canada and the age of conflict: a history of Canadian external policies.**
C. P. Stacey. Toronto: Macmillan, 1977-81. 2 vols.

A general history of Canadian external policies by a noted historian. Volume 1 of the set covers the period 1867-1921. Volume 2 deals with '1921-48, the MacKenzie King Era'. A landmark work of scholarship, of interest to scholars and the general reader alike.

543 **Canada 1984: a time of transition among nations.**
Edited by Brian W. Tomlin, Maureen Molot. Toronto: James Lorimer, 1985. 222p.

Intended to be the first volume of a series, produced by the Norman Paterson School of International Affairs at Carleton University, this focuses on the most recent complete calendar year and presents an analysis and assessment of Canada's international policies. It also examines significant developments in the internal domestic and the external international environments which have an impact on policy. This volume looks at 1984 and assesses the prospects for continuity in the critical areas selected for inclusion, which include structures of policy making, international security, political economy and development, and relations between Canada and the United States.

544 **Canadian foreign policy: contemporary issues and themes.**
Michael Tucker. Toronto: McGraw-Hill Ryerson, 1980. 244p.
(McGraw-Hill Ryerson Series in Canadian Politics).

As the editor of this volume states: 'When Pierre-Elliott Trudeau became Prime Minister in 1968, he resolved that Canada should have a rational foreign policy which would be designed to serve the national interest. His foreign policy White Paper in 1970 set down six priorities for Canada: fostering economic growth, safeguarding sovereignty and independence, working for peace and security, promoting social justice abroad, enhancing the quality of life, and ensuring a harmonious natural environment'. This work assesses Canada's success in these objectives, and concludes that in fact little changed through the 1970s to alter the character of Canada's foreign policy.

545 **Canada and the transition to Commonwealth: British–Canadian relations 1917-1926.**
Philip G. Wigley. Cambridge: Cambridge University Press, 1977. 294p. (Cambridge Commonwealth Series).

During the period cited in the title, Great Britain's relations with the overseas British dominions were profoundly modified. Between these two dates, the dominions moved away from a status of colonial autonomy under Britain's auspices to a position of practical independence in their international as well as domestic affairs, although still within the framework of the British Commonwealth. This study examines the particular relations between Britain and Canada, and the rôle that Canada played in this transition, both on her own behalf as well as on behalf of the other dominions.

Economics

Reference

546 **Canadian business and economics: a guide to sources of information =
Économique et commerce au Canada: sources d'information.**
Edited by Barbara Brown.   Ottawa: Canadian Library Association,
1984. 2nd ed. 469p.
Contains over 6,500 entries describing works of interest to the economist or the
business person.

547 **A dictionary of Canadian economics.**
David Crane.   Edmonton, Alberta: Hurtig, 1980. 372p.
Designed for the general reader, this work defines, in Canadian terms, traditional
economic and business terms, providing practical examples. Key areas of inclusion are
terms associated with: traditional economic and business areas; labour relations;
agriculture; the manufacturing and service industries; banking and investment;
telecommunications; resource industries; public finance and economic policy-making
and financial institutions.

548 **Economic history of Canada: a guide to information sources.**
Trevor J. O. Dick.   Detroit, Michigan: Gale Research Company,
1978. 174p. (Economics Information Guide Series, vol. 9).
Monographic and periodical literature which provide relevant information on the
background conditions of Canadian economic growth are included in this volume.
Entries are organized by chronological period in Canada's development.

549 **The new practical guide to Canadian political economy.**
Edited by Daniel Drache, Wallace Clement. Toronto: James
Lorimer, 1985. 243p.

An extremely useful introduction to the literature of 'political economy' defined
broadly to include aspects of the disciplines of economics, history, cultural studies,
political science, sociology and anthropology. Each section includes a brief textual
overview of the subject matter (i.e. resources and staples, labour conflict, imperialism
and dependency, English–Canadian nationalism, industrial and commercial policy,
etc.), followed by an enumerative, bibliographical listing.

General

550 **Canada's economic problems and policies.**
Maurice Archer. Toronto: Macmillan, 1975. 211p.

This noted academic explains and discusses firstly the major economic problems facing
Canada today, and secondly the different types of government policies that are being
used in order to cope with them. In this work the author synthesizes the work done in
his two substantial texts, entitled *Introductory microeconomics: a Canadian analysis*
(Toronto: Macmillan, 1974); and *Introductory macroeconomics: a Canadian analysis*
(Toronto: Macmillan, 1973). Another source for information on the subject is Archer's
Introduction to economics: a Canadian analysis (Toronto: Macmillan, 1978).

551 **The Canadian economy and its problems.**
Muriel Armstrong. Scarborough, Ontario: Prentice-Hall, 1982. 3rd
ed. 499p.

Designed for the student or general reader, this work attempts to explain
contemporary economic problems and their solutions; in this latter sense it is
concerned with economic policy. Recognition is given that to understand the economy
the reader must have some sense of history, laws and institutions. Significant historical
and institutional materials have thus been incorporated into the text.

552 **The Canadian economy: problems and options.**
Edited by R. C. Bellan, W. H. Pope. Toronto: McGraw-Hill
Ryerson, 1981. 394p.

Taken together, this collection of essays describes the main elements of the Canadian
economy, its problems and the options available to deal with those problems. Under
scrutiny here are topics such as the resource-based industries; energy; the industrial
system; transportation; the financial system; the labour force; regional economies;
international economic relations; unemployment and inflation; and the rôle of
government, particularly in areas such as education, health, welfare, labour legislation,
regional assistance, etc.

553 **Economic policies in Canada.**
Ingrid A. Bryan. Toronto: Butterworths, 1986. 2nd ed. 309p.
A reasonably current survey of economic problems and policies in Canada. The focus is on three areas of the economy, namely the allocation of resource, the distribution of income, and stabilization policies.

554 **Canadian Journal of Economics = Revue Canadienne d'Économique.**
Toronto: University of Toronto Press, 1968- . quarterly.
Scholarly articles and reviews on various aspects of economics, with some emphasis on Canadian topics.

555 **Initiative and response: the adaptation of Canadian federalism to regional economic development.**
Anthony G. S. Careless. Montreal; London: McGill-Queen's University Press, 1977. 244p. (Canadian Public Administration Series).
The theme of this work is the problem of regional disparities in economic growth and the ways in which the attitudes, structure and operation of Canada's federal system have had to be flexible in an effort to solve these disparities. The question as to whether all provinces should be treated equally in an economic and fiscal sense is also raised.

556 **Entering the eighties: Canada in crisis.**
Edited by R. Carty, Peter W. Ward. Toronto: Oxford University Press, 1980. 160p.
Noted economists, historians and political scientists provide thoughtful essays on four themes of interest: the nation and nationality, Quebec and the referendum, the economy and the state, and parliament and politicians. Given the economic crises of the late 1970s, the essays on economic themes are of particular importance.

557 **The next Canadian economy.**
Dian Cohen, Kristin Shannon. Montreal: Eden, 1984. 204p.
Popular economic journalists speculate on the future of the Canadian economy. Through interviews with key economic analysts, financiers, labour leaders, and business people, they construct a strategy and a vision for the future. Written in a journalistic style.

558 **Progress without planning: the economic history of Ontario from Confederation to the Second World War.**
Ian Drummond. Toronto: University of Toronto Press, 1987. 509p. (Ontario Historical Studies Series).
The second volume in a series of three which treats, from the late eighteenth century until the middle of the 1970s, the economic development of Ontario, Canada's largest and most industrially developed province. The author devotes considerable attention to matters of economic policy at the provincial level. The first volume remains to be published; the third volume is by K. J. Rea and is entitled *The prosperous years: the economic history of Ontario 1939-1975* (Toronto: University of Toronto Press, 1985).

559 **Canadian economic history.**
W. T. Easterbrook, Hugh G. J. Aitken. Toronto: Gage, 1988. 3rd ed.
606p.
A classic history which selects and arranges the major events and the processes of
Canadian economic history in a straightforward presentation directed at the interested
reader.

560 **Approaches to Canadian economic history.**
Edited by W. T. Easterbrook, M. H. Watkins. Toronto: Gage, 1980.
292p. (Carleton Library, vol. 31).
A collection of essays with a variety of approaches to Canadian economic history,
although focusing mainly on the impact made by the great staple trades, such as cod,
fur, newsprint and oil. Concludes with a bibliographic essay which reviews the
literature in the field. A more recent anthology, edited by Douglas McCalla,
supplements this earlier work and is entitled *Perspectives on Canadian economic
history* (Toronto: Copp Clark Pitman, 1987).

561 **Understanding the Canadian economy: a problems approach to
economic principles.**
Roy E. George. Peterborough, Ontario: Broadview, 1988. 252p.
A text designed for the general reader, which uses a problem-solving approach in order
to familiarize the reader with the broad range of problems and issues in the areas of
business and economic policy.

562 **The great economic debate: failed economics and a future for Canada.**
Cy Gonick. Toronto: James Lorimer, 1987. 425p.
A polemical discussion on the roots, nature and prospects of the Canadian economy.
The author presents first of all an ideological perspective, which tends to be critical of
the 'New Right'. The precepts of Keynesian economics and the traditional Canadian
interpretation thereof are examined, and tied in with the interventionist policies of the
1970s which were regarded as a revival of Keynesian economic thought. Finally he
takes a radical economic approach drawing on Marx and neo-Marx analysis, using this
theory to chart the course of the current economic crisis.

563 **Rescue: saving the Canadian economy.**
A. D. Hutcheon. Victoria, British Columbia; Toronto: Press
Porcépic, 1982. 171p.
A survey for the general reader of macroeconomic policy development in Canada,
through the 1960s, the 1970s and into the early 1980s. The author presents a somewhat
novel solution to the country's economic problems.

564 **Income distribution and economic security in Canada.**
Toronto: University of Toronto Press in cooperation with the Royal
Commission on the Economic Union and Development Prospects for
Canada and the Canadian Government Publishing Centre, Supply and
Services Canada, 1985. 319p.

This volume, included as part of the collected research of the Royal Commission on
the Economic Union and Development Prospects for Canada, examines income
distribution in Canada, the influence on it of factors such as sex, age and education,
and the effect of various government programmes, including current transfer
programmes in which the federal government collects taxes, transferring them later
back to the provincial governments, on the welfare of Canadians.

565 **The fur trade in Canada: an introduction to Canadian economic history.**
Harold A. Innis. Toronto: University of Toronto Press, 1975. rev. ed.
463p. (Canadian University Paperbacks, vol. 2).

Few would argue that this is a landmark in western and Canadian history, including as
it does several detailed and interlinked histories in one. The contents of this book
cover the familiar western theme: the clash between sophisticated and primitive
cultures as the movement westward advanced to satisfy eastern needs. This work also
charts the involvement of Indian participation in the fur trade, and explores some of
the ways in which an American empire began to displace a British one, presenting to
the reader much diplomatic, commercial and economic history.

566 **An economic history of Canada.**
Mary Quayle Innis. Toronto: Ryerson Press, 1954. rev. ed. 384p.

A work which contains much which is of use to the student of economic history.

567 **Regional economic policy: the Canadian experience.**
N. H. Litwick. Toronto: McGraw-Hill Ryerson, 1978. 368p.

This is an attempt to explain the problem of regional economic inequalities in Canada,
as well as providing an assessment of the policy efforts that have been made in Canada
to deal with this problem.

568 **Canadian macroeconomics: problems and policies.**
Brian Lyons. Scarborough, Ontario: Prentice-Hall, 1987. 2nd ed.
423p.

An introductory macroeconomic text that addresses itself to major economic problems
facing Canada and Canadians. Other texts of a similar type are: David A. Wilton and
David M. Prescott's *Macroeconomics: theory & policy in Canada* (Don Mills, Ontario:
Addison-Wesley, 1987), and Alexander MacMillan's *Macroeconomics: the Canadian
context* (Scarborough, Ontario: Prentice-Hall, 1983).

569 **Canada: an economic history.**
William L. Marr, Donald G. Paterson. Toronto: Macmillan, 1980.
539p. bibliog.
Criticized by reviewers for its thematic organization, this work does, nonetheless, provide the reader with a perspective on Canadian economic development, as well as other useful material, including a lengthy bibliography.

570 **Economic and social history of Quebec, 1760-1850: structures and conjonctures.** [sic]
Fernard Ouellet. Toronto: Gage in association with the Institute of Canadian Studies, Carleton University, 1980. 696p. (Carleton Library, vol. 120).
The English translation of Ouellet's classic economic history of Quebec. Ouellet moves from previous political preoccupations with regard to French-Canadian history, and instead develops a chronology which is socio-economic. Similarly useful as socio-economic history is Jean Hamelin's *Économie et société en Nouvelle-France* (Economy and Society in New France. Quebec: Les Presses de l'Université Laval, 1970).

571 **Northern development: the Canadian dilemma.**
Robert Page. Toronto: McClelland & Stewart, 1986. 360p. (Canada in Transition Series).
The author focuses on two key public policy debates of the 1970s which surrounded the hearings of the Commission on the Mackenzie Valley Pipeline and the National Energy Board hearings. Within the context of discussing these key issues, he outlines and examines the broader issue of northern economic development, both in the past and in the present. It is clear that the question is complex and is composed of a myriad of other disparate parts, such as environmental protection, native rights, economic nationalism, energy conservation and political sovereignty. Highly recommended.

572 **The politics and management of Canadian economic policy.**
Richard W. Phidd, G. Bruce Doern. Toronto: Macmillan, 1978.
598p.
The process of economic policy-making and policy itself can best be understood, contend the authors, within the context of understanding the processes (political, managerial and organizational) which have shaped the process and in consequence the policy. Examined here are the micro- and macrodimensions of economic management shedding light on the inter- and intradepartmental/governmental relations as well as those between the public and the private sectors.

573 **The economic development of Canada.**
Richard Pomfret. Toronto: Methuen, 1981. 216p.
Although Easterbrooke and Aitken's *Canadian economic history* (q.v.) is regarded by many as the standard work since its appearance in 1956, Richard Pomfret's volume brings together much recent research and a new framework to provide an introduction to, and interpretation of, the development of the Canadian economy since European settlement.

574 **Postwar macroeconomic developments.**
Toronto: University of Toronto Press in cooperation with the Royal
Commission on the Economic Union and Development Prospects for
Canada and the Canadian Government Publishing Centre, Supply and
Services Canada, 1986. 332p.

This is the second in a series of seven volumes (the first volume was never distributed)
dealing with macroeconomics, included as part of the collected research of the Royal
Commission on the Economic Union and Development Prospects for Canada. Other
titles in the series are: *Fiscal and monetary policy*; *Economic growth: prospects and
determinants*; *Long-term economic prospects for Canada: a symposium*; *Foreign
macroeconomic experience: a symposium*; and, *Dealing with inflation and unemployment in Canada*.

575 **Report of the Royal Commission on the economic union and
development prospects for Canada.**
Ottawa: Minister of Supply and Services Canada, 1985. 3 vols.

The charge of the Commission was to investigate and report on 'the long-term
economic potential, prospects and challenges facing the Canadian federation and its
respective regions, as well as the implications that such prospects and challenges have
for Canada's economic and governmental institutions, and for the management of
Canada's economic affairs'. In addition, the Commission was to recommend the
appropriate national economic goals and policies to facilitate the well-being of
Canadians and maintain a competitive economy. While the *Report* of the Commission
provided much of interest on the economy of Canada, the specialized, published
research reports which accompanied the *Report* (numbering seventy-two volumes) add
greatly to the literature in a number of related fields. Individual volumes, or series of
volumes are referenced in various sections of this compilation.

576 **The Canadian economy: problems and policies.**
Edited by G. C. Ruggeri.   Toronto: Gage, 1987. 3rd ed. 474p.

An anthology of seventy-five readings from academic, media and government sources
which collectively seek to outline the structure and functioning of the Canadian
economic system. Essays are grouped into five sections: Part One is a general
introduction to the mode of operations of a mixed economic system; Part Two deals
with economic growth; Part Three relates to the labour market; Part Four is a survey
of the main issues facing the economy, with attention to trade liberalization and
foreign investment; and, Part Five provides an overview of economic policy-making in
Canada.

577 **The Canadian economy: a regional perspective.**
Edited by Donald J. Savoie.   Toronto: Methuen, 1986. 291p.

This gathers together readings selected from some of the most important articles on
Canadian regional development policy and experiences. Divided into two parts, the
first part provides an overview of the theoretical frameworks guiding regional
development policies; the second part looks at the policies and programmes that have
been tried or suggested in Canada's regional development efforts.

578 **Economic analysis and Canadian policy.**
David Stager. Toronto: Butterworths, 1985. 5th ed. 577p.
This is one of many introductory texts which relates to the Canadian economy, to economics in Canada or to Canadian economic policy. Other excellent examples of this genre include: Bruce A. Forster and Clement A. Tisdell's *Economics in Canadian society: principles and applications* (Toronto: John Wiley, 1986); and, R. C. Bellan's *Principles of economics and the Canadian economy* (Toronto: McGraw-Hill Ryerson, 1985); and, Pierre Fréchette and Jean-P. Vezina's *L'économie du Québec* (The economy of Quebec. Montreal: Les Éditions HRW Ltee, 1985).

Finance and Banking

Reference

579 **Guide to the Canadian financial services industry.**
Toronto: Flagship Publishers Corporation, 1986- .
The *Guide* is intended to be a comprehensive directory of the institutions and individuals within this business sector. Includes information on the structure of each organization, and profiles of the executives and directors who are key players. Approximately 800 companies are listed, including banks, trust companies, general and life insurance companies, securities dealers, stock exchanges, mortgage loan companies, consumer loan and sales finance companies, factoring and financial leasing operations, venture capital companies, mutual fund management companies, credit card operations, credit unions and financial conglomerates. Over 10,000 individuals are listed. Supported by various indexes.

580 **Who's Who in Canadian Finance.**
Toronto: Trans-Canada Press, 1979- . annual.
This is a standard directory which provides biographical information about the country's financial executives.

General

581 **A matter of trust: power and privilege in Canada's trust companies.**
Patricia Best, Ann Shortell. Markham, Ontario: Viking, 1985. 352p.
Trust and loan companies have under their control assets which comprise a significant percentage of all financial market assets in Canada. But, the rules governing the industry are significantly different from those which regulate the chartered banks. As such there have been many questionable operators of these institutions with many trust

companies going bankrupt and leaving depositors unprotected. This work looks at the development of the trust business and concentrates on some of the newer and dominant players of the industry, particularly those in the business of mortgage lending and real estate development. The work was written shortly after the Greymac Affair, which saw the failure of a number of eastern-based companies, but before the collapse of the Alberta-centred Principal Group of trusts.

582 **Money, banking and finance: the Canadian context.**
Gordon F. Boreham, Ronald G. Bodkin.   Toronto: Holt, Rinehart & Winston, 1988. 716p.

The book's aim is to balance many varying approaches to money, banking and finance, including the theoretical, institutional, statistical and historical. While most of the material appearing in this edition is drawn from the body of knowledge common to the field of monetary economics, some areas are based on the author's own surveys of over eighty foreign banking systems, with the intention of establishing a comparative basis for studying more comprehensively the Canadian system.

583 **The IDB: a history of Canada's Industrial Development Bank.**
E. Ritchie Clark.   Toronto: University of Toronto Press, 1985. 435p.

The Industrial Development Bank (IDB) was the institution preceding the present Federal Business and Development Bank. The Bank was established in 1944 partly to assist Canadian businesses to adjust to peacetime conditions, and partly to provide a source of term financing to small and medium-sized businesses. Useful for an understanding of banking and business development in Canada.

584 **Money, inflation and the Bank of Canada.**
Thomas J. Courchene.   Montreal: C. D. Howe Institute, 1976-81. 2 vols.

Volume I is subtitled *An analysis of Canadian monetary policy from 1970 to early 1975*; Volume II is subtitled *An analysis of monetary gradualism, 1975-80*. This leading monetary policy analyst provides reviews of major monetary policy developments in Canada and assesses their significance. Within this framework the author comments also on such issues as the increasingly important rôle of Canada Savings Bonds in meeting federal government cash needs, the use of foreign currency assets and liabilities in the Canadian banking system, and the impact of revisions to the Bank Act.

585 **Ottawa and the provinces: the distribution of money and power.**
Edited by Thomas J. Courchene, David W. Conklin, Gail C. A. Cook.   Toronto: Ontario Economic Council, 1985. 2 vols. (Special Research Report/Federal–Provincial Relations Series).

The papers included here touch on all facets of the federal-provincial financial interface. The essays are broadly grouped by theme, including: 'The Fiscal Arrangements: Yesterday, Today, and Tomorrow'; 'The Fiscal Arrangements: An International Perspective'; 'The Social-Security System in the 1990s'; 'Postsecondary Education in the 1990s'; 'Health Care in the 1990s'; 'Equalization Payments'; and, 'The Federal-Provincial Consultation Process: 1987 and Beyond'.

586 **Financing the future: Canada's capital markets in the eighties.**
Arthur W. Donner. Ottawa: Canadian Institute for Economic Policy, 1982. 169p. (Canadian Institute for Economic Policy Series).

An examination, by an economic consultant, of seven capital market issues: the impact of central bank monetarism; the problems of raising sufficient capital in Canada to finance megaprojects; the barriers to Canadianization of the oil and gas industry; the shift of economic power to western Canada; the financing of pension funds; the state of housing finance; and the interaction between inflation and capital markets.

587 **The Financial Post.**
Toronto: Maclean–Hunter, 1907- . daily.

One of two key national financial and business newspapers in Canada. The other publication is the *Financial Times* (Toronto: Financial Times of Canada, 1912-).

588 **Merchants of fear: an investigation of Canada's insurance industry.**
James Fleming. Markham, Ontario: Viking, 1986. 409p.

There are four pillars of Canadian finance – the chartered banks, the investment dealers, the trusts and the insurance companies. This is a journalist's investigation of the last pillar, Canada's insurance industry. The author attempts to provide a balanced examination, but does not hesitate to criticize and to 'rattle skeletons' which have been identified. An equally good, and similar journalistic study, is Rod McQueen's *Risky business: inside Canada's $86-billion insurance industry* (Toronto: Macmillan, 1985).

589 **Canadian financial markets.**
W. T. Hunter. Peterborough, Ontario: Broadview, 1988. rev. ed. 220p.

A rudimentary introduction to various financial markets, including the changes to those markets which were wrought by inflation in the 1980s, and the integration of Canadian financial markets with world markets – the latter brought about by advancing technology, deregulation and the impact of institutional investors.

590 **An introduction to Canadian financial markets: an analytical approach.**
Alexander MacMillan. Scarborough, Ontario: Prentice-Hall, 1989. 429p.

Although designed as an introductory textbook, this work provides the general reader with a readable examination of the institutional aspects of money and banking in Canada, complete with an outline of the historical development of the Canadian financial infrastructure. Special features of the work include reprints of articles from the financial press and problem sets.

591 **Canadian monetary, banking and fiscal development.**
R. Craig McIvor. Toronto: Macmillan Company, 1958. 263p.

Though dated, this work remains a valuable and comprehensive introduction to many aspects of Canadian financial history. McIvor traces that history from New France through to the post-war years, the latter period laid the basis for present-day monetary and fiscal policy.

Finance and Banking. General

592 **The money-spinners: an intimate portrait of the men who run Canada's banks.**
Rod McQueen. Toronto: Macmillan, 1983. 276p.
A business publicist and journalist looks at the country's largest banking institutions and the key individuals who control them. The author also looks at the position and impact of the banking establishment on major business dealings in the country. Key CEOs (Chief Executive Officers) portrayed, include Rowlie Frazee (Royal Bank), Russ Harrison (Canadian Imperial Bank), Bill Mulholland (Bank of Montreal), Ced Ritchie (Bank of Nova Scotia), and Dick Thomson (The Toronto-Dominion Bank).

593 **Canada's financial system: a managerial approach.**
Edwin H. Neave, Jacques Préfontaine. Toronto: Methuen, 1987. 414p.
An introductory text which examines how the Canadian financial system is organized and how it performs its functions, including explanations as to how the major forces shaping Canada's financial enterprises are manifest. See also *Canadian financial management* (Toronto: Holt, Rinehart & Winston, 1987); *Public finance in theory and practice* (Toronto: McGraw-Hill Ryerson, 1987); and Peter Lusztig and Bernard Schwab's *Managerial finance in a Canadian setting* (Toronto: Butterworths, 1983).

594 **The financial system of Canada: its growth and development.**
E. P. Neufeld. Toronto: Macmillan, 1972. 645p.
Considered by many to be a masterful study of all varieties of Canadian financial institutions, this work contains a comprehensive examination of the growth and development of the Canadian financial system. That development is traced from the very beginning to the date of publication, and deals with all sectors, such as: the banks, building societies, mortgage loan companies, investment companies, insurance companies, trust companies, sales finance companies, money lenders, mutual funds, investment trusts, development companies, credit unions, pension funds, stock and bond dealers. Long-term trends in Canadian interest rates are also traced.

595 **Money and banking in Canada: historical documents and commentary.**
Edited by E. P. Neufeld. Toronto: McClelland & Stewart, 1964. 369p. (Carleton Library, vol. 17).
Original documents, contemporary commentary and essays which outline the major developments in the history of money and banking in Canada form the content of this volume. The forms and use of money in the pre-Confederation era are examined as well as the major problems of nineteenth- and twentieth-century monetary policy. A lengthy introductory essay places the developments within an historical perspective.

596 **Banking: the law in Canada.**
M. H. Ogilvie. Agincourt, Ontario: Carswell, 1985. 687p.
Deals with the law of banking within the context of the various Canadian bank acts, as well as the cases wherein the statutory provisions have been considered. For the legal practitioner or the informed reader.

597 **The traders: inside Canada's stock markets.**
Alexander Ross. Toronto: Collins, 1984. 269p.
A journalist's enquiry into Canada's capital markets. This readable work portrays all aspects of an industry on the point of fundamental change.

598 **Banking en français: the French banks of Quebec, 1835-1925.**
Ronald Rudin. Toronto: University of Toronto, 1985. 188p. bibliog.
(Social History of Canada, vol. 38).
While described as an institutional history of nine French banks from the establishment of the Banque du Peuple in 1835 to the emergence of the Banque Canadienne Nationale in 1925, this work is also an analysis of the rôle of francophones within the Canadian banking industry and the problems they encountered in achieving a larger capital market. Includes a bibliography.

599 **The money market in Canada: how it works . . . the arrangements, practices and instruments.**
S. Sarpkaya. Don Mills, Ontario: CCH Canadian Limited, 1984. 3rd ed. 194p.
A practical guide to money market arrangements and practices which incorporates a guide to various types of institutions. Useful for the layperson, as well as the professional, for managing investment funds.

600 **The economics of the Canadian financial system: theory, policy & institutions.**
Ronald A. Shearer, John F. Chant, David E. Bond. Scarborough, Ontario: Prentice-Hall, 1984. 2nd ed. 671p.
Though intended as a university or college text, this work provides a good introduction, for the informed reader, of the workings of Canadian financial institutions and the development of Canadian monetary policies.

601 **Adam Shortt's history of Canadian currency and banking 1600-1880.**
Adam Shortt. Toronto: Canadian Bankers' Association, [1986]. 904p.
This is a collection of forty-eight articles, originally published in series between 1896 and 1906 and again in a subsequent series between 1921 and 1925, in the periodical *Journal of the Canadian Bankers' Association*, now known as the *Canadian Banker*. The work provides a rich storehouse of information with regard to the origins of Canadian currency and the banking industry.

602 **Towers of gold: feet of clay: the Canadian banks.**
Walter Stewart. Toronto: Collins, 1982. 303p.
This noted investigative journalist takes a critical look at the Canadian banking industry, dominated as it is by a group of five companies which are allied in turn to a network of major corporations yet isolated from economic turbulence. As the author points out, this is an industry which shapes much of individual Canadian life and exercises a vast influence over government policy, while paying minimal taxes. It is also an industry which many Canadians experience as arrogant and uncaring.

Finance and Banking. General

603 **Canadian public finance.**
J. C. Strick. Toronto: Holt, Rinehart & Winston, 1978. 2nd ed. 198p.
Focuses on governmental financial institutions, their practices and their problems with emphasis on the federal level. Topics under discussion include: the rôle and growth of government; government decision-making and the budgetary process; tax structures; intergovernmental fiscal relations; and fiscal policy.

604 **The public purse: a study in Canadian democracy.**
Norman Ward. Toronto: University of Toronto Press, 1962. 334p.
(Canadian Government Series, vol. 11).
A classic work which chronicles the story, an often humorous one, of the federal parliament's attempts to monitor and control government spending.

Trade

605 The Canada–U.S. Free Trade Agreement.
Ottawa: International Trade Communications Group, Department of
External Affairs, 1988. 315p.

The Free Trade Agreement is the most significant bilateral trade arrangement ever
negotiated between trading partners. The relations entered into have affected, and will
continue to affect the country economically, socially and politically. In the period
leading to the signing of the Agreement, and since, much has been written with regard
to both its positive benefits and its negative effects on Canada. Never has such a
foreign policy issue led to such domestic debate. Literature exists on all sides of the
question. Some publications of note published after the ratification of the Agreement
are: A. R. Riggs and Tom Velk's *Canadian–American free trade: (the sequel):
historical, political and economic dimensions* (Halifax, Nova Scotia: Institute for
Research on Public Policy, 1988); Randall White's *Fur trade to free trade: putting the
Canada–U.S. Trade Agreement in historical perspective* (Toronto: Dundurn, 1988);
Steve Dorey's *Free trade on the prairies: the implications of the Canada–U.S. trade pact
for the three prairie provinces* (Regina, Saskatchewan: Canadian Plains Research
Centre, 1989); John Crispo's *Free trade: the real story* (Toronto: Gage, 1988); Duncan
Cameron's *The free trade deal* (Toronto: James Lorimer, 1988); Richard Lipsey and
Robert York's *Evaluating the free trade deal: a guided tour through the Canada–U.S.
Agreement* (Toronto: C.D. Howe Institute, 1988); and *Open borders: an assessment of
the Canada–U.S. Free Trade Agreement* (Ottawa: Economic Council of Canada, 1988).

606 The Canadian trade and investment guide.
Toronto: Financial Post Information Service, 1989. 572p.

Not only is this an overview of how to do business in Canada, it provides information,
by way of sixty-two informed, well-documented articles, on various issues relating to
Canada's economic performance, markets, technological infrastructure, and emerging
opportunities under the Free Trade Agreement with the United States. Articles have
been prepared to a standard format, with standardized headings and sub-headings for
easy reference. Highly recommended for Canadian as well as foreign business people.

Trade

607 **Canadian trade policies and the world economy.**
Toronto: University of Toronto Press in cooperation with the Royal Commission on the Economic Union and Development Prospects for Canada and the Canadian Government Publishing Centre, Supply and Services Canada, 1985. 147p. bibliog.

This is the first in a series of six volumes dealing with international trade, included as part of the collected research of the Royal Commission on the Economic Union and Development Prospects for Canada. This series deals with: trade policy, including the best strategies to improve and secure access to foreign markets, the question of protection of Canada's industries, the General Agreement on Tariffs and Trade (GATT), foreign investment, trade liberalization, free trade between Canada and the United States, and many other related topics. Includes a bibliography. Other titles in the series are: *Canada and the multilateral trading system*; *Canada–United States free trade*; *Domestic policies and the international economic environment*; *Trade, industrial policy and international competition*; and *Canada's resource industries and water export policy*.

608 **Canadian manufactured exports: constraints and opportunities.**
D. J. Daly, D. C. MacCharles. Montreal: Institute for Research on Public Policy/L'Institut de recherches politiques, 1986. 180p. bibliog. (Essays in International Economics).

Trade and industrial policy have been a major talking-point for over a century, but these matters have become increasingly important recently due to internal and external pressures which are challenging the Canadian economy. Access to foreign markets and, to a much lessser degree, the competitiveness of Canadian industry, have been the subject of most research and commentary to date. The authors add to the literature on this topic with this assessment as to whether changes in tariffs, exchange rates, wage rates and other factors in Canada have influenced the country's ability to compete internationally. A significant conclusion was that Canadian unit labour costs were notably higher than those of other countries. The authors direct a number of recommendations to the private sector with regard to increasing productivity and competing successfully in world markets. A bibliography is provided.

609 **Handbook of Canadian consumer markets.**
Edited by Carolyn R. Farquhar, Carole Fitzgerald. 32nd ed. Ottawa: Conference Board of Canada, 1984. 288p.

Though dated, this work remains useful. The *Handbook* brings together consumer market data from a variety of sources. Information on several thousand series of economic and demographic data is provided through 240 tables – 90 charts illustrate major trends, distributions and projections that describe Canadian consumer markets.

610 **Canada/United States trade and investment issues.**
Edited by Deborah Fretz (et al.). Toronto: Ontario Economic Council, 1985. 496p. (Canadian Trade at a Crossroads Series).

Papers presented at a workshop held 18-19 November 1983 at the University of Western Ontario organized for the purpose of analysing and discussing major issues between Canada and the United States. Papers deal with a broad range of issues ranging from the very general to discussion of sectoral trade issues, i.e. the automotive industry, energy, etc. See also *Canada and international trade* (Montreal: Institute for Research on Public Policy/L'Institut de recherches politiques, 1985).

611 **Trade policy making in Canada: are we doing it right?**
W. R. Hines.   Montreal: Institute for Research on Public Policy/L'Institut de recherches politiques, 1985. 113p. (Essays in International Economics).

In 1982 responsibility for the international trade function was shifted from the Department of Industry, Trade and Commerce to the Department of External Affairs. This change has had a profound impact on the process of formalizing and implementing economic policy. The author briefly examines the trade policy decision-making process prior to 1982 and examines in some detail the effects of the reorganization. He concludes that the change has not been in the best interests of Canadian business.

612 **The new protectionism: non-tariff barriers and their effects on Canada.**
Fred Lazar.   Ottawa: Canadian Institute for Economic Policy, 1981. 102p. (Canadian Institute for Economic Policy Series).

This interesting study, produced prior to the free trade debate of the middle 1980s, argues against freer trade with the United States, indicating that such a move would endanger the Canadian manufacturing sector. In the author's opinion the country was not capable of surviving in the international market. He urges the government to develop an industrial strategy to increase the competitiveness of Canadian firms.

613 **Importing: a practical manual for coping with Canadian customs.**
Ernest Y. Maitland.   Vancouver: International Self-Counsel Press, 1981. 372p. (Self-Counsel Series).

An array of regulations, coupled with appropriate forms, confront the importer in Canada. Knowing something of these rules and their paper manifestations is useful, both for the firm importing into the country, and for the exporter in the country of manufacture.

614 **Market opportunities catalogue: import trends = Catalogue des possibilités du marché: tendance des importations.**
Ottawa: Market Development Branch, Department of Regional Industrial Expansion, 1986. 675p.

The trade and commerce related offices of the federal and provincial governments in Canada produce a staggering array of documents relevant for the Canadian company, as well as the foreign company, wishing to penetrate the Canadian market. This is one example of such a publication produced by a federal agency; its purpose is to increase awareness of the enormous potential existing in the Canadian marketplace for domestic production. It covers approximately 89% of all products imported into Canada (thus of interest to potential Canadian manufacturers but also of use to foreign companies wishing to gain knowledge of Canadian markets). Information provided includes a description of the product, annual import quantities, average growth rate trends, and major foreign countries of export.

615 **Canada and the European Community: an uncomfortable partnership.**
N. G. Papadopoulos. Montreal: Institute for Research on Public
Policy/L'Institut de recherches politiques, 1986. 136p. bibliog. (Essays
in International Economics).
This study examines in detail Canada's neglected partnership with the European
Community, reviewing reasons for the weakening in the links between Canada and the
European market. The author comes to the conclusion that Canada can no longer
afford to disregard its ties with the European Community, the largest trading block in
the world, and whose member countries have many historical, economic, cultural and
political affiliations with Canada today. The author presents a number of proposals as
to how Canada's relationship with the EEC could be strengthened. A timely work.

616 **Canada's crippled dollar: an analysis of international trade and our
troubled balance of payments.**
H. Lukin Robinson. Toronto: James Lorimer with the Canadian
Institute for Economic Policy, 1980. 204p. (Canadian Institute for
Economic Policy Series).
This work deals with the question of Canada's balance of payments problem from the
early years following the Second World War to 1978. 'The argument of the study is
that the structure of Canada's exports and imports of goods and services is such that we
are at present unable to balance our imports with corresponding exports. We cannot at
present pay our way in the world, and depend on foreign borrowing to make up the
difference between what we earn and what we spend abroad'. Some of the problems
and suggested policy options identified by the author are as relevant today as they were
a decade ago.

617 **The Canadian import file: trade, protection and adjustment.**
G. E. Salembier, Andrew R. Moroz, Frank Stone. Montreal:
Institute for Research on Public Policy/L'Institut de recherches
politiques, 1987. 269p.
Canadian trade policy is an issue which has been the subject of intense public debate in
the 1980s. Domestic producers have traditionally worried about the maintenance of
tariffs and other import barriers. This study examines the pros and cons of
protectionism within the context of an increasing trend toward an interdependent
world economy.

618 **Federalism and the Canadian economic union.**
Edited by Michael Trebilcock (et al.). Toronto: University of Toronto
Press, 1983. 560p. (Ontario Economic Council Research Studies, vol.
28).
These essays study the various issues involved in securing an internal common market
within Canada; drawing upon the expertise of a number of disciplines they explore the
problems of limiting or eliminating the barriers to inter-provincial commerce which
exist in Canada.

619 **Not for export: toward a political economy of Canada's arrested industrialization.**
Glen Williams. Toronto: McClelland & Stewart, 1986. 213p. (Canada in Transition Series).

Although Canada has a high standard of living and a high level of technological know-how, there is also a surprisingly low level of industrial development. Many experts have referred to Canada as a 'rich industrialized underdeveloped country' due to its dependence on foreign investment and reserve based exports, and during its economic history, Canada has failed to develop both its markets abroad and a solid manufacturing base at home. The author develops a thesis calling for a re-shaping of economic priorities, with renewed vigour applied to Canadian manufacturing and a stronger emphasis on exports.

Business and Industry

Reference

620 **The Blue Book of Canadian Business.**
Toronto: Canadian Newspaper Services International Limited, 1976- .
annual.
This compilation provides information on Canadian companies. Section 1 profiles leading companies, providing in-depth studies of the nature of the company, its history, and its rôle in the Canadian economy and society. Section 2 ranks the largest companies in Canada in terms of sales, assets, net income, advertising expenditures and stock performance. Section 3 gives the reader quick and basic information on a broad group of companies, including company location, ownership and legal structure, relative size, nature of business and names of chief officers, etc.

621 **Canadian Business Index.**
Toronto: Micromedia Limited, 1980- . monthly.
Formerly the *Canadian Business Periodical Index*, this is a reference guide to Canadian periodicals and reports in business, industry and economics, administrative studies and related fields. Over 180 Canadian business periodicals are covered including also the weekly *Financial Post*, and the daily *Financial Times* and *Globe and Mail*. The *Index* provides access by subject, corporate name and personal name. The subject index is the primary listing. It is supported by a corporate name index, which covers corporations, unions, associations, governments, etc., by name, and a personal name index which encompasses chief executives and directors, public figures and prominent authorities mentioned in the indexed materials. An annual cumulation of this title is also published.

622 **Canadian key business directory 1989=Répertoire des principales entreprises canadiennes 1989.**
Toronto: Dun & Bradstreet, 1989.
A reference source of the top three per cent of all Canadian businesses. In total, more than 20,000 Canadian organizations are represented, selected from a database of over 670,000 establishments. Criteria for inclusion are firms with: $10,000,000 (£5,015,045) in sales; or, 100 total employees; or, $1,000,000 (£501,504) in net worth; or, branches having more than 500 employees. Each listing includes information as to company name, address, telephone number, names of top executive personnel and their function, annual sales volume, number of employees and parent company affiliation. Various indexes support the primary listing.

623 **Canadian Trade Index.**
Toronto: Canadian Manufacturers' Association, 1900- . annual.
This is an authoritative guide to Canadian manufacturers having more than a local distribution for their products. Over 16,000 firms are listed. Various sections provide access through a classified list of products, through geographical listing, by alphabetical listing, by trademark, and by distributorship.

624 **Directory of Directors.**
Toronto: Financial Post Information Service, 1931- . annual.
Section One is an alphabetical listing of approximately 16,000 Canadian business men and women. Entries include the executive positions and directorships of the individuals as well as their addresses. Section Two is an alphabetical listing of approximately 2,200 selected Canadian companies, with their boards of directors and executive officers.

625 **Financial Post Survey of Industrials.**
Toronto: Financial Post Information Service, 1949- . annual
This survey covers public, listed and unlisted, industrial corporations. The edition covers some 2,000 principal companies, with an additional 6,000 subsidiaries, affiliates, etc. Company profiles are prepared by companies themselves and include names, addresses, telephone numbers, stock symbols, transfer agents, details of operations, management, financial data, and information on subsidiaries.

626 **Fraser's Canadian Trade Directory.**
Toronto: Maclean-Hunter, 1913- . annual.
A comprehensive publication listing manufacturers and suppliers classified by product type, with various indexes including trade or brand names (over 12,000), product agents and distributors (over 37,000), and foreign manufacturers with agents or distributors in Canada (over 9,000).

627 **Guide to Canadian Manufacturers.**
Toronto: Dun & Bradstreet, 1980- . annual.
This directory provides marketing information on over 10,000 top manufacturing locations in Canada. It is divided into three cross-referenced sections. The 'Central Information Source' provides information such as company name, address, materials purchased, products, capital machinery used in operations, personal data, key officers, plant size, number of employees, etc. 'Line of Business Listing' lists companies firstly by geographical division, then alphabetically within each section. The 'Geographical

Business and Industry. Reference

Listing' lists companies alphabetically by name within city within province. The work includes a 'Standard Industrial Classification' index, and a 'Numerical Index'. Regional specific directories should also be consulted. *Scott's directories* are a primary source for regional manufacturers. Publications are available for Ontario, Quebec, western manufacturers and Atlantic manufacturers.

628　**Who's Who of Canadian Business.**
　　　Edited by Kim G. Kofmel.　Toronto: Trans-Canada Press, 1980/81- . annual.
This publication provides biographical information about the country's leading business executives.

629　**Market research handbook = Recueil statistique des études de marché.**
　　　Ottawa: Statistics Canada, 1931- .
A reference tool designed to aid market analysts and researchers interested in the depth and diversity of Canadian markets. Contains much information relating to the social and economic fabric of Canadian life.

General

630　**Canadian cases in business-government relations.**
　　　Edited by Mark C. Baetz, Donald H. Thain.　Toronto: Methuen, 1985. 407p.
There are numerous works which outline, explain or critically analyse the relationships between government and business in Canada. The involvement of government in business has taken many forms, has evolved for many reasons and has had both positive and negative consequences. This work, using a case methodology, attempts to develop an understanding of the interrelationships, describes the mistakes, and assesses the appropriateness of the responses. Other works for the interested reader are: K. J. Rea and Nelson Wiseman's *Government and enterprise in Canada* (Toronto: Methuen, 1985); Marsha Gordon's *Government in business* (Montreal: C. D. Howe Institute, 1981); James Gillies' *Where business fails: business government relations at the federal level in Canada* (Montreal: Institute for Research on Public Policy, 1981); K. J. Rea and J. T. MacLeod's *Business and government in Canada: selected readings* (Toronto: Methuen, 1976); and Philip Mathias' *Forced growth: five studies of government involvement in the development of Canada* (Toronto: James Lewis & Samuel, 1971).

631　**Business and society: Canadian issues.**
　　　David K. Banner.　Toronto: McGraw-Hill Ryerson, 1979. 388p.
The author identifies a number of distinctive Canadian issues and problems with regard to the relationship of business with society. Chapter headings include topics such as: 'Corporate Social Responsibility in Canada'; 'Business And Its Employees'; 'Business And Its Social Interfaces'; 'The Business/Government Interface in Canada'; 'The Multinational Phenomenon'; and 'The Changing Roles of Work/Leisure in Society'.

632 **Northern enterprise: five centuries of Canadian business.**
Michael Bliss. Toronto: McClelland & Stewart, 1987. 640p.

Superb scholarship destined to become a classic in the literature. This noted academic traces the whole history of business in Canada, from the earliest Atlantic fishermen in the 1480s to the pressure for free trade with the United States in the 1980s. Relevant for the general reader as well as the student of business history, the work also contains an excellent section on 'Sources and Further Reading'. Other useful works include: David S. Macmillan's *Canadian business history: selected studies, 1497-1971* (Toronto: McClelland & Stewart, 1972); Glenn Porter and Robert Cuff's *Enterprise and national development: essays in Canadian business and economic history* (Toronto: Hakkert, 1973); Michael Bliss's *A living profit: studies in the social history of Canadian business, 1883-1911* (Toronto: McClelland & Stewart, 1974); and Tom Travis's *Essays in Canadian business history* (Toronto: McClelland & Stewart, 1984).

633 **Business Quarterly.**
London, Ontario: University of Western Ontario, 1935- . quarterly.

A publication of scholarly, but readable, articles on a wide range of business, finance, and industry related topics. A more popular business magazine, published monthly, is *Canadian Business* (Toronto: CB Media, 1969-). Consult also: *Canadian Business Review* (Ottawa: Conference Board of Canada, 1973-); *Canadian Banker* (Toronto: Canadian Bankers' Association, 1893-); and *Moneywise* (Toronto: Financial Post, 1986-).

634 **Canadian business reader.**
Toronto: Stoddart, 1986. 306p.

Articles reprinted from Canada's premier business magazine, *Canadian Business*. The pieces included have been chosen in order to provide a true representation of the extent of Canadian business.

635 **Canadian industry in transition.**
Toronto: University of Toronto Press in cooperation with the Royal Commission on the Economic Union and Development Prospects for Canada and the Canadian Government Publishing Centre, Supply and Services Canada, 1986. 388p.

This is the first in a series of seven volumes dealing with the Canadian industrial structure, included as part of the collected research of the Royal Commission on the Economic Union and Development Prospects for Canada. This series deals with: the evolution of Canadian industry, with emphasis on the manufacturing sector; the diffusion of technological and organizational innovation; the performance of government enterprises and the effects of financial and economic regulation; an industrial strategy for Canada; productivity questions with regard to Canadian manufacturing; and competition policy. Other titles in the series are: *Technological change in Canadian industry; Canadian industrial policy in action; Economics of industrial policy and strategy; The rôle of scale in Canada–U.S. productivity differences in the manufacturing sector 1970-1979; Competition policy and vertical exchange;* and *The political economy of economic adjustment.*

636 **Continental corporate power: economic elite linkages between Canada and the United States.**
Wallace Clement. Toronto: McClelland & Stewart, 1977. 408p.
This work probes the structures or underpinnings of the economic relationship between Canada and the United States. It examines the organizations involved, i.e. the multinational corporations; it looks at the social dimensions of the relationship, i.e. the people controlling the dominant corporations. It also studies Canada's rôle within the North American business economy. In summary, the work is 'an analysis of corporate concentration and the economic elites in both Canada and the United States and of corporate and elite linkages between the two nations'.

637 **Business and politics: a study of collective action.**
William D. Coleman. Kingston, Ontario; Montreal: McGill-Queen's University Press, 1988. 336p.
Views relations between business and politics (government) through the eyes of the interest associations. Firms, in the opinion of the author, have used associations to gain special privilege within the policy process, rather than assuming a wider political responsibility. He concludes that business is 'not sufficiently accountable for its actions and not organized to assume the political responsibilities that should result from its economic power'.

638 **Controlling interest: who owns Canada?**
Diane Francis. Toronto: Macmillan, 1986. 352p.
Controlling interest outlines Canada's thirty-two wealthiest families who, along with five conglomerates, already control about one-third of the country's non-financial assets, which is nearly double what they controlled four years before. Their combined revenues in 1985 were nearly $123 billion (£61.6 billion), an amount greater than the federal government's income.

639 **Quebec inc.: French-Canadian entrepreneurs and the new business elite.**
Matthew Fraser. Toronto: Key Porter, 1987. 280p.
The author documents the transformation taking place in Quebec business and the resultant emergence of a French-Canadian corporate élite. This group is divided into five main categories: the dynasties, the old middle class, the new managers, the entrepreneurs, and the outsiders. While the work tends to be a series of personal portraits, the author is able to link the segments and produce an interesting commentary on the developing business community in the province.

640 **How Ottawa decides: planning and industrial policy-making 1968-1980.**
Richard D. French. Toronto: James Lorimer, 1984. 2nd ed. 225p.
An examination of the federal government's and the federal bureaucracy's attempts to develop an industrial strategy for Canada – and their failure.

641 **Business in the Canadian environment.**
Peter H. Fuhrman. Scarborough, Ontario: Prentice-Hall, 1989. 3rd ed. 789p.
This is an example of one of many good introductory texts designed for the student, but equally useful for the general and interested reader, which outline the nature of the

business system in Canada. Other similar works of interest are: *Introduction to Canadian business* (Toronto: Allyn & Bacon, 1987); *The world of business: a Canadian profile* (Toronto: Wiley, 1987); Lionel A. Mitchell's *Canadian business and management* (Toronto: Methuen, 1987); William A. Preshing's *Business management in Canada: an introduction* (Toronto: John Wiley, 1979); and Robert W. Sexty's *Issues in Canadian business* (Scarborough, Ontario: Prentice-Hall, 1979).

642 **The objectives of Canadian competition policy 1888-1983.**
Paul K. Gorecki, W. T. Stanbury.   Montreal: Institute for Research on Public Policy/L'Institut de recherches politiques, 1984. 236p.
The first restraint of trade legislation in Canada was passed in 1889. Since that time legislation, and amendments to this legislation have come forward as a result of political and economic imperatives. This work studies the objectives of these laws and how they have been adapted to changes in the economy, shifts in political priorities, new developments in theory, and refinements in the judicial system. The authors generally conclude that competition policy can be viewed as a form of political compromise between the conflicting interests of consumers and of business. The policy in practice, the authors go on to surmise, can amount to paying lip-service to such objectives as 'efficiency' and 'competition' while, at the same time, not seriously inconveniencing the business community's freedom to impose a wide variety of trade restraints.

643 **Canadian industrial organization and policy.**
Christopher Green.   Toronto: McGraw-Hill Ryerson, 1985. 2nd ed. 486p.
Directed at the university student, this work provides the general reader with a comprehensive treatment of Canada's industrial economics and policies. The topics handled here include the general economic setting in Canada, market structure, foreign ownership, industrial behaviour in Canada, public policy and business, competition policy, and public enterprise.

644 **Guts, greed and glory: a visual history of modern Canadian business.**
Toronto: Summerhill Press, 1988. 207p.
Designed for the general reader, this is a history in pictures and words representing six decades of Canadian business. Little content for the informed reader but interesting photographs and illustrations.

645 **Industrial policy.**
Toronto: University of Toronto Press in cooperation with the Royal Commission on the Economic Union and Development Prospects for Canada and the Canadian Publishing Centre, Supply and Services Canada, 1986. 379p.
This is the first of two volumes dealing with industrial policy in Canada, included as part of the collected research of the Royal Commission on the Economic Union and Development Prospects for Canada. Examined are the rôles of principal participants in the development of policy and the diverse national and international forces which have an impact on such development. The other title in the series is *The political sociology of industrial policy.*

646 **Canadian business law: principles in action.**
George B. Klippert. Toronto: Holt, Rinehart & Winston, 1987. 508p.
Using a hypothetical company, this text seeks to deal with issues of business and the law by approximating the realities of a business setting. Appropriate for the student or general reader. Other similar works are: Harold Sterling's *Business law for business people* (Toronto: Methuen, 1987); and John Willes' *Contemporary Canadian business law: principles and cases* (Toronto: McGraw-Hill Ryerson, 1986). Of interest also is the anthology of articles in Richard B. Miner's *Current issues in Canadian business law* (Toronto: Carswell, 1986). Also the informed reader may wish to consult: Ernest Amirault and Maurice Archer's *Canadian business law* (Toronto: Methuen, 1986); and Bruce Welling's *Corporate law in Canada: the governing principles* (Toronto: Butterworths, 1984).

647 **Business cycles in Canada: the postwar experience and policy directions.**
Maurice Lamontagne. Ottawa: Canadian Institute for Economic Policy, 1984. 194p. (Canadian Institute for Economic Policy Series).
The author examines Canada's attempts to respond to short- and medium-term business cycles, speculating also on the implications for the country with regard to the long-term. An interesting work by a career economist, policy advisor, parliamentarian, cabinet minister and senator.

648 **Silent surrender: the multinational corporation in Canada.**
Kari Levitt. Toronto: Macmillan, 1970. 185p.
The late 1960s were marked by a renewal of the discussion regarding foreign ownership and Canadian business. Much of this discussion revolved around such issues as free trade and nationalist *versus* continentalist debate. This work was one of the more widely-read and quoted works attacking foreign ownership. Interesting background reading in light of the developments of the 1980s. See also from the same period: *Dual loyalty: Canadian–U.S. business arrangements* (Toronto: McGraw-Hill, 1971); and Ian Lumsden's *Close the 49th parallel etc: the Americanization of Canada* (Toronto: University of Toronto Press, 1970).

649 **The Canadian multinationals.**
I. A. Litvak, C. J. Maule. Toronto: Butterworths, 1981. 184p.
Much has been written on the subject of foreign multinational corporations operating inside Canada; little has been written with regard to Canadian corporate investment outside Canada. This work focuses on investment abroad, identifies major corporate investors, discusses the economic impact of outward investment, and the existing policies which guide that investment. Particularly interesting also is the development of a code of conduct for the behaviour of foreign subsidiaries of Canadian companies. See also: Jorge Niosi's *Canadian multinationals* (Toronto: Between The Lines, 1985); and Patricia Marchak's *In whose interests: an essay on multinational corporations in a Canadian context* (Toronto: McClelland & Stewart, 1979).

650 **The politics of development: forests, mines & hydro-electric power in Ontario, 1849-1941.**
H. V. Nelles. Toronto: Macmillan, 1974. 514p.
One of the best accounts available dealing with the interaction of the political, governmental and business sectors – in this instance, the interrelationship of the three

in the development of the resource industries of Ontario. Solid background reading for an understanding of the forestry, mining and power industries in Canada's largest province. Of related interest is the older work by John H. Dales, entitled *Hydroelectricity and industrial development: Quebec 1898-1940* (Cambridge, Massachusetts: Harvard University Press, 1957).

651 The Canadian establishment.
Peter C. Newman. Toronto: McClelland & Stewart, 1975. 480p.

This journalist and popular historian focused, for some considerable period of his writing career, on documenting the rise and activities of Canada's corporate élite. This volume, and its companion entitled *The Canadian establishment: the acquisitors* (Toronto: McClelland & Stewart, 1981) chronicle this group. Related books written or edited by the same author are: *Bronfman dynasty: the Rothchilds of the new world* (Toronto: McClelland & Stewart, 1978); *The establishment man: a portrait of power* (Toronto: McClelland & Stewart, 1982); and Debrett's *Illustrated guide to the Canadian establishment* (Agincourt, Ontario: Methuen, 1983). Other interesting works of the same genre include: Allan Gould's *The new entrepreneurs: 80 Canadian success stories* (Toronto: Seal, 1986); Paul Grescoe and David Cruise's *The money rustlers: self-made millionaires of the new west* (Markham, Ontario: Viking, 1985); and Kenneth Barnes and Everett Banning's *Money makers: the secrets of Canada's most successful entrepreneurs* (Toronto: McClelland & Stewart, 1985).

652 Canadian capitalism: a study of power in the Canadian business establishment.
Jorge Niosi. Toronto: James Lorimer, 1981. 224p. bibliog.

A large body of Canadian nationalist literature sees foreign capital as the dominant economic and political force, whereas this study questions that view. The author puts forward the concept that it is in fact the Canadian middle class which plays the most significant rôle here, controlling at least seventy per cent of all corporate assets within the private sector and exerting a dominant influence even in government-owned corporations. An interesting perspective. See also by the same author *The economy of Canada: a study of ownership and control* (Montreal: Black Rose, 1981).

653 Prairie capitalism: power and influence in the new west.
John Richards, Larry Pratt. Toronto: McClelland & Stewart, 1979. 340p. (Canada in Transition: Crises in Political Development).

An important, scholarly and award-winning work, which examines resource development in the provinces of Alberta and Saskatchewan, and in the process provides the reader with an understanding of the emergence of an entrepreneurial outlook by the respective provincial governments. Central to this transition was also a spirited, if not vicious interplay between the provincial governments and institutions and their federal counterparts. The authors trace the growth of such industries as potash, natural gas and oil, as well as those associated with agriculture. It is their belief that 'provincialization' of resources is inevitable.

654 Megafirms: strategies for Canada's multinationals.
Alan M. Rugman, John McIlveen. Toronto: Methuen, 1985. 270p. bibliog.

The author identifies the twenty largest Canadian-owned megafirms and reviews their performance, examining their international operations and their intra-corporate links.

Competitive advantage is analysed in relation to foreign–owned rival corporations. The advantages peculiar to each company is evaluated in turn, particularly within the context of competitive strategy. The analysis is positive indicating the general well-being of this segment of Canadian business and industry. A bibliography is included.

655 **Foreign and domestic firms in Canada: a comparative study of financial structure and performance.**

Daniel M. Shapiro. Toronto: Butterworths, 1980. 142p.

Foreign-controlled firms have long dominated key manufacturing and resource-based industries in Canada, making up a total of sixty per cent of the total ownership of these industries. This high figure makes this subject of some concern to Canadians.

656 **Uneasy lies the head: the truth about Canada's crown corporations.**

Walter Stewart. Toronto: Collins, 1987. 266p. bibliog.

A noted journalist looks at, sometimes irreverently, publicly owned companies in Canada. The more serious reader may wish to consult J. Robert S. Prichard's *Crown corporations in Canada: the calculus of instrument choice* (Toronto: Butterworths, 1983) or Allan Tupper and G. Bruce Doern's *Public corporations and public policy in Canada* (Montreal: Institute for Research on Public Policy, 1981).

657 **The state and enterprise: Canadian manufacturers and the federal government, 1917-1931.**

Tom Traves. Toronto: University of Toronto Press, 1979. 175p.

This study provides the informed reader with a valuable insight into the Canadian regulatory system, and, thus the Canadian economy today, in that it shows how a modern interventionist state was arrived at due to competing claims on the part of manufacturers, industrial workers and farmers.

658 **Canada's industrial space-economy.**

David F. Walker. London: Bell & Hyman, 1980. 261p. (Advanced Economic Geographies).

A study of the rôle of manufacturing in the Canadian economy and on the policies of the federal government which influence its character and well-being. The work claims three objectives. It describes firstly the past and present pattern of industrial location in Canada, then interprets historical trends along with the current situation and future prospects. Finally, it evaluates planning and industrial development policies which have been designed to ensure the manufacturing industries benefit Canadians.

Resource Industries

General

659 **Natural resources in Canada: economic theory and policy.**
F. J. Anderson. Toronto: Methuen, 1985. 301p. bibliog.
In this study directed at the informed reader, the author applies economic theory to the study of natural resource use, i.e. minerals, oil and gas, forests, fisheries, etc.

660 **Managing Canada's renewable resources.**
Edited by Ralph R. Krueger, Bruce Mitchell. Toronto: Methuen, 1977. 333p.
Readings which attempt, firstly, to provide a perspective on resource management issues in general, and secondly, which provide case studies on specific issues. See also Basil A. Kalymon's *The management of Canadian resources: concepts and cases* (Toronto: McGraw-Hill Ryerson, 1981). Both works are directed at the informed reader.

661 **How to find information on Canadian natural resources: a guide to the literature.**
Gabriel Pal. Ottawa: Canadian Library Association, 1985. 182p.
This guide will direct the reader to the significant sources of information on resources, ranging from government documents, handbooks, statistical yearbooks and annual reports, to popular works on Canadian resources. More importantly, it also acquaints the user with the various methods of searching and finding information on Canadian sources. Citation groupings include: natural resources; energy resources; mineral resources; land resources; climate; water resources; and, fish, marine and wildlife resources.

Agriculture

662 **Remembering the farm: memories of farming, ranching and rural life in Canada, past and present.**
Allan Anderson. Toronto: Macmillan, 1977. 287p.
Only a generation ago the majority of the Canadian population was classed as rural. This is a nostalgic look at farm life, the good and the bad, as recounted by individuals across Canada.

663 **One hundred harvests: Research Branch, Agriculture Canada 1886-1986.**
T. H. Anstey. Ottawa: Research Branch, Agriculture Canada, 1986. 432p. (Historical Series, vol. 27).
The history of the Research Branch of Agriculture Canada (the federal government ministry of agriculture) is in great measure the history of agriculture in Canada. The research conducted represents much of the innovation, invention, and development in the agricultural food industry in Canada. This book was written on the occasion of the centenary of the Experimental Farm Station Act. These latter institutions are an integral part of the agricultural research infrastructure with a proud tradition and interesting individual histories.

664 **The political economy of agriculture in western Canada.**
Edited by G. S. Basran, David A. Hay. Toronto: Garamond Press, 1988. 247p.
Papers presented at a conference organized for the purpose of investigating contemporary social issues in agriculture during the 1980s. The agricultural sector was examined from a number of divergent perspectives and viewpoints, including: overviews of the state of agriculture in western Canada; state, class and agricultural policies; farm health and safety; issues relating to farm women; and, rural communities and services.

665 **The Canadian prairie west and the ranching frontier 1874-1924.**
David H. Breen. Toronto: University of Toronto Press, 1983. 302p.
The story of agricultural development in western Canada is most frequently told within the context of cereal agriculture. Although passing reference has always been given to the introduction and development of ranching, this reference has frequently been characterized as a picturesque interlude before the arrival of the homesteader, or worse, as a short-lived adjunct of the American ranching era. In this scholarly but readable study Breen recognizes a distinct ranching frontier in Canada, socially and culturally different from the American, and a powerful political and economic force in its own right.

666 **Canadian papers in rural history.**
Gananoque, Ontario: Langdale Press, 1978- .
These volumes of papers are not published on a regular basis, but the five volumes of scholarly papers published to date comprise an informative and authoritative record of various aspects of rural life in Canada.

667 **Will the bounty end?: the uncertain future of Canada's food supply.**
Garry Lawrence Fairbairn. Saskatoon, Saskatchewan: Western
Producer Prairie Books, 1984. 160p.
This is an exceptionally informative book for the general reader. The author, who was
commissioned by the Agricultural Institute of Canada, presents an alarming vision of a
possible future, based on his analyses of the current state of the agricultural industry. It
is the author's thesis that if the looming farm and food crisis is to be avoided some
decisive steps must be taken. These include environmental challenges such as the issue
of land use and soil erosion, and the protection of farmlands against encroaching
urbanization. Most importantly, an enhanced level of understanding of agriculture's
place in Canadian society must be fashioned together with a change in the country's
habits as consumers of agricultural produce.

668 **Canadian agricultural policy: the historical pattern.**
Vernon C. Fowke. Toronto: University of Toronto Press, 1978. 304p.
This early, but still relevant work of scholarship tests the assumption that agriculture
has been Canada's basic industry. Fowke demonstrates that agricultural interests have
always been secondary to other political considerations in the shaping of agricultural
policy, thus policy has always been influenced less by the needs of the farm community
than by other economic, political or international factors.

669 **The national policy and the wheat economy.**
Vernon C. Fowke. Toronto: University of Toronto Press, 1978. 312p.
This study of the agricultural development of western Canada, focusing on the wheat
economy, is considered a classic and is essential reading for the student or the
researcher of prairie agricultural or economic history.

670 **Men against the desert.**
James H. Gray. Saskatoon, Saskatchewan: Western Producer Prairie
Books, 1967. 250p.
The drought conditions on the prairies during the 1930s left as desert millions of acres
of land. Gray tells the story of the successful reclamation of the land and the people
and agencies responsible for the restoration of productivity to the region. In Gray's
words, these were the people who 'fought the scorching wind, the blowing dust, the
[drought], hail, frost, grasshoppers and rust from one crop failure to another, and
never gave up'. The many dedicated people who brought (and fought) the Prairie Farm
Administration into being included university researchers, soil scientists, entomologists,
plant breeders and animal husbandmen who often worked around the clock with the
farmers in the fields to make the reclamation of the stricken lands a success story.

671 **History of agriculture in Ontario 1613-1880.**
Robert Leslie Jones. Toronto: University of Toronto Press, 1977.
420p.
An early, but still important, history of agriculture in Ontario. This work attempts to
encompass all the facets of agricultural development, ranging from the forms of
agriculture engaged in by the Indians to the agricultural endeavours of the early
settlers and pioneers, to grain growing, the grain trade, the livestock industry, the
dairy industry, the fruit industry, farmers' organizations and movements and relevant
economic policies and forces which affected the farm community.

672 **Canadian agriculture in a global context: opportunities and obligations.**
Edited by Irene Knell, John R. English. Waterloo, Ontario:
University of Waterloo Press, 1986. 229p.

Canadian agriculture of today faces a crisis. Farmers have been receiving lower returns on their sales and on their equity and these conditions will inevitably affect the productivity and the international competitiveness of Canadian agriculture. This collection of papers by Canadian and other authorities on the international dimensions of Canadian agriculture has been compiled to examine the challenges and opportunities created by this present crisis.

673 **The Harrowsmith reader: an anthology from Canada's national award winning magazine of country life and alternatives to bigness.**
Edited by James Lawrence. Camden East, Ontario: Camden House
Publishing, 1978. 287p.

This volume, and its companion *The Harrowsmith reader, volume II* (Camden East, Ontario: Camden House Publishing, 1980), bring together a collection of the best articles from the Harrowsmith magazine, a magazine of country and alternative life style. Articles have been arranged under such headings as: 'Land', 'Country Careers', 'Shelter', 'The Garden', 'Husbandry', 'The Pantry', 'Rural Life'. The *Reader*, like the magazine, is beautifully illustrated, and the articles are well written and reflective of today's rural living.

674 **Between the Red and the Rockies.**
Grant MacEwan. Toronto: University of Toronto Press, 1952. 300p.

A popular and very readable history of the development of agriculture in western Canada, from the time of initial settlement through the first half of the twentieth century. MacEwan, better than most writers today, is able to tell this story within the context of the general history of the region, as well as with an eye to balance between the economic, social and technological aspects of this development. Regardless of its date of publication this is a work still relevant, particularly for the uninformed reader. Other of MacEwan's works which are of interest to the general and serious reader alike would be: *Illustrated history of western Canadian agriculture* (Saskatoon, Saskatchewan: Western Producer Prairie Books, 1980); *Power for prairie plows* (Saskatoon, Saskatchewan: Western Producer Prairie Books, 1971) which chronicles the dramatic development of farm power – from horse, to steam, to petrol driven tractors. and, *Harvest of bread* (Saskatoon, Saskatchewan: Western Producer Prairie Books, 1969), an account of the development of the wheat industry on the prairies.

675 **Unequal beginnings: agriculture and economic development in Quebec and Ontario until 1870.**
John McCallum. Toronto: University of Toronto Press, 1980. 148p.

A comparative economic history which examines the differences in agricultural, and to some extent resultant industrial development of the provinces of Ontario and Quebec. The author demonstrates that it was the success of Ontario agriculture, favoured in some measure by better soil and climate, which fostered a strong provincial economy by way of the local creation of capital, transportation facilities and other industrial infrastructure supports. Thus the pattern of development of the two regions diverged as growth in Quebec was based mainly on external forces and elements, i.e. a dependence on the uncertainty of external markets. Ultimately this led to the greater stability and prosperity of the Ontario economy. For a focused examination of agriculture in Quebec as it related particularly to settlement in the province, see Normand Séquin's *Agriculture et colonisation au Québec: aspects historiques* (Montreal: Boreal Express, 1980).

676 **The politics of food.**
Don Mitchell. Toronto: James Lorimer, 1975. 235p.
An analysis of agribusiness in Canada at a point in the mid-1970s. The author looks at this sector from the point of view of the consumer as well as the producer. He devotes a lengthy discussion to the perceptions of the former group, as well as the economic uncertainties of the latter, commenting also on what he perceives to be over-capacity and inefficiency in the processing sector. Ultimately, the issues and conflicts within the industry must be dealt with at the political and policy levels, and the discussion turns to the political stage. This is most definitely a one-sided treatise, but useful for the student or informed reader.

677 **Chosen instrument: a history of the Canadian Wheat Board: the McIvor years.**
William E. Morriss. Edmonton, Alberta: Reidmore Books, 1987. 292p.
The Canadian Wheat Board marked its fiftieth anniversary in 1985. It is the best known, but probably least understood, of Canada's marketing agencies. Certainly it is a key player in the agricultural economy of western Canada. This work provides a history of its formative years. The author begins with the early development of agriculture, before turning to the birth of the Board during the depression years and the rôle of the Board during the Second World War. The Board's part in Canada's broader agricultural policy objectives and the opening of export markets for Canadian grain are also covered. The story of another key agency in the grain trade, the Winnipeg Grain Exchange, is told in Allan Levine's *The Exchange: 100 years of trading grain in Winnipeg* (Winnipeg, Manitoba: Peguis Publishers, 1987). Established in 1887 the Exchange acted as a commodity exchange, an advocate for improvement in transportation facilities, a supporter of more efficient farming techniques and a lobby for a fair and workable grain inspection system.

678 **A history of agriculture in Ontario.**
G. Elmore Reaman. Toronto: Saunders, 1970. 2 vols.
An historical overview of agriculture in the province from 1615 to 1967. The work lacks scholarly documentation, but provides a starting point for the interested student. The examination is presented in a chronological fashion and does attempt to introduce elements of effect into the discussion; for example, the concurrent development of agricultural education, and the evolution of government policy as it was related to agricultural matters.

679 **Prairie lives: the changing face of farming.**
Lois L. Ross. Toronto: Between the Lines, 1985. 172p.
A photo-journalist documents in prose and photographs the present state of agriculture in western Canada. The author undertook a four month trek through the region interviewing farmers and exploring with them their views on food production and the direction of agriculture, commodity prices, food quality, soil quality, farm size and the

impact of modern agricultural techniques and technology on the environment. The response is mixed, but on the whole there is a regressive tone which should be disturbing to the concerned citizen.

680 **The politics of agricultural policy-making in Canada.**
Grace Skogstad. Toronto: University of Toronto, 1987. 229p.
A political scientist examines how the agricultural sector has been served by government policy, at the federal and provincial levels, as well as by the interaction between the various levels. Three issues are examined in some detail: the transportation question, focusing on the handling of grain and including a discussion of the Crow's Nest freight rate issue; national marketing plans and supply management in the poultry and dairy sectors; and commodity price stabilization. Within these areas she addresses the questions of concurrent federal/provincial jurisdiction over agriculture – its benefits and its disadvantages.

681 **Agriculture on the prairies, 1870-1940.**
David Spector. Ottawa: National Historic Parks and Sites Branch, Parks Canada, Environment Canada, 1983. 260p. (History and Archaeology Series, vol. 65).
Between 1880 and 1920 animal husbandry played a supportive rôle to the dominant cereal grain agriculture on the Canadian prairies. Livestock raising became feasible in the West as the ability to improve livestock breeding, disease control and animal shelter provided farmers with an ancilliary income as a form of security against poor harvests. Yet the predominantly rich black and brown soils of the prairies proved more profitable in the cultivation of wheat and other field crops. Despite the encouragement of W. R. Motherwell and other agricultural officials to diversify, prairie farmers showed a persistent reluctance to adopt mixed farming on a significant scale.

682 **The future of grain: Canada's prospects for grains, oilseeds and related industries.**
Terry Veeman, Michele Veeman. Ottawa: Canadian Institute for Economic Policy, 1984. 130p.
This commissioned study reviews the future of the grain economy within the context of a rapidly changing international economy while not leaving out of account the limitations of the Canadian resource base i.e. soil deterioration, etc. The authors review the position of Canadian grain exports, providing a wealth of information on production, transportation and handling systems, international competition and the functions of various government agencies. They also examine the status of the various industries connected to the grain economy, such as the manufacturing of agricultural machinery, the production of pesticides and fertilizers, the processing industries, etc. Prophetically, they caution against over-optimism as to the future of wheat and the export market.

683 **Rhetoric and roses: a history of Canadian gardening 1900-1930.**
Edwinna Von Baeyer. Markham, Ontario: Fitzhenry & Whiteside, 1984. 197p. bibliog.
Rhetoric and roses is the history of an era characterized by a variety of horticultural innovations as well as an abundant rhetoric, frequently forceful, or moralistic, which affected the creation of Canada's ornamental gardens, school grounds, vacant lots and

back yards. Included is a bibliography as well as an afterword by Susan Buggey, Chief of Historical Research, Prairie Region, Parks Canada on 'The Preservation of Historic Gardens in Canada'.

684 **Western Canadian agriculture to 1990.**
Calgary, Alberta: Canada West Foundation, 1980. 302p.
To describe and analyse the present status of western Canadian agriculture – to discuss the potential for further growth and development – to identify risks, constraints and impediments to further development – to suggest policies, programmes and conditions required for the optimum development of agriculture in the economy of western Canada – these were the objectives of this study. Its conclusions would be of interest to the serious reader, particularly in light of the drought and market realities of the 1980s.

685 **The Western Producer.**
Saskatoon, Saskatchewan: Western Producer Publications, 1923- . weekly.
This tabloid format periodical, includes news and feature articles relating to agriculture and the farm community in Canada (particularly western Canada). Other publications with a similar focus include: *Farm & Country: Ontario's Farm Business and Management Publication* (Toronto: Agricultural Publishing, 1891-); *Farm Light & Power* (Regina, Saskatchewan: Farm Light & Power Publications, 1959-); and, *Country Guide* (Winnipeg, Manitoba: Public Press, 1982-).

686 **Farm gate defense: the story of the Canadian Farmers Survival Association.**
Allen Wilford. Toronto: NC Press, 1984. 242p.
A combination of factors including low commodity prices, high production costs, erosion of traditional markets, drought and financial problems have made the 1980s a difficult time for the agricultural producer. This is the story of one group's response to some of these forces. While the treatise is one-sided it provides the reader with a sense of the frustrations experienced by some of Canada's present-day farmers.

687 **Beyond the harvest.**
Barry Wilson. Saskatoon, Saskatchewan: Western Producer Prairie Books, 1981. 289p.
The late twentieth century is a time of many challenges for the prairie grain farmer in Canada. This study explores some of the issues of farming, such as rising costs of production, commodity prices, marketing systems, soil depletion, cultivation techniques, fuel costs and availability, government agricultural policies, agricultural research, political action, and farm image.

688 **Canadian grain marketing.**
C. F. Wilson. Winnipeg, Manitoba: Canadian International Grains Institute, 1979. 456p.
A comprehensive and technical review of the development of Canada's grain industry, with emphasis on its marketing systems. For additional historical context the reader should refer to two works by Duncan Alexander MacGibbon: *The Canadian grain trade 1931-1951* (Toronto: University of Toronto Press, 1952), and *The Canadian grain*

trade (Toronto: Macmillan, 1932). In addition, a great deal can be learned about the economic and social aspects of early agriculture in western Canada from G. E. Britnell's *The wheat economy* (Toronto: The University of Toronto Press, 1939).

689   **A century of Canadian grain: government policy to 1951.**
C. F. Wilson.   Saskatoon, Saskatchewan: Western Producer Prairie Books, 1978. 1138p.

A detailed account, synthesized from a staggering amount of primary documentation, of the policy formulation process, and the resulting government policy relating to the grain industry in Canada, at least until 1951. Part I of the work outlines the development of the trade and government involvement in the trade up to 1930; Part II looks at the period of the early 1930s and the fevered government response to the drought and the realities of the depression years, such as the price-support systems which were put into place at this time; Part III covers the period 1935-43 which saw the transition from a voluntary to a compulsory wheat board; and Part IV deals with the immediate post-war period as Canada began to develop a more aggressive international grain trading policy. This is a work for the informed and academic reader.

690   **A history of farmers' movements in Canada.**
Louis Aubrey Wood.   Toronto: University of Toronto Press, 1975. 372p. (Social History of Canada, vol. 25).

Still the best study of the origins and early development of the agrarian protest movement in Canada, reissued with a scholarly introduction by Foster Griezic. In the late nineteenth century, beginning in Ontario and working outward to Quebec, the Maritimes and the West, Canadian farmers came to believe they were being exploited and ill-rewarded for their labours. Groups such as the Grange, the Farmers' Alliance and later provincial farmers' associations came to be organized and agitated for political, economic and social reforms. They were concerned with such issues as equality for women, rural depopulation, cheaper transportation, improved marketing facilities, availability of farm credit, business government interdependence among many others. Their methods ranged from cooperative ventures, to pressure group tactics, to political action. See also Paul F. Sharp's *The agrarian revolt in western Canada* (Minneapolis, Minnesota: University of Minnesota Press, 1948).

Fisheries

691   **The war against the seals: a history of the North American seal fishery.**
Briton Cooper Busch.   Kingston, Ontario; Montreal: McGill-Queen's University Press, 1985. 374p. bibliog.

A scholarly historical examination of this controversial segment of the fishery industry. Three major units comprise the story: the activities of the New England sealers in the eighteenth and nineteenth centuries; the Newfoundland sealing industry in the nineteenth and twentieth centuries; and the northern fur seal controversies, centred primarily on the North Pacific, in the late nineteenth century. The reader interested in a popular account of the more recent controversy surrounding the industry should review works such as Pol Chantraine's *The living ice: the story of the seals and the men who hunt them in the Gulf of St. Lawrence* (Toronto: McClelland & Stewart, 1980).

692 **The struggle to organize: resistance in Canada's fishery.**
Wallace Clement. Toronto: McClelland & Stewart, 1986. 219p.

In an industry affected by social change and ruthless corporate restructuring, loosely directed by state policies, and subject to turbulent economic conditions, Canadian fishers have created a complex of organizations to defend themselves. These can be categorized as unions, cooperatives, and associations, although such groupings do not do justice to the complexity of the actions, ideologies, and politics of these organizational forms. This book provides information on the conditions underlying the formation and behaviour of these organizations and the people they represent. Organizations considered include the United Fishermen and Allied Workers' Union, the Prince Rupert Fishermen's Co-operative, the Newfoundland Fishermen, the Food and Allied Workers' Union, and the Eastern Fishermen's Federation.

693 **Turning the tide: a new policy for Canada's Pacific fisheries.**
Commission on Pacific Fisheries Policy. Vancouver: The Commission, 1982. 292p.

This Royal Commission was mandated to find ways to improve Canada's Pacific fisheries. A variety of circumstances led to the creation of the Commission, including a growing concern as to the precarious condition of fish stocks, increasing anxiety among Indians about their traditional fishing rights, and economic problems resulting from deficiencies in fisheries policy. Presents a good deal of background information about the industry, its problems and its potential.

694 **The Atlantic salmon in the history of North America.**
R. W. Dunfield. Ottawa: Department of Fisheries and Oceans, 1985. 181p. (Canadian Special Publication of Fisheries and Aquatic Sciences, vol. 80).

Initially the Atlantic salmon was a principal food source for the Amerindian cultures which shared its range. Both chronologically and cumulatively, the salmon became an increasingly important factor in the domestic and commercial life of the developing colonies, but its history is largely comprised of repetitive instances of over-exploitation, careless destruction of stocks and their environment, and ineffectual conservation actions.

695 **The cod fisheries: the history of an international economy.**
Harold A. Innis. Toronto: University of Toronto Press, 1978. rev. ed. 522p. (Canadian University Paperbacks, vol. 212).

When first published this work presented a new interpretation of European and North American history that has since become a classic. Here Innis shows how the exploitation of the cod fisheries from the fifteenth to the twentieth century has been closely tied up with the whole economic and political development of Western Europe and North America. Still relevant today as the fishing industry of Canada, and the maritime communities dependent on that industry, go through a period of fundamental social and economic change.

696 **Uncommon property: the fishing and fish-processing industries in British Columbia.**
Edited by Patricia Marchack, Neil Guppy, John McMullan. Toronto: Methuen, 1987. 402p.

A commentary on the Canadian west coast fisheries in the 1980s, focusing on the social and economic structure of the industry. The work describes the history of the industry, the rôle of the various levels of government, the nature of markets, and the importance of the processing sector. It also considers the labour process, including discussions on shoreworkers and fishers, with some recognition and perspective on the Union of Fishermen and Allied Workers' Union. The viability of the communities dependent on the fishery, particularly in light of the depletion of fish stocks, is also dealt with here.

697 **Rising to the challenge: a new policy for Canada's freshwater fisheries.**
Peter H. Pearse. Ottawa: Canadian Wildlife Federation, 1988. 180p.

The report of an inquiry charged with examining and making recommendations on, the recreational, native and commercial fisheries and the waters that support them in Canada. This independent investigation was sponsored by the Canadian Wildlife Federation. The report deals mainly with policy, and makes a plea for better fisheries' management in Canada. The work provides a description of the resources, the fishing dependent on them, and how governments manage them.

698 **Economic resurgence and the constitutional agenda: the case of the east coast fisheries.**
A. Paul Pross, Susan McCorquodale. Kingston, Ontario: Institute of Intergovernmental Relations, Queen's University, 1987. 156p.

A survey and analysis of events that provide an excellent overview and appreciation of the contemporary situation with regard to the control and development of the east coast fisheries. The authors show why the control of the fisheries is a subject of heated constitutional controversy, what is at stake, and the problems involved with transfer of responsibility from the federal government to the provinces.

699 **Seals and sealing in Canada.**
Royal Commission on Seals and the Sealing Industry in Canada.
Ottawa: Ministry of Supply and Services Canada, 1986. 3 vols.

'During the past 20 years the management of seals in Canada has changed from being viewed as essentially a technical matter that concerned a few fishermen on the east coast and a handful of scientists and fishery administrators, to a responsibility which has aroused considerable interest, and sometimes strong feelings, among a great many Canadians. Canada's approach to seals and sealing has also evoked public interest in a number of other countries [and has] threatened Canada's image in other countries'. This Commission reviewed all aspects of the industry, including social, economic and biological matters.

700 **Navigating troubled waters: a new policy for the Atlantic fisheries.**
Task Force on Atlantic Fisheries = Groupe d'étude des pêches de
l'Atlantique. Ottawa: Minister of Supply and Services Canada, 1982.
152p.
The Atlantic fisheries are today, and have been for some time, in a state of disarray.
The depletion of fish stocks, taken together with various issues, such as ill-advised
government initiatives of regional and economic development, have brought about a
disharmonious situation. The recommendations of this Task Force have guided fishery
policy in the past few years but the result has been less than satisfactory. The situation
is resulting in economic, and thus social disintegration for the Atlantic region. See also
Ernie Weeks and Leigh Mazany's *The future of the Atlantic fisheries* (Montreal:
Institute for Research on Public Policy, 1983).

Forestry

701 **Canadian Forest Industries.**
Don Mills, Ontario: Southam Business Information and
Communications Group, 1880- . monthly.
This magazine serves operative and administrative management sectors of the logging,
sawmilling and related wood products industries. It is intended to alert its readers to
new production and operating techniques and equipment, and to improved management methods for the overall benefit of the forest industry in Canada.

702 **Stumped: the forest industry in transition.**
Ken Drushka. Vancouver, Toronto: Douglas & McIntyre, 1985.
280p.
A journalist critically examines the history, theory, economics and institutional
structure of today's forest management policies. The focus is on British Columbia.

703 **Lost initiatives: Canada's forest industries, forest policy and forest
conservation.**
R. Peter Gillis, Thomas R. Roach. New York: Greenwood Press,
1986. 326p. bibliog. (Contributions in Economics and Economic
History, vol. 69).
A comprehensive, scholarly historical analysis of the forest industries, forest
conservation and forest policy (with emphasis on the latter), beginning with the year
1800 and continuing to the period immediately after the Second World War. The
authors point to the apathy of the Canadian public in terms of their indifference to the
manner in which resources have been used and abused. Highly recommended. Includes
a comprehensive bibliographical essay.

704 **Logging: British Columbia's logging history.**
Ed Gould. Saanichton, British Columbia: Hancock House, 1975.
221p.
A popular historical treatment, profusely illustrated with photographs, of the logging and lumbering industry in British Columbia. See also: Wilmer Gold's *Logging as it was: a pictorial history of logging on Vancouver Island* (Victoria, British Columbia: Morriss, 1985).

705 **The newsprint paper industry: an economic analysis.**
John A. Guthrie. Cambridge, Massachusetts: Harvard University Press, 1941. 274p. (Harvard Economic Studies, vol. 68).
Though very dated, this remains the best study of the early development of pulp and paper as a dominant forest product industry in Canada and the United States.

706 **Forests of Nova Scotia.**
Ralph S. Johnson. Halifax, Nova Scotia: Nova Scotia Department of Lands and Forests/Four East Publications, 1986. 407p.
Forests of Nova Scotia relates how the province's forests evolved and how man assumed the rôle of major caretaker. The author takes the reader from the end of the Ice Age to the complex world of 1982, showing how man affected the forests as native inhabitant, early settler, logger, timber merchant and politician. Woven through this chronicle of developing forest industries, transportation, legislation and colourful characters is the obvious concern of the author for the future of this essential resource and those dependent upon it.

707 **Renewing nature's wealth: a centennial history of the public management of lands, forests & wildlife in Ontario 1763-1967.**
Richard S. Lambert, Paul Pross. Toronto: Ontario Department of Lands and Forests, 1967. 630p.
While primarily the history of a government, or series of government departments, this work provides useful and interesting background with regard to the individual's, or an institution's impact on the forest environment, ranging in this regard from the needs of the settler, to the activities of forest product companies, and then to the wider issue of managing the competing industrial and recreational uses of the land.

708 **The North American assault on the Canadian forest: a history of the lumber trade between Canada and the United States.**
A. R. M. Lower. Toronto: Ryerson Press, 1938. 377p. (Relations of Canada and the United States).
A classic study in economic history which, though difficult to obtain, should be required reading for the interested researcher. Lower sees the development of the forest industry, as a by-product of the growth of the United States which, as a major centre of trade and commerce, made correspondingly major demands upon nearby supply areas. See also the author's *Great Britain's woodyard: British America and the timber trade, 1763-1867* (Montreal; London, Ontario: McGill-Queen's University Press, 1973).

709 **Empire of wood: the MacMillan Bloedel story.**
Donald MacKay.   Vancouver; Toronto: Douglas & McIntyre, 1982.
361p.
The corporate history of one of the largest, and most dominant of the lumber/forest products companies in Canada, centred in British Columbia. Of necessity, the author deals in general with the development of the industry over the course of the period under examination; that is from the late nineteenth century to 1981. A corporate history of a similar nature is Sue Baptie's *First growth: the story of British Columbia Forest Products Limited* (Vancouver: British Columbia Forest Products, 1975).

710 **Heritage lost: the crisis in Canada's forests.**
Donald MacKay.   Toronto: Macmillan, 1985. 272p.
Many people find it hard to believe that Canada, of all places, is running short of timber, or at least of the sort of timber vital to Canada's industrial needs and to prevent serious silvicultural depletion. This book is a layman's effort to examine the problem, its causes, its size and ubiquity, and how it affects people's lives, wallets, and well-being.

711 **The lumberjacks.**
Donald MacKay.   Toronto: McGraw-Hill Ryerson, 1986. paperback
ed. 319p.
An excellent, well illustrated study and dissection of the development of the lumbering industry in Canada, encompassing the period from the birth of the industry in the eighteenth century, to the 1950s. Deals with lumbering primarily in New Brunswick, Quebec, Ontario and British Columbia.

712 **Cut and run: the assault on Canada's forests.**
Jamie Swift.   Toronto: Between the Lines, 1983. 283p.
This book attempts to explain how the Canadian forest has been systematically abused. The subject-matter of the book ranges from the history of Canadian forest management and exploitation through public policy, technological changes in logging and their effects, forest ecology and forest administration, to ways in which economic and political forces have determined the treatment of Canadian forests.

713 **Timber: history of the forest industry in B. C.**
G. W. Taylor.   Vancouver: J. J. Douglas, 1975. 209p.
The author depicts this work as an overall picture of the timber industry in this region. The emphasis, however, is on the lumbermen and those pioneers from such states as Michigan, Wisconsin and Washington whose talents and organizational abilities went into the development of the massive and complex British Columbia forest industry of today.

714 **Timber colony: a historical geography of early nineteenth century New Brunswick.**
Graeme Wynn. Toronto: University of Toronto Press, 1981. 224p.

The author examines the transformation of a colony under the impact of British capitalism in the first half of the nineteenth century. Discussed here are the swift rise and growth of the timber trade and the unstable nature of the dependent colonial economy, revealing the impact of this fluctuation on provincial development. Graeme Wynn also examines the connections between lumbering, settlement, farming and individual economic opportunity.

Mining

715 **Fortunes in the ground: Cobalt, Porcupine & Kirkland Lake.**
Michael Barnes. Erin, Ontario: Boston Mills Press, 1986. 263p.

Presented here is the colourful, and historically important, story of three great gold mining discoveries, and their impact on the Canadian mining industry, the Canadian economy, and the land.

716 **Eldorado: Canada's national uranium company.**
Robert Bothwell. Toronto: University of Toronto Press, 1984. 470p.

The fascinating corporate history of an important company and industry in Canada, a company which not only took the lead in mineral prospecting and uranium mining and processing, but which also became heavily involved in many aspects of related policy, public administration and international matters.

717 **Canadian Minerals Yearbook.**
Ottawa: Energy, Mines and Resources Canada, 1901- . annual.

Reports on the activity of the mineral industry during the year under review, as well as identifying the predominant economic events relating to or affecting the industry in that year. Particular chapters feature commodity profiles, including information on developments, uses, prices, exports and production consumption figures, etc. An 'Outlook' section under each commodity review provides a forecast of the industry's future position.

718 **Canadian Mines Handbook.**
Toronto: Northern Miner, 1931- . annual.

This reference source provides information on over 2,400 companies engaged within the mining industry. Entries are comprehensive, providing company addresses, the names of officers, assets, an outline of properties, and financial data. The *Handbook* also provides a wide range of general information on the mining industry in Canada. See also *Mining in Canada: facts & figures* (Ottawa: Mining Association of Canada, 1967-).

719 **Canadian Mining Journal.**
Don Mills, Ontario: Southam Business Information and
Communications Group, 1879- . monthly.

Articles and information directed to those who work in the technical, administrative
and supervisory aspects of exploration, mining and processing in the Canadian mineral
industry. See also *The Northern Miner* (Toronto: Northern Miner, 1915-); and *The
Northern Miner Magazine* (Toronto: Northern Miner Press, 1986-).

720 **Hardrock mining: industrial relations and technological changes at Inco.**
Wallace Clement. Toronto: McClelland & Stewart, 1981. 392p.

In the first instance this study portrays the mining industry, particularly from the
perspective of those engaged in that industry; in the second instance it examines class
transformations within a work force, and then tests the resulting propositions against
the broader community. Using one of Canada's oldest and largest mining companies as
a case study allowed the author to develop a good cross-section of the past and future
of the industry as a whole.

721 **Controlling interest: the Canadian gas and oil stakes.**
David Crane. Toronto: McClelland & Stewart, 1982. 336p.

Much discussion has occurred over the past two decades with regard to energy issues,
policy, etc. in Canada. The oil and gas industry, plus the related refining and
associated product industries, account for a substantial percentage of the country's
gross national product, as well as a considerable component of Canada's export trade.
Many works, like this one, examine the industry from any number of perspectives.
Further examples are: Roger Voyer's *Offshore oil: opportunities for industrial
development and job creation* (Ottawa: Canadian Institute for Economic Policy, 1983);
J. D. House's *The last of the free enterprisers: the oilmen of Calgary* (Toronto:
Macmillan, 1980); and Peter Foster's *The blue-eyed sheiks: the Canadian oil
establishment* (Toronto: Collins, 1979).

722 **Geology and economic minerals of Canada.**
Edited by R. J. W. Douglas. Ottawa: Department of Energy, Mines
and Resources, 1970. 5th ed. 838p. (Economic Geology Report, vol.
1).

Directed at the informed inquirer, this volume with its accompanying charts and maps,
is a brief and handy reference to important facts, concepts and interpretations of
geology and mineral resources in Canada. The contents are treated either by major
geological region, or by individual subjects. Investigators should also be aware of the
many reports and studies produced by the Geological Survey of Canada.

723 **The Financial Post Survey of Mines and Energy Resources.**
Toronto: Financial Post Information Service, 1926- . annual.

Reviews approximately 2,910 mining and energy companies in Canada, including those
companies involved in exploration, development and production of oil, gas and
minerals, as well as hydroelectric power generation. Listings include: information on
the details of operations, management and financial status; production and reserve
tables for minerals, oil and gas by company; selected industry statistical data taken
from government sources; and rankings of Canadian oil and gas producers.

724   **From rigs to riches: the story of Bow Valley Industries Ltd.**
Peter Foster.   Calgary, Alberta: Bow Valley Industries, 1985. 203p.
Though a commissioned work, this corporate portrait tells not only the story of one of
the country's more colourful independent producers, but also provides insight into the
industry in general.

725   **The sorcerer's apprentices: Canada's super-bureaucrats and the energy
mess.**
Peter Foster.   Toronto: Collins, 1982. 287p.
The National Energy Program, introduced in 1980, has been described as one of the
most revolutionary, controversial, and even disastrous policies in Canadian history.
The author depicts here how the NEP adversely affected stock markets, the Canadian
dollar, foreign investment and Canadian–U.S. relations. He examines whether this was
a matter of fraud, incompetence or misfortune and concludes it was a mixture of all
three. Further information can be obtained from G. C. Watkins and M. A. Walker's
Reaction: the National Energy Program (Vancouver: Fraser Institute, 1981).

726   **The great Canadian oil patch.**
Earle Gray.   Toronto: Maclean-Hunter, 1970. 355p.
A popular account, for the general reader, of the history of the petroleum industry in
Canada, focusing on western Canada in particular. See also Ed Gould's *The history of
Canada's oil & gas industry* (Saanichton, British Columbia: Hancock House, 1976).

727   **Wildcatters: the story of Pacific Petroleums and Westcoast
Transmission.**
Earle Gray.   Toronto: McClelland & Stewart, 1982. 306p.
When written, the twentieth century history of western Canada will include a chapter
(or more) on oil companies and oil and gas transmission pipelines. This popular
examination combines the two in chronicling the history of two related companies, and
the individuals associated with them (the McMahon family).

728   **Golden giant: Hemlo and the rush for Canada's gold.**
Matthew Hart.   Vancouver; Toronto: Douglas & McIntyre, 1985.
176p.
A journalistic account of the discovery and development of the richest gold–bearing
ore body in Canada, and one of the richest in the world. A more recent work, in the
same journalistic style, by Ken Lefolii and entitled *Claims: adventures in the gold trade*
(Toronto: Key Porter Books, 1987) provides additional insight into the controversy
surrounding the companies involved, including the colourful legal challenges.

729   **Oil and gas: Ottawa, the provinces and the petroleum industry.**
James Laxer.   Toronto: James Lorimer, 1983. 221p. (Canadian Issues
Series).
A polemic study which presents and provides commentary on the tensions between the
federal and provincial levels of government, particularly in the wake of the shocks to
the industry, and the economy, precipitated by the OPEC price revolution in 1973.
During the years following this upheaval Ottawa evolved policies of an interventionist

nature, whereas the oil-producing provinces sought to maintain control and world level prices.

730   **Metals and men: the story of Canadian mining.**
D. M. LeBourdais.   Toronto: McClelland & Stewart, 1957. 416p.

Dated, but still a useful popular treatment of the development of mining in Canada, this work focuses primarily on the discovery and development of particular mines or mineral deposits. Also of some interest is Roy M. Longo's *Historical highlights of Canadian mining: including Canadian personalities* (Toronto: Pitt, 1973).

731   **Dome: the rise and fall of the house that Jack built.**
Jim Lyon.   Toronto: Macmillan, 1983. 227p.

A colourful story of one of Canada's premier, albeit for a brief span of time, oil companies, with a particular interest in exploration and development in the Canadian north. For a short period before 1982, Dome was a concern with the largest corporately-owned marine fleet and the biggest private air force in Canada with a gigantic operation at the edge of the world. It was characterized as having 'an energy, a vision and a single-mindedness that was unmatched among companies in Canada'. But the great bubble was to burst. The decline of the company is outlined in greater detail by Peter Foster in *Other people's money: the banks, the government and Dome* (Toronto: Collins, 1983).

732   **Fuels and the national policy.**
John N. McDougall.   Toronto: Butterworths, 1982. 199p. bibliog.

The author looks at various past issues in Canada's energy policy development. Issues include: coal policies in the period 1867-1913 and again for the period 1919-46; questions relating to oil and gas pipelines in the period 1949-58; decisions made by the National Energy Board from 1960-71; and the National Energy Policy of the 1970s and early 1980s.

733   **The impact of the mining industries on the Canadian economy.**
Kingston, Ontario: Centre for Resource Studies, Queen's University, 1977. 117p. (The National Impact of Mining Series).

This title is the first in a multidisciplinary programme of research dealing with the nature and extent of the effects of the mining industry on the economy and other aspects of Canadian society. Titles and topics include: *The transportation impact of the Canadian mining industry* (1977); *Health and safety in the Canadian mining industry* (1978); *Human resources in Canadian mining: a preliminary analysis* (1977); *The Canadian nonferrous metals industry: an industrial organization study* (1978); *Economic impacts and linkages of the Canadian mining industry* (1978); and, *Environmental impact of mining in Canada* (1978).

734   **Technology on the frontier.**
Dianne Newell.   Vancouver: University of British Columbia Press, 1986. 220p.

A treatise about economic transition in a frontier mining industry. Focuses on the adoption of new technology to the economic and engineering aspects of the mining industry in Ontario up to 1890.

735 **The tar sands: Syncrude and the politics of oil.**
Larry Pratt. Edmonton, Alberta: Hurtig, 1976. 197p.
Much of the political controversy of the 1970s was associated with energy issues, and oil policy in particular. Syncrude and the tar sands development was central to much of the debate in Canada. This study is as much an examination of policy development, and federal–provincial relations as it is about alternate sources for oil. The author provides an historical overview of the tar sands resource; he examines United States, Canadian, and world oil policies and the structure of the international oil industry; he deals with the politics of oil; and finally, he argues for public ownership of the resource.

736 **Profitability in the Canadian mineral industry.**
Charles H. Pye. Kingston, Ontario: Centre for Resource Studies, Queen's University, 1981. 178p.
This study of profitability in the mineral industry divides the industry into four sectors: gold mining; iron mining; other metal mining; and, nonmetal mining. The analysis looks at level of profitability, trends in profitability, risk, excess profits, transfer pricing, size of firm and productivity. Directed at the informed reader.

737 **Canada's oil and the American empire.**
Ed Shaffer. Edmonton, Alberta: Hurtig, 1983. 296p.
A social scientist looks at the problems posed by variations in the production and consumption of oil. He traces: the rise in use of oil in the United States; the ascendancy of the United States to a position of world dominance in terms of production and recovery technology; the impact of U. S. oil policies on Canada; and, the erosion of the' American position in terms of world production, as well as the impact on, and response by, Canada as a result of that erosion of position.

738 **Harvest from the rock: a history of mining in Ontario.**
Philip Smith. Toronto: Macmillan, 1986. 346p.
The first harvests reaped by European settlers in the land which became Ontario were mainly beaver furs and masts for Nelson's navy. But the real riches were to be found in the rock of the Precambrian Shield, which covers two-thirds of the province. This tells the story of the prospectors, geologists, explorers and miners who reaped this harvest from the wilderness.

739 **The treasure-seekers: the men who built Home Oil.**
Philip Smith. Toronto: Macmillan, 1978. 310p.
Much can be learned about the oil industry in Canada from the story of the founding (in 1925) and development of one of Canada's surviving independent oil companies.

740 **Canadian mineral policy, past and present: the ambiguous legacy.**
David Yudelman. Kingston, Ontario: Centre for Resource Studies, Queen's University, 1985. 176p.
A systematic study of mineral policy through the nineteenth and twentieth centuries. The author identifies the trends over the period and from this base takes a critical look at policy of recent years. Future policy initiatives are recommended.

Transport

General

741 Canadian transportation economics.
A. W. Currie.   Toronto: University of Toronto, 1967. 719p.
A scholarly treatment, to the date of its publication, of the economics of transportation in Canada, whether rail, highway, inland and coastal waterway, ocean, air or pipeline. Still a solid and reliable overview for the student, researcher or general reader.

742 A history of transportation in Canada.
G. P. deT. Glazebrook.   Toronto: McClelland & Stewart, 1964. 2 vols. (Carleton Library, vol. 11).
The classic history of transportation in Canada first published by the Ryerson Press as a volume in *The Relations of Canada and the United States: A Series of Studies Prepared Under the Direction of the Carnegie Endowment for International Peace Division of Economics and History.*

743 Paddles & wheels: everyday life and travel in Canada.
L. M. Grayson, J. Paul Grayson.   Toronto: Oxford University Press, 1974. 192p.
A delightful and informative book which will take the general reader or the student from the era of canoe and snowshoe travel in Canada through to the modern day era of automobiles and trucks. Not meant for the academic reader.

Water

744 **Sailing ships of the Maritimes: an illustrated history of shipping and shipbuilding in the Maritime provinces of Canada 1750-1925.**
Charles A. Armour, Thomas Lackey. Toronto: McGraw-Hill Ryerson, 1975. 224p.
During the period under study Canada had developed a huge shipbuilding industry supplying nearly one-third of all British shipping in the 1860s, and having built over 26,000 ships by the close of the nineteenth century. This work traces the growth and development of shipping and shipbuilding in the Maritimes and shows, by way of text and numerous illustrations, the evolution of ship design.

745 **Bluenose.**
Brian Backman, Phil Backman. Toronto: McClelland & Stewart, 1965. 112p.
A nostalgic, somewhat anecdotal but nonetheless interesting story of Canada's most famous sailing vessel. As the blurb would suggest, this is 'The tale of a ship, her exploits and triumphs that took her to greatness, and of the men who planned her, who built and sailed her . . . and of those who loved her enough to bring her back again'.

746 **Lifeline: the story of the Atlantic ferries and coastal boats.**
Harry Bruce. Toronto: Macmillan, 1977. 249p.
Most of the smaller, as well as many of the larger, communities on the eastern seaboard of Canada are served primarily, if not exclusively, by the ferries and coastal boats which transport goods and people from location to location. This is a readable popular history of the service concentrating on the twentieth century and combining the political/administrative/social aspects into the chronicle. The reader is treated also to a colourful description of the life in coastal communities as well as a portrait of the inhabitants.

747 **Sternwheelers & sidewheelers: the romance of steamdriven paddleboats in Canada.**
Peter Charlebois. Toronto: NC Press, 1978. 142p.
Inland waterway transportation, while belonging to an era fancied today as romantic, was also a vital component of the transportation system in Canada up until the first part of the twentieth century. This illustrated work provides an overview of the rôle and romance of the vessels which were a part of this system. The work is organized by region. It includes a selected reading list and for the real enthusiast includes a listing of still operating paddlewheelers. Various works look at the paddleboats from a regional perspective. A few of these are: Theodore Barris' *Fire canoe: prairie steamboat days revisited* (Toronto: McClelland & Stewart, 1977); Bruce Peel's *Steamboats on the Saskatchewan* (Saskatoon, Saskatchewan: Western Producer, 1972); and, Art Downs' *Paddlewheels on the frontier: the story of British Columbia and Yukon sternwheel steamers* (Sidney, British Columbia: Gray's Publishing, 1972).

748 **The Welland Canals: a comprehensive guide.**
John N. Jackson, Fred A. Addis. St. Catharines, Ontario: Welland
Canals Foundation, 1982. 140p.

The Canal was originally opened in 1829, constructed to by-pass a turbulent portion of
the Niagara River as well as Niagara Falls. Its purpose was to provide a transportation
waterway thus making possible trade and commerce into the inland part of the
continent. The Canal has been a part of the St. Lawrence Seaway since 1959, open for
lake and ocean-going vessels. In 1973 a significant upgrade to the Canal was completed
effectively retiring a significant portion of the original winding Canal. This work is an
illustrated history of the Canal for the general reader. A more scholarly study of the
1973 project can be found in the author's *Welland and the Welland Canal* (Belleville,
Ontario: Mika, 1975). Additional visual materials can be found in Roberta M. Styran
and Robert R. Taylor's *The Welland Canals: the growth of Mr. Merritt's ditch* (Erin,
Ontario: Boston Mills Press, 1988).

749 **Rideau waterway.**
Robert Legget. Toronto: University of Toronto Press, 1986. 2nd ed.
312p.

While the Rideau Canal was first proposed as a secure interior water route for moving
troops for the defence of Canada during the War of 1812, construction was not actually
begun until 1826, and was completed in 1832. When completed the Canal played a
major rôle in the commercial transportation system of the Ottawa and Rideau valley
interiors. Lieutenant Colonel John By was selected to superintend the construction of
the waterway, and operated the Canal until 1856. Much controversy surrounded this
colourful historical figure. Bytown, a small community at the junction of the Rideau
and Ottawa Rivers was named after By. In 1855 the name was changed to Ottawa – the
nation's capital. Today the Rideau Canal is used entirely by pleasure craft and is one of
the most beautiful areas of the country. The interested reader is directed also to the
beautifully illustrated work by Robert Passfield published to celebrate the 150th
anniversary of the Canal entitled *Building the Rideau Canal: a pictorial history*
(Toronto: Fitzhenry & Whiteside/Parks Canada, 1982); or Edward Forbes Bush's
Commercial Navigation on the Rideau Canal, 1832-1961 (Ottawa: National Historic
Parks and Sites Branch, Parks Canada, Environment Canada, 1981); or *The Rideau: a
pictorial history of the waterway* (Brockville, Ontario: Besancourt, 1981).

750 **Canals of Canada.**
Robert F. Legget. Vancouver: David & Charles, 1976. 261p. (Canals
of the World).

An overview history of the development of canals and other waterways in Canada.
Systems discussed include the Chambly Canal, the Rideau Canal, the Trent Canal
system and the St. Lawrence Seaway system to name only a few. Essential reading for
the student or researcher on water transportation in Canada.

751 **The Seaway.**
Robert F. Legget. Toronto: Clarke, Irwin & Co., 1979. 92p.

An informative, illustrated survey of the history of the St. Lawrence Seaway produced
to commemorate the 20th anniversary of the Seaway and the 150th anniversary of the
first Welland Canal. The Seaway was a monumental feat of engineering and
construction which links the five Great Lakes and the St. Lawrence River to the

Atlantic Ocean. Funded by Canada and the United States, the Seaway is today administered by the St. Lawrence Seaway Authority. It is a major contributor to the economic and industrial development of Canada in that it permits economical water transport of goods and raw materials to and from major centres deep within the heart of the continent.

752 **Canadian Pacific: the story of the famous shipping line.**
George Musk. Toronto: Holt Rinehart & Winston, 1981. 272p.

Another important dimension of the history of the multi-modal transportation system created by Canadian Pacific. While the work is not definitive, it does contribute much information and insight into ocean, coastal and inland shipping services in Canada. More than 300 ships are described, ships that played an important rôle in the development of the country.

753 **Sails of the Maritimes: the story of the three- and four-masted cargo schooners of Atlantic Canada 1859-1929.**
John P. Parker. Toronto: McGraw-Hill Ryerson, 1976. 226p.

This presents the story of cargo schooners built in Atlantic Canada during the eighty years of their existence, a period of time extending up to the 1920s, although some did not die out until after the Second World War. Further reading includes: Stanley T. Spicer's *Masters of sail: the era of square-rigged vessels in the Maritime provinces* (Toronto: Ryerson Press, 1968).

754 **The Pacific Empresses: an illustrated history of Canadian Pacific Railway's Empress liners on the Pacific Ocean.**
Robert D. Turner. Victoria, British Columbia: Sono Nis Press, 1981. 290p.

'The steamship service that was developed on this route by the Canadian Pacific was the ultimate extension of the transcontinental railway – the link to the Orient. The Empresses brought tea, silk, spices and produce from the Orient and in return took the products of a growing Canada back. They transported thousands of immigrants, missionaries, dignitaries, travellers, soldiers and businessmen back and forth between the Orient and North America and at the same time contributed carloads of passengers and freight to the railway that was their benefactor'. A beautiful book chronicling a romantic dimension of transportation history.

755 **Wooden ships and iron men: the story of the square-rigged merchant marine of British North America, the ships, their builders and owners, and the men who sailed them.**
Frederick William Wallace. Belleville, Ontario: Mika, 1973. 356p.

This is a reprint of a classic work of maritime history. Told here, by way of anecdotal recollection combined with antiquarian recitation of sailing and ship-building data, is the story of Canadian merchant mariners primarily during the nineteenth century. The work would interest the reader truly addicted to maritime lore and history.

Railways

756 The national dream: the great railway 1871-1881.
Pierre Berton. Toronto: McClelland & Stewart, 1970. 439p.
The companion volume to this work is *The last spike: the great railway 1881-1885* (Toronto: McClelland & Stewart, 1971). Together these two volumes comprise a well researched history of a colourful chapter of Canadian history – the building of the Canadian Pacific Railway. Berton is Canada's premier popular historian and through his works, the railway books in particular, he awoke in Canadians an interest in their own history. A major television docu-drama was developed from the books, and other publications were produced to take advantage of the book's popularity; notable among these was an abridged version of the works entitled: *The national dream/the last spike* (Toronto: McClelland & Stewart, 1974); and an illustrated version entitled: *The great railway: illustrated* (Toronto: McClelland & Stewart, 1972).

757 The Grand Trunk Railway of Canada.
A. W. Currie. Toronto: University of Toronto Press, 1957. 556p.
The Grand Trunk Railway was formerly incorporated in 1858, with the purpose of building a railway from Toronto to Montreal. A companion corporation, the Grand Trunk Railway East was also incorporated to build a rail line from Quebec City to Trois-Pistoles, Quebec. Over time, through additional building projects and the acquisition of smaller lines, the Railway came to be the largest railroad in Canada. Indeed, in 1867 the line was the largest in the world. However, disastrous competition with the Canadian Pacific Railway in the west, by way of the subsidiary Grand Trunk Pacific, combined with bad management, saw the financial collapse of the Railway in 1919 and take over by the federal government, its major creditor. In 1923 it was absorbed into the Canadian National Railways system.

758 The politics of freight rates: the railway freight rate issue in Canada.
Howard Darling. Toronto: McClelland & Stewart, 1980. 258p.
(Canada in Transition: Crises in Political Development).
Few subjects are likely to engage the various regions of Canada in heated debate more than that of the economics and politics of rail freight rates. The rhetoric of the issue is frequently at hand in any discussion of federal/provincial relations, particularly with regard to issues mobilizing provincial (primarily western and maritime) opinion against the federal government or against central Canada. This work presents the history of the freight rate issue and places the problem within the broader context of transport policy.

759 The selling of Canada: the CPR and the beginnings of Canadian tourism.
E. J. Hart. Banff, Alberta: Altitude Publishing, 1983. 180p.
'If we can't export the scenery, we'll import the tourists'. Such was the philosophy which accounted for the development of the Canadian Pacific Railway's tourist operations, its campaigns, and its network of hotel and tourist facilities in the latter years of the nineteenth century. The realization of the CPR's extraordinarily successful and lucrative tourist and settlement programmes amounted also to the first time Canada had been promoted to the rest of the world. The world's view of Canada, then

and today, owes much to the positive and somewhat romantic image first devised by railway publicists, and examined and illustrated in this beautifully produced work.

760   **A history of the Canadian Pacific Railway.**
Harold Adams Innis.   Toronto: University of Toronto Press, 1971. 365p.
There are any number of scholarly and popular histories of the Canadian Pacific Railway. Innis, a distinguished historian and economist, wrote one of the earliest histories of the company, reprinted from the 1923 edition with a scholarly introduction by Peter George. Other works of interest are: Omer Lavallee's *Van Horne's road: an illustrated account of the construction and first years of operation of the Canadian Pacific Transcontinental Railway* (Toronto: Railfare Enterprises, 1981); W. Kaye Lamb's *History of the Canadian Pacific Railway* (New York, London: Macmillan, 1977); and J. Lorne McDougall's *Canadian Pacific: a brief history* (Montreal: McGill University Press, 1968). Of regional interest would be John A. Eagle's *The Canadian Pacific Railway and the development of western Canada, 1896-1914* (Kingston, Ontario; Montreal: McGill-Queen's University Press, 1989); and Robert D. Turner's informative *West of the great divide: an illustrated history of the Canadian Pacific Railway 1880-1986* (Victoria, British Columbia: Sono Nis Press, 1987); and Hugh A. Dempsey's *The CPR west: the iron road and the making of a nation* (Vancouver; Toronto: Douglas & McIntyre, 1984).

761   **Railways of Canada.**
Robert F. Legget.   Vancouver; Toronto: Douglas & McIntyre, 1987. 2nd ed. 255p.
An historical overview of railways in Canada. A good introduction to the topic for the general reader.

762   **The railway game: a study in socio-technological obsolescence.**
J. Lukasiewicz.   Toronto: McClelland & Stewart, 1976. 302p.
A critical examination of Canadian railways. The author provides a general overview of the development of railways in Canada, and examines and explains the origins of the industry's deficiencies. He compares the Canadian railway system, in terms of developments and quality of service, to railways abroad – particularly in Europe and Japan. Finally, he suggests various remedies for the observed deficiencies, including recommendations on forms of organization, financing, technical modernization and long range strategic policy.

763   **Illustrated history of Canadian railways.**
Nick Mika, Helma Mika, Donald M. Wilson.   Belleville, Ontario: Mika, 1986. 288p.
An attractively produced work, illustrated with over 500 photographs, drawings and maps in black and white and colour. This tells the story of rail transportation in Canada from the first railway inaugurated in 1836 through to the building of the Grand Trunk Railway, the Canadian Pacific Railway, the Canadian Northern, the National Transcontinental, the Intercolonial, and the Canadian National Railway. A less handsome work, but also of interest is Robert F. Legget's *Canadian railways in pictures* (Vancouver: David & Charles, 1977).

764 **The Canadian Northern Railway: pioneer road of the northern prairies 1895-1918.**
T. D. Regehr.   Toronto: Macmillan/Maclean-Hunter Press, 1976.
543p. bibliog.

The story of the agricultural colonization of a vast area of the western parkland region of the prairie provinces, as well as the opening of various areas of the mineral belt, were tied up in the history of the Canadian Northern Railway. This well-researched study chronicles the history of this short-lived but vitally important enterprise, and the activities of the two promoters, William MacKenzie and Donald Mann, who built and ran the railroad over its twenty year life. In 1918 transcontinental competition, combined with unprofitable expansion had left the company in debt, primarily to the federal government. In that year the company was nationalized and became a major part of the new publicly owned Canadian National Railways. Includes an extensive bibliography.

765 **History of the Canadian National Railways.**
G. R. Stevens.   New York, London: Macmillan, 1973. 538p.
(Railroads of America).

Canadian National Railways had its origins in the amalgamation of five financially troubled railways during the period 1917-23; these were the Grand Trunk, the Grand Trunk Pacific, the Intercolonial, the Canadian Northern and the National Transcontinental. Today the publicly owned crown corporation is the longest railway system in North America. This work is a popular survey of the history and development of the line, written in the formula style of the series. The interested reader will also wish to read a larger two–volume history by Stevens entitled *Canadian National Railways* (Toronto: Clarke Irwin, 1960, 1962) which chronicles the histories of the companies which ultimately formed the CNR from 1836 to 1922. Patrick Dorin's illustrated *The Canadian National Railways' story* (Saanichton, British Columbia: Hancock House, 1975) also complements the Stevens volumes.

Air

766 **Wings over the West: Russ Baker & the rise of Pacific Western Airlines.**
John Condit.   Madeira Park, British Columbia: Harbour, 1984. 235p.

This is the story of Pacific Western Airlines, today Canadian Airlines International, Canada's second largest commercial carrier, and of Russell Baker, a pioneer aviator and bush pilot, who began the company and guided it through its early years.

767 **Canada in space.**
Lydia Dotto.   Toronto: Irwin Publishing, 1987. 371p.

A well-known science writer looks at the US/international manned space programme but from the perspective of Canadian involvement, including the examination of: the Canadian astronaut programme; the development and rôle of the Canadarm (a remotely controlled cargo manipulator) aboard the space shuttle; Canada's scientific and technological involvement in the shuttle programme and the space station; and the potential for development of Canadian scientific research, commerce and industry during the space station era. Of interest also is Doris H. Jelly's *Canada: 25 years in space* (Montreal: Polyscience Publications/National Museum of Science and Technology, 1988); and Theodore Hertz and Irvine Paghis' *Spacebound* (Ottawa: Minister of Supply and Services Canada, 1982).

768 **125 years of Canadian aeronautics: a chronology 1840-1965.**
G. A. Fuller, J. A. Griffin, K. M. Molson. Willowdale, Ontario: Canadian Aviation Historical Society, 1983. 328p.

A chronological table of dates marking significant aeronautical events occurring within Canada or Newfoundland (the latter administered by Britain during some of this period), and achievements of Canadians in the field of aeronautics elsewhere. The first date, 10 August 1840 marks the first aerial voyage (in a balloon) in what is now Canada, although almost fifty years earlier a Canadian, William B. Jarvis, of Upper Canada, witnessed the ascension of Vincent Lunardi's balloon on 15 September 1784.

769 **Deregulation of the Canadian airline industry: a charade: the missing theory, the distorted facts.**
Fred Lazar. Toronto: Key Porter Books, 1984. 155p. bibliog.

The present debate of airline regulation *versus* deregulation is more than a decade old in Canada, and was sparked in large measure by the deregulation of the US industry in the late 1970s. This analysis by a proponent of regulation presents arguments supporting his position. Considerable space is devoted to a review of the literature relating to the debate. The interested reader may also wish to view *Perspectives on Canadian airline regulation*, edited by G. B. Reschenthaler and B. Roberts (Montreal: Butterworth for the Institute for Research on Public Policy, 1979).

770 **Voyageurs of the air: a history of civil aviation in Canada 1858-1967.**
J. R. K. Main. Ottawa: Queen's Printer, 1967. 397p.

This work was commissioned by the federal Department of Transport as a centennial project. Here a veteran flier, and senior government official, relates the story of aviation from the era of ballooning, to the pioneering period of the early twentieth century with its bush pilots, to the advances occasioned by the two World Wars, to the era of modern aviation. A readable work which not only chronicles the major advances and the romanticism of early flying, but also documents and credits the ground–based advances such as airport development, weather reporting, navigation technology, government aviation policy, and so forth. Another work of interest which concentrates on the earlier pioneering era of aviation (1907-30) is Frank Ellis's *Canada's flying heritage* (Toronto: University of Toronto Press, 1968). Also recommended is Larry Milberry's general overview history, told in prose and photograph, entitled *Aviation in Canada* (Toronto: McGraw-Hill Ryerson, 1979).

771 **Pioneering in Canadian air transport.**
K. M. Molson. [Altona, Manitoba]: D.W. Friesen & Sons for James Richardson & Sons, 1974. 315p.

The story of the transportation of goods to the more remote regions of Canada, especially the north, is in large measure the story of early aviation in Canada. This work chronicles this enterprise, in prose and photograph, and looks particularly at the corporate history of Western Canada Airways, (founded in 1926 by grain merchant

James A. Richardson), and its successor Canadian Airways. While the work is a commissioned history, it adds much to our understanding of early aviation in Canada.

772 **Canadian aircraft since 1909.**
K. M. Molson, H. A. Taylor. Stittsville, Ontario: Canada's Wings, 1982. 530p.
For the real enthusiast, this is a history of the individual major aircraft companies and their products in Canada. The book deals with fixed-wing powered aircraft that have been built for commercial sale, or intended for commercial sale, up to 1979. Considerable technical detail is included.

773 **Canada's National Aviation Museum.**
Kenneth M. Molson. Ottawa: National Aviation Museum, National Museum of Science and Technology, 1988. 291p.
The story of how the National Aviation Museum came to be, and indirectly much of the story of aviation in Canada.

774 **It seems like only yesterday: Air Canada: the first 50 years.**
Philip Smith. Toronto: McClelland & Stewart, 1986. 368p.
Air Canada was founded in 1937 with the name Trans-Canada Airlines. Until the recent privatization of the airline, it was 100% owned by the Canadian government as a crown corporation. In this regard, and as the author indicates 'Air Canada succeeded despite its government ownership, not by virtue of any advantage this conferred'. This work tells the story from the days of the bush pilots and corporate visionaries to the vast and multifaceted business of today, replete with accounts of the strategies, negotiations and corporate manoeuvring which resulted in the growth and development of the company.

775 **The politics of Canada's airlines from Diefenbaker to Mulrony.**
Garth Stevenson. Toronto: University of Toronto Press, 1987. 236p. (State and Economic Life, vol. 9).
Historically, transportation policy has preoccupied Canadian policy makers – whether relating to water, railway or road transportation. The objective of the author is to provide a comprehensive analysis of domestic air transport policy, examining the technological and social changes that have influenced policy, including how public policy has in turn contributed to changes to the industry. Stevenson outlines the geographical, technical, legislative and institutional backdrops to air policy, and then presents, by way of case studies, specific issues in domestic air policy, including among others: the relationship between the two major carriers; the evolution of air policy in Quebec; and the influence of trends toward competition and deregulation. A comprehensive work directed to the informed reader.

776　Canada's aviation pioneers: 50 years of McKee Trophy winners.
Alice Gibson Sutherland.　Toronto: McGraw-Hill Ryerson, 1978.
304p.
The McKee trophy dates back to 1927, commemorating the first trans-Canada seaplane flight made in September 1926, by Captain James Dalzell McKee. The intent of the award was to recognize those who contributed to the advancement of aviation in Canada and this collection of profiles of the winners constitutes a history of Canadian aviation.

Road

777　Cars of Canada.
Hugh Durnford, Glenn Baechler.　Toronto: McClelland & Stewart, 1973. 384p.
This is a comprehensive, illustrated history of Canadian cars and the Canadian automotive industry. For the purposes of the study a car was Canadian if it met three of these four criteria: designed in Canada; built in Canada; built by a Canadian-owned company; having a Canadian name. A work equally appealing for the general reader as well as the automotive authority.

778　The story of Canadian roads.
Edwin C. Guillet.　Toronto: University of Toronto Press, 1966. 246p.
In seeking to connect two oceans by road, Canada faced any number of land-related problems such as extended mountain ranges, permafrost, swamps, and vast distances through forests. This scholarly study, profusely illustrated, documents road building, and the various movements, most notably the Canadian Good Roads Association, which promoted roadways in Canada. A fascinating, and at the same time, entertaining work.

Labour Movements
and Trade Unions

Reference

779 **Directory of labour organizations in Canada = Répertoire des organisations de travailleurs et travailleuses au Canada.**
Bureau of Labour Information = Bureau de renseignements sur le travail. Ottawa: Minister of Labour, Government of Canada, 1980- . annual.
The *Directory* contains brief, statistical data on union membership, and an alphabetical list of unions, congresses and other labour organizations. Also included are the names and addresses of principal officers, the titles of union publications, upcoming conventions and the geographic distribution of union local branches in Canada.

780 **The labour companion: a bibliography of Canadian labour history based on materials printed from 1950 to 1975.**
G. Douglas Vaisey. Halifax, Nova Scotia: Committee on Canadian Labour History, 1980. 126p.
A 'working' bibliography of items in the areas of labour history, industrial relations and related social studies, published between 1950 and 1975. Entries are in alphabetical order, with a subject index.

General

781 **On strike: six key labour struggles in Canada 1919-1949.**
Edited by Irving Abella. Toronto: James Lewis & Samuel, 1974.
196p.

It was the editor's purpose to introduce the reader to the significant and colourful events of the Canadian labour past. The period covered was the most turbulent in Canadian labour history. The strikes examined were important both as turning points in the labour movement but also as significant for their political impact. They include the Winnipeg General Strike of 1919, the Estevan Miners Strike of 1931, the Stratford Furniture Workers Strike of 1933, the Oshawa General Motors Strike of 1937, the Ford Workers Strike of 1945 and the Asbestos Workers Strike of 1949.

782 **Nationalism, communism, and Canadian labour: the CIO, the Communist party, and the Canadian Congress of Labour 1935-1956.**
Irving Martin Abella. Toronto: University of Toronto Press, 1973.
256p.

This is a study of the interaction of the Canadian Congress of Labour and the C10 (Congress of International Organizations) in which they both struggled to rid themselves of their Communist-dominated affiliates, and, in the case of the Congress, sought to resist aggressive interference from American unions. Within the context of this interaction the work deals with the history of the labour movement during the period.

783 **The Canadian worker in the twentieth century.**
Edited by Irving Abella and David Millar. Toronto: Oxford
University Press, 1978. 310p.

An anthology of documents compiled for the purpose of reconstructing, from first-hand accounts, the daily lives of Canadian workers. In selecting materials the guiding principle was to give preference to eyewitness accounts of the activities of work, home, and leisure rather than the 'official' documents of labour history. The material also provides a variety of workers' settings, such as the home, the workplace, the bush camp, mine and homestead, the small town and the city. A similar anthology was prepared by Michael S. Cross and is entitled *The workingman in the nineteenth century* (Toronto: Oxford University Press, 1974). These collections are valuable and interesting supplements to general studies on working class history.

784 **Canadian labour law: a comprehensive text.**
George W. Adams. Aurora, Ontario: Canada Law Book, 1985. 983p.

A general text emphasizing and illustrating the common labour relations principles underlying Canadian labour law from all Canadian jurisdictions (provincial and territorial). Of interest also to the informed reader is Innis Christie's *Employment law in Canada* (Toronto: Butterworths, 1980) and James E. Dorsey's *Canada labour relations board: federal law and practice* (Toronto: Carswell, 1983).

785 **Labour pains: women's work in crisis.**
Pat Armstrong. Toronto: Women's Press, 1984. 273p.
The author provides a detailed examination of the crises within the labour force with the emphasis on women's work, both in the labour force and in the household. Various sectors are examined, and in general a pessimistic future is presented. An excellent companion volume by Patricia Connelly entitled *Last hired, first fired: women and the Canadian work force* (Toronto: The Women's Press, 1978), provides an historical context, based on a Marxian orientation, of the involvement of women in the Canadian work force from 1901 to the 1970s.

786 **A working majority: what women must do for pay.**
Pat Armstrong, Hugh Armstrong. Ottawa: Canadian Advisory Council on the Status of Women, 1983. 280p.
By way of interviews with women holding a wide range of jobs, complemented by other research techniques, the authors investigated the quality of women's work in Canada. The result is a description of what it is like to be a woman working for pay in Canada in the 1980s. The results of the investigation were not encouraging – low wages, high unemployment, differential treatment in the work place, poor working conditions, displacement through microtechnology, etc., all contributed to a depressed outlook. The interested researcher is also directed to another work by the authors entitled *The double ghetto: Canadian women and their segregated work* (Toronto: McClelland & Stewart, 1978).

787 **Labour law and industrial relations in Canada.**
H.W. Arthurs, D.D. Carter, H.J. Glasbeek. Toronto: Butterworths, 1984. 316p.
'An overview of all aspects of Canadian labour law, and, to some extent, of its social, economic and political context'. The work is aimed at an audience of lawyers, personnel administrators, general management, labour management, and students.

788 **Putting the Charter to work: designing a constitutional labour code.**
David M. Beatty. Kingston, Ontario; Montreal: McGill-Queen's University Press, 1987. 252p.
The entrenchment of a Charter of Rights and Freedoms in the constitutional order of the Canadian government has affected the body of law in Canada by introducing a set of formal, procedural requirements which qualify the legal authority of the state. The author works through the implications of the Charter with regard to the labour laws of the country. In the process the study indicates the impact which various interest groups will now have on the everyday life of working Canadians.

789 **Fools and wise men.**
David J. Bercuson. Toronto: McGraw-Hill Ryerson, 1978. 300p.
The One Big Union (OBU) was established as a post-First World War outgrowth of the response to working conditions, primarily in the mines, logging camps and various industrial enterprises of western Canada. It grew from a desire of these groups to secede from such bodies as the American Federation of Labour and the Trades and Labor Congress of Canada, and form a new Canadian industrial union. The OBU was launched in June of 1919 during the same period as the Winnipeg General Strike. Initially it enjoyed great success. At its peak over 50,000 workers were members. By

the mid-1920s counterattacks by the craft unions, by the Communist Party, by governments and by employers resulted in rifts in the leadership and among the members. By 1923 the membership had been reduced to under 5,000. A fascinating interlude in Canadian labour history.

790 **Confrontation at Winnipeg: labour, industrial relations, and the General Strike.**
David Jay Bercuson. Montreal: McGill-Queen's University Press, 1974. 227p.

One of Canada's leading labour historians analyses the industrial background to the Winnipeg General Strike of 1919 – Canada's best known labour confrontation and a pivotal point in the labour movement. This work traces the worsening labour-management conditions of the pre- and post-First World War period which, combined with the impact of depression and war, was manifested by a rapidly rising cost of living and dreadful working conditions, and the desire for increased political power on the part of organized labour, set the stage for the strike. The interested reader should also note the following works: D.C. Masters' *The Winnipeg General Strike* (Toronto: University of Toronto Press, 1950); Norman Penner's *Winnipeg 1919: the strikers' own history of the Winnipeg General Strike* (Toronto: J. Lorimer, 1975); and, Kenneth McNaught & David J. Bercuson's *The Winnipeg Strike: 1919* (Don Mills, Ontario: Longman, 1974).

791 **Union sisters: women in the labour movement.**
Edited by Linda Briskin, Lynda Yanz. Toronto: The Women's Press, 1983. 421p.

Union sisters documents the struggles and triumphs of the movement of union women, providing some direction to women and unions in the struggle to defend the interests of working people. The work provides an overview of the contemporary situation of women in the workplace, looks at particular issues such as affirmative action, microtechnology, sexual harassment, as well as discussing the obstacles facing women in organizing unions, and recounting the experiences of women unionists. It also examines the relationship between the trade union movement and other women's movements such as the daycare movement, political parties, etc. The interested reader is also directed to: Barbara K. Latham and Roberta J. Pazdro's *Not just pin money: selected essays on the history of women's work in British Columbia* (Victoria, British Columbia: Camosun College, 1984); Jennifer Penney's *Hard earned wages: women fighting for better work* (Toronto: The Women's Press, 1983); and, *Women at work: Ontario, 1850-1930* (Toronto: Canadian Women's Educational Press, 1974).

792 **The anatomy of poverty: the condition of the working class in Montreal 1897-1929.**
Terry Copp. Toronto: McClelland & Stewart, 1974. 192p. (Canadian Social History Series).

The definition of 'working class' as used in this work covers two-thirds of the population of Montreal who received wages, rather than salaries or who were self-employed. This is a watershed socio-economic study which examines the conditions of this group during a period which is popularly considered to be a time of Canadian prosperity and expansion.

793 **'An impartial umpire': industrial relations and the Canadian state 1900-1911.**
Paul Craven.   Toronto: University of Toronto Press, 1980. 386p.
(State in Economic Life, vol. 3).

An analysis of Canadian labour policy, and particularly the policy and practice of state intervention in industrial relations, in what was a critical period of the labour movement – the first decade of the century. Central in this study is the rôle of Mackenzie King, primarily in relation to his activities in the Department of Labour and his rôle in moulding Canada's official position in the relations between capital and labour. Key in this regard was the legislative activity which led to the passage of the Industrial Disputes Investigation Act, legislation which ultimately set the tone of the Canadian method of state intervention in labour disputes.

794 **Trade unions in Canada 1812-1902.**
Eugene Forsey.   Toronto: University of Toronto Press, 1982. 600p.

A somewhat encyclopaedic, but nonetheless valuable, account of the evolution of trade unions in Canada. In the words of the author, the study 'presents few opinions or arguments, and attempts few analyses'. Commissioned by the Canadian Labour Congress as its centennial project the work does make a substantial contribution to the literature by providing the foundation of fact and documentation for the further study of Canadian labour history. It presents profiles of all unions of the period – craft, industrial, local, regional, national, and international – as well as the Knights of Labor and the local and national central organizations. It provides a complete account of unions and organizations in every province including their formation and function, time and place of operation, as well as any political activity in which they were engaged.

795 **The history of the labour movement in Quebec.**
Montreal: Black Rose, 1987. 299p.

A useful summary of labour history in Quebec over 150 years. Includes commentary on the state of the economy, the political situation, the state of development of the trade unions and the nature of workers' political actions during each major historical period. Written from a left-wing perspective.

796 **Canadian labour in politics.**
Gad Horowitz.   Toronto: University of Toronto Press, 1968. 273p.

Based on the files of the federal New Democratic Party and the archives of the Canadian Labour Congress Political Education Department, the author studies the relationship between the labour movement and the socialist party in Canada. He traces that relationship from the birth of modern industrial unionism.

797 **Industrial relations in Canada.**
Stuart Jamieson.   Toronto: Macmillan, 1973. rev. ed. 156p. bibliog.

A revised and somewhat enlarged edition of a classic survey of the development of industrial relations in Canada. A good introduction to the general or informed reader touching on the origin and growth of the Canadian labour movement, the nature of Canadian unionism, a survey of labour unrest and industrial conflict from 1900 to 1972, and an analysis of changing and evolving government labour legislation and administrative policies.

798 **Organized labour and pressure politics: the Canadian Labour Congress 1956-1968.**
David Kwavnick. Montreal; London: McGill-Queen's University Press, 1972. 287p.
The author examines the origins, rôle, development, activities and effectiveness of the Canadian Labour Congress within the framework of the operative factors and basic determinants of interest group dynamics. A work for the informed reader.

799 **Labour-management cooperation in Canada.**
Toronto: Published by the University of Toronto Press in cooperation with the Royal Commission on the Economic Union and Development Prospects for Canada and the Canadian Government Publishing Centre, Supply and Services Canada, 1986. 205p.
This is the first in a series of four volumes dealing with labour markets and labour relations in Canada, included as part of the collected research of the Royal Commission on the Economic Union and Development Prospects for Canada. This series deals with: the current state of labour-management cooperation in Canada, with an assessment of prospects for a less adversarial labour-relations climate; aspects of industrial relations (union growth and development, strikes, collective bargaining, etc.), with emphasis on the rôle of public policy; and, changes in the Canadian labour market. Other titles in the series are: *Canadian labour relations*; *Work and pay: the Canadian labour market*; and, *Adapting to change: labour market adjustment in Canada*.

800 **Labour/Le Travail.**
St. John's, Newfoundland: Department of History, Memorial University of Newfoundland, 1976- . bi-annual.
Scholarly articles on Canadian labour studies, both contemporary and historical. Includes book reviews. For the reader interested in the views of organized labour in Canada, refer to the publication *Canadian Labour* (Ottawa: Canadian Labour Congress, 1956-).

801 **Canada's unions.**
Robert Laxer. Toronto: James Lorimer, 1976. 341p.
Laxer examines the Canadian labour movement, with a focus on Ontario, during the 1970s. His thesis highlights two merging components – nationalism and militancy; the former is examined within the context of the rapid growth of independent Canadian unions, the latter within the context of an emerging new leadership coming not from the traditional manufacturing and industrial unions, but from public service workers, particularly teachers, hospital workers and government employees. Introductory and concluding sections place Canadian unions within an historical context as well as within the context of Canadian political economy.

802 **The long winding road: Canadian labour in politics.**
Morden Lazarus. Vancouver: Boag Foundation, 1977. 103p.
A slight but personal work outlining labour's relationship with politics, political parties and politicians from the 1870s to the establishment of the New Democratic Party in 1961. A work for the uninformed reader. The serious researcher is directed to Martin

Robin's comprehensive *Radical politics and Canadian labour, 1880-1930* (Kingston, Ontario: Queen's University, Industrial Relations Centre, 1968).

803   **The trade union movement of Canada 1827-1959.**
Charles Lipton.   Toronto: NC Press, 1978. 4th ed. 387p.
A classic comprehensive history of Canadian trade unionism.

804   **Trade unions in Canada: their development and functioning.**
H.A. Logan.   Toronto: Macmillan, 1948. 639p.
A classic of Canadian labour history, although because it is now quite dated, should be read in conjunction with other titles in this section.

805   **Work in the Canadian context: continuity despite change.**
Edited by Katherina Lundy, Barbara Warme.   Toronto: Butterworths, 1981. 392p.
This anthology has as its purpose the examination of various work dimensions as well as the differentiation of issues and characteristics exclusive to Canada from those common to all industrial nations. This collection would be most useful to the informed or academic reader.

806   **The company store: James Bryson McLachlan and the Cape Breton coal miners 1900-1925.**
John Mellor.   Toronto: Doubleday, 1983. 362p. bibliog.
The story of the Cape Breton miners is a shameful and sordid chapter of Canadian history. Miners worked in the most disheartening of circumstances with pitiful wages, backbreaking toil, long hours, few basic safety measures, and degrading labour practices. Forced to buy food and other necessities from company stores, the miner and his family were effectively slaves in a feudal system. The author chronicles the rising militancy of the miners as led by James Bryson McLachlan, a Scottish immigrant miner, and their struggles against the mine owners and government establishment for better working conditions and terms of employment. A well written but disturbing book.

807   **We stood together: first-hand accounts of dramatic events in Canada's labour past.**
Gloria Montero.   Toronto: James Lorimer, 1979. 261p.
Ten major events in Canadian labour history are recalled by those who participated, and they are recounted in vivid journalistic style. Events range from the Winnipeg General Strike of 1919, through to the Canadian Seamen's Strike of 1949, to the Asbestos Miners' strike of 1978. Photographs add to the work.

808   **Working people.**
Desmond Morton, Terry Copp.   Ottawa: Deneau & Greenberg, 1980. 349p.
A chronicle of the development over 150 years of working class movements in Canada. The book has over 170 illustrations and is enhanced by a comprehensive, annotated section of further reading.

Labour Movements and Trade Unions. General

809   **Labour economics in Canada.**
Sylvia Ostry, Mahmood A. Zaidi.   Toronto: Macmillan, 1979. 418p.
There are any number of works which deal with the subject of labour economics or labour market theory in Canada. In addition to the above the interested researcher or student might look at Stephen Peitchinis' *The Canadian labour market* (Toronto: Oxford University Press, 1975). A more recent introductory textbook of interest is Byron Eastman's *Labour market theory and the Canadian experience* (Toronto: Harcourt Brace Jovanovich, 1987).

810   **The character of class struggle: essays in Canadian working-class history, 1850-1985.**
Edited by Bryan D. Palmer.   Toronto: McClelland & Stewart, 1986.
239p. (Canadian Social History Series).
An anthology of essays which collectively attempt to deal with the evolving nature of class struggle in Canada. The transformation is discussed within the contexts of economic and political developments with individual essays focusing on specific aspects of class struggle such as regional differences, gender, trade union leadership, industry specific conflict, etc. See also other collections such as: W.J.C. Cherwinski and Gregory S. Kealey's *Lectures in Canadian labour and working-class history* (St. John's, Newfoundland: Committee on Canadian Labour History & New Hogtown Press, 1985); and, Gregory Kealey and Peter Wallian's *Essays in Canadian working class history* (Toronto: McClelland & Stewart, 1976).

811   **Working-class experience: the rise and reconstitution of Canadian labour, 1800-1980.**
Bryan D. Palmer.   Toronto: Butterworth, 1983. 347p.
Palmer seeks to portray the collective experience of Canadian workers; to provide, through synthesis, a unified portrait of working class Canadians in their communities, with their families, as well as in the union halls and as represented by political parties. The emphasis is on the 'totality of the working-class experience'.

812   **Collective agreement arbitration in Canada.**
Earl Edward Palmer.   Toronto: Butterworths, 1983.
2nd ed. 805p.
A *Supplement* to this work was published in 1986. Of interest primarily to lawyers and human resource specialists, this work deals with the law and established practices in the areas of employment, grievance arbitration, collective agreements, employee and employer rights and obligations, relations with unions and union activity, and liabilities. A parallel work, of interest to the same audience, is Donald Brown and David Beatty's *Canadian labour arbitration* (Agincourt, Ontario: Canada Law Book Limited, 1977).

813   **Labour and capital in Canada 1650-1860.**
H. Clare Pentland.   Toronto: James Lorimer, 1981. 280p.
A seminal work of scholarship which was published posthumously from the manuscript of the author's doctoral dissertation. This work deals with the emergence of the Canadian industrial working class. It traces the evolution of the labour supply in colonial Canada, discussing the question of early slavery, indentured and convict

labour, pre-industrial labour, as well as the skilled artisan. Although Pentland himself denied being influenced by Marxism, it is clear that his work can be so characterized. A thoughtful introduction to the book by Paul Phillips comments on the life and writings of the author.

814   **Labour relations and the collective bargaining cycle.**
Gerald E. Phillips.   Toronto: Butterworths, 1981. 2nd ed. 333p.
Originally published in 1977 under the title *The practice of labour relations and collective bargaining in Canada.* This is a readable introduction to the practice of labour relations in Canada, although included is considerable detail on the historical and legal aspects of collective bargaining. The reader is introduced to various topics, including: the collective bargaining process; practices and institutions that influence employees, for example labour market trends, labour standards, labour policy and trade unionism. A similar text focusing somewhat more on industrial relations and less on actual collective bargaining is John Crispo's *The Canadian industrial relations system* (Toronto: McGraw-Hill Ryerson, 1978). A recent text book of interest is Alton Craig's *The system of industrial relations in Canada* (Scarborough, Ontario: Prentice-Hall, 1986).

815   **Women and work: inequality in the labour market.**
Paul Phillips, Erin Phillips.   Toronto: James Lorimer, 1983. 205p.
(Canadian Issues Series).
Here is a report card as to the progress made by women in the paid work force (the book does not deal with work in the home) since the 1970 report of the Royal Commission on the Status of Women in Canada. The report is not a positive one. The authors discuss such questions as the reasons why women have not been able to acquire the skills and behaviour patterns that are valued in the marketplace, or why social organization, attitudes and institutions wittingly or unwittingly discriminate against women. The authors also analyse the contemporary market situation with regard to the challenges and opportunities for women; two areas are given attention, the impact of the new microelectronic technology on the work place and the participation of women in the union movement.

816   **The condition of the working class in Toronto – 1900-1921.**
Michael J. Piva.   Ottawa: University of Ottawa Press, 1979. 190p.
bibliog. (Cahiers d'histoire de l'Université d'Ottawa, vol. 9).
The period under study was unquestionably one of growth and domestic prosperity for Canada. However, examination indicates that the wealth generated was not evenly distributed. Piva examines the standard of living of blue-collar workers in Toronto (Toronto and Montreal were the two most industrialized centres in Canada), including analyses of wage rates, housing, public health, and employment patterns.The work inevitably deals also with a number of social and political reform movements. The work complements Terry Copp's *The anatomy of poverty: the condition of the working class in Montreal 1897-1928* (Toronto: McClelland & Steward, 1974).

817 **Radical politics and Canadian labour 1880-1930.**
Martin Robin. Kingston, Ontario: Industrial Relations Centre, Queen's University, 1968. 321p.
Prior to the appearance of this work there had been little scholarship on the relationship of unions and socialist politics. Indeed, there was an impression that prior to the formation of the Co-operative Commonwealth Federation unions had only a cursory involvement with socialist political parties. Three forms of radical politics are examined: socialism or the ideology and structure of the early socialist movements; labourism or the attempts from time to time to launch a labour party; and syndicalism or the opposition to electoral political action in favour of the general strike or revolutionary industrual unionism.

818 **Saturday's stepchildren: Canadian women in business.**
Sybil Shack. Toronto: Faculty of Education, University of Toronto, 1977. 184p.
The author reports on conversations with over 150 men and women and from this distills a picture of working women in Canada. Among the questions and issues raised are: equal pay for work of equal value; pension and insurance benefits; day care; recognition of dignity and worth; and advancement of women into positions of authority.

819 **From contact to contract: a study of labour relations in Canada.**
Trevor R. Smith, Diane M. Smith. Toronto: D.C. Heath, 1977. 71p.
A popular and personal description of the collective bargaining process in Canada. A useful introduction for the general reader but too simplistic for the labour relations specialist or professional.

820 **Strike!**
Walter Stewart. Toronto: McClelland & Stewart, 1977. 224p.
A noted journalist examines industrial relations in Canada particularly the adversarial nature of the system leading, as so often is the case, to job actions and strikes. The author is sympathetic to the union movement but, in general, is critical of the adversarial system. Despite exploring some models in other countries, Stewart makes few useful recommendations for change. Generally a worthwhile book for both the informed and uninformed reader.

821 **Reconcilable differences: new directions in Canadian labour law.**
Paul Weiler. Toronto: Carswell, 1980. 335p.
Drawing from his experience as the first Chairman of the British Columbia Labour Board this Harvard professor attempts to examine various aspects of Canadian labour law and presents principles which should be pursued when governments confront the need for policy in areas of industrial relations. The author begins each section with a real-life labour dispute which illuminates a particular policy dilemma. Given the subject matter, the author presents the material in a most readable manner.

Statistics

822 **Bibliography of federal data sources excluding Statistics Canada.**
Ottawa: Statistics Canada, User Services Division, Reference Products
Section, 1982. 189p.
This brings together, for the first time, sources of social and economic data produced
on a regular basis by federal departments and agencies. This work, together with the
Statistics Canada catalogue, provide the key to locating federally-produced data.

823 **Historical catalogue of Statistics Canada publications 1918-1980.**
Ottawa: Statistics Canada, User Services Division, 1982. 337p.
Knowledge of the corpus of publications produced and available from Statistics Canada
is absolutely essential for those engaged in research requiring statistical compilations.
This catalogue provides, a complete record of all the catalogued publications of
Statistics Canada and the Dominion Bureau of Statistics. It has been designed as an aid
for researchers, librarians and those whose work requires searches for statistical data.

824 **Historical statistics of Canada.**
Edited by F.H. Leacy. Ottawa: Statistics Canada, 1983. 2d ed. [n.p.]
This is a compilation of economic, social and political statistical data, including some
descriptive information for the period from Confederation (1867) to approximately
1975. The volume is divided into twenty-one sections, each representing a field.
Sections include a brief descriptive text with bibliographical information relating to
sources of information and data. This text is followed by statistical tables. Researchers
are advised that some series of information in the first edition have been dropped from
the second edition. Also, the descriptive texts and the bibliographic references have
been substantively reduced between editions. Researchers may thus also wish to access
the first compilation, edited by M.C. Urquhart and K.A.H. Buckley.

825 **Perspectives Canada.**
Ottawa: Office of the Senior Advisor on Integration, Statistics Canada, 1980-
This series was intended to provide a variety of perspectives on core social and economic features of Canadian life – features such as health, education, rights and property. Each topic was supported by relevant statistics. Publication has been suspended but available volumes are useful as reflections of the characteristics of Canadian life at the time.

826 **Statistics Canada catalogue 1987-1988.**
Ottawa: Minister of Supply and Services Canada, 1988. 137p.
Previously referred to as the *Current publications index*. The *Catalogue*, produced regularly, is the official listing of 'Statistics Canada' publications. Supplemented between editions, it is essential for those requiring statistical information. Bibliographical information relating to publications of Statistics Canada is also made available through *Canadiana, the national bibliography* (q.v.).

Environment

Architecture

827 **No mean city.**
Eric Arthur. Toronto: University of Toronto Press, 1965. 280p.
A book on the origins and early architectural history of Toronto. This leading architectural historian begins his study with the prehistory of the Toronto area and concludes his examination at the end of the nineteenth century. The work is profusely illustrated. It also includes brief essays on 'The architectural profession in the nineteenth century', which incorporates brief biographical sketches on practicing architects, and 'The origin of street names in Toronto' with a listing of names and their significance.

828 **Contemporary Canadian architecture: the mainstream and beyond.**
William Bernstein, Ruth Cawker. Toronto: Fitzhenry & Whiteside, 1988. 2nd ed. 216p.
This book forms an important contribution to the literature of Canadian architecture. The authors initiate an informed discussion about modern architecture in Canada by examining selected projects, which were major public commissions. The six sections of this book are devoted to a number of these projects, one of which is the new National Gallery in Ottawa. The work is illustrated with photographs and architectural plans. See also the authors' *Building with words: Canadian architects on architecture* (Toronto: Coach House Press, 1981).

829 **Gothic revival in Canadian architecture.**
Mathilde Brosseau. Ottawa: Minister of Supply and Services Canada, 1980. 208p. bibliog. (Canadian Historic Sites: Occasional Papers in Archaeology and History, vol. 25).
'This study deals with the evolution of Gothic Revival in Canadian architecture. It goes back to the origins of the style, marks its arrival in the country and traces its four

mutations ranging over the greater part of the 19th century and even into the first decades of the 20th century'. The main text is followed by 124 plates, along with a commentary, illustrating examples of the style in Canada. A bibliography is included.

830   **Second Empire style in Canadian architecture.**
Christina Cameron, Janet Wright.   Ottawa: National Historic Parks and Sites Branch, 1980. 247p. (Canadian Historic Sites: Occasional Papers in Archaeology and History, vol. 24).
Describes the Second Empire architectural style, which is recognized by its characteristic mansard or broken roof, and the opulent sculptural ornamentation. This style of architecture was originally associated with the court of Emperor Napoleon III of France, and reached Canada via the United States and to a lesser extent, via England. Many major public and institutional buildings erected in Canada during the 1870s and 1880s exemplify Second Empire design. However, by the end of the nineteenth century this architectural style, was no longer favoured by Canadian architects and builders.

831   **The Canadian Architect.**
Don Mills, Ontario: Southam Business Publications Ltd., 1955- . monthly.
Contains articles relating to architects and the aesthetics of architecture in Canada and includes items on related fields such as urban planning.

832   **Early Canadian court houses.**
Compiled by Margaret Carter.   Ottawa: National Historic Parks and Sites Branch, Parks Canada, Environment Canada, 1983. 258p. (Studies in Archaeology, Architecture and History).
Examines the early Canadian court houses against the background of the court systems they were built to serve. The author notes the variety of designs and methods of construction employed in various parts of the country during its formative years. She comments on the prominence of these buildings and their rôles performed within their respective communities. Buildings are grouped and described by region.

833   **Pioneer churches.**
John De Visser, Harold Kalman.   New York: W. W. Norton, 1976. 192p. bibliog.
This book examines the development of the church architecture of pioneers from 1600 to the early 20th century. The authors note that the study of their architecture can provide an insight into the pioneers, their society and the values they held. The beautiful photographs and reproduced plans and drawings are accompanied by an authoritative text. A full bibliography is included.

834   **Canadian architecture 1960-1970.**
Carol Moore Ede.   Toronto: Burns & MacEachern, 1971. 264p.
This work examines a number of buildings which the compiler claims make a great step forward in interpreting new needs without negating architecture as a visual art. The twenty-four projects depicted and discussed are arranged by function: educational,

public, commercial, industrial, religious, and residential. This work is more interesting for its photographs of the projects identified than for its commentary on these projects. Biographies are provided of the eighteen architects represented.

835 **The architecture of Arthur Erickson.**
Arthur Erickson.   Vancouver; Toronto: Douglas & McIntyre, 1988.
228p.

This renowned architect examines and comments on his own work. Erickson has been honoured with numerous honourary degrees and has been awarded the Auguste Perret Award, International Union of Architects (1974), the Companion of the Order of Canada (1981), the Gold Medal of the Royal Architectural Institute of Canada (1984), the Chicago Architecture Award (1984), the Gold Medal of the Académie Française d'Architecture (1984), and the Gold Medal of the American Institute of Architects (1986). The work is attractively illustrated with photographs and plans. See also Edith Iglauer's *Seven stones: a portrait of Arthur Erickson, architect* ([Vancouver]; Seattle: Harbour Publishing; University of Washington Press, 1981).

836 **Building Canada: an architectural history of Canadian life.**
Alan Gowans.   Toronto: Oxford University Press, 1966. rev. ed. 412p.

This was a pioneering work in the field of Canadian architectural history (it was first published in 1958 under the title *Looking at architecture in Canada*) and it remains a good starting point for the student or researcher working in the field.

837 **Picture book of log homes.**
B. Allan Mackie.   Prince George, British Columbia: Log House Publishing, 1983. 180p.

The past twenty years has seen the development, or perhaps better termed the renaissance, of log home construction in Canada. This work describes some of the best log homes in Canada, with information on design, construction etc. Of equal interest is the work by Donovan Clemson entitled *Living with logs: British Columbia's log buildings and rail fences* (Saanichton, British Columbia: Hancock House, 1974). This latter work provides an historical perspective to the log buildings of the west coast.

838 **The ancestral roof: domestic architecture of Upper Canada.**
Marion MacRae.   Toronto: Clarke, Irwin, 1963. 258p.

The ancestry of Ontario domestic buildings constructed between 1784 and 1867 is outlined in the text and depicted in photographs. This is a handsome book but primarily of interest to the knowledgeable reader.

839 **Hallowed walls: church architecture of Upper Canada.**
Marion MacRae.   Toronto: Clarke, Irwin, 1975. 304p.

This is a book about the churches of Ontario. This volume is illustrative of similar works for other provinces, most notably Quebec. The work is of a scholarly nature, but is well illustrated. For the churches listed every attempt has been made to identify designers, builders and craftsmen.

840 **Neoclassical architecture in Canada.**
Leslie Maitland. Ottawa: National Historic Parks and Sites Branch, Parks Canada, Environment Canada, 1984. 150p. (Studies in Archaeology, Architecture and History).
An account of the Neoclassical movement in architecture which enjoyed great popularity in Canada from the 1820s to the 1850s. The principal examples of the style are the public buildings of the era, although some domestic and religious architecture was well influenced by it.

841 **Small churches of Canada.**
Kim Ondaatje. Toronto: Lester & Orpen Dennys, 1982. 195p.
A noted photographer illustrates the diversity of religious traditions in Canada through the architecture of the small churches.

842 **Old Ontario houses.**
Kim Ondaatje, Lois Mackenzie. [Agincourt, Ontario]: Gage, 1977. [n.p.]
Beautiful colour photographs depict 170 historical houses in Ontario, most of which date from the nineteenth century. A brief commentary outlining the background, style and notable features of the structure accompanies each photograph. See also *Ontario towns* (Ottawa: Oberon, 1974).

843 **Art in architecture: art for the built environment in the province of Ontario.**
Jeanne Parkin, edited by William J.S. Boyle. Toronto: Visual Arts Ontario, 1982. 276p.
In 1979 the Committee of Visual Arts Ontario was established with the belief that the artist and the architect might be brought closer together for the betterment of the built environment. This text was a project of that Committee and was intended to be a 'practical attempt to provide specific information about the incorporation of art into architecture to architecture and design firms in the Province'. The result is a most interesting work which documents a number of case studies of existing art and architecture, and in the process of analysing each case draws conclusions from the experience. It also provides a practical guide for the implementation of art in architecture projects, including a discussion of contracts and available government assistance. Particularly useful also is an 'Index of Artists' which documents the relevant work of Canadian artists previously commissioned to work within the built environment.

844 **Building with wood and other aspects of nineteenth-century building in central Canada.**
John I. Rempel. Toronto: University of Toronto Press, 1980. rev. ed. 454p.
This book focuses on the practical aspects of construction, discussing the technical methods used in the erection of ordinary buildings. The author traces the history of various European and North American influences on methods of building, particularly in Ontario. The work is enhanced by 475 photographs and drawings in support of the text.

845 **Canada builds 1867-1967.**
T. Ritchie. Toronto: University of Toronto Press, 1967. 406p.
This is an account of the history of building in Canada from its beginnings. The author demonstrates here the simple constructions of the early settlers to the modern complexes of today.

846 **Early Indian village churches: wooden frontier architecture in British Columbia.**
Edited by John Veillette, Gary White. Vancouver: University of British Columbia Press, 1977. 195p.
This work chronicles the tradition of the mission church within the built environment of the west coast. The first section of this work is made up of three essays. The first, by Robin Fisher, places the churches within the context of the growth of missionary activity among the Indians of British Columbia. The second, by Warren Sommer, outlines how the churches were built and the technology and traditions which influenced the various building styles. The third, by the editors, describes contemporary Indian village life and the present state of the village church. The second section of the work organizes the churches by region within British Columbia and describes each in turn.

847 **Modern Canadian architecture.**
Edited by Leon Whiteson, foreword by Raymond Moriyama. Edmonton, Alberta: Hurtig, 1983. 272p.
Four leading architects provide an introduction to the modern architecture of the four major regions of the country. Ron Thom discusses 'Modern architecture on the West Coast', Peter Hemingway provides an introduction to 'Prairie architecture', John C. Parkin writes about 'Modern architecture in Ontario', and Raymond Affleck comments on 'Modern architecture in Quebec'. Within this framework some sixty architectural projects are examined. Biographies of the forty-nine architects represented are provided in an appendix. Plans and photographs complement the text.

848 **Architecture of the picturesque in Canada.**
Janet Wright. Ottawa: National Historic Parks and Sites Branch, Parks Canada, Environment Canada, 1984. 183p. (Studies in Archeology, Architecture and History).
An account of the 'picturesque' influence on Canadian architecture. The author traces the origins of this aesthetic back to late 18th-century Britain, where it sought to reconcile landscape design and nature, and reviewed architecture as secondary to the natural environment.

Urban planning

849 **Canada's urban past: a bibliography to 1980 and guide to Canadian urban studies.**
Alan F. J. Artibise, Gilbert A. Stelter. Vancouver: University of British Columbia Press, 1981. 396p.

The purpose of this work is to facilitate study and research in urban history. To this end the book provides a bibliographic guide, with more than 7,000 entries, which brings together many kinds of urban and urban related materials. The selection criteria used for the listing is broad, looking at the Canadian urban environment within regional, national and even international contexts. Also in support of its stated purpose, the introduction to the work includes an extended essay entitled 'Guide to approaches in urban history'. Finally, the work includes a 'Guide to approaches in urban history studies' which serves as a handbook for the researcher. The authors provide a critique of research tools and sources, such as newsletters and journals, archival repositories, special libraries and information centres.

850 **Town and city: aspects of western Canadian urban development.**
Edited by Alan F. J. Artibise, L. G. Crossman. Regina, Saskatchewan: Canadian Plains Research Center, University of Regina, 1981. 455p. (Canadian Plains Studies, vol. 10).

A collection of commissioned essays on urban development in western Canada. While western history has been clearly focused on an agrarian dimension, 'the urban frontier was one of the vital elements in Canada's western expansion. Towns and cities introduced a dynamic and aggressive element into the West and played a key role in transforming a sparsely settled fur-trading expanse into a settled and well-integrated region'.

851 **City for sale.**
Henry Aubin. Montreal; Toronto: Éditions l'ÉTINCELLE in association with James Lorimer, 1977. 389p.

The author, an investigative reporter, examines the 'ownership of major development companies, public works contractors, building supply manufacturers and moneylending institutions', in a city in Canada. 'It is the interrelationships between these and other sectors which produce power'. While this is a case study, the implications of the ownership patterns of real estate and large residential and commercial developments in major urban centres are relevant for most other cities.

852 **Contemporary cathedrals: large-scale developments in Canadian cities.**
Robert W. Collier. Montreal: Harvest House, 1974. 201p. (Environment Series).

The development boom of the late 1950s and 1960s put predictable strains on municipal legislative and planning machinery. This was particularly true when municipal governments were asked to approve and make significant decisions about urban projects. This study examines eleven such major downtown 'high-rise' projects from Vancouver to Halifax and discusses and analyses the civic legal and administrative procedures established to deal with such developments, the relationships between different levels of government in dealing with the projects, the form, if any, by which public opinion was sought and expressed, and the rôle of the public official in the development process.

853 **Planning the Canadian environment.**
Edited by L. O. Gertler. Montreal: Harvest House, 1968. 311p. (Environment Series).
'The papers presented in this volume are selections from the first five years of *PLAN, Canada*, the journal of the Town Planning Institute of Canada. Spanning a period from the end of 1959 to the first quarter of 1965, they have been chosen for the way they illuminate the evolution of planning in Canada'. This is a useful volume for historical reasons, as it represents the thinking of active Canadian planners during a period of intense activity in urban and regional development.

854 **Urban issues.**
Leonard O. Gertler. Toronto: Van Nostrand Reinhold, 1976. 124p. (Making Man's Environment).
Urban issues introduces the Making Man's Environment series. It begins with a brief historical survey of the development of Canadian cities, then provides a detailed examination of the most critical problems related to land, transportation, regional development, and the formulation of planning principles and policies.

855 **Changing Canadian cities: the next 25 years.**
Leonard O. Gertler, Ronald W. Crowley. Toronto: McClelland & Stewart, 1977. 474p.
This work attempts to deal with contemporary urban issues. It initially describes the forces that have shaped Canada's urban environment, and then studies various aspects of that environment: the inner city neighborhoods; land use; quality of life; etc. Case studies are used to illustrate particular circumstances. Charts, graphs and maps have been used to illustrate the text.

856 **Men of property: the Canadian developers who are buying America.**
Susan Goldenberg. Toronto: Personal Library, 1981. 320p.
A series of profiles of Canadian developers operating in both Canada and the United States. The text is based on interviews with company directors, business associates, banks, insurance and pension companies, accountants, lawyers and the like. Among the companies included are Olympia & York Developments Limited, Trizec Corporation, Oxford Development Group, and Campeau Corporation.

857 **The history of Canadian cities.**
Toronto: James Lorimer, Canadian Museum of Civilization, in collaboration with the Secretary of State, 1977- . 8 vols.
This series was developed in response to a perceived need to make available, for the general reader, books which provide, in a readable and attractive format a systematic, interpretative and comprehensive account of the urban experience in a variety of key Canadian communities. Each volume in the series is expected to include commentary on such issues as ethnic relationships, regionalism, provincial-municipal interaction, social mobility, labour management relationships, urban planning and general

economic development. Eight volumes have been published to date, including: *Regina* by J. William Brennan; *Ottawa* by John Taylor; *Winnipeg* by Alan Artibise; *Calgary* by Max Foran; *Vancouver* by Patricia Roy; *Hamilton* by John Weaver; *Toronto to 1918* by J.M.S. Careless; and, *Toronto Since 1918* by James Lemon.

858 **Planning Canadian communities: an introduction to the principles, practice and participants.**
Gerald Hodge. Toronto: Methuen, 1986. 386p.
This noted scholar in the field of planning examines the Canadian response to the task of planning for the building and rebuilding of communities of all sizes in the country. The author examines the roots of Canadian planning since the Second World War, he describes the practice of community planning today, and he looks at the persons and groups who participate in planning activities in this country – with a particular focus on the decision makers.

859 **The developers.**
James Lorimer. Toronto: James Lorimer, 1978. 307p.
This exposé of the development industry was sparked by this author/publisher's early involvement in community and civic politics, and later by the results of a major research report undertaken by Peter Spurr for the Central Mortgage and Housing Corporation of the federal government entitled *Land and urban development: a preliminary study* (Toronto: James Lorimer, 1976). This study is critical, not only of the developers but also of the various levels of government for not adequately regulating the activities of these entrepreneurs, as well as of financial institutions for not ensuring the best use of investment capital. The work is well documented.

860 **After the developers.**
Edited by James Lorimer and Carolyn MacGregor. Toronto: James Lorimer, 1981. 136p.
An anthology of articles which purports to look critically at the experiences of the citizen movement and reform politics with particular reference to the developers of large scale projects. The collection is informative, though there is no balance of viewpoint. The four sections of the work deal with 'The industrial strategy issue', 'Shopping and cities', 'Reform and power at city hall', and 'City planning'.

861 **The city book: the politics and planning of Canada's cities.**
Edited by James Lorimer, Evelyn Ross. Toronto: James Lorimer, 1976. 223p. bibliog.
This collection of articles from the *City Magazine* provides a glimpse of urban Canada in the mid-seventies and is intended as a casebook illustrating the current trends in Canadian cities with real-life examples of the processes and political forces which operate in Canada. An annotated, selected bibliography is included of Canadian reform-oriented literature on urban studies. A sequel to this work is *The second city book: studies of urban and suburban Canada* (Toronto: James Lorimer, 1977).

862 **Minetown, milltown, railtown: life in Canadian communities of single industry.**
Rex A. Lucas. Toronto: University of Toronto Press, 1971. 433p.

By way of personal interviews and questionnaires, over 500 individuals in three communities, a mining town in the Maritimes, a milling town in Quebec and a railway town in Ontario (all communities of under 30,000 residents), were involved in this study which attempted to identify patterns of similarity and variation in Canada's small towns. The study deals as much with the social environment of the communities as it does with the physical environment.

863 **Montreal in evolution: historical analysis of the development of Montreal's architecture and urban environment.**
Jean-Claude Marsan. Montreal: McGill-Queen's University Press, 1981. 456p. bibliog.

First published in French under the title: *Montréal en evolution* (Montreal: Editions Fides, 1974). This is a synthesis, or overview of the development of Montreal from the time of its foundation to the modern city of today. It focuses particularly on the evolution of the city's architecture and of the urban environment generally. The work is in four parts: part I deals with the ever present factors of location, geography and physical environment; part II covers the pre-industrial period up to the 1840s; part III deals with the impacts of the industrial revolution and its effects on urban economics, society and culture; and part IV provides a commentary on twentieth century Montreal and its future. There is an extensive bibliography.

864 **Urban sociology in Canada.**
Peter McGàhan. Toronto: Butterworths, 1986. 2nd ed. 334p. bibliog.

The author states that the aim of urban sociology is to analyse the evolution and structure of the urban community as a sociospatial system. This analysis is undertaken from dynamic and structural perspectives. In the case of the former this includes such topics as rural-urban migration, and the consequent process of assimilation; and in the case of the latter, this includes such topics as the future of the local communities and neighbourhoods in the urban system, particularly as it relates to the characteristics of the wider system. This is a scholarly study and is supported by an extensive bibliography.

865 **Cities of Canada.**
George A. Nader. Toronto: Macmillan, 1975-76. 2 vols. bibliog.

Volume one of this set is subtitled *Theoretical, historical and planning perspectives.* It attempts to describe the major forces operating on the contemporary urban system as well as the evolution of the Canadian urban system through history and to look at possible solutions to the problems which face Canada's cities. In Volume two, subtitled *Profiles of fifteen metropolitan centres*, the foci of historical development, the economic base, land-use structure and planning policy have been applied to the case studies of fifteen metropolitan centres. Bibliographies are included in each volume. This is a work of major importance to the lay and informed reader.

866 **Canadian urban growth trends: implications for a national settlement policy.**
Ira M. Robinson. Vancouver: University of British Columbia Press, 1981. 154p. (Human Settlement Issues, vol. 5).
The author advocates the need for a national settlement policy for the country. Such a programme, at the federal level, would control or reduce some of the effects of current urbanization patterns, such as the social and environmental consequences of continued concentration of populations, the desire to raise living standards above some minimum standard in disadvantaged cities and regions, and the need to maintain economic growth rates commensurate with rising social needs.

867 **Essays on Canadian urban process and form.**
Lorne H. Russwurm, Richard E. Preston, L. R. G. Martin. Waterloo, Ontario: Department of Geography, Faculty of Environmental Studies, University of Waterloo, 1977. 377p. (Department of Geography Publication Series, vol. 10).
The essays in this book were commissioned as background studies for sections of *Changing Canadian cities: the next 25 years* (q.v.) by Len Gertler and Ron Crowley. They focus on alternative settlement forms for urban areas, on the changes at work on the regional environments which surround our cities, and the behaviour of land dealers and land developers with regard to the urban fringe. Additional related essays can be found in the work *Essays on Canadian urban process and form II* (Waterloo, Ontario: Department of Geography, Faculty of Environmental Studies, University of Waterloo, 1980) by the same editors. These nine essays deal in more general terms with urbanization in Canada.

868 **Saving the Canadian city: the first phase 1880-1920: an anthology of early articles on urban reform.**
Edited by Paul Rutherford. Toronto: University of Toronto Press, 1974. 366p. (The Social History of Canada, vol. 22).
Canada's earliest urban reform movement began in the 1880s and 1890s, peaking immediately following the First World War. Many concerns were raised during this period, including the problems of vice and crime, social justice, a healthy environment, the regulation of utilities, beautification of the industrial city, town planning, tax reform, and the reshaping of municipal government. The pieces in this collection were originally published in the aforementioned period. They have been organized thematically: the debate over the municipal control of public utilities; the efforts to make the city healthy, moral and equitable for all its citizens; the desire for a planned urban environment; and municipal reform. The editor introduces the work with an historical summary of the reform movement in Canada.

869 **Urban Canada.**
James Simmons, Robert Simmons. Toronto: Copp Clark, 1974. rev. ed. 188p.
An overview of urban development in Canada, directed to the general reader. While dated, it remains useful as a quick survey which highlights major issues, particularly of the post-war period. Selected reading lists following each chapter direct the reader to additional resource materials.

870 **The Canadian city: essays in urban and social history.**
Edited by Gilbert Stelter, Alan F. J. Artibise. Ottawa: Carleton
University Press, 1984. rev. ed. 503p. (Carleton Library Series,
vol. 132).
A collection of original essays which, through an interdisciplinary approach, shed light
on Canada's urban past. Essays represent jurisdictions from across the country. The
editors preface each of the sections of the work with a brief introductory essay. An
earlier collection published in 1977 included many of the same essays. Similar
anthologies produced by the same editors include *The usable urban past: planning and
politics in the modern Canadian city* (Toronto: Macmillan, 1979), and *Shaping the
urban landscape: aspects of the Canadian city-building process* (Ottawa: Carleton
University Press, 1982).

871 **Power and place: Canadian urban development in the North American
context.**
Edited by Gilbert Stelter, Alan F. J. Artibise. Vancouver: University
of British Columbia Press, 1986. 398p.
The authors of this collection of essays attempt to address the relatively neglected
questions regarding power in urban development. They feel that 'there is a particular
value in looking at Canadian development from a larger perspective: in this case, the
North American context'.

872 **Urban History Review = Revue d'Histoire Urbaine.**
Toronto: City of Toronto Archives, 1972- . three times a year.
This journal provides a vehicle for the exchange of information, theories and
techniques relating to the development of urban communities over time. Emphasis is
placed on the historical evolution of urban Canada.

873 **Main street: Windsor to Quebec City.**
Maurice Yeates. Toronto: Macmillan, 1975. 431p.
This work was commissioned by the Ministry of State for Urban Affairs of the federal
government of Canada. It provides an analysis of the implications of the concentration
of economic and population activity in the corridor which runs from Windsor to
Quebec City, which encompasses well over half of Canada's population. The problems
associated with the growth of this area as the service/industrial centre for the nation are
as prevalent in the 1980s as they were when the book was commissioned. This is a
work aimed at the informed reader.

Rural planning

874 **The barn: a vanishing landmark in North America.**
Eric Arthur, Dudley Witney. Toronto: McClelland & Stewart, 1972. 256p.
This is a record in prose and photography of an indigenous architectural form of fundamental importance within the rural built environment. It deals with the barn in North America, although a significant proportion of the work is concerned with Canada. It is a scholarly volume and is enhanced by beautiful colour and black-and-white photographics. Interested readers might also wish to refer to Bob Hainstock's *Barns of western Canada – an illustrated century* (Victoria: Braemar Books, 1985). Completely different, yet equally important as a rural architectural feature in the history of the country were the sawmills and flour mills. These are documented in the work by Carol Priamo entitled *Mills of Canada* (Toronto: McGraw-Hill Ryerson, 1976).

875 **Rural Ontario.**
Verchoyle Benson Blake, Ralph Greenhill. Toronto: University of Toronto Press, 1969. 173p.
By way of words and pictures the authors attempt to explain the characteristic appearance of the Ontario countryside. Rural is interpreted strictly here and excludes towns and larger villages. The work provides insights into the spread of settlements in the province, as well as comments on the succession of building styles and the development of farm practices. The ninety black-and-white photographs are of exceptional quality.

876 **Prairie giants.**
Hans Dommasch. Saskatoon, Saskatchewan: Western Producer Prairie Books, 1986. 127p.
The grain elevator is a powerful symbol of economic and social stability in the west as it is the only form of man-made structure to be found on the prairies. This work is a photographic tribute to these sentinels.

877 **Regional planning in Canada: a planner's testament.**
L. O. Gertler. Montreal: Harvest House, 1972. 186p.
A planner outlines some of the theories and realities of regional planning in Canada, including an analysis of then current federal and provincial policies. Several regional planning initiatives are discussed, such as the Mactaquac Regional Development Plan in New Brunswick. Despite its title, the work focuses on eastern Canada.

878 **Towns and villages in Canada: the importance of being unimportant.**
Gerald Hodge, Mohammad A. Qadeer. Toronto: Butterworths, 1983. 250p.
An exploration into the form of small communities in contemporary Canada numbering in excess of 9,500 centres. The study examines the demographic, social, and economic bases of Canada's small towns and villages, it produces baseline information as to the status and developmental trends of these communities, comments on their

place and rôle within the existing settlement trends in the country, and suggests ways in which the habitat may be sustained in the future.

879 **Land Use in Canada Series.**
Ottawa: Lands Directorate, Environment Canada, 1974- .
To date twenty-eight volumes have been published in this series, the purpose of which is to address major land use issues and problems in Canada. Volumes deal with the causes and consequences of major land problems and land use trends throughout Canada, and the rôle of various government programmes in effecting solutions. Provides information on land use trends, analyses the effects of current and proposed means to influence the use of the land and reviews the impact of various laws, regulations and government programmes on land use in Canada.

880 **Man's impact on the western Canadian landscape.**
J. G. Nelson. Toronto: McClelland & Stewart, 1976. 205p. (Carleton Library, vol. 90).
Presents a collection of essays by Nelson, a leading geographer, focusing on humanity's impact on the environment. The earlier pieces deal with the Caucasian invasion, public land policy, parks and recreation in Canada, and changing relationship between society and the natural world. The later essays indicate a change in approach basing his study on the research of biologists, psychologists, lawyers, political scientists and economists.

881 **Stress on land in Canada.**
Produced and coordinated by Wendy Simpson-Lewis, Ruth McKechnie, V. Neimanis. Ottawa: Policy Research and Development Branch, Lands Directorate, Environment Canada, 1983. 323p. bibliog.
This publication focuses on how the Canadian population uses its land resource. The authors examine several of the activities which put pressure on the land and contribute to land degradation and reduce the utility of the land. They provide an analysis of land use in Canada and what the results of these practices mean for the resource as a whole. A number of bibliographical references are included.

Protection

882 **The late, Great Lakes: an environmental history.**
William Ashworth. New York: Alfred A. Knopf, 1986. 274p.
This is a frightening account in which the author pulls no punches in exposing the environmental mistreatment of one of North America's greatest water resources. He notes the complacent attitude of the people of North America, for whom the Lakes have 'always' existed and would continue to do so. He points out that geography is not immutable, and that the Lakes, which were formed only 'a geological eyeblink ago', could be destroyed just as quickly.

883 **Much is taken, much remains: Canadian issues in environmental conservation.**

Rorke Bryan. North Scituate, Massachusetts: Duxbury, 1973. 307p.

Though dated this text provides valuable and wide-ranging background to the issues concerning the environment in Canada. Various sections deal in turn with pollution in relation to industrial and resource development, water as a resource and commodity, wildlife conservation, and the rôle of national parks in Canada.

884 **Still waters: report of the Sub-committee on Acid Rain of the Standing Committee on Fisheries and Forestry.**

Sub-committee on Acid Rain of the Standing Committee on Fisheries and Forestry. Ottawa: Ministry of Supply and Services Canada, 1981. 150p. bibliog.

Of the many environmental issues facing Canada at this time, the problems associated with acid rain rank at the top of the list. This investigation brought the problem to the attention of the political community. It includes a selective bibliography. Many works have since been published on the issue, including: Ross Howard and Michael Perley's *Acid rain: the North American forecast* (Toronto: Anansi, 1980), Thomas Pawlick's *A killing rain: the global threat of acid precipitation* (San Francisco: Sierra Club Books, 1984), John E. Carroll's *Acid rain: an issue in Canadian-American relations* (Toronto: C. D. Howe Institute, 1982), *Rain of death: acid rain in western Canada* (Edmonton, Alberta: NeWest Press, 1981) and Phil Weller's *Acid rain: the silent crisis* (Toronto: Between the Lines, 1980).

885 **Environment and good sense: an introduction to environmental damage and control in Canada.**

M. J. Dunbar. Montreal: McGill-Queen's University Press, 1971. 92p. (Environmental Damage and Control in Canada).

This series, though dated, provides a still regrettably, relevant analysis, of aspects of Canada's environmental problems. Other volumes in the series are David V. Bates' *A citizen's guide to air pollution* (1974), P. A. Larkin's *Freshwater pollution, Canadian style* (1974), and Milton M. R. Freeman's *People pollution* (1974).

886 **Resources and the environment: policy perspectives for Canada.**

Edited by O. P. Dwivedi. Toronto: McClelland & Stewart, 1980. 346p.

A collection of essays which 'is based on the view that the exploitation, use, and transportation of natural resources create, and have created, environmental problems'. The authors believe that an 'understanding of these problems can benefit from the examination of political, legal, and institutional forces which shape the policy process'. They point out that while economic factors greatly influence the nature of the use and exploitation of resources, it is ultimately the responsibility of political and bureaucratic devices for policy implementation and the consequences. The work is divided into two sections: the first includes essays which define, explain and analyse the policy process; the second provides an examination of particular case studies, such as the uses of coastal waters, hydroelectric development in James Bay, northern pipelines, mercury contamination, and nuclear energy. An earlier similar collection by the same editor was entitled *Protecting the environment: issues and choices – Canadian perspectives* (Toronto: Copp Clark, 1974).

887 **The sociology of natural resources.**
John Elliott. Toronto: Butterworths, 1981. 232p.
The author examines pollution as the end product of various social, economic and political processes. The author prefers the term 'environment' to 'pollution' in that the environment effectively becomes a direct consequence of various types of pollution plus other occupational hazards, diseases, land use, etc. The author contends that the environmental issues which are today's concerns are but the product of this country's particular brand of economic growth and development.

888 **Poison's in public: case studies of environmental pollution in Canada.**
Ross Howard. Toronto: James Lorimer, 1980. 173p.
This work documents four serious but representative instances of massive industrial pollution. Each case is used in turn to note the nature of relationships between big business and government in Canada and the obstacles which interest groups must overcome in order to halt these destructive practices.

889 **Chemical nightmare: the unnecessary legacy of toxic wastes.**
John Jackson, Phil Weller, Waterloo Public Interest Research Group.
Toronto: Between the Lines, 1982. 128p.
The authors describe a number of cases of chemical waste mismanagement and analyse the problem as 'one of today's major environmental tragedies'. They present 'a history of corporate negligence compounded by government inaction, as well as the organizing of citizen's groups in response to this danger to communities'.

890 **Lead in the Canadian environment: science and regulation.**
Ottawa: Royal Society of Canada, 1986. 374p.
The final report of the Commission on Lead in the Environment, which was established with the purpose of reporting on: the sources of lead releases in Canada; the pathways by which lead enters the Canadian environment; the toxicity of lead; the potential risks; practical corrective measures; and the economic, technical, social and labour implications of reductions in lead releases.

891 **Ecology versus politics in Canada.**
Edited by William Leiss. Toronto: University of Toronto Press, 1979. 282p.
Presents twelve essays which focus on the relationships between ecology and politics, current government activity, and received economic theory. They discuss governmental apathy on questions of industrial and occupational diseases; and examine social and environmental problems caused by the search for energy, notably nuclear electricity. The editor concludes with an essay on 'Political aspects of environmental issues'.

892 **Acid rain and friendly neighbors: the policy dispute between Canada and the United States.**
Edited by Jurgen Schmandt, Hilliard Roderick. Durham, North Carolina: Duke University Press, 1985. 332p.
Presents the findings and conclusions of a research team charged with examining the question of United States-Canada relations with regard to the acid rain issue. Specifically the project sought answers to the following questions: What is the extent of

agreement and disagreement between Canada and the United States, as evidenced in published documents, about the nature of acid rain and its environmental effects? What domestic policy developments are underway in Canada and the United States aimed at controlling acid rain, and what additional measures would be helpful? and what joint measures have the two countries taken to resolve the issue?

893 **The conserver solution.**
Lawrence Solomon.   Toronto: Doubleday Canada, 1978. 220p.
The author describes an ideal conserver society and the benefits that would accrue. He points out that the economy has become 'skilled at expanding', without learning to distinguish between good and bad growth; the drive to produce more has made society complacent about waste.

894 **Environmental rights in Canada.**
Edited by John Swaigen.   Toronto: Butterworths, 1981. 447p.
These essays attempt to contribute to an understanding and resolution of issues that relate to environmental law and policy. Topics include environmental impact assessment, class actions and freedom of information to name but a few. All of the authors are critical of the mechanisms in place to curb pollution; 'it is still impossible to be sure that toxic substances and dangerous technologies will be identified before they are marketed'. Members of the public do not know whether they will be involved in the decision-making process concerning developments that might destroy their environment.

895 **No safe place.**
Warner Troyer.   Toronto: Clarke, Irwin, 1977. 267p.
Mercury levels in the Canadian environment have been, and remain one of Canada's more significant environmental problems. This well researched work of investigative journalism reveals the magnitude of the problem in northwest Ontario, although the resultant insights and perceptions of the author can be extrapolated more generally with regard to the tension between industry, public concern and government action.

896 **The Canadian environment: data book on energy and environmental problems.**
Madelyn F. Webb.   Toronto: W. B. Saunders, 1980. 166p.
A useful reference tool which provides information pertaining to Canadian energy and environmental problems. Topics covered include supply and demand data for various energy sources, Canada's pattern of energy use, alternative energy sources, population, water pollution, metals, pesticides, air pollution, solid waste and land use. The work functions as a directory, directing the reader to other sources.

Education

Reference

897 **Canadian education index = Répertoire canadien sur l'éducation.**
Toronto: Micromedia Limited, 1965- .
An author/subject index to Canadian educational periodicals (200), as well as report and monographic literature, published three times between October and June, including an annual cumulation. Reference works of related interest include *The directory of education studies in Canada* (Toronto: Canadian Education Association, 1968/69-), *Inventory of research into higher education in Canada* (Ottawa: Association of Universities and Colleges of Canada, 1975-), *A bibliography of higher education in Canada [with supplements]* (Toronto: University of Toronto Press, 1960-), and *EDUQ* (Quebec: Gouvernement du Quebec, Ministère de l'éducation, Direction de la recherche, 1981-).

898 **Education in Canada: a bibliography = L'éducation au Canada: une bibliographie.**
E. G. Finley. Toronto; Oxford: Dundurn Press in cooperation with the National Library of Canada and the Canadian Government Publishing Centre, Supply and Services Canada, 1989. 2 vols.
This bibliography contains over 14,000 references to literature covering the development of Canadian education from the seventeenth century to the early 1980s. Material on the formal system from pre-primary through post-secondary levels, with both academic and technical streams included as well as adult education and its life-long dimensions.

899 **A source book of royal commissions and other major governmental inquiries in Canadian education 1787-1978.**
Cary F. Goulson. Toronto: University of Toronto Press, 1981. 406p.
A listing of 367 inquiries into Canadian education. These include investigations into education generally, into specific aspects of education and into matters which impacted educational concerns in a significant way. Each entry provides a synopsis as to the conclusions or recommendations of the inquiry.

History

900 **Histoire de l'enseignement au Québec.** (History of education in Quebec.)
Louis-Philippe Audet. Montreal; Toronto: Holt, Rinehart & Winston, 1971. 2 vols.
The standard, historical overview of education in Quebec. The first volume covers the period 1608-1840; the second one deals with the period 1840-1971. See also Roger Magnuson's *A brief history of Quebec education: from New France to Parti Québécois* (Montreal: Harvest House, 1980).

901 **The one-room school in Canada.**
Jean Cochrane. Toronto: Fitzhenry & Whiteside, 1981. 168p.
The cloaking mist of nostalgia is a wonderful feeling; nostalgia in relation to one's school days is more wonderful yet as it permits the recreation of a flavour of youth, the bitter and the sweet. This work will provide such an experience for those who have memories of the one-room schoolhouse, particularly in a rural or small-town environment. Another work equally compelling is John C. Charyk's *Syrup pails and gopher tails: memories of the one-room school* (Saskatoon, Saskatchewan: Western Producer Prairie Books, 1983).

902 **Educating Canadians: a documentary history of public education.**
Edited by Douglas A. Lawr, Robert D. Gidney. Toronto: Van Nostrand Reinhold, 1973. 284p.
The documents in this collection provide the reader with a sense of educational issues from the vantage point of the politicians in the provincial legislatures and the federal parliament, and from the thoughts of our educators and other administrators. Although education in Canada has traditionally been the responsibility of the provincial or regional authorities, one is struck by the commonality of experience across the country as jurisdictions sought to establish, and then expand and develop their school systems.

903 **Schools in the West: essays in Canadian educational history.**
Edited by Nancy M. Sheehan, J. Donald Wilson and David C. Jones. Calgary, Alberta: Detselig Enterprises, 1986. 323p.
This collection, taken together with an earlier collection by the same editors and entitled *Shaping the schools of the Canadian West* (Calgary, Alberta: Detselig Enterprises, 1979), enhances the understanding of educational developments in western Canada.

904 **The schools of Ontario, 1876-1976.**
Robert M. Stamp. Toronto: University of Toronto Press, 1982. 293p.
(Ontario Historical Studies Series).

This book describes and analyses the development of the school system of Ontario in the first century following the retirement of Egerton Ryerson as Chief Superintendent of Schools in 1876. For this period the image of Ontario education has been one of extreme centralization, and of a supposedly superior system. Certainly it was a system which was used as a model for many other Canadian jurisdictions. Stamp presents both the illusion and the reality, documenting the accomplishments and the shortcomings of the system. Key in his examination was the rôle played by community groups which shaped local and provincial actions. Other studies which deal with Ontario education include Bruce Curtis' *Building the educational state: Canada West, 1836-1871* (London, Ontario: The Althouse Press, 1988); *The house that Ryerson built: essays in education to mark Ontario's bicentennial* (Toronto: OISE Press, 1984); Michael B. Katz and Paul H. Mattingly's *Education and social change: themes from Ontario's past* (New York: New York University Press, 1975); and, Robin S. Harris's *Quiet evolution: a study of the educational system of Ontario* (Toronto: University of Toronto Press, 1967). The influence Egerton Ryerson had on education is also documented in: *Egerton Ryerson and his times* (Toronto: Macmillan, 1978).

905 **Children in English-Canadian society: framing the twentieth-century consensus.**
Neil Sutherland. Toronto: University of Toronto Press, 1976. 336p.

The late nineteenth century saw the emergence of a new generation of reformers dedicated to freeing Canadian society from a variety of social problems by committing to a programme of social improvement based on the more effective upbringing of children. This work examines the growth of the public health movement, developments within the new juvenile courts, and the development of the school systems, the latter of which was considered the main underpinning of the new society. Other works of interest in this general area are Alison L. Prentice and Susan E. Houston's *Family, school & society in nineteenth-century Canada* (Toronto: Oxford University Press, 1975), Alison Prentice's *The school promoters: education and social class in mid-nineteenth century Upper Canada* (Toronto: McClelland & Stewart, 1977), and J. Donald Wilson's *An imperfect past: education and society in Canadian history* (Vancouver: Centre for the Study of Curriculum and Instruction, University of British Columbia, 1984).

906 **Education in Canada: an interpretation.**
Edited by E. Brian Titley, Peter J. Miller. Calgary, Alberta: Detselig Enterprises, 1982. 228p.

A collection of essays which identify educational arrangements at crucial stages of Canada's past and examine a number of contemporary issues arising from these experiences. The pieces are weighted in their attention to western Canada.

907 **Canadian education: a history.**
Edited by J. Donald Wilson, Robert M. Stamp, Louis-Phillippe Audet. Scarborough, Ontario: Prentice-Hall, 1970. 528p.

A collaborative anthology which provides a textbook in Canadian educational history. The editors and contributing writers have placed the history of education in Canada in the mainstream of social history. A unifying thread within the work is the relationships between the political, economic, social, cultural and intellectual aspects of Canadian history and educational development. This is an able successor to the pioneering work in this field, by C. E. Phillips, *The development of education in Canada* (Toronto: W. J. Gage, 1957). Readers wishing a shorter synthesis might consult F. Henry Johnson's *A brief history of Canadian education* (Toronto: McGraw-Hill, 1968).

General

908 **Immigrant children and Canadian schools.**
Mary Ashworth. Toronto: McClelland & Stewart, 1975. 228p.
Discusses the the rôle of Canada's schools in the development and education of non-English speaking immigrant children. The author, after lengthy study, suggests there is much work to do; he describes the present approach to immigrant education as generally unsystematic and ill-informed. Although many places have good intentions, shortages of money, trained teachers and advisors have impeded progress. Additional reading on this topic would include Aaron Wolfgang's *Education of immigrant students: issues and answers* (Toronto: Ontario Institute for Studies in Education, 1975), and Mary Ashworth's *The forces which shaped them: a history of the education of minority group children in British Columbia* (Vancouver: New Star Books, 1979).

909 **Indian education in Canada.**
Edited by Jean Barman, Yvonne Hebert, Don McCaskill. Vancouver: University of British Columbia Press, 1986. 2 vols. (Nakoda Institute Occasional Paper, vol. 2).
Indian education is undergoing rapid changes. This work was designed to facilitate discussion on the developments in this field. The first volume, subtitled *The legacy*, analyses the history of Indian education in Canada. Volume 2, subtitled *The challenge*, focuses on recent developments. The volumes are a combination of critical commentary, case studies and position statements.

910 **Children's rights: legal and educational issues.**
Edited by Heather Berkeley, Chad Gaffield, W. Gordon West. Toronto: Ontario Institute for Studies in Education, 1978. 177p. (Symposium Series, vol. 9).
An anthology of essays which provide a general overview of children's rights, focusing on legal and educational issues.

911 **Canadian Journal of Education = Revue Canadienne de l'Éducation.**
Ottawa: Canadian Society for the Study of Education/Société canadienne pour l'étude de l'éducation, 1976- . quarterly.
This journal contains scholarly articles on all aspects of Canadian education. It also includes reviews. See also: *Education Canada* (Toronto: Canadian Education Association, 1948-); and, *Educational digest* (Unionville, Ontario: Zanny Limited, 1969-). For information on education in French see *Revue de l'assocation canadienne*

d'éducation de langue française (Quebec: L'association canadienne d'éducation de langue française, 1971-).

912 **Philosophy of education: Canadian perspectives.**
Edited by Donald B. Cochrane, Martin Schiralli. Don Mills, Ontario: Collier Macmillan Canada, 1982. 322p.
Dimensions of the philosophy of education are discussed within the Canadian context. Many of the issues in this field, of course, can hardly be characterized as Canadian, however, the compilers have attempted to use recent Canadian experience as the basis for the examination of many universal problems. This is an excellent text aimed at the informed reader.

913 **Education in Canada: an analysis of elementary, secondary and vocational schooling.**
Stephen T. Easton. Vancouver: Fraser Institute, 1988. 122p. bibliog. (Economics of the Service Sector in Canada).
Commissioned by the right-wing Fraser Institute, this study uses various measures to examine the value of educational expenditure in Canada at the elementary and secondary school levels. Value of expenditure is measured by the contribution made to the growth of national income, its rate of return, etc. The author also probes into such issues as costs and productivity in the education sector. A bibliography is included.

914 **Education: Ontario's preoccupation.**
W. G. Fleming. Toronto: University of Toronto Press, 1972. 330p.
This work was written as a companion volume to the comprehensive, multi-volumed work entitled *Ontario's educative society* (Toronto: University of Toronto Press, 1971-1972). The two works have the identical objective of exploring the development of education in the province of Ontario, Canada's largest province, concentrating on the period following the Second World War, although this summary has less emphasis on fact and more on interpretation. The primary investigation itself is encompassed in seven volumes: volume 1, *The expansion of the educational system;* volume 2, *The administrative structure;* volume 3, *Schools, pupils, and teachers;* volume 4, *Postsecondary and adult education;* volume 5, *Supporting institutions and services;* volume 6, *Significant developments in local school systems;* and volume 7, *Educational contributions of associations*

915 **Constitutional language rights of official-language minorities in Canada: a study of the legislation of the provinces and territories respecting education rights of official-language minorities and compliance with Section 23 of the Canadian Charter of Rights and Freedoms.**
Pierre Foucher. Ottawa: Ministry of Supply and Services Canada, 1985. 460p.
A work which could also be classified as relating to language, minorities and constitutional issues in Canada. This thorough study is the first attempt to examine the record of each province in education with attention on the official minority language groups, and specifically to analyse the effects of the rights conferred by the new Charter on official language minorities in Canada. The author also brings together the constitutional rights relating to education in order to 'facilitate future interpretation in

the courts and, most importantly, to begin the process of giving concrete expression to these rights, in legislation that will comply with the requirements of the Constitution . . .' This work is very much directed to those with some legal background.

916   **Social change and education in Canada.**
Edited by Ratna Ghosh, Douglas Ray.   Toronto: Harcourt Brace Jovanovich, 1987. 288p.
'Presents a collection of original essays, written specifically for this volume, that reflects the state of the art in Canadian educational studies. The book is especially intended for those with no formal background in the sociology of education and identifies the major trends and issues in the relationship between education and social change' . For an earlier and similar collection see *Education, change, and society: a sociology of Canadian education* (Toronto: Gage Educational Publishing 1977).

917   **Educational administration in Canada.**
T. E. Giles, A. J. Proudfoot.   Calgary, Alberta: Detselig Enterprises, 1984. 3rd ed. 286p.
The authors examine the school and the rôle of the teacher within the legal and structural settings in Canada, 'as provided by the neighborhood, municipal, provincial, national and professional communities'. The text deals with the development of the Canadian design for education, the structure and financing of Canadian education, the legal concerns of the teacher and school administrator, teacher relationships with various publics, and the teacher as professional.

918   **An introduction to educational administration in Canada.**
Leslie R. Gue.   Toronto: McGraw-Hill Ryerson, 1985. 2nd ed. 274p.
While designed as an undergraduate text, this work is useful in providing the general reader, or the reader unfamiliar with the Canadian educational environment, with a view of educational administration in Canada. The author covers the philosophical background, information on the structure of Canada's educational systems, the nature of the school environment, and an outline of, and constraints upon, the curriculum.

919   **A sociology of Canadian education.**
Pat Duffy Hutcheon.   Toronto: Van Nostrand Reinhold, 1975. 282p.
The nature and the relationships of the disciplines of education and sociology are discussed within a Canadian context. The author deals with a number of sociological concepts, and explores the usefulness of these in terms of selecting or developing the content of curricula for Canadian schools. This textbook is particularly useful for its critical introductions to readings on various educational issues. Collectively these contributions, scattered throughout the work, comprise an overview of Canadian research in this field.

920   **Federal-provincial relations: education Canada.**
Edited by J. W. George Ivany, Michael E. Manley-Casimir.   Toronto: OISE Press, 1981. 150p. (Symposium Series, vol. 14).
A selection of papers presented at the national symposium in 1981, entitled *Education Canada: federal–provincial relations in education*. The symposium was organized in response to the lack of debate on education, and the rôle of education in shaping

Canadian life and society, within the constitutional debates. Organizers saw the repatriation debates as an opportunity to review and redefine education within our national life. Various themes were examined, including the context and nature of federal–provincial interactions, the rôle of education in building or maintaining a national and cultural identity, the examination of alternative governance structures, and speculation on various scenarios for the future.

921 **The nation in the schools: wanted: a Canadian education.**
Rowland M. Lorimer. Toronto: OISE Press/Ontario Institute for Studies in Education, Canadian Learning Materials Centre, 1984. 113p. (Research in Education Series, vol. 11).
Provides a survey of Canadian content in language, arts, literature, and social studies curricula. The author examines the procedures used in the selection of learning materials and teacher – training programmes and addresses the degree to which they foster Canadian studies in the classroom. Generally, the author is critical of progress made and suggests strategies to encourage and ensure Canadian content in the formal curriculum.

922 **Education law in Canada.**
Wayne A. MacKay. Toronto: Emond-Montgomery, 1984. 416p. bibliog.
This first attempt to examine the legal complexities of education in Canada. Although primarily a provincial responsibility, the work looks at laws from all jurisdictions. The author brings together excerpts from statutes, policy manuals, and cases. He provides extensive notes as well as a comprehensive bibliography.

923 **The politics of education: a study of the political administration of the public schools.**
Frank MacKinnon. Toronto: University of Toronto Press, 1962. 187p.
This volume is considered somewhat of a classic in the literature. The author examines the control of education by the State and the effect of that control on the schools and the teaching profession. 'It is written in favour of state ownership, on the side of the public schools, and in support of democracy in education . . .'

924 **Cultural diversity and Canadian education: issues and innovations.**
Edited by John R. Mallea, Jonathan C. Young. Ottawa: Carleton University Press, 1984. 555p. (Carleton Library Series, vol. 130).
This is a substantial and informative anthology for the student or researcher, as well as for the informed reader, which attempts to clarify the issues surrounding language, culture and education in Canada's culturally diverse society.

925 **Canadian education: a sociological analysis.**
Wilfred B. W. Martin, Allan J. Macdonell. Scarborough, Ontario: Prentice-Hall, Canada, 1982. 2nd ed. 429p.
Despite the fact that the Canadian educational scene is characterized by diversity, given such factors as geography, population distribution, political and constitutional structures, etc., the author searches out and focuses on the commonalities, which tend

to be the interrelationships of education with other components of the social structure of Canadian society. The author deals with common social characteristics of Canadian education, including the organization of the school, encompassing such topics as groups and group processes, the teacher in the school, the formal organization of the school, legal and fiscal controls, the rôle of interest groups, and the changing school.

926 **The long road to reform: restructuring public education in Quebec.**
Henry Milner. Kingston, Ontario; Montreal: McGill-Queen's University Press, 1986. 170p.

The author '. . . analyses attempts to change the sectarian nature of schooling in Quebec, focusing on the fate of the radical proposals advanced by the Parti québécois in their White Paper of June 1982. The then minister of education . . . proposed to reform the existing system of "confessional" school boards, with its separate networks of schools for Catholics and Protestants, replacing it with school boards divided along regional lines . . . Widespread opposition to this proposal led to its eventual modification and to the substitution of a much scaled-down version of these reforms, Bill 3, which was declared unconstitutional . . . in May 1985'. This is an interesting work drawing attention to the many dimensions and problems involved in reform, particularly when those individuals and institutions committed to maintaining the *status quo* are formidable.

927 **The organization and administration of education in Canada.**
David Munroe. Ottawa: Education Support Branch, Secretary of State, 1976. 219p.

Though somewhat dated, this work is still very useful as an introduction to the various areas and levels of education in Canada. The author provides a description of the organization and operation of schools and post-secondary education, a chapter on the national organizations and another on general trends of the time in the field of education.

928 **The failure of educational reform in Canada.**
Edited by Douglas Myers. Toronto: McClelland & Stewart, 1973. 200p.

Although dated, this collection of essays commissioned originally for publication in the journal *Canadian Forum*, provides a reflective statement and assessment of the activities with regard to education in the 1960s, as well as interesting speculation as to approaches to follow. The pieces, written as they were in a period of some malaise, predictably reflect disenchantment and scepticism. It is of interest to the educator today.

929 **Introduction to the economics of Canadian education.**
Donald M. Richards, Eugene W. Ratsoy. Calgary, Alberta: Detselig Enterprises, 1987. 127p.

An examination of the relationship between education and the national economic system. Various problems and issues are examined, for example the economics of education and its implications for students, teachers, parents, school systems and governments. It would be of most use to the informed reader.

930 **Culture and adult education: a study of Alberta and Quebec.**
Hayden Roberts. Edmonton, Alberta: University of Alberta Press,
1982. 274p.
A comparative study of adult education in two Canadian provinces, which provides
much insight into the delivery of such programmes throughout the country.

931 **Contemporary educational issues: the Canadian mosaic.**
Edited by Leonard L. Stewin, J. H. Stewart McCann. Toronto: Copp
Clark Pitman, 1987. 636p.
A substantial book of original readings focusing on the Canadian educational issues
that are receiving most attention in professional journals, conferences, and symposia as
well as those that are attracting popular attention in newspapers, magazine articles,
radio talk shows, and television documentaries. Broad areas covered include human
rights in Canadian education, computers in Canadian education, standards and
standardized testing, ethnic diversity for Canadian education, value conflicts, social
problems and issues, education for the exceptional child, teacher training, and
Canadian education in the future.

932 **What's so Canadian about Canadian educational administration?: essays
on the Canadian tradition in school management.**
Edited by Richard G. Townsend, Stephen B. Lawton. Toronto: OISE
Press, 1981. 220p. (Informal Series, vol. 27).
A collection of insightful essays which question the ideas, concepts and assumptions
used in educational administration. Many of the essays are comparative, looking at
both the United States and Europe, and seeking from that examination to define a
distinctiveness for Canada.

933 **Canadian education in the 1980s.**
Edited by J. Donald Wilson. Calgary, Alberta: Detselig Enterprises,
1981. 282p.
Presents a collection of essays by senior scholars in universities across the country.
Although the authors deal with topics and issues seen to be relevant and pressing for
the decade of the 1980s, it is interesting that many incorporate a significant historical
perspective as they attempt to define and elucidate the present and the immediate
future. A list of readings accompanies each contribution.

934 **The political economy of Canadian schooling.**
Edited by Terry Wotherspoon. Toronto: Methuen, 1987. 327p.
The current trend in Canada is to attack the state of the present education system
which is seen to be beset with major problems. Unfortunately, critics air their
grievances, while failing to suggest any solutions and lose sight of the fundamental
nature of Canada's education system. 'This book is about the political economy of
education. It reveals, in large part, the story of our public education system as a story
of domination and struggle'.

Higher education

935 **Academic futures: prospects for post-secondary education.**
Toronto: OISE Press, 1987. 172p. (Symposium Series, vol. 16).
In this anthology of essays university administrators and educators examine present trends and future directions in North American post-secondary education, with emphasis on Canada. Not surprisingly, many of the authors note that the future of post-secondary education will be shaped by forces and influences outside institutions rather than by education-oriented issues.

936 **Scholars and dollars: politics, economics, and the universities of Ontario 1945-1980.**
Paul Axelrod. Toronto: University of Toronto Press, 1982. 270p.
(State and Economic Life, vol. 4).
Higher education went through a period of major growth in the 1960s. This growth was propelled by buoyant economic conditions buttressed by wide-spread public support. Within a decade, however, there had been a reversal in spending priorities. In this study the author examines the impact of economic changes since the Second World War. He examines public perception of the universities, the reasons for their support during the period of expansion, their plans to realize their prescribed functions, and the effect of the 'diminished opportunities and the cooler economic climate of the 1970s'. Axelrod points out 'that not only did the universities prove to be imperfect instruments of economic development, but the efforts expended in the task compromised their vital roles as islands of culture and critical thought in a materialistic society'.

937 **The great brain robbery: Canada's universities on the road to ruin.**
David J. Bercuson, Robert Bothwell, J. L. Granatstein. Toronto:
McClelland & Stewart, 1984. 160p.
A controversial polemic which was much discussed when published. The authors contend that the quality and value of undergraduate education being offered in Canadian universities has declined drastically. Entrance requirements have been relaxed, grades are inflated, scholarship is poor, and standards of all sorts have deteriorated. The work examines the structures of universities, government funding, the impact of democratization of higher education and the development of unions and collective bargaining by faculty. In the eyes of the authors all of these factors have contributed to mediocrity in Canada's universities.

938 **Canadian Journal of Higher Education=La Revue Canadienne d'Enseignement Supérieur.**
Ottawa: Canadian Society for the Study of Higher Education/La Société canadienne pour l'étude de l'enseignement supérieur, 1971- .
quarterly.
This journal is intended to serve as a medium of communication among persons directly involved in higher education in Canada. Its principal focus is on Canadian higher education.

939 **Canada's community colleges: a critical analysis.**
John D. Dennison, Paul Gallagher. Vancouver: University of British
Columbia Press, 1986. 360p. bibliog.

A diversity of factors – historical, socio-economic, political and educational –
contributed to the development of college systems in Canada, systems with distinctive
goals and structures from other institutions of higher learning. The authors describe
provincial and territorial college systems as they have evolved to 1985, discussing
problems particular to each system and evaluating the extent to which often idealistic
early goals have been realized. This comprehensive study identifies a number of key
issues, including accessibility, identity, relations with governments, managment and
leadership, and evaluation and accountability. Also included is a most thorough
bibliography.

940 **Les collèges classiques au Canada français (1620-1970).** (Classical
colleges of French Canada [1620-1970].)
Claude Galnarneau. Montreal: Fides, 1978. 287p.

The origins and development of these post-secondary institutions is presented,
including a systematic analysis of graduates and assessment of course content.
Understanding the rôle of le collège classique is essential for a complete understanding
of Quebec social history.

941 **A history of higher education in Canada 1663-1960.**
Robin S. Harris. Toronto: University of Toronto Press, 1976. 715p.
bibliog.

Harris traces the development of higher education in Canada, through a detailed
description and analysis of what was being taught and the nature of research
opportunities available to professors in the years from 1860 to 1960. The opening
chapters provide background, outlining the origins of post-secondary education, the
establishment of new institutions, and the growth of existing institutions. Considerable
attention is given to an examination of the curricula in arts and science, professional
education, and graduate studies, using benchmark years for comparative purposes. A
full bibliography, and a number of statistical appendices are included.

942 **Canadian universities 1980 and beyond: enrollment, structural change
and finance.**
Peter M. Leslie. Ottawa: Association of Universities and Colleges of
Canada, 1980. 446p.

An internal report to the Board of Directors of the Association which was intended to
examine financing alternatives for universities, recommending alternative positions on
the matter. While attention is paid to the financing question, the report contains much
of interest on the rôles of federal and provincial governments with regard to funding
and other strategic policy issues related to higher education. This report is directed to
the informed reader.

943 **Financing Canadian universities: for whom and by whom?**
Edited by David M. Nowlan, Richard Ballaire. Toronto: Institute for
Policy Analysis and the Canadian Association of University Teachers,
1981. 244p.

Papers and perspectives from a conference held in Toronto on 3 March 1981 which
focused on issues relating to financing, as well as more narrowly on questions of
federal–provincial relations as they might relate to universities.

944 **"Please, sir, I want some more": Canadian universities and financial
restraint.**
Michael L. Skolnik, Norman S. Rowen. Toronto: OISE Press, 1984.
216p. (Informal Series, vol. 59).

There are few jurisdictions in Canada where funding has kept pace with inflation since
the 1970s. This has given rise to an interest in the financial problems of universities, as
well as the impact and implications of funding shortfalls. The authors explore these
issues not only from a strict financial perspective, but also with a sensitivity to the
interaction of financial factors with larger social, political and cultural issues; issues
such as the balance between scholarship and service, autonomy of institutions,
collegiality and the concept of tenure, the contribution of higher education to society
generally, and the maintenance of public confidence in universities.

945 **University Affairs/Affaires Universitaires.**
Ottawa: Association of Universities and Colleges of Canada, 1959- .
ten times a year.

Contains news and articles relating to higher education in Canada. Also of interest are
the viewpoints expressed in the *CAUT Bulletin* (Ottawa: Canadian Association of
University Teachers, 1953- . ten times a year).

946 **But can you type?: Canadian universities and the status of women.**
Jill McCalla Vickers, June Adam. Toronto: Clarke, Irwin in
association with the Canadian Association of University Teachers,
1977. 142p. (A CAUT Monograph Series).

Examines in considerable detail the rôle of women in Canadian universities. Within the
context of this discussion much is revealed about Canadian universities in general, and
about the values of contemporary Canadian society.

947 **Higher education in Canada: an analysis.**
Edwin G. West. Vancouver: Fraser Institute, 1988. 122p. (Economics
of the Service Sector in Canada).

This study analyses the economic issues associated with the allocation of resources to
higher education. The study provides information on the general statistical background
of the post-secondary sector since 1975, the productivity of universities over the
previous ten year period, education as a capital investment, educational loan services,
such as tuition fees, and future policy issues.

Science and Technology

948 **'Mind, heart, and vision': professional engineering in Canada 1887 to 1987.**
Norman R. Ball. Ottawa: National Museum of Science and Technology, National Museums of Canada, 1987. 176p.
Chronicles the development of engineering and the rôle of engineers in Canadian history. The work. was written on the occasion of the centennial of the Canadian Society of Civil Engineers. Of related interest is J. Rodney Millard's *The master spirit of the age: Canadian engineers and the politics of professionalism 1887-1922* (Toronto: University of Toronto Press, 1988). This latter scholarly work 'examines the engineer's struggle to acquire power and prestige. It covers the relatively short, yet crucial period between the founding of the CSCE [Canadian Society of Civil Engineers] in 1887 and the granting of registration laws to Ontario's engineers in 1922 . . . This book is the story not so much of how engineers changed society but of how they survived that change through collective action'.

949 **Research and development in Canada: a practical guide to financing, protecting and exploiting new technology.**
Edited by Daniel R. Bereskin. Toronto; Vancouver: Butterworths, 1987. 264p.
A guide to 'financing, protecting and exploiting new technology', with 'information of practical use to lawyers, accountants, managers and scientists who are engaged from time to time in planning, managing and administering research and development projects in Canada'.

950 **Science, God, and nature in Victorian Canada.**
Carl Berger. Toronto: University of Toronto Press, 1983. 92p.
These essays by a noted historian seek 'to explore the rise, expression, and relative decline of the idea of natural history' in Canada. Three essays deal, in turn, with the emergence of scientific institutions, especially natural history societies, the sense of

wonder and reverence evoked by natural history for Victorian society, and the reception of Darwin's theory among Canadian naturalists.

951   **Banting: a biography.**
      Michael Bliss.   Toronto: McClelland & Stewart, 1984. 336p.

The life story of one of Canada's best known scientists, credited with many discoveries in the area of medical research but identified with the discovery (with others) of insulin used in treatment for diabetes. The author provides an objective portrait, identifying the myth as well as analysing the man. It should be required reading for all Canadians as well as those seeking to know more about Canadian science.

952   **Nucleus: the history of Atomic Energy of Canada Limited.**
      Robert Bothwell.   Toronto: University of Toronto Press, 1988. 524p.

The history of nuclear power in Canada is a story focused on the use of nuclear energy in the production of electricity, and not on its use for military purposes. A prominent Canadian historian chronicles the history of the Crown corporation, Atomic Energy of Canada, and its predecessor division within the National Research Council. Embodied within this history at one and the same time is a discussion of technological development and transfer from the private to the public sector, of economic development, international relations, and of federal-provincial relations, at least as it was manifest in the interplay of science with politics.

953   **Ideas in exile: a history of Canadian invention.**
      J. J. Brown.   Toronto; Montreal: McClelland & Stewart, 1967. 372p.

Though dated this remains one of the best overviews of the subject yet produced. In this highly readable account the author concludes that 'great things are usually done by great men. The story of the disasters and triumphs of Canadian invention is for the most part the story of the struggles of individuals to achieve recognition from an indifferent society'. More popular accounts of Canadian inventions can be found in such works as Janis Nostbakken and Jack Humphrey's *The Canadian inventions book: innovations, discoveries and firsts* (Toronto: Greey de Pencier, 1976); and, J. J. Brown's *The inventors: great ideas in Canadian enterprise* (Toronto: McClelland & Stewart, 1967).

954   **Canadian Journal of Botany = Journal Canadien de Botanique.**
      Ottawa: National Research Council of Canada/Conseil national de recherches Canada, 1951- . monthly.

The National Research Council of Canada publishes numerous scientific journals, including, but not limited to the *Canadian Journal of Chemistry*; the *Canadian Journal of Earth Sciences*; the *Canadian Journal of Forest Research*; the *Canadian Journal of Microbiology*; the *Canadian Journal of Physics*; and, the *Canadian Journal of Zoology*. All include scholarly articles not necessarily restricted by the nationality of the author or of the subject matter, but tending to deal frequently with Canadian research and topics when appropriate.

955 **Histoire des sciences au Québec.** (History of the sciences in Quebec.)
Luc Chartrand, Raymond Duchesne, Yves Gingras. Montreal:
Boréal, 1987. 487p.

Traces the development of science in Quebec from the period of New France
(approximately 1608-1763), with its surveyors, navigators and hydrographers through
the centuries focusing on some of the areas where particular contributions were made
by Quebec scientists. Particularly noteworthy is the work of geologists, naturalists,
medical researchers and environmental scientists. The authors also chronicle the
development and contribution of learned societies, research agencies and universities.

956 **Science and politics in Canada.**
G. Bruce Doern. Montreal: McGill-Queen's University Press, 1972.
238p.

An examination of the relationships between science and politics in Canada. The
author analyses the scientific community as a political system unto itself, comments on
the effectiveness of its response to the federal bureaucracy, and examines the science
policy-making and decision-making mechanisms in Canada.

957 **Traces through time: the history of geophysical exploration for
petroleum in Canada.**
David Finch. Calgary, Alberta: Canadian Society of Exploration
Geophysicists, 1985. 182p.

Documents the major developments in geophysical exploration for petroleum in
Canada, with an attempt to 'capture the spirit, the sense of adventure, indeed the very
passion of the people that made these events possible'.

958 **Biological sciences at the National Research Council of Canada: the early
years to 1952.**
N. T. Gridgeman. Waterloo, Ontario: Wilfred Laurier University
Press, 1979. 153p. bibliog.

Describes the work of the Division of Biological Sciences in three primary areas:
scientific research in agriculture from 1916 until 1939; research into special problems
connected with the Second World War, including the preservation and packaging of
food for long-distance transportation; and administrative developments in the agency
including the establishment of branch laboratories in various parts of Canada. There is
little critical comment, but a valuable chronicle of accomplishments is included. A
bibliography as well as a listing of publications related to work accomplished in the
Division are included.

959 **The chaining of Prometheus: evolution of a power structure for
Canadian science.**
F. Ronald Hayes. Toronto: University of Toronto Press, 1973. 217p.

Provides the reader with a perspective on the evolution of science policy in Canada.
Though set in the mid-1970s the issues of the day remain relevant in that they reflect
the need for, advisability of, or even possibility of, imposing national planning and
controls over the historical free-enterprise system of scientific research and development.

Science and Technology

960 The cold light of dawn: a history of Canadian astronomy.
Richard A. Jarrell. Toronto: University of Toronto Press, 1988. 251p.
A general history which describes the main points of interest in the evolution of Canadian astronomy, together with the appropriate framework in which to explain the rise of astronomical science in Canada. The author notes that there was little in Canadian astronomy which was original until the twentieth century. He does survey the period between 1534 and 1905 in as much depth as sources permit, but gives greater emphasis to the modern period. Of related interest is Malcolm M. Thomson's *The beginning of the long dash: a history of timekeeping in Canada* (Toronto: University of Toronto Press, 1978). Historically, formal timekeeping was a specialized branch of astronomy, though today it is a branch of physics.

961 Science, technology, and Canadian history=Les sciences, la technologie et l'histoire canadienne.
Edited by Richard A. Jarrell, Norman R. Ball. Waterloo, Ontario: Wilfred Laurier University Press, 1980. 246p. bibliog.
Papers presented at the first Conference on the Study of the History of Canadian Science and Technology, held in Kingston, Ontario in November 1978. Essays discuss the nature of this emerging field of study, dealing more with the nature and potential of the field rather than with specific scientific or technological accomplishment. A selective bibliography is included. See also *Critical issues in the history of Canadian science, technology and medicine: second conference on the history of Canadian science, technology and medicine* (Thornhill, Ontario; Ottawa: HSTC Publications, 1983). Here the papers give historical treatment to various developments within the discipline.

962 History of the Medical Council of Canada.
Robert B. Kerr. Ottawa: Medical Council of Canada/Le Conseil Médical du Canada, 1979. 131p.
Chronicles the development of the Council, particularly focusing on activities relating to medical education and medical licensure in Canada.

963 A curious field-book: science & society in Canadian history.
Edited by Trevor H. Levere, Richard Jarrell. Toronto: Oxford University Press, 1974. 233p.
Presents a collection of readings excerpted from primary documentation, ranging from 1616 to 1919, which is intended to illustrate major themes in Canadian social history, as related by salient aspects of science. In an informative and lengthy introduction, the editors contend that 'Canadian science – or, more precisely, science as it has been practised and developed in the territories and provinces that constitute contemporary Canada – has been and is unique'. The readings support this claim. A companion volume entitled *Let us be honest and modest: technology and society in Canadian history* (Toronto: Oxford University Press, 1974) brings together a representative selection of documents, ranging from 1620 to 1952, which 'indicate some of the ways in which Canadians have dealt with their material environment over the past three and a half centuries'. Taken together these works should provide the general reader with a good introduction to the history of science and technology in Canada. Both volumes provide lists of further reading.

964 **Physics at the National Research Council of Canada, 1929-1952.**
W. E. K. Middleton. Waterloo, Ontario: Wilfred Laurier University
Press, 1979. 238p.

Describes the work of the Physics Division by sub-discipline: aeronautics, light, radiology, optics, theoretical physics, etc. Although the work lacks critical comment or integration into a broader historical context, it is useful as a chronicle of activities and personalities within the Council as well as within the community of Canadian physicists. Includes a listing of the publications of the Division during the time period under review.

965 **The mirrored spectrum: a collection of reports for the non-scientist and non-engineer about achievements in Canadian science and technology.**
Ottawa: Ministry of State, Science and Technology, 1973-74. 2 vols.

A collection of short articles, intended for the general reader, which present a selection of achievements in Canadian science and technology. Items included were submitted by working scientists, engineers, professional associations, industrial groups, universities and government agencies.

966 **The earth sciences in Canada: a centennial appraisal and forecast.**
Edited by E. R. W. Neale. Toronto: University of Toronto Press in
cooperation with The Royal Society of Canada, 1968. 259p. (Royal
Society of Canada Special Publications, vol. 11).

Presents a collection of papers produced for a symposium held by the Earth Science Division of the Royal Society of Canada in 1967 on the occasion of Canada's centennial celebrations. Collectively they provide the informed reader with a chronicle of the country's activities and accomplishments in the various disciplines represented generally as the earth sciences. Several of the papers speculate on trends for the future.

967 **Science and technology in Canadian history: a bibliography of primary sources to 1914.**
R. Alan Richardson, Bertrum H. MacDonald. Thornhill, Ontario:
HSTC Publications, 1987. 18p. (Research Tools for the History of
Canadian Science and Technology, No. 3).

This reference work enumerates over 58,000 entries relating to the history of science and technology in Canada. For the purposes of the compilation Canadian science was defined as any scientific or technological work published in or outside of Canada by a Canadian, or published in Canada or abroad by a non-Canadian provided the work contained some substantial material about Canada.

968 **[Background studies].**
Science Council of Canada. Ottawa: Canadian Government Publishing
Centre, 1967- .

The Science Council of Canada is Canada's national advisory agency on science and technology policy. Its primary responsibilities are to analyse science and technology policy issues, recommend policy directions to government, alert Canadians to the impact of science and technology on their lives, and stimulate discussion of science and

Science and Technology

technology policy among governments, industry and academic institutions. Various of this agency's series (i.e. also the Report Series) are essential reading for an understanding of science and technology issues and policies in Canada.

969 **A science policy for Canada: report of the Senate Special Committee on Science Policy.**
Ottawa: Queen's Printer, 1970-77. 4 vols.

In November, 1967 a special Committee of the Senate was instructed to 'consider and report on the science policy of the Federal Government with the object of appraising its priorities, its budget and its efficiency in the light of the experience of other industrialized countries and of the requirements of the new scientific age'. The Committee reviewed the trends in research expenditure in Canada, the research activities undertaken by the federal government at the time, the existing level of federal assistance to research activities, and the long-term financial requirements and the structural underpinnings for a dynamic national science policy. Much can be learned with regard to science policy today from reading this report. The various volumes of the report are subtitled: *A critical review: past and present* (1970); *Targets and strategies for the seventies* (1972); *A government organization for the seventies* (1973); and, *Progress and unfinished business* (1977).

970 **Scientia Canadensis: Journal of the History of Canadian Science, Technology and Medicine.**
Thornhill, Ontario; Ottawa: HSTC Publications, 1976- . semi-annual.

This publication contains scholarly historical articles in all scientific disciplines.

971 **The technical entrepreneur: inventions, innovations & business.**
Edited by Donald S. Scott, Ronald M. Blair. [Victoria, British Columbia]: Press Porcépic, 1979. 288p.

This volume is 'intended to serve as an introduction to the problems and techniques of new venture creation in technology-based business enterprises . . . designed to give an awareness to the student of the many kinds of technical and business activities which take place in setting up a new enterprise containing a technological component'.

972 **Pioneers of Canadian science=Les pionniers de la science canadienne.**
Edited by G. F. G. Stanley. Toronto: University of Toronto Press for the Society, 1966. 146p. (Royal Society of Canada 'Studia Varia' Series, vol. 9).

Publishes the proceedings of a symposium presented to the Royal Society of Canada in 1964. Papers include an overview of the history of science in Canada, the background and development of biological research in Canada, and individual papers on four noted scientists, Abbé Léon Provancher, Dr George Lawson, Rev. Dr James Bovell, and Sir John William Dawson.

973 **Science in Canada: selections from the speeches of E. W. R. Steacie.**
E. W. R. Steacie, edited by J. D. Babbitt. Toronto: University of Toronto Press, 1965. 198p.

Edgar Steacie was a nationally and internationally acclaimed scientist. His primary reputation, however, was made as a scientist-statesman and senior government administrator, eventually becoming President of the National Research Council. Through his efforts Canada developed its post-war science policies, as well as developing the infrastructure for the programme of government grants to the university and public sectors which, with modifications, remains in place today. Steacie's speeches provide the reader with considerable insight into the background and development of science policy in Canada.

974　The development of biochemistry in Canada.
E. Gordon Young.　Toronto: University of Toronto Press, 1976. 129p.
Traces the development of the discipline in Canada from its beginnings to the 1970s. Biochemistry itself is seen as an interdisciplinary subject, incorporating aspects of other disciplines, primarily chemistry and physiology, but also agriculture, biology and medicine. The author organizes his subject by chronicling development in universities, agricultural colleges, in government laboratories, and special institutes. He also examines the growth of biochemical societies and special journals.

975　Reading the rocks: the story of the Geological Survey of Canada 1842-1972.
Morris Zaslow.　Ottawa: Macmillan, in association with the Department of Energy, Mines and Resources and Information Canada, 1975. 599p.
The Geological Survey of Canada was founded in 1842, with a mandate to assist in the development of a mineral industry in Canada. In the course of this activity the Survey was responsible for much of the geological mapping of the country, and was instrumental in the exploration of vast tracts of unexplored territory. Today, the Survey is involved in earth science studies in all parts of the country, and is responsible for ensuring that geological, geophysical and geochemical information is recorded and disseminated for Canada and its sovereign off-shore. This work is concerned with the history of the Survey, incorporating an examination of the administrative and political environments in which it operated, its relationships with mining and other industries, and with the academic and scientific communities. Of related interest is A. Ignatieff's history of the Mines Branch of the Department of Energy, Mines and Resources entitled *A Canadian research heritage: an historical account of 75 years of federal government research and development in minerals, metals and fuels at the Mines Branch* (Ottawa: Supply and Services, 1981).

976　Inventing Canada: early Victorian science and the idea of a transcontinental nation.
Suzanne Zeller.　Toronto: University of Toronto Press, 1987. 356p.
The author documents Victorian science in Canada, focusing on four areas: geology; terrestrial magnetism; meteorology; and botany. Within this context she explores the rôle of key individuals of the nineteenth century including Sir William Edmond Logan, Sir John Henry Lefroy, and George Lawson among many other scientists, educators, journalists, businessmen, and agriculturalists.

Literature

Reference

977 **Archives des lettres canadiennes.** (Archive of Canadian literature.) Ottawa: Centre de recherches de littérature canadienne-française, Éditions de L'Université d'Ottawa, 1961-76. 5 vols.

Taken collectively or individually, this set provides valuable commentary and resource material on various aspects of Quebec literature. Of particular interest are volumes three, four, and five. Volume three entitled *Le roman canadien-français* (The French-Canadian novel. Montreal: Fides, 1971) provides a critical survey of Quebec fiction, and includes sketches of contemporary writers and a chronology of novels from 1837 to 1962. Volume four entitled *La poésie canadienne-française* (French-Canadian poetry. Montreal: Fides, 1969) gives similar focus to Quebec poetry and poets, including a chronology from 1803 to 1967. Finally, volume five entitled *Le théâtre canadien-français* (French-Canadian theatre. Montreal: Fides, 1976) deals with Quebec theatre and dramatists, with a listing of plays from the seventeenth century to 1976.

978 **Canadian Literature Index: a Guide to Periodicals and Newspapers.** Toronto: ECW Press, 1985- . quarterly.

The *Index* has two objectives: 'one, to access all Canadian primary materials (poems, short stories, novels, plays and literary essays), and two, to access all Canadian secondary materials (critical articles, book reviews, interviews and bibliographies)'. Included in the *Index* are literary periodicals which meet the editors' criteria of quality and reliability. Also included are general interest periodicals and newspapers and international publications selected on the basis of literary content, quality and circulation.

979 **Bibliographie de la critique de la littérature québécoise et canadienne-française dans les revues canadiennes (1974-1978).** (Bibliography of Quebec and French-Canadian literacy criticism in Canadian journals [1974-78]).
René Dionne, Pierre Cantin. Ottawa: Les Presses de l'Université d'Ottawa, 1988- .

This is the first volume in a bibliographical series which will enumerate literary criticism of Quebec and French-Canadian literature, both retrospectively as well as ongoing. The interested reader is alerted also to the authors' *Bibliographie de la critique de la littérature québécoise dans les revues des XIX et XX siècles* (Bibliography of Quebec literary criticism in 19th- and 20th-century journals. Ottawa: Centre de recherche en civilisation canadienne-française, 1979).

980 **Histoire de la littérature française du Québec.** (History of French literature of Quebec.)
Pierre de Grandpré. Montreal: Librairie Beauchemin Limitée, 1967. 4 vols.

A survey of French-Canadian literature, superseded in terms of its encyclopaedic use by the *Dictionnaire des oeuvres littéraires du Québec* (q.v.) (Dictionary of literary works of Quebec), but still widely available and useful for the general reader.

981 **Dictionnaire pratique des auteurs québécois.** (Practical dictionary of Quebec authors.)
Réginald Hamel, John Hare, Paul Wyczynski. Montreal: Fides, 1976. 723p.

A bio-bibliographical reference tool, with very brief articles on some 600 French language writers in Canada. The arrangement is alphabetical with each entry including biocritical articles, followed by works by and about the writer. This is a fundamental source of information for libraries and for individual researchers in the field.

982 **Bibliographie critique du roman canadien-français, 1837-1900.** (Critical bibliography of the French-Canadian novel 1837-1900.)
David M. Hayne, Marcel Tirol. Toronto: University of Toronto Press, 1968. 141p.

This descriptive bibliography lists the monographic works of French-Canadian novelists for the period under study, including the first edition of each work, as well as translations, serializations, etc. Entries are arranged alphabetically and then chronologically by date of publication. Included within each author's entry are notes relating to the publication of the works and a listing of sources consulted. There is a lengthy introductory section devoted to general biographical and critical materials.

983 **Profiles in Canadian literature.**
Edited by Jeffrey Heath. Toronto; Charlottetown, Prince Edward Island: Dundurn Press, 1980-86. 6 vols. bibliog.

Leading scholars have written a series of eighty-seven profile studies of significant Canadian, primarily but not exclusively, novelists and poets. Each essay familiarizes the reader with each author's work and provides valuable insights into themes, techniques and special characteristics. A commentary by and about each author provides additional information and provides advice for further research. This publication is most suitable for the student or the interested, but uninformed, general reader.

984 **Modern English-Canadian prose: a guide to information sources.**
Helen Hoy. Detroit, Michigan: Gale Research Company, 1983. 605p.
(American Literature, English Literature, and World Literatures in English: An Information Guide Series, vol. 38).
A checklist of twentieth-century Canadian fiction and nonfiction prose written in English. Included are writers (sixty-eight in number) whose work 'rests squarely within the twentieth century, omitting those . . . who may have published in this century but only as the continuation of an established literary career'. The emphasis for inclusion is on novelists and short story writers; non-fiction writers have been included particularly if their writing is closely related to literary pursuits, i.e. essay writers, literary critics, nature writers, biographers, writers of memoirs and humourists. The first two sections list reference sources and works of literary history, criticism and theory respectively. The volume is supported by separate author, title and subject indexes.

985 **Literary history of Canada: Canadian literature in English.**
General ed., Carl F. Klinck, edited by Alfred G. Bailey, Claude
Bissell, Roy Daniells, Northrop Frye, Desmond Pacey. Toronto:
University of Toronto Press, 1976. 2nd ed. 3 vols.
The *Literary history of Canada* is a classic of Canadian scholarship. A cooperative undertaking, the purpose of the work was 'to publish a comprehensive reference book on the (English) literary history of this country, and to encourage established and younger scholars to engage in a critical study of that history both before and after the appearance of the book'. The three volumes deal not only with works classified as 'literature' but also with 'other works which have influenced literature or have been significantly related to literature in expressing the cultural life of the country'. The work is divided into parts according to historical period: the Old World and the new found lands, settlement to Confederation, Confederation to the First World War, 1920 to 1960, and 1960-73. The introductory chapter to each part consolidates the historical essays. Each volume is indexed.

986 **The annotated bibliography of Canada's major authors.**
Edited by Robert Lecker, Jack David. Downsview, Ontario: ECW
Press, 1979- . 7 vols.
In 1987 seven volumes in the ongoing, multi-volume series had been published. Lecker and David's bibliography will encompass, when complete, a broad array of significant French- and English-Canadian authors, from the nineteenth and twentieth centuries, and because it presents such a compilation within one bibliographic series, it seems prudent to note its existence for the reader. Each bibliography in the series includes entries of primary and secondary works by and on specific writers. Each entry contains standard enumerative, bibliographic information, as well as an annotation of the critical writings which are 'designed to furnish an informed, but objective, summary of the arguments advanced in each secondary source'. A detailed justification of the arrangement of individual bibliographies is well described in the 'Introduction' to each volume.

987 **Dictionnaire des oeuvres littéraires du Québec.** (Dictionary of literary works of Quebec.)
[Edited by] Maurice Lemire. Montreal: Fides, 1978- . 5 vols.
This is a monumental piece of scholarship, and absolutely essential to the student or researcher of francophone Quebec or Canadian literature and history. Each volume contains a series of bio-biblio-critical entries, varying in length depending upon the importance attached to the individual or work under discussion (these range from 250 to 3,000 words). Each volume is introduced by a critical essay on the period, and the volumes are concluded with extensive general bibliographies for the respective periods encompassed by each volume. In total the five volumes cover literature from its origins up until 1975.

988 **Index to Canadian poetry in English.**
Compiled by Jane McQuarrie, Anne Mercer, Gordon Ripley.
Toronto: Reference Press, 1984. 367p.
This *Index* is patterned after *Granger's index to poetry*, a standard reference work published by the Columbia University Press, New York. This volume indexes approximately 7,000 Canadian poems (and a sample of French-Canadian poems in translation) in fifty-one collections. The compilers note that the work is a beginning and make no claim to being inclusive. Their intent was 'to include a broad array of anthologies, particularly those anthologies one might expect to find on the shelves of public libraries in Canada and the United States'. The 'Title and First-Line Index' is the principle index of the compilation. Here can be found the full reference for each poem. A 'Subject Index' utilizing broad subject headings, and an 'Author Index' provide additional access to the listed poems. For additional access to works of Canadian poetry, researchers are directed to Margery Fee's *Canadian poetry in selected English-language anthologies: an index and guide* (Halifax, Nova Scotia: Dalhousie University Libraries and Dalhousie University School of Library Service, 1985).

989 **English-Canadian literature to 1900: a guide to information sources.**
R. G. Moyles. Detroit, Michigan: Gale Research Company, 1976. 346p. (American Literature, English Literature, and World Literatures in English: An Information Guide Series, vol. 6).
This bibliography introduces the researcher to the primary and secondary sources considered necessary for the study of pre-1900 Canadian literature. The compiler divides his work into sections including: general reference guides, literary histories and criticism, anthologies, major authors (listing works and criticism of twelve key writers), minor authors (listing works and criticism of thirty-six writers), the literature of exploration, travel and description, and the journals of the period. Individual author sections are prefaced by short biographies.

990 **Canadian writers since 1960: first series.**
Edited by W. H. New. Detroit, Michigan: Gale Research Company, 1986. 445p. (Dictionary of Literary Biography, vol. 53).
The objective of the host *Dictionary of Literary Biography* is 'to make literature and its creators better understood and more accessible to students and the literate public, while satisfying the standards of teachers and scholars'. This volume is the first of at least four volumes focusing on the writers of Canada who use English or French as

their language of artistic expression. Entries typically include works by the author, an extensive, critical biography, and a listing of bibliographies, reference works and critical work about the author. Supplementary reading lists are included in the volumes. Related works include: *Canadian writers since 1960: second series* (1987); *Canadian writers, 1920-1959: first series* (1989); *Canadian writers, 1920-1959: second series* (1989).

991   **Modern English-Canadian poetry: a guide to information sources.**
Edited by Peter Stevens.   Detroit, Michigan: Gale Research
Company, 1978. 216p. (American Literature, English Literature, and
World Literatures in English: An Information Guide Series, vol. 15).
This publication is offered as a 'working bibliography' of major and some minor English-Canadian poets of the twentieth century. The work is divided into three major divisions: 'The Beginnings: 1900-1944'; 'Poetic Renaissance: The 1940's and Beyond'; and, 'Contemporary Poetry: The 1960's and '70's'. Within these divisions the works and criticism (the latter primarily limited to Canadian work) of individual authors are listed. Entries give all pertinent bibliographic information and annotations have been provided for those titles 'which mark an advance in a poet's development, a change of direction, or a gathering of the poet's work'. Brief biographical notes are also included. The full effectiveness of the work is somewhat limite by its selectiveness, however it is an easily available starting point for the informed reader or researcher in Canada or abroad.

992   **The Oxford companion to Canadian literature.**
Edited by William Toye.   Toronto: Oxford University Press, 1983.
843p.   ·
This standard reference tool provides a guide to Canadian authors and creative writing and supersedes the *Oxford companion to Canadian history and literature* (1967). The *Companion* is organized alphabetically, with articles mainly on writers and genres. It covers in detail 'the outlines of, and critical responses to, a rich literary culture in two languages'. Of interest also, particularly to the general reader, is Albert and Theresa Moritz's *The Oxford illustrated literary guide to Canada* (Toronto: Oxford University Press, 1987).

993   **A checklist of Canadian literature and background materials 1628-1960.**
Reginald Eyre Watters.   Toronto: University of Toronto Press, 1972.
rev. ed. 1085p.
'Watters' remains the most comprehensive listing of separately published works, with imprints from 1960 or earlier, that constitutes the literature of English-speaking Canada. Approximately 16,000 entries are divided into two categories. 'Part one ' of the *Checklist* is an inventory of all known titles in the genres of poetry, fiction and drama, produced by English-speaking Canadians. 'Part two' is a more selective listing of books which the compiler sees to be valuable to the study of literature and culture in Canada. The books are divided into sub-categories of biography, essays and speeches, local histories, religion and morality, social history, scholarship, and travel and description. Library locations are provided for those titles with an imprint date prior to 1951. The work has an index of anonymous titles as well as a general author index.

994 Who's who in Canadian literature, 1987-88.
'Toronto: Reference Press, 1987. 360p.
A general reference work, which is updated and published every second year, combines bibliographical data with biographical information. The individuals selected for listing had to be living Canadian poets, playwrights, story writers, novelists, children's writers, critics, editors or translators who have made some contribution to Canadian literature. Excluded are writers who died before the date of publication, as well as journalists, historians, biographers (with the exception of literary biographers) and essayists. A typical entry contains information about: literary vocation, place and date of birth, parents and family, education, memberships in literary associations, awards, occupation, magazine publications, anthologies, monograph publications, works in progress, home address, mailing address, sources of biographical and critical information, and general notes (editorships, unpublished work, war service, etc.). Also included is a list of the Governor General's Literary Awards.

Criticism

995 Survival: a thematic guide to Canadian literature.
Margaret Atwood. Toronto: Anansi, 1972. 287p.
Survival has been heralded as a landmark work of criticism. However regarded, it is a highly readable, witty and insightful treatise which has lasting qualities. It identifies and comments upon 'key patterns' which taken together 'constitute the shape of Canadian literature insofar as it is Canadian literature'. Intended primarily for educators and students of Canadian literature, each chapter is concluded with a 'Short List' of works as well as a 'Long List' which includes all works mentioned in the chapter. A later work by Atwood entitled *Second words: selected critical prose* (Toronto: Anansi, 1982), serves as a companion volume, though it did not have the same impact as *Survival*.

996 Surrealism and Quebec literature: history of a cultural revolution.
André G. Bourassa, translated by Mark Czarnecki. Toronto: University of Toronto Press, 1984. 374p. bibliog.
'What was the impact of the surrealist movement in Quebec? Does the cultural history of Quebec include a surrealist phase? Did the movement in Quebec define itself in any special way? Did Quebec play a role in the movement on an international level?'. The author requests the reader to consider these questions from the outset of the book. Through study of the literature of Quebec, from the first novel in 1837, through the Quiet Revolution of the 1950s and 1960s, to the mid 1980s the author examines the nature of Quebec surrealism. Key to the study is the understanding of the circumstances leading to the publication in 1948 by Quebec artist Paul-Emile Borduas of his manifesto *Refus global* – a plea for rejection of rationalization, mechanization, and other restraining influences in society, including the Church. Originally published in 1977 with the title *Surréalisme et littérature québécoise*, this is a work of importance for those wishing to gain another perspective on the culture of Quebec, as well as its politics. The work is supported by an extensive bibliography.

997 **On Canadian poetry.**
     E. K. Brown. Ottawa: Tecumseh Press, 1973. 172p.

This critical essay, first published in 1943, seeks to answer three questions pertaining to the peculiar difficulties faced by the Canadian writer, the state of Canadian poetry and the means by which the masters of Canadian poetry have achieved their success and the nature of this success. The focus on the latter question is on three poets – Archibald Lampman, Duncan Campbell Scott, and E. J. Pratt.

998 **Responses and evaluations: essays on Canada.**
     E. K. Brown.   Toronto: McClelland & Stewart, 1977. 314p. (New
     Canadian Library, vol. 137).

This is an important work of literary criticism, for it brings together much of the writing of an early and influential Canadian critic. Of Brown, B. K. Sandwell wrote 'no one, I think, in his generation made a more lasting imprint upon Canadian literary taste than this brilliant native of Toronto . . . he was a man of delicate literary perception, catholic critical taste, and extremely well-informed judgement in all matters relating to expression in both the English and French languages'. The collection includes thirteen diverse essays, a series of fifteen annual reviews of Canadian poetry (1935-49) which appeared in the *University of Toronto Quarterly*, and a section of 'Causeries', an informal and colloquial form of criticism taken primarily from the *Winnipeg Free Press*.

999 **Canadian Literature = Littérature canadienne.**
     Vancouver: University of British Columbia, 1959- . quarterly.

Regarded as the premier journal of Canadian literary criticism this publication incorporates some òriginal poetry and fiction. It also includes an extensive book review section. Canadian literary studies are served by a wide variety of other journals, including: *Studies in Canadian Literature* (Fredericton, New Brunswick: Department of English, University of New Brunswick, 1975-); *Essays on Canadian Writing* (Toronto: ECW Press, 1974-); *Canadian Fiction Magazine* (Toronto: Canadian Fiction Magazine, 1971-); *Journal of Canadian Fiction* (Montreal: JCF Press, 1972-); *Canadian Poetry* (London, Ontario, Department of English, University of Western Ontario, 1977); *Journal of Canadian Poetry* (Nepean, Ontario: Journal of Canadian Poetry, 1986-); and, *Canadian Children's Literature/Littérature canadienne pour la jeunesse* (Guelph, Ontario: Canadian Children's Press, 1975-). Quebec literature is served by such journals as: *Voix & Images* (Voices & Images. Montreal: Université du Québec, 1975-); and, *Revue d'Histoire Littéraire du Québec et du Canada Français* (Journal of Literary History of Quebec and French Canada. Ottawa: Les Presses de l'Université d'Ottawa, 1981-).

1000 **Surviving the paraphrase: eleven essays on Canadian literature.**
      Frank Davey.   Winnipeg, Manitoba: Turnstone, 1983. 193p.

Presents eleven essays by a noted poet/critic. In the words of another highly regarded poet/critic, Eli Mandel, Davey has 'added his voice on behalf of post-modern writing, and perhaps as clearly as any other writer has articulated the theory of post-modernism. He has given our criticism its contemporary voice, its sound and its rhythms, and to the mood of our most recent critical writing added his generous and welcoming spirit'. This work is an important contribution to Canadian literary criticism.

1001   **Canadian novelists and the novel.**
· Edited by Douglas Daymond, Leslie Monkman.   Ottawa: Borealis
Press, 1981. 284p.

Thirty-two English-Canadian novelists of the last one hundred and fifty years comment on the 'theory and practice of their art'. The volume is divided into five parts: 'The Pre-Confederation Novel'; 'The Novel in the New Dominion'; 'The Rise of Realism'; 'Regionalism and Nationalism'; and 'The Contemporary Novel'. Each section is introduced by a notable present-day critic of the period. An excellent work for the reader interested in the development of the Canadian literary tradition.

1002   **Towards a Canadian literature: essays, editorials and manifestos.**
Edited by Douglas M. Daymond, Leslie G. Monkman.   Ottawa:
Tecumseh Press, 1984-85. 2 vols.

These two volumes provide fascinating reading for the informed academic and general reader alike. The work is made up of a selection of writings about literature in English in Canada ranging from 1752 to 1983. Its purpose is to examine the development of Canadian English-language literature by means of a 'collection of documents by Canadian editors, essayists, poets, novelists and anthologists. It includes addresses, manifestos, editorials, introductions and essays selected from newspapers, magazines, anthologies and volumes of literary criticism'. The pieces are generally arranged chronologically, in five divisions, and where appropriate are grouped by journal title.

1003   **Selected essays and criticism.**
Louis Dudek.   Ottawa: Tecumseh Press, 1978. 380p.

A collection of essays and articles by one of Canada's best known poets/critics. Spanning the period from 1942 to 1976 these pieces provide reflection on the Canadian literary scene from the point of view of one of its more respected insiders.

1004   **The republic of childhood: a critical guide to Canadian children's literature in English.**
Sheila Egoff.   Toronto: Oxford University Press, 1975. 2nd ed. 335p.

A critical examination of Canadian children's books, most published after 1950. The purposes of the work are varied; to indicate standards by which children's reading can be guided; to guide parents, teachers and librarians who purchase and make available books for children; to credit achievement for recognizably good writing for children in Canada. Coverage includes Indian and Eskimo legends, folk tales, fiction, animal stories, poetry and plays, as well as history. Each chapter is followed by an annotated list of the works discussed as well as a selection of related work. Essential reading for those interested in children's literature. Less authoritative, but a handy reference, is Irma McDonough's *Profiles* (Ottawa: Canadian Library Association, 1975) which contains biographical profiles of Canadian authors and illustrators of children's books.

1005   **The bush garden: essays on the Canadian imagination.**
Northrop Frye.   Toronto: Anansi, 1971. 256p.

This collection has been regarded as a classic, given that it brings together a great deal of writing, spanning a thirty year period, on Canadian culture by one of Canada's eminent literary critics. Half of the work reprints the ten annual surveys of Canadian poetry written during the decade of the 1950s for the journal *University of Toronto Quarterly*, in its 'Letters in Canada' issue. The remaining pieces are drawn from a

Literature. Criticism

variety of sources and include two insightful articles on Canadian art. It is essential
reading for the student of Canadian literature, and important also for an understanding
of the question of Canadian 'identity'.

1006   **Unnamed country: the struggle for a Canadian prairie fiction.**
Dick Harrison.   Edmonton, Alberta: University of Alberta Press,
1977. 250p. bibliog.

Offers insights into the development, or 'struggle' as the author states in his subtitle,
for an indigenous prairie fiction. The work 'begins before the first prairie novel, with
the encounter between the civilized imagination and an unnamed country. It then
traces the growth of prairie fiction over the past century as part of our imperfect and
often self-defeating efforts to humanize that country'. In tracing this development the
author concentrates on the 'unique challenge the plains environment presents to the
writer's imagination' and at the same time takes into account 'the influence of culture
on man's reaction to the landscape'. A substantial bibliography complements the work.

1007   **Butterfly on rock: a study of themes and images in Canadian literature.**
D. G. Jones.   Toronto: University of Toronto Press, 1970. 197p.

This is not so much a survey as it is a discussion of recurring themes and images which
themselves serve to define the Canadian imaginative life – themes and images such as
the land, the concept of exile and of garrison culture. It is required reading for those
seriously interested in Canadian literature. The introductory essay, 'The Sleeping
Giant', has itself become a classic piece.

1008   **Canadian literature in English.**
W. J. Keith.   London; New York: Longman, 1985. 287p. (Longman
Literature in English Series).

This is an important book for it subsumes a concise, but comprehensive, historical
survey or guide of Canadian literature in English by one of the country's leading
critics. Keith explores the development of Canadian literature, which began as a
continuation of what was produced in Great Britain, and how it defined itself against
the American tradition evolving 'as a distinctive literature related to but independent
of both parent and neighbour'. The bibliography is particularly good both as an
introduction to general critical literature, as well as to works by and about over 128
major writers.

1009   **Canadian Writers and Their Works: Fiction Series.**
Edited by Robert Lecker, Jack David and Ellen Quigley. Downsview,
Ontario: ECW Press, 1983- . 10 vols. bibliog.

Each volume in this series contains five critical essays on writers important to the
development of Canadian fiction over the past two centuries. A unifying essay by
George Woodcock introduces each collection. The bio-critical essays also incorporate
'a discussion of the tradition and milieu influencing [the writer's] work, a critical
overview section which reviews published criticism on the author, a long section
analyzing the author's works, and a selected bibliography listing primary and secondary
material'. It comprises an essential collection for libraries or for the serious researcher.

1010   **Canadian Writers and Their Works: Poetry Series.**
Edited by Robert Lecker, Jack David, Ellen Quigley.   Downsview,
Ontario: ECW Press, 1982- . 10 vols. bibliog.
Similar to the fiction series by the same editors (q.v.), each volume contains five
critical essays on writers important to the development of Canadian poetry over the
last two centuries. Again, a unifying essay by George Woodcock introduces each
collection. The essays are similar in form to those of the companion series.

1011   **Les grands thèmes nationalistes du roman historique canadien-français.**
(The main nationalistic themes of the French-Canadian historical
novel.)
Maurice Lemire.   Quebec: Les Presses de L'Université Laval, 1970.
281p. bibliog. (Vie des Lettres canadiennes, vol. 8).
The author poses a question concerning the roots of neo-nationalism; is it the modern
equivalent of traditional nationalism or simply its continuation? He then examines the
historical fiction of Quebec, and identifies and proceeds to discuss the major themes of
French-Canadian nationalism. He divides these themes into two broad categories
reflecting two periods (designated the positive and the negative) of Quebec's history.
The themes in the former category, which tend to reflect the period of the French
régime, include heroic illusions such as 'La Légende de l'Iroquoise', 'Les Missionnaires',
'Les Pionniers', 'Les Soldats'; the latter are associated with the events and period
relating to or following the defeat by the English. The work includes a *tableau
chronologique* which identifies works of historical fiction mirroring the thematic
categories of the text. A bibliography is also included.

1012   **Introduction à la littérature québécoise (1900-1939).** (Introduction to
the literature of Quebec.)
Maurice Lemire.   Montreal: Fides, 1981. 171p.
A very readable survey of literary development in Quebec, concentrating on a period
which had lost its appeal for many critics. In this work the author has been able to
place the literature of the province within the economic, social and cultural contexts. It
is of particular interest to the student or the general reader with some background in *la
littérature québécoise.*

1013   **Histoire de la littérature acadienne: de rêve en rêve.** (History of
Acadian literature: from dream to dream.)
Marguerite Maillet.   Ottawa: Les Éditions d'Acadie, 1983. 262p.
bibliog.
Increasingly Canadians are beginning to take notice of the depth and richness of their
national literature. Maillet explores a significant component of this tradition in her
work on Acadian (New Brunswick) literature. Those interested in this ara would be well
advised to use the present volume as a companion to the author's 1979 multi-volume
anthology of Acadian texts. In the work in hand four stages of development are
identified. The first 'Du Rêve à la Réalité (1604-1866)' (From a dream to reality)
records the emergence of a written literature from a rich oral tradition; stage two 'Sur
les Chemins de l'Histoire (1867-1928)' (Making history) sees the emergence of a new
identity through the work of a generation of historians, essayists and other nationalist
writers; 'Sous le Signe du Souvenir (1929-1957)' (A time for remembrance) chronicles
the development of traditional genres of *belles lettres*, such as fiction, poetry and

drama, and finally, 'Récupération et Contestation' (Recovery and contention) discusses the development of this distinct literary tradition as it moves to distinguish itself from the literary traditions of Quebec. The volume includes a useful *tableau chronologique* which identifies and dates key literary benchmarks and places them within the context of contemporary events, and is also supported by a substantial bibliography.

1014   **Another time.**
Eli Mandel.   Erin, Ontario: Press Porcépic, 1977. 160p. (Three Solitudes: Contemporary Literary Criticism in Canada, vol. 3).
Poet/critic Mandel presents a collection of materials which he characterizes as 'reflections rather than arguments' on modern Canadian writing. The essays within the work are grouped into three parts: the first sets out a general framework; the second explores the images, romance, realism and regionalism in the literature of the west; and the last examines various problems of Canadian writing.

1015   **Contexts of Canadian criticism.**
Edited by Eli Mandel.   Chicago: University of Chicago Press, 1971. 304p. (Patterns of Literary Criticism).
In this collection poet/critic Eli Mandel frames patterns of literary and critical development in 'essays on historiography and on social, as well as cultural, history'. He argues that 'Canadian literary criticism consistently seeks its organizing principles not only in theories of literature but in historical and social contexts. It may be that Canadian concern with historiography, social structure, and esthetics can be viewed best as an expression of an almost paranoiac self-consciousness . . . Whatever the explanation . . . any collection of critical essays that aspires to represent Canadian critical writing fairly and accurately will obviously present selections concerned not only with traditional comments on patterns of literary development but with the history and form of Canadian society'. Essays are reprinted from a variety of sources and are by noted writers such as W. L. Morton, H. A. Innis, F. H. Underhill, George Grant, Northrop Frye, Marshall McLuhan, Henry Kreisel and Dorothy Livesay, to name a few.

1016   **Harsh and lovely land: the major Canadian poets and the making of a Canadian tradition.**
Tom Marshall.   Vancouver: University of British Columbia Press, 1979. 184p.
A survey work examining the major English-Canadian poets and the development of their poetic tradition in Canada. The author devotes most attention to the work of the twentieth century, and within that context, to the post-war period.

1017   **The wacousta syndrome: explorations in the Canadian langscape.**
Gaile McGregor.   Toronto: University of Toronto Press, 1985. 473p.
This work is difficult to characterize. It is a book about Canada. In the publisher's words, it is a book about our creation of Canada. In the author's words the coining of the word 'langscape', evident in the subtitle, is meant 'to underline the extent to which nature, like other aspects of reality, is not simply perceived but socially constructed'. Ultimately, the author attempts to find the accommodation between 'self' and 'other' through analysis of Canadian literature.

1018   L'Age de la littérature canadienne: essai. (The era of Canadian
literature: an essay.)
Clément Moisan.   Montreal: Éditions HMH, 1969. 193p. (Collection
Constantes, vol. 19).
This was an important work at the time of its publication in that it was the first
monographic comparative treatment of English and French-Canadian literature. While
dated, it remains of interest to the student and the general reader concerned with the
development of such comparative studies. It stands alone as a general survey of the
two literatures.

1019   A poetry of frontiers: comparative studies in Quebec/Canadian
literature.
Clément Moisan.   Victoria, British Columbia; Toronto: Press
Porcépic, 1983. 219p. bibliog.
A translation of the author's *Poésie des frontières: étude comparée des poésies
canadienne et québécoise* (LaSalle, Québec: Éditions Hurtubise HMH, 1979), and an
expansion of his earlier work *L'Âge de la littérature canadienne* (q.v.). Here he focuses
on the similarities and differences with regard to form, structure and theme of English-
Canadian and Quebec poetry. Moisan's conclusions tend to be predictable as he
exposes the common themes of identity, survival and the garrison mentality, among
others. This is a work for the well informed or academic reader. There is a substantial
bibliography.

1020   A native heritage: images of the Indian in English-Canadian literature.
Leslie Monkman.   Toronto: University of Toronto Press, 1981. 193p.
Until the appearance of this work there had been no comprehensive study of the rôles
and stereotypes to which the Indian was relegated in Canadian literary tradition. The
author points out that there are comparatively few works by white writers which
directly concern the Indian and his culture. He goes on to note in the introduction that
'if white writers offer relatively few insights into the red man's world, they have
repeatedly found in the confrontation of native and non-native heritages a unique focus
for the exploration of their own concerns and culture . . . writers have turned to the
Indian and his culture for standards by which to measure the values and goals of white
Canadian society, for patterns of cultural destruction, transformation, and survival,
and for new heroes and indigenous myths'.

1021   Here and now.
Edited by John Moss.   Toronto: NC Press, 1978. 204p. (The
Canadian Novel, vol. 1).
Here and now is the first of four independently titled volumes in The Canadian Novel
series. These anthologies of criticism combine published work (taken primarily from
the *Journal of Canadian Fiction*) with previously unpublished work, and focus on the
work of selected writers of achievement. This first volume deals with contemporary
writers. Volume two, entitled *Beginnings: a critical anthology* (1980) includes articles
on seven prose classics; volume three, entitled *Modern times: a critical anthology*
(1982) identifies ten writers characterized as representative of a transitional phase in
Canadian literature; and volume four, entitled *Present tense* (1985) illuminates the
work of thirteen writers described by the editor as postmodern.

1022 **Patterns of isolation in English-Canadian fiction.**
John Moss. Toronto: McClelland & Stewart, 1974. 256p.

It is noted in the introduction that 'the patterns of isolation in English-Canadian fiction provide one of a number of its distinguishing characteristics'. With isolation as a 'linking bond' the author takes notable works of fiction as his point of departure. The interested reader would be well advised to sample other examples of this author's work, for example *Sex and violence in the Canadian novel: the ancestral present* (Toronto: McClelland & Stewart, 1977).

1023 **A reader's guide to the Canadian novel.**
John Moss. Toronto: McClelland & Stewart, 1981. 399p.

An invaluable guide for scholars, students and the general public alike. This work is a 'critical reference work, consisting of separate commentaries on over two hundred Canadian novels'. Novels, published from 1769 to 1980, were selected on the basis of their 'significance within the Canadian literary tradition, as seen from a present perspective'. The author notes the mercurial nature of significance (whether historical, thematic, innovative, etc.) and in a well-reasoned introduction defends his approach and his decisions for the novels' inclusion. The work is limited to novels published originally in English and thus excludes québécois literature.

1024 **Articulating West: essays on purpose and form in modern Canadian literature.**
W. H. New. Toronto: New Press, 1972. 282p.

The author seeks to understand, through literary example, the tensions at the heart of the Canadian experience and their influence on Canada's writers.

1025 **Dramatists in Canada: selected essays.**
Edited by William H. New. Vancouver: University of British Columbia Press, 1972. 204p. (Canadian Literature Series).

Through the medium of connected essays, this work provides a retrospective survey of and introduction to Canadian drama. The essays examine the writers and the audience, discuss the ideas and techniques of Canadian drama and trace the historical developments and current trends. While the volume examines the work of leading nineteenth-century dramatists, its primary focus is on the twentieth century and in particular the period from 1940 to 1965.

1026 **Creative writing in Canada: a short history of English-Canadian literature.**
Desmond Pacey. Toronto: Ryerson Press, 1961. 314p.

The work of such a noteworthy observer as Pacey must be included in any collection of recommended works on Canadian literature. It must be recognized, however, that this work's importance lies not only in its critical comments, but perhaps more in its usefulness as a marker along the road of development of Canadian literary criticism. Such statements as 'the distinctiveness of Canadian literature thus far has been almost wholly an inevitable response to a geographical, climatic and social situation, and thus it should and must remain' remind us as to how mature Canadian literature is and the concomitant evolution of critical analysis. The readers may also wish to consult the author's collected work in *Essays in Canadian criticism 1938-1968* (Toronto: Ryerson

Press, 1969); also, *Ten Canadian poets: a group of biographical and critical essays* (Toronto: Ryerson Press, 1958).

1027 **First people, first voices.**
Edited by Penny Petrone. Toronto: University of Toronto Press, 1983. 221p.
Presents a selection of writing and speeches by Canadian Indians from the 1630s to the 1980s, this book aims to record the origins and development of an Indian literary tradition in English. A study of this literature can provide an important insight into the Indian view of Canadian history.

1028 **Wilderness writers.**
James Polk. Toronto; Vancouver: Clarke, Irwin, 1972. 147p.
The wilderness and the place of wild animals within the natural setting has always been an important component in Canadian writing. Here is discussed the work in this genre of three key Canadian writers of the twentieth century: Ernest Thompson Seton, Charles G. D. Roberts, and Grey Owl.

1029 **Vertical man horizontal world: man and landscape in Canadian prairie fiction.**
Laurence Ricou. Vancouver: University of British Columbia Press, 1973. 151p.
By way of the metaphor, 'vertical man, horizontal world' Ricou is able to focus his analysis on the prominence of landscape in the works of prairie writers. As he points out in the preface the very obvious contrast of man to land, man's dramatic vertical presence in an entirely horizontal world, presented itself in an intriguing variety of contexts and was used for remarkably different artistic purposes'.

1030 **Contemporary Quebec criticism.**
Edited and translated by Larry Shouldice. Toronto: University of Toronto Press, 1979. 217p.
This work contains much of interest for the informed reader who enjoys some background to the literature and practices of literary criticism. The collection is comprised of English translations of ten articles representative of the body of criticism which has grown alongside the development of French-Canadian literature itself. Articles are divided into two sections. 'Backgrounds' views Quebec literature from an historical, cultural, ideological and national perspective. 'Themes and Genres' focuses on critical trends and approaches from the period 1958-78. All articles are general in nature and do not concentrate on any single writer. The editor introduces the anthology with a general overview of the development of Quebec criticism. He provides perspective on the importance of nationalism in Quebec writing and discusses some of the influences on Quebec literature, particularly the French.

1031   **Towards a view of Canadian letters: selected critical essays 1928-1971.**
A.J.M. Smith.   Vancouver: University of British Columbia Press,
1973. 230p.
This collection of essays reprinted from a variety of sources reflects the work of one of
the country's eminent poets/critics. It makes essential reading, not only for its
comment with relation to the works under discussion, but also as an expression as to
the nature and development of literary criticism over the period from which the
materials were drawn.

1032   **Writers of the prairies.**
Edited by Donald G. Stephens.   Vancouver: University of British
Columbia Press, 1973. 208p. (Canadian Literature Series).
In a brief introduction the compiler of this collection of essays captures the prairie
environment and the literary reflection of that environment. He writes 'it is a landscape
that is never merely tolerated; it is loved and hated with equal intensities. People hate
the bitter piercing cold of the winter, but praise the clear blue skies and the dazzling
sun on the purple-tinged banks of snow. They dislike the blowing dust and bleak
landscape of August but luxuriate in the never-ending sunsets and the rippled seas of
grain. The pure physicality of the landscape is always with the people on the prairies,
and its writers consciously and unconsciously reflect this world'.

1033   **Major Canadian authors: a critical introduction.**
David Stouck.   Lincoln, Nebraska: University of Nebraska Press,
1984. 308p.
This collection of seventeen short, critical essays is designed to introduce a selection of
Canada's most important authors writing in English. The essays are arranged
chronologically thus situating the authors within an historical context. The author
attempts to provide some insight into each writer's work and 'offers a description of
works that includes mode, structure, and style, as well as moral or social vision'. Each
essay is concluded by a short listing of selected readings. An appendix entitled 'Guide
to Other Canadian Writers' supports the text, in which is included a brief biographical
capsule on seventy other Canadian writers. This work is useful as an introduction to
Canadian literati.

1034   **All the polarities: comparative studies in contemporary Canadian
novels in French and English.**
Philip Stratford.   Toronto: ECW Press, 1986. 109p.
The author has chosen what he has determined to be remarkable works of fiction, six
French and six English novels, and used comparative techniques to explore a shared
focus. It is principally of interest to the informed reader seeking to find the common
ground which has evolved from two centuries of a shared history, geography and
government.

1035   **Second image: comparative studies in Quebec/Canadian literature.**
Ronald Sutherland.   Toronto: New Press, 1971. 189p.
Although dated, this work is still of interest and use for those interested in comparative
Canadian literature, that is the application of literary analysis to the works of Canadian
writers, both those writing in English and those writing in French. This area of

scholarship has progressed considerably in the intervening years. However, although there is much which can be criticized about Sutherland's analysis, its publication still represents a benchmark in the development of Canadian literary criticism. *The new hero: essays in comparative Quebec/Canadian literature* (Toronto: Macmillan, 1977) serves as a companion volume to this one.

1036 **Destin littéraire du Québec.** (Literary development of Quebec.)
Gérard Tougas. Montreal: Éditions Québec/Amérique, 1982. 208p.
This noted scholar reviews the development of Quebec literature within the context of western civilization and finds the literature to be thriving, supported as it is by vibrant socio-economic institutions. In his view it is fast becoming an important and accepted francophone literature, second only, perhaps, to that of France.

1037 **History of French-Canadian literature.**
Gerard Tougas, translated by Alta Lind Cook. Toronto: Ryerson Press, 1966. 2nd ed. 301p.
First published in 1960 under the title *Histoire de la littérature canadienne-française*, this is an enduring, very readable work which provides a critical survey of the literature.

1038 **The long journey: literary themes of French Canada.**
Jack Warwick. Toronto: University of Toronto Press, 1968. 172p.
(University of Toronto Romance Series, vol. 12).
Though an earlier work, this English-language discussion remains of interest particularly to the uninformed reader.

1039 **Survey: a short history of Canadian literature.**
Elizabeth Waterston. Toronto: Methuen, 1973. 215p. (Methuen Canadian Literature Series).
This book is aimed at the high-school and college student, or uninformed reader. It contains eleven short essays which explore various themes in Canadian literature. Each is concluded by a study guide which directs the reader to a selection of accessible literary and critical works. In the author's words 'this book proposes to explore some of the "hows" and the "whys" of Canadian art. Why certain topics caught the consciousness of writers. . . how particular writers or groups of writers shaped those topics into artworks'. It provides a reasonably good introduction to the field for the above audience. A work similar in nature and purpose is Clara Thomas' *Our nature – our voices: a guidebook to English-Canadian literature* (Toronto: New Press, 1972).

1040   **Odysseus ever returning: essays on Canadian writers and writing.**
George Woodcock.   Toronto: McClelland & Stewart, 1970. 158p.
(New Canadian Library, vol. 71).
Woodcock claims a special status among Canadian literary critics. As William New
states in the introduction, 'In this book we do not find essays on every Canadian
literary figure with pretensions to artistry, but we do find excursions into the literary
milieu and examples of fine criticism. Through the bluntness and humour with which
George Woodcock expresses himself, we approach his exploration of the applicability
of international theories and standards of art towards a regional literature. We see also
the stylish peregrinations of a humane critic, as he returns across Odyssean waters to
his often inhospitable native land'. Later similar collections serve to provide more of
Woodcock's insights, for example, *The world of Canadian writing: critiques &
recollections* (Vancouver: Douglas & McIntyre, 1980). Woodcock also compiled and
edited numerous anthologies, many of which included articles reprinted from the
journal *Canadian Literature*.

Arts

General

1041 Who's afraid of Canadian culture?
S.M. Crean.   Don Mills, Ontario: General Publishing, 1976. 296p.
Crean is strident in her condemnation of arts organizations in Canada and presents the view that they in effect exclude Canadian culture, while educational establishments and the mass media become increasingly Americanized. Although the work is almost fifteen years old, it is, in many ways, timeless. The problems discussed are as real today as they were fifteen, twenty-five, or even more years ago. It is a good readable examination of the problem for the uninitiated.

1042 An introduction to the arts in Canada.
Robert Fulford.   Toronto: Copp Clark, 1977. 135p.
A simply presented primer on the arts in Canada written particularly for new Canadians or those outside Canada. Fulford was a long-time editor of *Saturday Night*, one of the premier current affairs and cultural publications in Canada. The text covers native arts, literature, music, theatre, painting and sculpture, dance, film, architecture and broadcasting. Somewhat out-of-date today.

1043 Performing Arts in Canada.
Toronto: Canadian Stage and Arts Publications, 1961- . quarterly.
Articles in this publication deal with all areas of the arts, including dance, theatre and music.

1044 Strange bedfellows: the state and the arts in Canada.
George Woodcock.   Vancouver, Toronto: Douglas & McIntyre, 1985. 207p.
One of Canada's most distinguished literary critics and a general cultural commentator, provides an historical and critical assessment of current Canadian arts policy. He

reviews the relationship between the arts and the state throughout the world and then, focusing on Canada, assesses the progress made since the Massey Commission and the impact of such cultural agencies as the Canada Council, arts commissions and other vehicles of promotion.

Visual arts

1045 **Printmaking in Canada: the earliest views and portraits = Les débuts de l'estampe imprimée au Canada: vues et portraits.**
Mary Allodi. Toronto: Royal Ontario Museum, 1980. 244p.
A catalogue, with commentary, prepared for an exhibition held at the Royal Ontario Museum, April-May, 1980. The catalogue, with text, catalogues and comments upon separately issued views and portraits printed in Canada up to 1850, and develops from this a history of pictorial printmaking in the country. The text is bilingual.

1046 **Painters in a new land: from Annapolis Royal to the Klondike.**
Selected by Michael Bell. Toronto: McClelland & Stewart, 1973. 224p.
The water-colours and drawings reproduced in this book chronicle eighteenth- and nineteenth-century life in Canada. Originally produced by amateur artists who were primarily British travellers, military personnel or journalists, many of the prints were published in the form of engravings, aquatints, and lithographs which illustrated travel narratives and English popular journals, or graced the drawing rooms of English society. The plates are juxtaposed with text drawn from contemporary travel literature, diaries and newspaper accounts. Taken together the work is a beautifully produced visual and narrative record of our cultural and historical heritage.

1047 **From the heart: folk art in Canada.**
Jean-François Blanchette (et al.). Toronto; Ottawa: McClelland & Stewart in cooperation with the National Museum of Man, National Museums of Canada, 1983. 256p. bibliog.
This handsome book records the exhibition of Canadian folk art held by the National Museum of Man and sponsored by the Allstate Foundation of Canada. The introduction observes: 'Folk art in Canada reveals a feeling for life, a feeling nurtured by memories, drawn from moments of tenderness, and expressed in the restless stirrings of countless imaginations'. The book, reflecting the exhibition, is divided into four sections: 'Reflection' incorporates the artifacts of traditional everyday life; 'Commitment' contains the art created to express the emotions of devotion or loyalty; and, 'Fantasy' is devoted to works of imagination. The final section focuses on four folk artists whose work represents one or more of the aforementioned themes. The artists are Nelphas Prévost, Sam Spencer, Frank Kocevar and George Cockayne. Each of the exhibits is catalogued and includes descriptive commentary.

1048   **The Canadian earth: landscape paintings by the Group of Seven.**
Roger Boulet.   Toronto: Cerebrus/Prentice-Hall, 1982. 226p.

This is a coffee table art book, but it is one of the best of its type and provides the reader with plates of the highest quality. The limited text is informative but not critical, thus the work is directed in the first instance to the general reader. Short biographies of the members of the Group have been prepared by Paul Duval. In the words of A. J. Casson, member of the Group, 'in a very real sense, the landscape paintings of the Group of Seven represent a critical turning point in Canadian art. For the first time, Canadians dared to venture beyond the restrictive confines of the European academic tradition and paint as Canadians. For the first time, they dared to view native landscapes through Canadian eyes and paint with the fire and conviction required to record the breathtaking vistas of this country'. Another similar work, with somewhat more critical commentary, is Peter Mellen's *The Group of Seven* (Toronto: McClelland & Stewart, 1981). Of interest also is the catalogue by Dennis Reid entitled *Le Groupe des sept=The Group of Seven* (Ottawa: The National Gallery of Canada, 1970). Many additional works have been published on individual members of the Group.

1049   **"Bo'jou, Neejee!": profiles of Canadian Indian art.**
Ted J. Brasser.   Ottawa: National Museum of Man, 1976. 204p.

This catalogue was prepared for the travelling exhibition of Indian and Métis art, comprising the collection of collector Arthur Speyer. Over 200 artifacts are depicted. A scholarly essay introduces the catalogue, and relates the individual items to the ethno-cultures of the peoples represented.

1050   **Visions: contemporary art in Canada.**
Edited by Robert Bringhurst (et al).   Vancouver: Douglas & McIntyre, 1983. 239p.

Six noted critics/curators/art historians examine the post-war art scene in Canada. In general it was the editors' intention that following an introductory survey essay, most ably executed by Alvin Balkind, the remaining essays would 'investigate postwar art along five of the paths which recent artists have taken: art as response to place, art as art, art as social response, art as personal statement, art as idea'. Most interesting and useful essays, supported by over one hundred colour plates.

1051   **Contemporary Canadian art.**
David Burnett, Marilyn Schiff.   Edmonton, Alberta: Hurtig, 1983. 300p. bibliog.

Modern art in Canada is given a scholarly, critical examination from the period beginning in 1945 to the mid-1980s. Emphasis in the work has been given to the most significant radical developments and the artists responsible for these developments. The initial chapters deal with the modernist influence in the centres of Toronto and Montreal, with subsequent chapters devoted to the Maritimes and the West. The final chapters survey the achievements of post-modern Canadian sculptures and painters. The text is appropriately supported by black-and-white, as well as colour, illustrations.

1052   **Canadian Art.**
Toronto: Maclean-Hunter, 1984- . quarterly.

A colour illustrated magazine dealing with art and artists in Canada. Other publications essential to the interested reader include: *Canadian Art Review = Revue*

Arts. Visual arts

d'Art Canadienne (Montreal: Société pour promouvoir la publication en histoire de l'art au Canada/Society for the Promotion of Art History Publications in Canada, 1974-); and, *The Journal of Canadian Art History = Annales d'Histoire de l'Art Canadien* (Montreal: Concordia University, 1974-   ).

1053   Canadian art: its origins & development.
William Colgate.   Toronto: Ryerson, 1967. 278p.

A survey history of art in Canada which, while dated, is still one of the best overviews available in paperback for the general reader. Ninety illustrations of early paintings and engravings contribute to the work.

1054   Indian arts in Canada.
Olive Patricia Dickason.   Ottawa: Indian & Northern Affairs, 1972. 137p.

This work poses the question whether Indian artists should derive inspiration solely from their own culture, or express creativity completely independently of their own particular cultural background. The book examines some of these forces, i.e. the utilitarian nature of 'primitive art' *versus* the non-utilitarian nature of art for commercial considerations. The author surveys the artistic history of the North American Indian, examines the influences of the European culture, and discusses the future for the art form.

1055   Four decades: the Canadian Group of Painters and their contemporaries – 1930-1970.
Paul Duval.   Toronto: Clarke, Irwin, 1972. 191p.

For some forty years the Canadian Group of Painters (founded in 1933 by the Group of Seven members) served as a focus society providing its membership, which included almost every significant painter working in the period, with a creative community of interest and an outlet to exhibit. Within this broad survey of the main developments in Canadian painting (examining the work of more than 200 painters), there is encompassed a history of the Canadian Group. The work is beautifully produced with the vast majority of the almost 200 plates in colour.

1056   High realism in Canada.
Paul Duval.   Toronto: Clarke, Irwin, 1974. 175p.

For the purposes of this work 'high realism' is seen as an art form characterized by objectivity of vision, high definition, technical precision, accurate detail and excellent craftsmanship. Duval introduces his subject in a lengthy introduction which traces the origins of the style in Canada. He then examines the work of thirteen artists, among these Alex Colville, Ken Danby, Ernest Lindner and Christopher Pratt. Colour plates enhance the work.

1057   Documents in Canadian art.
Edited by Douglas Fetherling.   Peterborough, Ontario: Broadview, 1987. 327p.

A collection of significant essays relating to Canadian art, which were originally published between 1809 and 1986, and include the commentary of, among others,

Marius Barbeau, J.E.H. MacDonald, A.J. Casson, Bertram Brooker, Emily Carr, Northrop Frye, Wyndham Lewis and Paul-Emile Borduas.

1058 **Enjoying Canadian painting.**
Patricia Godsell. Don Mills, Ontario: General Publishing, 1976. 275p.

An attempt to place a set of selected Canadian maps, prints and paintings within the context of their own history and within the context generally of the art of the western world. The book, representing the work of approximately ninety artists, is organized in sections which reflect chronological periods of Canadian history. Each commentary embraces biographical information on the artist as well as the author's interpretation and considered reaction to the work. In brief essays preceding the sections there is an attempt to treat the effects on Canadian art and artists of major artistic movements of the nineteenth and twentieth centuries. Includes seventy colour and fifty black-and-white plates.

1059 **Early painters and engravers in Canada.**
J. Russell Harper. Toronto: University of Toronto Press, 1970. 376p. bibliog.

A biographical directory of artists who painted in early Canada, and whose birth dates were before 1867, the year of Confederation. Entries include date and place of birth, known details of the life of the artist, a listing of public exhibitions where works have appeared, and some biographical references.

1060 **Painting in Canada: a history.**
J. Russell Harper. Toronto: University of Toronto Press, 1977. 2nd ed. 463p.

Harper provides a scholarly treatment of art history in Canada from its beginnings in the seventeenth century through to the early 1960s, including the results of research ongoing since the original publication of the work in 1966. Incorporated into the chronicle are entertaining anecdotes and considerable biographical information on known and little known painters. While the author successfully places the development of Canadian painting within the context of artistic movements and national events and circumstances, he provides little critical judgement in the work. A selection of 175 black-and-white plates (over 400 plates, many in colour, illustrated the first edition) provide a visual narrative to complement the text. Brief biographies of artists are included as a final section to the book.

1061 **A people's art: primitive, naïve, provincial, and folk painting in Canada.**
J. Russell Harper. Toronto: University of Toronto Press, 1974. 176p.

This work takes as its focus art produced for the enjoyment of ordinary people, rather than for connoisseurs, and as such, its subject matter is plain, its expression is frank, its air is unpretentious. It therefore provides a direct reflection of life as it is experienced by people at work and at leisure. This study of vernacular art is lavishly produced with over 125 illustrations, many of which are in colour.

1062　A heritage of Canadian art: the McMichael Collection.
Toronto: Clarke, Irwin, 1979. 208p.

The McMichael Canadian Collection is now a national treasure containing countless works of art, prints and sculptures. Its nucleus is its collection of Group of Seven paintings, the largest collection anywhere. In 1965 Robert and Signe McMichael donated their collection to the Province of Ontario, in addition they donated their home (a marvelous log structure named Tapawingo) and their property in the rural village of Kleinburg, Ontario. The collection remains at this location although the structure has been expanded as many more works have been added to the collection. This is a catalogue of representative works, with bio-critical sketches of the Group of Seven. The interested reader is also referred to Robert McMichael's autobiography entitled *One man's obsession* (Scarborough, Ontario: Prentice-Hall Canada, 1986).

1063　Northwest coast Indian art: an analysis of form.
Bill Holm. Seattle, Washington: University of Washington Press, 1982. 115p. (Thomas Burke Memorial Washington State Museum, Monograph No. 1).

This leading authority brought over twenty years of study to this synthesis of the characteristics of northwest coast Indian art. Another authoritative source for the general or informed reader would be *Indian art traditions of the northwest coast* (Burnaby, British Columbia: Archaeology Press, Simon Fraser University, 1976). Also worthwhile is the beautifully produced work entitled *The legacy: tradition and innovation in northwest coast Indian art* (Vancouver: Douglas & McIntyre; Seattle, Washington: University of Washington Press, 1985). This latter work is a richly illustrated catalogue documenting an exhibition which first toured in 1970 and was so popular it continued on tour until 1982.

1064　Indian art of the northwest coast: a dialogue on craftsmanship and aesthetics.
Bill Holm, Bill Reid. Houston, Texas: Institute for the Arts, Rice University, 1975. [n.p.]

Two accomplished artists shed light on the art of the Indians of the northwest coast. Over one hundred objects are examined in a lively and informal discussion which illuminates the themes embodied by the art and helps the reader to appreciate both the creativity and the technical ability of the exhibited artists. This volume was originally published under the title *Form and freedom: a dialogue on northwest coast Indian art*, in conjunction with an exhibition organized by the Institute for the Arts, Rice University. See also Hilary Stewart's *Looking at Indian art of the northwest coast* (Seattle, Washington: University of Washington Press, 1979).

1065　Eskimo prints.
James Houston. Barre, Massachusetts: Barre Publishers, 1971. 110p.

Houston served fourteen years, 1948-62, in the Canadian Arctic, much of this time as the Canadian federal government's civil administrator on Baffin Island. During this period he also acted as the Arctic representative for the Canadian Handicrafts Guild. Houston is generally credited with assisting the Inuit artists in the techniques of printmaking and guided and fostered their efforts to bring their work to the art markets of North America and the world. This is Houston's account of this period. The work includes forty-eight prints from the period with brief commentaries.

1066   A story of the Group of Seven.
Harry Hunkin.   Toronto: McGraw-Hill Ryerson, 1976. 160p.
Directed to the student or the reader with an awakening interest in Canadian art generally, and the Group of Seven in particular. Employing colour and black-and-white prints, captioned with comments by members of the Group drawn from a variety of private (letters, memorabilia) or public (newspaper articles) sources, the compiler has been able to produce an interesting and useful introduction to this important movement in Canadian art. Also published under the title *The Group of Seven: Canada's great landscape painters* (Edinburgh: Paul Harris, 1979).

1067   A compendium of Canadian folk artists.
Terry Kobayashi, Michael Bird.   Erin, Ontario: Boston Mills Press, 1985. 241p.
In their introduction the compilers provide a definition of folk art and folk artists which defines the inclusion criteria for the work. The amount of biographical detail for each individual reflects the nature of the information available to the compilers. Each entry includes a listing of sources for the individual as well as the museums, galleries, libraries, archives or other public institutions where the work of the artist can be found.

1068   A dictionary of Canadian artists.
Compiled by Colin S. MacDonald.   Ottawa: Canadian Paperbacks, 1967- . 7 vols.
An extremely valuable work which provides biographical information on Canadian painters, sculptors and printmakers. The scope of entries varies from a few lines to several pages depending upon the reputation and achievements of the individual. A list of references is provided with each entry in order to direct the inquirer.

1069   Folk art: primitive and naïve art in Canada.
Blake McKendry.   Toronto: Methuen, 1983. 288p. bibliog.
A dealer and collector provides a survey of modern folk art in Canada, incorporating into the survey a history of the form and its influences on, and from, the mainstream of art. The author addresses such questions as the recognition and definition of the folk art style as a genre distinct from academic art; he examines 'primitive' art within the context of the magic and rituals of prehistoric peoples; and he looks at the simplistic attitudes and forms which characterize 'naïve' art. A section is also devoted to 'folk artifacts' such as quilts, hand-made utensils etc. which 'please the eye and enrich the drabness of everyday routine'. Over 260 objects are displayed in either black-and-white or colour plates. Included are a checklist of Canadian folk artists and a bibliography. See also the author's *A dictionary of folk artists in Canada from the 17th century to the present . . .* (Elginburg, Ontario: Blake McKendry, 1988).

1070   Landmarks of Canadian art.
Peter Mellen.   Toronto: McClelland & Stewart, 1978. 260p. bibliog.
This is a beautifully produced catalogue of 116 works, with scholarly commentary, of the treasures of the Canadian heritage. The selection of these exceptional works was made by a distinguished editorial board. They illustrate the development of Canadian art and include works of the Inuit and Indians, and those who emigrated to the country, or those who descended from those who emigrated. Most of the works are

from the nineteenth and twentieth centuries, although some prehistoric art and some sixteenth, seventeenth and eighteenth century religious works from Quebec are included. The works are reproduced in full colour and in large format.

1071 **The best contemporary Canadian art.**
Joan Murray. Edmonton, Alberta: Hurtig, 1987. 201p.
The work of 100 artists are represented by their prints and commentary. Works included were selected by the artists themselves, with the commentary being a distillation of interviews by the compiler. Provides a cross-sectional view of art in the country today, providing a sense of the themes and concerns of the artists represented. Colour plates throughout.

1072 **Modernism in Quebec art, 1916-1946.**
Jean-René Ostiguy. Ottawa: National Gallery of Canada, 1982. 167p.
Ostiguy traces artistic development in Quebec earlier this century, discovering common bonds and a unity between diverse artistic styles.

1073 **Canadian native art: arts and crafts of Canadian Indians and Eskimos.**
Nancy-Lou Patterson. Don Mills, Ontario: Collier-Macmillan, 1973. 179p. bibliog.
A scholarly survey of native art in Canada. The author deals with her subject by regional groupings of native peoples. She views native art as an outgrowth of the everyday life of these people, but at the same time notes the dynamic, ever-changing nature of the art, influenced in the first instance by geography and changes in the physical environment over time, as well as by the influence of other native cultural groups, and ultimately the European presence. The work is illustrated by black-and-white as well as some colour plates.

1074 **Land of earth and sky: landscape painting of western Canada.**
Ronald Rees. Saskatoon, Saskatchewan: Western Producer Prairie Books, 1984. 148p. bibliog.
This is a geographer's view of prairie painting, and thus the paintings and drawings are used here in terms of evoking the nature of the relationship of the people with the land, rather than in terms of the purely aesthetic. Rees's essay displays perceptive observation as he discusses the ways in which the prairie landscape has been portrayed by painters. The work is divided into discussions of 'Art Before the Settlement' and 'The Art of the Settlement'. Eighty colour and twenty-five black-and-white prints illustrate the work.

1075 **A concise history of Canadian painting.**
Dennis Reid. Toronto: Oxford University Press, 1988. 2nd ed. 418p.
This survey history, beginning in 1665 and ending in 1980, chronicles the movements and styles of Canadian painting, as well as outlines and evaluates the accomplishments of significant artists. In this way, it also conveys to the reader a sense of Canada's cultural evolution. This work is considered required reading for the student or researcher of Canadian art history.

1076 **"Our own country": being an account of the national aspirations of the principal landscape artists in Montreal and Toronto 1860-1890.**
Dennis Reid. Ottawa: National Gallery of Canada, 1979. 454p.

This thoroughly documented and illustrated study is an outgrowth of the research conducted for an exhibition of the same title presented by the National Gallery of Canada in 1978. Within the context of the forces of expansion and settlement which existed in central Canada, and which were manifested even more dramatically in the westward expansion which characterized the period, Reid presents to the reader the vision of Canada as seen by the landscape artists and in particular the landscape artist-photographers of the late nineteenth century. Reid outlines at length the special rôle played by Scottish photographer William Notman. This work is essential reading, for student and researcher of art history, as well as for the social and economic historian.

1077 **The mountains and the sky.**
Lorne E. Render. [Calgary]: Glenbow-Alberta Institute/McClelland & Stewart West, 1974. 223p.

The extraordinary nature of the western countryside has produced a deep artistic interest. This interest is represented here by plates and prose selected to show a multitude of artistic styles – romantic, formalized, idyllic, passionate, naturalistic and abstract – to reflect the moods and scenes which comprise this beautiful land.

1078 **Arts of the Eskimo: prints.**
Edited by Ernst Roch. Montreal: Signum Press in association with Oxford University Press, 1974. 240p.

There are any number of books which comment on, or chronicle the development of Inuit graphic art and sculpture. Other titles of interest are: Carson I.A. Ritchie's *Art of the Eskimo* (South Brunswick; New York: A.S. Barnes, 1979); Cottie Burland's *Eskimo art* (Toronto: Hamlyn, 1973), Edmund Carpenter's *Eskimo realities* (New York: Holt, Rinehart & Winston, 1973); Ian Christie Clark's *Indian and Eskimo art of Canada* (Toronto: Ryerson, 1971); and W.T. Larmour's *The art of the Canadian Eskimo* (Ottawa: Indian Affairs and Northern Development, 1967).

1079 **Passionate spirits: a history of the Royal Canadian Academy of Arts, 1880-1980.**
Rebecca Sisler. Toronto: Clarke, Irwin, 1980. 296p.

The RCA was founded in 1880 with impetus and under the patronage of the Governor General, the Marquis of Lorne. The Academy at that time reflected the needs of its founding membership for public recognition of art in Canada. For most of the period encompassed by this history the Academy saw itself as an arbiter of artistic taste in Canada, serving as an institutional framework for practical initiatives, such as the founding of the National Gallery of Canada, the sponsorship of courses designed to improve the quality of art in the country, the promotion of Canadian art by means of annual and travelling exhibitions, and the awarding of prizes and scholarships. Sisler's history is enriched by many colour and black-and-white plates of members' work. A 'List of Presidents and Members 1880-1979' is included.

1080   **The spirit sings: artistic traditions of Canada's first peoples.**
Toronto; Calgary, Alberta: McClelland & Stewart/Glenbow Museum,
1987. 264p. bibliog.

This magnificent volume was prepared in support of a major exhibition held
concurrently with the 1988 Winter Olympics in Calgary, Alberta. The exhibition of art
and artifact illustrated the diversity of cultures among Canada's native peoples yet
emphasized too the similar views to be found among these separate cultures i.e. the
necessity of harmony between man and nature. The continuity and strength of native
culture in the face of European influence and oppression is also made apparent. The
authoritative text and beautiful plates (many in colour) support these themes.

1081   **Sculpture of the Eskimo.**
George Swinton.   Toronto: McClelland & Stewart, 1987. 255p.
bibliog.

A visual and prose record of Eskimo sculpture, covering a time-span from prehistory
to the present. Over 800 plates and photographs.

1082   **Contemporary Canadian painting.**
William Withrow.   Toronto: McClelland & Stewart, 1972. 223p.
bibliog.

Twenty-four contemporary Canadian painters are profiled. Contemporary, in this
context, is defined to mean those individuals active in the period since 1945. Those
artists included are selected according to 'quality', 'a persistant and unique visual
image' or 'a catalytic function'. Each artist is afforded a bio-critical essay, which
incorporates statements by the artists on their works. High quality colour reproductions
complement each profile. The introductory essay chronicles the development of
painting in the post war period.

Music

Reference
1083   **Directory of musical Canadiana.**
Compiled by Wayne Gilpin.   Agincourt, Ontario: GLC Publishers,
1981. 363p.

This volume is patterned after a work entitled: *The American music handbook*, and
like the latter attempts to provide access to diverse musical information sources with
sections devoted to sectors such as government and community agencies and
organizations, educational institutions, performing groups, festivals, competitions,
libraries, media agencies and publishing companies.

1084 **Canadian music: a selected checklist 1950-73 = La musique canadienne: une liste sélective 1950-73.**
Edited by Lynne Jarman. Toronto: University of Toronto Press, 1976. 170p.

Over the years a number of catalogues of Canadian music have been produced, among these are the *Complete list of Canadian copyright musical compositions: (entered from 1868 to January 19th, 1889)* (Toronto? 1889?), *Canadian music* (Toronto: Oxford University Press, 1946), the *CBC's catalogue of Canadian composers* (Toronto?: Canadian Broadcasting Corporation, 1952), and the *Catalogue of orchestral music* (Toronto?: Canadian League of Composers, 1957). The volume here is a successor to these and compiles, for convenience, records taken primarily from the national bibliography *Canadiana*, as well as the publication *Fontes artis musicae*. A survey of issues of *Canadiana* under the appropriate classification will provide researchers with updates to this *Checklist*. Works are represented by descriptive catalogue records and are arranged by Dewey Decimal class number; two indexes are included, one by composer and the other by title of composition.

1085 **Encyclopedia of music in Canada.**
Edited by Helmut Kallmann, Gilles Potvin, Kenneth Winters. Toronto: University of Toronto Press, 1981. 1076p. bibliog.

This is an invaluable piece of scholarship about music in Canada. In one large volume of over 3,300 entries is a description of Canada's musical culture covering popular, folk, religious and concert music, past and present. The educational, critical and commercial aspects of these musical forms are also dealt with. The work is supported by a comprehensive index.

1086 **The Canadian jazz discography 1916-1980.**
Jack Litchfield. Toronto: University of Toronto Press, 1982. 945p.

An attempt to list every jazz record recorded by a Canadian jazz artist. Information provided includes: biographies of the artists; names of musicians and instruments played; dates and places of recordings; label names and serial numbers; tune titles and composers. The compiler defines 'jazz' broadly, including such allied music as ragtime, blues, rhythm 'n' blues, boogie-woogie, and gospel. To qualify for inclusion a record must either have been recorded in Canada, or recorded elsewhere by an artist who was a resident (temporary or permanent) of Canada at the time of recording. The term 'record' is intended to encompass tape (both audio and video), piano rolls, and motion pictures.

1087 **Music directory Canada**
Toronto: CM Books, 1982- . 607p.

Intended to serve as a comprehensive guide to the music industry in Canada.

1088 **Contemporary Canadian composers.**
Edited by Keith MacMillan, John Beckwith. Toronto: Oxford University Press, 1975. 248p.

A standard reference tool for the student or researcher. Information is provided on Canadian composers of the twentieth century (defined as composers who have produced all or most of their works since 1920). Included are 144 composers, who, in the opinion of the compilers represent 'the most active and prominent professional composers from all parts of the country in the period covered'. Generally not included are composers or arrangers of popular or commercial music, jazz, band and church music. The biographies incorporate basic biographical information, brief critical and stylistic comments, a listing of musical works, and published works about the individual.

1089 **Musicians in Canada: a bio-bibliographical finding list = Musiciens au Canada: index bio-bibliographique.**
Edited by Kathleen M. Toomey, Stephen C. Willis. Ottawa: Canadian Association of Music Libraries/Association canadienne des bibliothèques musicales, 1981. 184p.
This reference tool provides access to information about Canadian musicians. Part One of the work is an alphabetical listing by name entry, and contains some biographical information, most often birth and death dates as well as place of residence. Included in each entry are alpha-numeric references which direct the user to other published sources of bio- or bibliographical information. Part Two lists individuals by groupings of musical contributon as categorized by other alpha-numeric codes.

General

1090 **R. Murray Schafer.**
Stephen Adams. Toronto: University of Toronto Press, 1983. 240p. bibliog. (Canadian Composers/Compositeurs Canadiens, vol. 4).
Murray Schafer is one of the few Canadian composers who have achieved an international reputation. But Schafer's career is one of more than music, as he has accomplishments in the areas of the graphic arts, drama, writing, education, literary criticism and journalism. This work chronicles many of these accomplishments but concentrates on music. The author traces the development of Schafer's music from his early works in a mild neo-classical vein to his experimentation with various modernist procedures. The study is supported by a catalogue of compositions, a discography and a bibliography. Other volumes of the Canadian Composers Series include: *Harry Somers* by Brian Cherney (1975); *Jean Papineau-Coutre* by Louise Bail-Milot (Montreal: Les Editions Fides); and *Barbara Pentland* by Sheila Eastman and Timothy J. McGee (1983).

1091 **Music in Canada 1600-1800.**
Willy Amtmann. [Montreal]: Habitex Books, 1975. 320p.
A scholarly and well researched (given the paucity of readily available sources) survey of musical life in early Canada. Clearly the author has been diligent in locating documentary evidence, combing it for appropriate references and then constructing from the evidence the story of a dimension of Canada's cultural history.

1092 **Musical Canada: words and music honouring Helmut Kallmann.**
Edited by John Beckwith, Frederick A. Hall. Toronto: University of
Toronto Press, 1988. 369p.

A collection of informative but critical and scholarly essays on broad themes relating to
the history of music and musical lore in Canada. The contributions have been brought
together to honour Helmut Max Kallmann, whose own scholarly activities, such as his
History of music in Canada, 1534-1914 (q.v.) and the *Encyclopedia of music in Canada*
(q.v.), will long remain as seminal works in the field.

1093 **Chansons de voyageurs, coureurs de bois et forestiers.** (Songs of
travellers, trappers and lumberjacks.)
Madeleine Béland. Quebec: Les Presses de L'Université Laval,
1982. 432p. (Ethnologie de L'Amérique Française).

The *coureurs de bois* or 'wood-runners' were itinerant fur traders prevalent in the
interior trade through the seventeenth and eighteenth centuries. Working out of
centres such as Montreal these woodsmen, both individually and collectively, played an
important rôle in the exploration of the interior of North America, particularly the
northern portion of the continent, by establishing trading and social contacts with the
Indian bands. Similarly, those engaged in the lumber trade in Quebec were also
instruments in the expansion of the frontier. This is an academic treatment of the songs
of these primarily French-speaking groups (compiled from other sources), with
scholarly emendations.

1094 **Twentieth century Canadian composers.**
Ian L. Bradley. Agincourt, Ontario: GLC Publishers, 1977-82.
2 vols. bibliog.

These volumes were compiled for the student or interested but uninformed researcher.
Each volume provides analysis of ten Canadian composers, chosen for their
contribution and selected to represent the different regions of Canada. Besides the
biographical and critical information provided, each piece presents a descriptive
analysis of works by the composer recorded by the Canadian Broadcasting
Corporation, and available for public and educational use from that agency's Canadian
Collection. Each sketch also includes a list of references. Each volume also has a
general bibliography.

1095 **Music publishing in the Canadas, 1800-1867 = L'édition musicale au
Canada, 1800-1867.**
Maria Calderisi. Ottawa: National Library of Canada/Bibliothèque
nationale du Canada, 1981. 128p. bibliog.

This historical/bibliographical study of music publishing in the nineteenth century
contributes much to our understanding of the development of cultural taste as well as
publishing enterprise. Calderisi adds much by way of detail to our knowledge of
publishers and the relationship between book publishing and music publishing; she
examines music publishing in periodicals as well as the growth of the sheet music form.
Music printing and distribution is discussed as is the growth of copyright conventions.
A number of useful appendices are included, among these a publisher/printer index, a
chronological list of books containing musical notation, a list of newspapers known to
contain music, and a directory of sheet music publishers and printers. There is a
bibliography and the text is bilingual.

1096 **Canada's music: an historical survey.**
Clifford Ford. Agincourt, Ontario: GLC Publishers Limited, 1982. 278p. bibliog.
This work is a general historical overview of the development of music in Canada. It purports to concentrate primarily on the period from 1918 to the present, and thus complements the earlier work of Helmut Kallman in *A history of music in Canada, 1534-1914* (q.v.). On the whole it is a scholarly treatment of the subject, but is suitable for the general reader. A selected bibliography is included.

1097 **Glenn Gould: a life and variations.**
Otto Friedrich. Toronto: Lester & Orpen Dennys, 1989. 441p.
Glenn Gould is not without his detractors in the world of Canadian music. Many would question inclusion of materials relating to his life and accomplishments. However, despite his garrulousness and his facetiousness, Gould does remain one of a few Canadian musicians whose exploits have gained international recognition. This work was authorized by the musician's estate. An earlier author, Geoffrey Payzant, in *Glenn Gould: music & mind* (Toronto: Van Nostrand Reinhold, 1978) claimed Gould to be an 'original and profound musical thinker', despite 'his terrible puns, extended jokes and lapses into literary opulence'. Gould is to be taken seriously.

1098 **Songs of the dream people: chants and images from the Indians and Eskimos of North America.**
Edited and illustrated by James Houston. New York: Atheneum, 1972. 83p.
The author explains in the foreword that 'the songs of the Indians and Eskimos are often set to the stroke of a paddle, to the flight of birds, to the rhythm of a running horse, or the thump of the corn grinding stone. These songs have a rich vitality about them, voicing with passion an endless search for the magic of life'. Houston is one of the more knowledgeable authorities in this field and has compiled this collection of poetry and song texts of native peoples. The pieces are in four groupings: Eskimo, northwest coast, central plains and eastern woodland.

1099 **A history of music in Canada 1534-1914.**
Helmut Kallmann. Toronto: University of Toronto Press, 1987. 317p.
This landmark work of scholarship is a description of music at various stages of Canadian history. The study 'takes as its subject not creative giants who determine the course of world music history but humble musicians who instill a taste for their art among pioneers preoccupied with establishing the physical and economic foundations of a new nation; instead of mirroring the entertainment of the élite in the world's musical capitals, it reflects the musical pastimes and aspirations of the many; and instead of noting the changing styles which express the spirit of the age and nation, it deals with the collecting and assimilating of traditional forms from outside sources'.

1100 **Heart of gold: 30 years of Canadian pop music.**
Martin Melhuish. Toronto: CBC Enterprises, 1983. 200p.
Who does have the 'Bop in Beaver Land'? The author attempts to chronicle the growth of the Canadian popular music industry from its beginnings to the mid-1980s.

Special profiles are given to our international stars, and a section is devoted to the unique development of the Quebec rock music scene. The work is profusely illustrated.

1101   **Jazz in Canada: fourteen lives.**
Mark Miller.   Toronto: University of Toronto Press, 1982. 245p.
A biographical study of fourteen Canadian jazz musicians chosen by the author on the basis of their artistic excellence and the innovative qualities of their styles. While each piece is interesting in its own right, the book provides little synthesis or analysis of jazz activity in Canada. Neither does it effectively examine the common themes which run through the lives of the individuals chosen, i.e. lives of personal crises, professional frustrations, drugs, alcohol and untimely deaths – factors which the author suggests make the characters interesting, 'and their lives colourful, often darkly so'. Much of the 'why' is missing from the study, though it remains essential reading for the music enthusiast. Also of interest is the noted commentator, John Gilmore's *Swinging in paradise: the story of jazz in Montreal* (Montreal: Véhicule Press, 1988).

1102   **Roll back the years: history of Canadian recorded sound and its legacy: genesis to 1930.**
Edward B. Moogk.   Ottawa: National Library of Canada, 1975. 443p.
Despite the difficulties inherent in research without a substantial body of documentary evidence upon which to draw, this author has nonetheless produced a first-rate piece of scholarship which attempts to tell the story of recorded sound in Canada for the period beginning in 1878 to 1930. Together with the study is included: a section of biographical notes, much of the information being unique, on Canadian artists who had made a name for themselves outside of Canada; and, a discography of Canadian born, adopted, or trained performers, including the title of each performance, the accompaniment, the record company, the size and type of record, the catalogue number and the name of the composer. A number of interesting historical documents have been included as appendices to the text.

1103   **Musicanada.**
Ottawa: Canadian Music Council, 1976- . quarterly.
Follows the trends and events within the classical music community in Canada. Readers interested in other segments of this community should consult: *Canadian Musician* (Toronto: Norris Publications, 1978-); *The Canadian Composer* (Toronto: Composers, Authors and Publishers Association of Canada, 1965-); *Music Scene* (Don Mills, Ontario: Performing Rights Organization of Canada, 1967-); *Music Magazine* (Toronto: Future Perfect Publishing, 1978-); or, *Opera Canada* (Toronto: Foundation for Coast to Coast Opera Publications, 1960-).

1104   **Canadian music of the twentieth century.**
George A. Proctor.   Toronto: University of Toronto Press, 1980. 297p. bibliog.
This is a study of Canadian music: that is, an introduction to the music itself, analysing the style of composers without reverting to a documentary of the lives of these composers. It is restricted to what normally is referred to as classical music, although discusses when appropriate the direct or indirect impact of the country's folk songs, jazz, popular music, paintings, literary works, political events, or geography. Canadian

composers are defined as practising composers who are Canadian citizens or others who have been resident in Canada for at least five years. The work follows a chronological order, with each chapter followed by an appropriate listing of selected works. An appendix supplies 'A Chronological Table of Canadian History, Music, and Other Arts 1900-1979'.

1105 **Remembered moments of the Canadian Opera Company 1950-1975.**
[Toronto]: Canadian Opera Company, [1976].
Primarily a photographic record of the Company with a brief outline of its history. Included is a list of productions, with cast notes, as well as statistics on attendance, performances and box office receipts.

1106 **On Canadian music.**
R. Murray Schafer. Bancroft, Ontario: Arcana Editions, 1984. 105p.
A collection of essays written over twenty years by one of Canada's most noteworthy composers. They deal, in the main, with Canadian music and the music of the composer himself. If there is a theme to the collection it is a lament for more concern on behalf of Canadians for our own music and the work of our composers.

1107 **Aspects of music in Canada.**
Edited by Arnold Walter. Toronto: University of Toronto Press, 1969. 336p.
This volume of essays provides insight into a number of areas of musical history in Canada. Contributions deal with general history, folk and aboriginal music, the history of music composition, performers, music education, and national organizations. The work is a continuation of that by Ernest MacMillan entitled *Music in Canada* (Toronto: University of Toronto Press, 1955).

1108 **The unlikely pioneer: building opera from the Pacific through the prairies.**
David Watmough. Oakville, Ontario: Mosaic Press, 1986. 186p.
This is the story of the development of opera in Winnipeg, Edmonton and Vancouver as told by way of a biographical treatment of Irving Guttman, who was instrumental in the development of the Vancouver Opera, the Edmonton Opera and the Manitoba Opera Company.

Dance

1109 **The National Ballet of Canada: a celebration.**
Ken Bell, Celia Franca. Toronto: University of Toronto Press, 1978. 284p.
Essentially a pictorial record, this work does include a significant textual component which provides an anecdotal and personal account of the founding and development of Canada's national ballet company, by its first director. The production photography, by Ken Bell, is excellent, including its layout and presentation.

1110   **Visions: ballet and its future: essays from the International Dance Conference to commemorate the 25th anniversary of the National Ballet of Canada.**
Edited by Michael Crabb.   Toronto: Simon & Pierre, 1978. 189p.

In examining this work one laments at having missed the opportunity to attend what Vincent Tovell terms 'a celebration and exploration, a celebration of the National Ballet of Canada's 25th anniversary and an exploration of ballet's future here and around the world'. Contributors to the gala conference, as represented in these published proceedings, included such commentators, performers, musicians, in the world of dance as Dame Ninette de Valois, Ludmilla Chiriaeff, Veronica Tennant, Timothy Porteous, Clive Barnes, John Percival, Louis Applebaum and more. The work is an interesting chronicle of achievement in the field. Contributions are divided into sections such as: 'Ballet and Dancers', 'Music and Dance', 'Design', 'Criticism', 'Funding', 'Film', 'Television and Video', and 'Choreography'. Short biographies of the principals are provided, as is a short reading list.

1111   **Dance in Canada = Danse au Canada.**
Toronto: Dance in Canada Association, 1973- . quarterly.
Features articles on dance, dance troupes and dancers in Canada.

1112   **Dance as dance: selected reviews and essays.**
Graham Jackson.   Scarborough, Ontario: Catalyst, 1978. 128p.
A useful and readable collection of previously published, as well as unpublished reviews and articles written by an astute observer and critic of dance. Taken together they provide also an overview of the development of Canadian dance as it began to come of age in the mid-1970s.

1113   **Les Grands Ballets Canadiens: ou cette femme qui nous fit danser.** (Les Grands Ballets Canadiens: or the woman who inspired us.)
Roland Lorrain.   Montreal: Éditions du Jour, 1973. 219p.
The establishment and development of one of Canada's premier and world renowned ballet companies is documented in this profusely illustrated work.

1114   **Dance today in Canada.**
Andrew Oxenham, Michael Crabb.   Toronto: Simon & Pierre, 1977. 228p.
This volume combines a short overview history of dance in Canada written by Michael Crabb with a photographic portfolio of Canadian dance by Andrew Oxenham. The latter comprises the bulk of the work, with the photographs representative of a variety of Canadian dance companies. Included in an appendix, is a list of dance companies giving information as to the establishment of the company, key officers at the time of publication, address, and number of dancers.

1115   **Canada's National Ballet.**
Herbert Whittaker.   Toronto: McClelland & Stewart, 1967. 105p.
A history of the National Ballet produced within the context of Canada's centenary celebrations in 1967. Despite the resulting lack of critical comment in the work, it is a

useful record of the development of the company and does record the significant highs and lows of the first twenty years. A listing of artists of the ballet, by season, and the company's repertoire is reproduced as an appendix.

1116 **The Royal Winnipeg Ballet: the first forty years.**
Max Wyman. Toronto: Doubleday, 1978. 275p.
Only one North American ballet company is older than the Royal Winnipeg Ballet (the San Francisco Ballet). This prairie-based company has an impressive catalogue of firsts, for example, it was the first 'royal' company in the Commonwealth, and was the first Canadian company to tour Russia, Europe and Australia. On top of these accomplishments, 'this has always been a company for the people, and come flood, 'flu or howling blizzard they're always there, quivering – ready to dance, as if that's all the world was made for. They project an innocent excitement, and that is something an audience can smell. There's something about the RWB that warms your heart'. Even in light of this endorsement, this is an objective, profusely illustrated account of the founding (by Gweneth Lloyd and Betty Farrally), the development (led primarily by artistic director Arnold Spohr), and accomplishments of the company. Two appendices complement the work: the first lists ballets chronologically, highlighting those created for the company; the second, provides a capsule chronology of significant events in the history of the company.

Theatre

Reference

1117 **A bibliography of Canadian theatre history 1583-1975.**
John Ball, Richard Plant. Toronto: Playwrights Co-op, 1976. 160p.
The work contains over 2,000 entries which span some 400 years. Entries are arranged in thirteen sections and within each section the arrangement is chronological by year of publication, and within each chronological year the items are listed alphabetically by author. An update of the bibliography is under preparation and is to be published in the autumn of 1990. Materials in the work include monographic and periodical literature (not including newspapers). Excluded, in general, are unpublished studies, manuscript materials, materials dealing with ballet, music, opera, and radio drama. (For this latter genre the researcher may wish to refer to the work done by Howard Fink and the Concordia Radio Drama Project, as well as Pierre Pagé and Renée Legris' *Repertoire des dramatiques québécoises à la télévision 1953-1977* [Directory of Quebec television drama 1953-1977. Montreal: Fides, 1977] or Édouard Rinfret's *Le théâtre canadien d'expression française: répertoire* . . . [French-Canadian theatre: a directory. Montreal: Leméac, 1975-1978] Another source is *Vingt-cinq ans de dramatiques à la télévision de Radio-Canada 1952-1977* [Twenty-five years of television drama from Radio-Canada 1952-1977. Montreal: La Société Radio-Canada, 1978]). The *Supplement* lists an additional 1,040 items covering the same period, using the same principles of arrangement, and an additional *Supplement* was published in 1979 covering the years 1975-76.

1118   **The Oxford companion to Canadian theatre.**
Edited by Eugene Benson, L.W. Conolly.   Toronto: Oxford
University Press, 1989. 662p.

A comprehensive history and analysis of theatrical activity in Canada, from the use of drama in the cultures of Canada's native peoples to the present day. The work documents theatre not only in English Canada, but in French Canada as well, including Acadian and other French-language theatre. Of particular interest also are the chapters 'Amerindian and Inuit Theatre' and 'Multicultural Theatre'. The over 700 entries encompass genres, major subjects, theatres and theatre companies, biography and criticism, as well as criticism on major plays. Entries are enhanced by lists of suggested readings.

1119   **Canada's playwrights: a biographical guide.**
Edited by Don Rubin, Alison Cranmer-Byng.   Toronto: Canadian
Theatre Review Publications, 1980. 191p.
A selective listing of seventy Canadian playwrights containing biographical/bibliographical information. Photographs are included with each entry. Cited plays are categorized by genre, i.e. stage writing, radio writing, television writing, novels, short stories, and miscellaneous. Other categories are secondary sources and work in progress at the date of publication. While the work is dated, it remains a very useful starting point for information about Canada's playwrights.

1120   **The Brock bibliography of published Canadian plays in English 1766-
1978.**
Anton Wagner.   Toronto: Playwrights Press, 1980. 375p.
This bibliography encompasses and expands upon the work begun in *The Brock bibliography of published Canadian stage plays in English 1900-1972* (St. Catherines, Ontario: Brock University, 1972. 35p) and its *First supplement* . . . (St. Catherines, Ontario: Brock University, 1973. 32p). It is intended to be a companion volume to *A bibliography of Canadian theatre history 1583-1975* (q.v.), and its *Supplement*. It attempts to record and annotate the corpus of English-Canadian drama and French-Canadian drama in translation. English-Canadian drama is defined as plays written by Canadians, native, naturalized or landed immigrant. Entries are arranged first by century and then alphabetically by author. There is also a short title index of the plays listed.

General
1121   **English-Canadian theatre.**
Eugene Benson, L.W. Conolly.   Toronto: Oxford University Press,
1987. 134p. (Perspectives on Canadian Culture).
A succinct survey of the history of theatre and drama in English Canada, chronicling the dominance in the nineteenth century of foreign plays, companies, and stars; and the development in the twentieth century of an indigenous Canadian theatre. Directed to the general reader interested in an overview perspective.

1122 **Canada on stage.**
Toronto: PACT Communications Centre, 1974- .
This irregularly published work includes information from most theatre groups in Canada with regard to productions. Entries include the name of the play or production, credits, and cast, and includes a comprehensive index. A preliminary editorial section provides feature contributions from knowledgeable theatre writers as to the state of theatre in the various regions of the country. The last edition, published in 1989, covers the theatrical seasons 1982-86.

1123 **Canadian Theatre Review.**
Toronto: University of Toronto Press, 1974- . quarterly.
An illustrated journal relating to Canadian drama, playwrights, and dramatic criticism. Includes interviews and reviews. See also such publications as: *Canadian Drama = L'Art Dramatique Canadien* (Guelph, Ontario: University of Guelph, 1975-); and, *Theatre History in Canada = Histoire du Théâtre au Canada* (Toronto: University of Toronto Graduate Centre for Study of Drama, 1980-).

1124 **Robertson Davies the well-tempered critic: one man's view of theatre and letters in Canada.**
Robertson Davies, edited by Judith Skelton Grant. Toronto: McClelland & Stewart, 1981. 285p.
Significant and typical observations on Canadian theatre and letters by Canada's most noted writer and critic. The pieces included were published in various sources through the 1940s, 1950s, 1960s and 1970s. The collection is evenly drawn from work in both fields. From reading the work a great deal can be learned about the Canadian identity as 'frequently his grapplings with Canadian culture produced insights of continuing relevance'.

1125 **Not bloody likely: the Shaw Festival: 1962-1973.**
Brian Doherty. Toronto: J. M. Dent & Sons, 1974. 160p.
A pictorial record of the first ten years of the Shaw Festival, with memoirs relating to the establishment and early years of the festival written by the founder and first President. Included are cast and company lists for each of the production seasons.

1126 **A mirror of our dreams: children and the theatre in Canada.**
Joyce Doolittle, Zina Barnieh. Vancouver: Talonbooks, 1979. 214p.
This is a book about professional theatre for children in Canada. The authors attempt to present the significant challenges facing theatre for young audiences. The work is in three parts. Part One entitled 'Today's Child and the Theatre', is a history of the development of children's theatre in Canada, discussing the changing concepts of childhood, arts and children in Canada, live theatre, television, theatre in schools and professional theatre. In Part Two the authors examine, in some detail, a select number of companies working in the medium, while Part Three incorporates a chapter on children's theatre in Quebec written by Hélène Beauchamp, expert and critic on the subject.

1127 **Theatre in French Canada: laying the foundations 1606-1867.**
Leonard E. Doucette. Toronto: University of Toronto Press, 1984.
290p. bibliog. (University of Toronto Romance Series, vol. 52).
This is a scholarly analysis of the evolution of theatre in French Canada from 1606, marking the first performance of Marc Lescarbot's Théâtre de Neptune en la Nouvelle-France, to Confederation. The author identifies and concentrates on three dramatic forms: the religious-pedagogic; the political; and the social theatre. Much emphasis is given in particular to the struggles surrounding the presentation of the latter, in that it faced at various times a genuine but often dogmatic attitude towards it on the part of the clergy, coupled with French and British-American colonialism. There were also demographic and geographic problems and a degree of civic indifference to be overcome. Attempts to politicize it and what is termed here 'its own apparent self-descructive urge' are also issues dealt with in this work. The work boasts an extensive bibliography.

1128 **The festivals of Canada.**
Arnold Edinborough. Toronto: Lester & Orpen Dennys, 1981.
223p.
A noted critic documents the seven key summer theatre festivals in Canada: the Guelph Spring Festival, the Stratford Festival, the Shaw Festival, the Charlottetown Festival, the National Arts Centre Festival, Festival Lennoxville, and the Banff Festival of the Arts. The work is dominated by production photographs with each section introduced by a short essay outlining the development and nature of the festival. This work is of interest to the student of theatre but is most valuable to the theatre-goer.

1129 **A stage in our past: English-language theatre in eastern Canada from the 1790s to 1914.**
Murray D. Edwards. Toronto: University of Toronto Press, 1968.
211p.
A broad general history of Canadian theatre up to the beginning of the First World War. The study is divided into four parts: 'Players and Playhouses', which includes much factual information about the various playhouses and the communities of which they were a part; 'Touring Days', discusses the touring companies, native and foreign, which were very much a part of theatrical life in Canada; 'The Poetic Drama', an interesting examination of the development of the Canadian theatre; and 'The Canadian Reflection', an analysis of significant regional plays. As the title notes, the work deals only with English theatre in eastern Canada, although the latter is seen to include the western city of Winnipeg (here pre-war theatre touring companies and the present Canadian Football League share a unique geographical view of Canada).

1130 **Frontier theatre: a history of nineteenth-century theatrical entertainment in the Canadian far west and Alaska.**
Chad Evans. Victoria, British Columbia: Sono Nis Press, 1983.
326p.
This work is best described by its sub-title, for it is not strictly an examination of theatre, but a study of the spectrum of theatrical entertainments (theatre, minstrel shows, opera, circuses, etc.) which were prevalent primarily as touring companies in the communities of the Pacific northwest, British Columbia, the Yukon and Alaska

through the nineteenth century. The reader will learn a great deal of frontier social history from this readable and entertaining work.

1131 **Collective encounters: documentary theatre in English-Canada.**
Alan Filewood. Toronto: University of Toronto Press, 1987. 214p.

The collectively created documentary play is an important Canadian dramatic genre which flourished from the late 1960s onwards, coinciding with a major revival of nationalism, in Canadian culture. These plays are typically inspired by a community or political issue which is then researched by a group of actors, resulting in a play orientated towards a specific audience. The author examines this genre as it has developed nationally.

1132 **Le théâtre québécois.** (The Quebec theatre.)
Jean-Cléo Godin, Laurent Mailhot. Ville LaSalle, Quebec: Éditions Hurtubise-HMH, 1970-80. 2 vols.

The authors of these two volumes provide some of the best analysis and interpretation of Quebec theatre available to the academic and general reader for the period of the 1960s and 1970s. The first volume introduces ten Quebec dramatists to the reader, while the second continues by discussing the continuing work of the already established writers, as well as exploring the work of new dramatists and the emergence of new forms of theatre, particularly that represented by the Grand Cirque Ordinaire. Refreshing in their analysis is the recognition of theatre as more than the written word – reflections on acting and audience response is an integral part of the examination.

1133 **Le théâtre et l'État au Québec: essai.** (Theatre and State in Quebec: an essay.)
Adrien Gruslin. Montreal: VLB Éditeur, 1981. 413p.

This study is replete with tables, charts and graphs, each supporting the well researched and well written text, and all presented within the context of imaginative book design (which has become a hallmark of VLB Éditeur). The thesis of the work was simply to produce an 'attempt to describe the intervention of the State in matters of stage theatre in Quebec. This step has its origins in a simple intention: to put at the disposal of the public, of the stage theatre and of people interested in cultural matters, the statistics of the subsidies granted to the stage theatre by the authorities, something that no one had ever attempted to do before'. Predictably the work is not so objective, and the study shows the effects, over a twenty year period (1961-81), of government policy, both its actions and inactions, on culture in general and theatre particularly.

1134 **Renown at Stratford: a record of the Shakespeare Festival in Canada 1953.**
Tyrone Guthrie, Robertson Davies, Grant MacDonald. Toronto: Clarke, Irwin, 1953. 127p.

Probably still the best account of the founding of the Stratford Festival, and the first season of the Festival as described by its first artistic director and by noted critic, author and commentator Robertson Davies. The first part of the work is devoted to a discourse by Guthrie on the establishment of the Festival. The second part is made up of 'notes' by Davies, first on Guthrie and then on the players of the first season among them: Alec Guinness, Irene Worth, Robert Goodier, Douglas Campbell, Eleanor Stuart and many others. The latter section is illustrated by a collection of coloured drawings by Grant Macdonald. Davies refers to these as 'powerfully evocative records' which 'paint an actor in character in such a way that, even if we have not seen the actor play that part we sense the truth of the portrait, and receive a strong impression of what the performance was like'. A theatre classic which was reprinted in 1971 to mark the Festival's twentieth anniversary.

1135 **A Stratford tempest.**
Martin Knelman. Toronto: McClelland & Stewart, 1982. 240p.
This is the story of a particularly tempestuous period in the recent history of Canada's premier theatre. And although it revolves around the years 1980 and 1981, when the Stratford Theatre was in crisis following the resignation of the artistic director Robin Phillips and preceding the appointment of his successor, Canadian John Hirsch, it chronicles also the artistic development of a gradually maturing nation struggling to achieve a national cultural autonomy.

1136 **L'Église et le théâtre au Québec.** (The Church and the theatre in Quebec.)
Jean Laflamme, Rémi Tourangeau. Montreal: Fides, 1979. 355p. bibliog.
This pioneering work explores the stormy relationship between the theatre and the paternalistic Catholic Church. The work was intended to serve a threefold purpose: to provide a knowledge of the relations and attitudes of the Church toward the theatre; extensive research which will prove helpful to researchers planning to undertake other projects on the topic; the moral and social evolution of a still young nation, more and more concerned with self-examination, in the process of establishing itself. Within this context the work ·is arranged into three periods (1606-1836, 1837-96, 1837-1962) marking distinct stages of development for the relationship. The work is supported by an excellent bibliography of secondary and primary sources.

1137 **Le théâtre à Montréal à la fin du XIXe siècle.** (The theatre in Montreal at the end of the nineteenth century.)
Jean-Marc Larrue. Montreal: Fides, 1981. 139p.
The period under study here is important in that it witnessed the permanent establishment of theatre, particularly French Canadian theatre, in Montreal, initially by way of amateur societies and eventually with the founding of professional companies. This study discusses the background and context of the unprecedented growth in the number of performances in the 1890s which eventually led to this situation.

1138 **Love and whisky: the story of the Dominion Drama Festival and the early years of theatre in Canada 1606-1972.**
Betty Lee. Toronto: Simon & Pierre, 1982. 335p.
The DDF was created in 1932 and came to an end in 1978. During this period it played a significant rôle in the development of theatre in Canada. For a time, it was Canada's national theatre, made up as it was of a network of amateur theatres in all parts of the country. Annually, following a lengthy system of adjudication and regional competitions, finalists met, each year in a different city, for a week long competition. Awards were made for best production, acting, directing, set design, etc. The DDF is credited with much of the development of professional theatre, in that it was instrumental in

developing many actors and directors, as well as providing an opportunity for Canadian playwrights to have their plays produced.

1139 **Theatre and politics in modern Quebec.**
Elaine F. Nardocchio. Edmonton, Alberta: University of Alberta Press, 1986. 157p.

Another recommended work for the serious student of the theatre. The aim of the book is to provide a better understanding of the socio-political nature and implications of French-language theatre in Quebec. The relationship between art and nationalism is of particular significance within Quebec where artistic creation not only reflects political and socio-cultural struggles, but is an active part of them. Thus Quebec's national identity depends to some extent on her cultural identity. The work traces the socio-political context of theatre from the seventeenth century to the middle of the twentieth century. For the more recent period it concentrates on the evolution of French-language theatre in Montreal, and the work also of eight prominent playwrights.

1140 **Stratford: the first thirty years.**
John Pettigrew, Jamie Portman. Toronto: Macmillan, 1985. 2 vols.

A scholarly treatment of the founding and development of the Stratford Festival through the first thirty years of its history. The work chronicles the genesis, and the determination of visionaries like Tom Patterson, it continues systematically examining the contributions of other early principals, like the legendary first artistic director, Tyrone Guthrie. Year by year it documents the work of the subsequent directors, Cecil Clarke, Michael Langham, Jean Gascon, Robin Phillips, and John Hirsch. Throughout this artistic fabric is woven other aspects of the Festival's history, ranging from its periodic financial difficulties to the crises of the early 1980s. Two useful appendices complement the work. 'The Seasons 1953-1982' lists the theatrical productions including the members of the company and musical performances. 'Out-of-Season Activities' describes other events such as tours, television productions, etc. Those interested in reading more about the Festival are directed to: Tom Patterson's *First stage: the making of the Stratford Festival* (Toronto: McClelland & Stewart, 1987); Maurice Good's *Every inch a Lear* (Victoria, British Columbia: Sono Nis Press, 1982); Grace Lydiatt Shaw's *Stratford under cover: memories on tape* (Toronto: NC Press, 1977); James Forsythe's *Tyrone Guthrie: a biography* (London: Hamish Hamilton, 1976); Peter Raby's *The Stratford scene, 1958-1968* (Toronto; Vancouver: Clarke, Irwin, 1968); Nicholas Monsarrat's *To Stratford with love* (Toronto: McClelland & Stewart, 1963); and, Robertson Davies' *Thrice the brindled cat hath mewed* (Toronto: Clarke, Irwin, 1955).

1141 **Too soon the curtain fell: a history of theatre in Saint John 1789-1900.**
Mary Elizabeth Smith. Fredericton, New Brunswick: Brunswick Press, 1981. 244p.

The rich history of an important local theatre is revealed in this well documented and readable account of theatre in one of the country's oldest communities, Saint John, New Brunswick. This work is a significant contribution to the understanding of regional theatre and its place within the context of theatre development generally.

1142 **The history of prairie theatre: the development of theatre in Alberta, Manitoba and Saskatchewan 1833-1982.**
E. Ross Stuart. Toronto: Simon & Pierre, 1984. 291p. bibliog. (Canadian Theatre History Series, vol. 2).

Stuart's study observes the history of the prairie theatre through its most significant people, theatres, companies, institutions, and organizations. Although the work points out that much prairie theatre was imported, it concentrates on showing how the movements, events and personalities outside the region had an impact upon the West. This is a valuable contribution to theatre history in Canada. The author achieves his aims by organizing his study within a chronological framework: Part I examines theatre prior to the Depression years, including pioneer entertainment, touring companies, stock companies and vaudeville; Part II chronicles the amateur theatre movement; Part III comments upon the theatre within schools and universities; and Part IV discusses the re-emergence of professional theatre in the 1960s and 1970s.

1143 **Second stage: the alternative theatre movement in Canada.**
Renate Usmiani. Vancouver: University of British Columbia Press, 1983. 173p. bibliog.

Second stage examines the development and importance of alternative theatre in Canada. The Canadian scene is put within its own cultural/historical context as well as an international context. Various chapters provide an overview of developments, first from an international perspective, then as experienced in English Canada and in French Canada. The remainder of the book focuses on important companies which the author views as particularly representative of developments in the major cultural regions. These include: Passe-Muraille (Toronto), Tamahnous (Vancouver), Savage God (Vancouver/York/Edmonton), the Mummers' Troupe (Newfoundland), and Le Théâtre d'Aujourd'hui (Montreal). A modest bibliography supports the work.

Film

1144 **Canada's cultural industries: broadcasting, publishing, records and film.**
Paul Audley. Ottawa: Canadian Institute for Economic Policy, 1983. 346p.

A systematic, sector by sector examination of the state of Canada's cultural industries, including a comprehensive examination of trends in each of these industries through the 1970s and early 1980s. The study identifies major issues and makes suggestions for changes in government policy which would encourage and reinforce cultural expression and the cultural organizations in Canada.

1145 **The handbook of Canadian film.**
Eleanor Beattie. Toronto: Peter Martin Associates in association with Take One Magazine, 1977. 2nd ed. 355p.

Primarily entries on film makers, arranged in alphabetical order, with filmographies and suggestions for further reading. Includes a number of sections which will be of use to various interested groups. For example, film students will find useful the section on

'Film Study'; similarly, 'Making Films' lists sources of information of interest to the film maker; finally, teachers and librarians will find helpful information in the section 'Using Films'.

1146 **Hollywood's Canada: the Americanization of our national image.**
Pierre Berton.   Toronto: McClelland & Stewart, 1975. 303p.
A critical but entertaining and readable examination of the distorted or misleading identity created by Hollywood film makers of Canada, written by one of Canada's leading writers. Berton is concerned here with the effect produced by Hollywood's interpretation of the Canadian character, heritage and environment. His purpose is to establish what kind of impression the film-goer would form of Canada from these films and to comment upon this. Included is a list of Hollywood movies about Canada arranged by date.

1147 **Cinema Canada.**
Outremont, Quebec: Cinema Canada Magazine Foundation, 1969- .
monthly.
Includes feature articles on film in Canada, as well as reviews of films and books.

1148 **Canadian film.**
David Clanfield.   Toronto: Oxford University Press, 1987. 136p.
bibliog.
A concise historical overview of English and French Canadian film. Although modest in extent, the work provides an authoritative and readable discussion of all modes of film, ranging from the documentary tradition of the National Film Board to new wave film and television docudrama. An excellent book for all levels, but particularly useful for students of film and the lay reader.

1149 **Censored! only in Canada: the history of film censorship – the scandal off the screen.**
Malcolm Dean.   Toronto: Virgo Press, 1981. 276p.
As noted by Gerald Pratley 'the history of film censorship in Canada is long and peculiar and marked by comic absurdities the like of which no satirist could ever hope to come to grips with'. This is a well documented history of film censorship in Canada; that is, well documented understanding the limitations of the historical records made available to the author. Interesting and entertaining reading.

1150 **Motion pictures and the arts in Canada: the business and the law**.
Garth H. Drabinsky.   Toronto: McGraw-Hill Ryerson, 1976. 201p.
The focus of this text is summarized in the sub-title of the work. It is a practical guide to motion picture production and can be used as a primer to understand appropriate legal concepts, rights and obligations of film making. It is also a synthesis of some of the economic realities of making films for theatrical release. Topics discussed include: consideration of the laws of defamation; invasion of privacy; insurance; copyright, literary or dramatic property rights; writer agreements; and obscenity, censorship and film classification laws and regulations. Additional chapters provide information on financing and the motion picture, coproductions, distribution agreements, and, an overview of theatrical markets. While some of the information is now dated, it remains

a good starting point for the aspiring film maker. The author clearly profited from his own advice for he went on to become Chairman, President, and Chief Executive Officer of the Cineplex Odeon Corporation, a highly successful film distribution, theatre and production conglomerate.

1151 **John Grierson and the National Film Board: the politics of wartime propaganda.**
Gary Evans. Toronto: University of Toronto Press, 1984. 329p.
Grierson is best known for his rôle in the establishment of the National Film Board. The Board became, under Grierson and during the war years, the national film propaganda agency. Two important series produced during this period, 'Canada Carries On' and 'The World in Action', are analysed as indicative of the work of the Board during this period. But under Grierson, propaganda took on a different face from that of the other protagonists. This unique orientation was, in part, responsible for the Board's post-war success in the field of documentary production. While this is a study of wartime film propaganda, it is also a study of the impact of cinema in the pre-television age. A must book for those interested in the history of Canadian cinema.

1152 **Take two.**
Edited by Seth Feldman. Toronto: Irwin, 1984. 310p.
An anthology of twenty-seven articles examining the spectrum of film in Canada. The articles are well researched, written by film critics and scholars, and discuss various industry issues. They deal in addition with individual films, and serve as a guide to the work of some of Canada's major directors. This is a companion volume to the *Canadian film reader* (q.v.).

1153 **Canadian film reader.**
Seth Feldman, Joyce Nelson. Toronto: Peter Martin, 1977. 405p. bibliog.
This collection of essays is 'designed as a source book, providing some of the most lucid commentary available on this area of national culture . . . a gathering place of ideas, a dialogue, an exploratory tool, a reference work and a preserve for an endangered species of criticism . . . an inspiration and a companion piece to future comprehensive histories of the Canadian cinema'. These lofty goals are met by the contributors in this volume. An excellent compilation which introduces Canadian film to the scholar and lay reader alike.

1154 **Foreign ownership and Canada's feature film distribution sector: an economic analysis.**
Steven Globerman, Aidan Vining. [Vancouver]: Fraser Institute, 1987. 104p.
Produced by a business orientated think tank, the conclusions of this study challenge current government policies which support and subsidize film production in Canada as well as question the need for intervention by governments in film distribution and the policies so proposed for that purpose. The study doubtless takes positions unacceptable to many Canadian film makers, but does give the uninitiated a different perspective on an ongoing debate.

1155 **John Grierson: a documentary biography.**
Forsyth Hardy. London: Faber & Faber, 1979. 298p.
This is the standard biography of Grierson. The author, a life-long friend and film critic, documents Grierson's life and assesses his contributions to the cinema, and particularly to documentary film making, in Great Britain and Canada. With the effective establishment of the National Film Board in 1939, this extraordinary man was credited with inspiring and instilling new life into the Canadian film industry. See also *John Grierson and the NFB* (Toronto: ECW Press, 1984). The latter includes papers presented by scholars and filmmakers on the occasion of a conference held 29-31 October 1981. Papers dealt with Grierson's work within the history of the documentary movement.

1156 **Making it: the business of film and television production in Canada.**
Edited by Barbara Hehner. [Toronto]: Academy of Canadian Cinema and Television; Doubleday, 1987. 328p. bibliog.
This is a 'how to' book for Canadian producers or would-be producers offering a step-by-step guide through the complicated process of transforming an idea into a screen production. Contributions are by leading Canadian film experts commissioned to write material in their areas of expertise. The work includes a glossary of production terminology in addition to a modest bibliography.

1157 **Inner views: ten Canadian film-makers.**
John Hofsess. Toronto: McGraw-Hill Ryerson, 1975. 171p.
This film critic explores, in the form of interviews, the work of ten Canadian film makers: Claude Jutra; Alan King; Don Shebib; Jack Darcus; Graeme Ferguson; Frank Vitale; William Frùet; Paul Almond; Denys Arcand and Pierre Berton. The author provides an introduction which looks at the development of the film industry in Canada. A readable work primarily for the general public.

1158 **Dictionnaire du cinéma québécois.** (Dictionary of the Quebec cinema.)
Michel Houle, Alain Julien. Montreal: Fides, 1978. 363p.
Here Quebec cinema is defined as French-language film produced in Quebec. The work combines into one alphabetical sequence entries on Quebec film and film makers (the latter defined as the major participants in the production process), as well as relevant film associations, government offices dealing with film, etc. The entries for films include credit information as well as plot or content summaries. Entries for individuals include brief commentary as well as a list of film credits.

1159 **Who's who in Canadian film and television = Qui est qui au cinéma et à la télévision au Canada.**
Edited by Chappelle Jaffe, Marie-Claude Poulin. Toronto: Academy of Canadian Cinema and Television = Académie canadienne du cinéma et de la télévision, 1987. 519p.
Over 1,400 entries of individuals associated with film making in Canada. The entry for each person includes union/guild memberships, address and phone number, genres of interest, basic biographical information and a selective filmography. The entries are organized by function, i.e. writers, producers, directors, production managers, cinematographers, art directors, editors and composers. The work was produced from

a database developed and kept current by the Academy of Canadian Cinema and Television.

1160 **Film as a national art: NFB of Canada and the film board idea.**
C. Rodney James. New York: Arno Press, 1977. 760p. (Dissertations on Film Series).

While but one step removed from being a dissertation, this work is nonetheless useful as a general introductory history of the National Film Board.

1161 **Movies and memoranda: an interpretive history of the National Film Board of Canada.**
D.B. Jones. Ottawa: Canadian Film Institute/Institut canadien du film, 1981. 240p. (Canadian film series, vol. 5).

How did the National Film Board of Canada achieve the internationally unique position of becoming the leader in documentary film so early on, and then sustain this position through decades of filmmaking? This is the question posed and answered in a favourable treatment of the NFB. The author acknowledges the work of John Grierson, and his contribution both to the Board and also to the development of the commercial film industry. Moreover, he attempts to place the accomplishment and influence of the NFB's films within an international context.

1162 **Home movies: tales from the Canadian film world.**
Martin Knelman. Toronto: Key Porter, 1987. 248p.

An engaging book, examining the love-hate relationship between Canadian film makers (writers, directors, producers, actors, etc.) and Hollywood. The author tells the reader much about the past and present of the Canadian film industry, as well as much about Canadian participation in the affairs of Hollywood. While entertaining reading, employing a vignette style, the book may not be immediately comprehensible for the uninitiated. Some knowledge of the cultural scene in Canada would be helpful in order to fully appreciate the personalties and the thesis of the book.

1163 **This is where we came in: the career and character of Canadian film.**
Martin Knelman. Toronto: McClelland & Stewart, 1977. 176p.

A 'Canadian movie imperative' emerged out of the author's developing awareness. Based on youthful experience, Knelman felt increasingly that Canadian films should define the differences inherent in, and particular to, Canadian life, as well as shedding light on the country's shared experiences, and thereby providing an impression of Canada. It is to this end that Knelman labours, within the context of an anecdotal look at the development of Canadian film. The book concentrates on the post-Grierson era of film and it is particularly good at explaining the developments and personalities of the 1960s and 1970s.

1164 **Histoire générale du cinéma au Québec.** (General history of the Quebec cinema.)
Yves Lever. Montreal: Les Éditions du Boréal, 1988. 551p. bibliog.

In this authoritative, readable general history of film making in Quebec, the author covers all periods of development, putting the work of Quebec film makers within the national context, as well as within the political realities of the province. He also gives attention to genre and to the personalities of the Quebec film community. The work is well illustrated. A book for the general reader and the student of cinema.

1165   **Turn up the contrast: CBC television drama since 1952.**
Mary Jane Miller.   Vancouver: University of British Columbia Press; CBC Enterprises, 1987. 429p. bibliog.
Much of CBC television drama is generally of a high quality and is deservedly popular, so concludes the author. Without doubt, the dramatic work produced by the Corporation has contributed markedly to the country's cultural and literary fabric. This professor of dramatic literature takes a systematic look at CBC television drama and brings this perspective to a critical analysis of the forms and subject matter of the genre. The author presents at one and the same time a history and analysis of CBC television drama. The first part of the book uses genre (copshows and mysteries, family adventure, sitcoms and domestic comedy, series and miniseries) as a reference point; the second part chronologically looks at plays found in anthologies and drama specials. Contained in the work are a number of useful appendices, including a chronology of major series and anthologies, and a checklist of programmes.

1166   **Embattled shadows: a history of Canadian cinema 1895-1939.**
Peter Morris.   Montreal: McGill-Queen's University Press, 1978. 350p.
A scholarly chronicle of film activities in Canada before the establishment of the National Film Board, this work attempts a comprehensive examination of the early period of Canadian film. The narrative begins with the travelling showmen who brought the movies to communities across the country, examines the efforts to establish a film industry in the inter-war years, discusses the establishment and eventual collapse of the Motion Picture Bureau of the federal government, and finally, explores the activities of John Grierson at the National Film Board. The work concludes with a brief examination of the relationship of pioneer film making to later developments in the industry. Two interesting appendices supplement the work: the first is 'A Chronology of Film in Canada, 1894-1913'; and the second is a 'Filmography', selectively listing Canadian films produced before 1939.

1167   **The film companion.**
Peter Morris.   Toronto: Irwin, 1984. 335p.
This work serves two purposes: it provides biographical and credit information on over 300 film makers, including directors, screen writers, cinematographers, composers, art directors, editors, sound technicians, producers and administrators; and, it also gives brief synopses and critical evaluations for over 300 Canadian films. A useful reference tool.

1168   **The colonized eye: rethinking the Grierson legend.**
Joyce Nelson.   Toronto: Between the Lines, 1988. 197p.
The author attempts to bring a different perspective to the Grierson legend. It is her contention that Grierson was effectively a defender of multinational capitalism and that he used film to advance the ready acceptance of the new economic order which came to typify the post-war world.

1169 **Torn sprockets: the uncertain projection of the Canadian film.**
Gerald Pratley. Toronto: Associated University Presses, 1987. 330p.
An overview of the development of film making in Canada. The work is divided into three sections: Part 1, 'Early Canadian Film-making, 1900-1939'; Part 2, 'Success and Struggle, 1940-1984'; and Part 3, 'The Credits, Canadian Films, 1945-1984'. The first two parts encompass a well illustrated narrative, while the final, and largest part, also illustrated, lists films made in Canada which were primarily made for showings in cinemas. Information provided on the films includes: the premiere or release date; the title; the production or releasing company; credits; place of premiere; running time; distributor; cast; and brief description. The work also includes an 'Index to the Films of the NFB Producers and Directors'.

1170 **A pictorial history of the Canadian film awards.**
Maria Topalovich. Toronto: Stoddart, 1984. 182p.
Awards for film making in Canada were established in 1949 and have remained an annual tradition since that time. This work chronicles the award winning films from each year. A short chapter is devoted to each year, introduced by an essay which highlights the awards and the award ceremony for that year. The essay is then followed by a list of the award winners by category. A number of useful appendices supplement the work: the 'National Film Board of Canada's Canadian Film Award Winners'; the 'Canadian Broadcasting Corporation's Canadian Film Award Winners'; the 'Canadian Film Awards to films made with the participation of Telefilm Canada (Canadian Film Development Corporation 1968*-1984)'; the 'Winning Films and Their Awards 1949-1984'; and the 'Winning Filmmakers and Their Awards 1949-1984'.

1171 **Canadian feature film index=Index des films canadiens de long métrage 1913-1985.**
D.J. Turner, Micheline Morisset. Ottawa: Public Archives Canada; National Film, Television and Sound Archives, 1987. 816p.
This list documents 1,222 Canadian feature films produced between 1913 and 1985. For the purpose of the list a feature film is defined as a motion picture running more than sixty minutes. Information provided in the index includes titles, date of the shoot, film stock used, laboratory which developed the film, filming location, studio, language of dialogue, version, production company or companies, production credits, source of material, music, genre, actors, budget, cost, length, distributor, release information, and more.

1172 **Self portraits: essays on the Canadian and Quebec cinemas.**
Edited by Pierre Veronneau, Piers Handling. Ottawa: Canadian Film Institute/Institut canadien du film, 1980. 257p. bibliog. (Canadian Film Series, vol. 4).
An anthology of twelve essays which deal with specific aspects of film, and at the same time provide a survey of the evolution of Canadian cinema from 1898 to 1980. The stated intention of the editors was to combine the history of the Canadian and Quebec cinemas together with a consideration of related themes, perennial factors and resultant problems. The work includes: 'A Chronology of Canadian and Quebec Cinema: 1896-1979'; biographical entries on 75 film makers; credit information on 125 films; and a select bibliography.

Folklore

1173 **Canadian Folk Music Journal = Revue de Musique Folklorique Canadienne.**
Calgary, Alberta: Canadian Folk Music Society/Société canadienne de musique folklorique, 1973- . annual.
Scholarly articles on folklore and folk music.

1174 **Canadian folklore canadien: journal of the folklore studies association of Canada = Folklore canadien = Revue de l'association canadienne d'ethnologie et de folklore.**
Nepean, Ontario: Folklore Studies Association of Canada/L'Association canadienne d'ethnologie et de folklore, 1979- .
This journal, published irregularly, contains articles relating to folklore studies, including book reviews, and research notes.

1175 **A bibliography of Canadian folklore in English.**
Compiled by Edith Fowke, Carole Henderson Carpenter. Toronto: University of Toronto Press, 1981. 272p.
A comprehensive bibliography of Canadian folklore in English to the date of its publication. The 3,877 entries are arranged by genre: folktales; folk music and dance; folk speech and naming; superstitions, popular beliefs, folk medicine and the supernatural; folklife and customs; and, folk art and material culture. Within genres items are arranged by ethnic groups: anglophone and Celtic; francophone; Indian and Inuit; and, other ethnic groups. A variety of source materials such as reference books, periodicals, records, films, and graduate theses are included in this bibliography. A not altogether successful attempt is made to provide judgements on each work based on criteria of audience, importance to scholarship, and whether the work is suitable for young people. The work is intended primarily for scholars of folklore, but would also be of interest to scholars in anthropology, cultural geography, oral history, and other areas of Canadian studies. Includes a brief survey of Canadian folklore studies.

1176 **Explorations in Canadian folklore.**
Edith Fowke, Carole H. Carpenter. Toronto: McClelland & Stewart, 1985. 400p.
An anthology of articles that deal with various types of oral traditions drawn from many groups, including Canadians of English, Scottish, Irish, French, German, Jewish, Mennonite, Ukrainian, Amerindian and Inuit ancestry.

1177 **Canadian folklore.**
Edith Fowke. Toronto: Oxford University Press, 1988. 149p.
bibliog. (Perspectives on Canadian Culture).
Canada's premier folklorist has written a compact survey on Canadian folklore, the people associated with Canadian folklore, the collections that record it, the methods of studying it, and the materials that make it up. This overview looks at: the pioneer collectors; the tales, songs and music; the minor genres such as folk speech, place

names, proverbs, riddles, childlore, and adult diversions; beliefs and superstitions; folklore and customs; and, folk art and crafts. The text is supplemented by an extensive bibliography.

1178 **Folklore of Canada.**
Edited by Edith Fowke.   Toronto: McClelland & Stewart, 1976.
349p.
'The aim of this anthology is to present a representative cross-section of the various kinds of folklore found in Canada. Some genres, notably folk song, have inspired many books, but most types are sparsely represented and often buried in obscure out-of-print sources . . . this sampling will give some idea of our unwritten lore'. Material is arranged by ethnic origin.

1179 **The Penguin book of Canadian folk songs.**
Selected and edited by Edith Fowke.   Harmondsworth, England: Penguin Books, 1973. 224p.
A representative selection of over eighty Canadian folk-songs. Most of the songs included were composed in Canada, rather than having been imported. Also, most come from the traditions of Ontario and Newfoundland, with only a sampling from French Canada or the West. Other compilations representing various regions of the country, include: Helen Creighton's *Maritime folk songs* (St. John's, Newfoundland: Breakwater, 1979) and her *Songs and ballads from Nova Scotia* (New York: Dover Publications, 1966). See also Maud Karpeles' *Folk songs from Newfoundland* (Hamden, Connecticut: Archon Books, 1970); Edith Fowke's *Traditional singers and songs from Ontario* (Don Mills, Ontario: Burns & MacEachern, 1965); and, Kenneth Peacock's *Songs of the Newfoundland outports* (Ottawa: Queen's Printer, 1965).

1180 **Singing our history: Canada's story in song.**
Edith Fowke, Alan Mills.   Toronto: Doubleday Canada, 1984. 249p.
This book presents a view of Canada's history through its folk-songs. These folk-songs have been preserved, in the main, through an oral tradition. They are arranged in chronological order, beginning with songs of the Indian and Inuit cultures, through the period of the French colonies to the British influx, Confederation and the settlement and development of the West. Brief essays precede each section and place the songs in an historical context. They also inform the reader what information is available about the selected songs. The book includes a section on 'Sources and References' and a 'Record List'. For additional Canadian folk-songs see other of Fowke's compilations, including: *Lumbering songs from the northern woods* (Toronto: NC Press, 1985); *Canadian vibrations – Vibrations canadiennes* (Toronto: Macmillan, 1972); and, *Folk songs of Canada* (Waterloo, Ontario: Waterloo Music Company, 1966).

1181   **Tales told in Canada.**
       Edith Fowke.   Toronto: Doubleday, 1986. 174p. bibliog.
A collection of various kinds of tales that have been told in Canada, including myths, animal tales, supernatural tales, romantic tales, jokes and anecdotes, formula tales, legends, and personal experience narratives. The selections come from diverse ethnic groups, including Indian, Inuit, English, Scottish, Irish, French, German, Ukrainian, Doukhobor, Polish, Italian, Jewish, Greek, Swedish, Icelandic, West Indian, and others. Introductory notes to the individual groupings and tales give detail about the storytellers and the collectors. An interesting introduction orientates the reader to the field, while a lengthy bibliography lists useful reference works as well as most works of traditional Canadian folktales published in English with the addition of works which classify or analyse Canadian tales. This work is a good introduction to Canadian folklore. For further interest, see also Fowke's *Folktales of French Canada* (Toronto: NC Press, 1981).

Sport and Recreation

Reference

1182 **Who's who in Canadian sport.**
Bob Ferguson. Toronto: Summerhill Press, 1985. 354p.
A handy reference work for the sports enthusiast. Brief biographical sketches of over 2,800 athletes and sports figures, both amateur and professional, living and deceased. A typical entry includes personal history, education, amateur and professional sports affiliations, records, achievements and awards.

1183 **Sport Canadiana.**
Compiled by Barbara Schrodt, Gerald Redmond, Richard Baka.
Edmonton, Alberta: Executive Sport Publications, 1980. 224p.
bibliog.
A chronological record of the significant dates in the development of seventy-three sports played in Canada, from the early nineteenth century to 1978 (when the XI Commonwealth Games were held in Canada). Each sport is prefaced by a short historical introduction. The work is illustrated and has a short, selected bibliography.

1184 **Sport bibliography = Bibliographie du sport.**
Ottawa: Sport Information Resource Centre/Centre de documentation pour le sport, 1981- .
The original eight volume set of this reference tool was published in 1981-82. It contained over 70,000 entries (books, periodical articles, thesis, microforms, conference proceedings, etc.), relating to sport and physical activity, worldwide, published during the period 1974–80 inclusive, with a substantial number of entries for the period prior to 1974. Published in 1983 was the two volume *Sport bibliography*, *update* 1983 (Ottawa: Sport Information Resource Centre, 1983). This work contains over 28,000 entries representing materials from 1979 onwards. Three subsequent volumes were published (Volumes 11, 12, and 13), each with approximately 15,000

entries. No further hard copy volumes of the *Bibliography* have been published since Volume 13 (1984), instead researchers can gain access to the file through the SPORT database, available from the standard vendors.

General

1185   **Fly fishing: the Canadian Rockies.**
Joey Ambrosi.   Calgary: Rocky Mountain Books, 1987. 218p.
This work is in two parts. The first is a general introduction to fly fishing as a sport. The second section lists 700 lakes, rivers and streams in the Canadian Rockies with information on individual waters, location, setting, access, type and size of fish present, plus applicable and recommended tactics. A book for the enthusiast.

1186   **Sports and the law in Canada.**
John Barnes.   Toronto: Butterworths, 1983. 370p.
An introductory survey of issues in Canadian sports law and sports policy. The approach used in the presentation is one of 'law in context', that is, taking into account some wider social, economic and administrative issues, along with the legal questions raised. Mainly of interest to the sports administrator and the student of physical education.

1187   **L'église et le loisir au Québec avant la revolution tranquille.** (The Church and leisure in Quebec before the Quiet Revolution.)
Michel Bellefleur. Quebec: Presses de l'Université du Quebec, 1986. 221p.
The Catholic Church in Quebec has long been a dominant force in all aspects of French-Canadian society. This socio-historical study looks at the more recent rôle assumed by the Church and the Quebec clergy in the leisure time and recreational activities of the Quebec people. An interesting commentary with regard to a significant segment of the Canadian community.

1188   **CAHPER/ACSEPL Journal.**
Gloucester, Ontario: Canadian Association for Health, Physical Education and Recreation/L'Association canadienne pour la santé, l'éducation physique et le loisir, 1934- . bi-monthly.
This incorporates a magazine format with feature articles on health and fitness. See also *Recreation Canada* (Vanier, Ontario: Canadian Parks/Recreation Association/ Association canadienne des loisirs/parcs, 1949-).

1189   **The game: a thoughtful and provocative look at a life in hockey.**
Ken Dryden.   Toronto: Macmillan, 1983. 248p.
There are many books which can be classified within the genre of sport memoirs – the insider's story if you like. This is one; but it is also much more. It is the story of nine days in the life of one of hockey's superstars playing in the 1970s, but it is also an articulate and absorbing commentary on 'the game' – for many Canadians the only

game – as seen through the eyes of a thoughtful and literate professional athlete. Certainly an important book for sports enthusiasts, but also recommended reading for the general reader interested in discovering another dimension of the Canadian national identity.

1190   **Images of sport in early Canada = Images du sport dans le Canada d'autrefois.**
Compiled by Nancy J. Dunbar.   Montreal: McGill-Queen's University Press, 1976. 95p.
A picture book which chronicles early Canadians (native and European ancestry) at play and engaging in sport, with a short but observant introduction by noted writer Hugh MacLennan. The works represented are historical works of art or photographs. The reproductions are in black-and-white as well as colour.

1191   **The Canadian rodeo book.**
Claire Eamer, Thiza Jones.   Saskatoon, Saskatchewan: Western Producer Prairie Books, 1982. 124p.
The rodeo events of today evolved from the skills needed to work the cattle ranches of the American and Canadian West. Today the sport has grown to be international in nature. This work traces the Canadian development of the sport, it 'carries the reader from the momentous first Calgary Stampede [an agricultural fair and rodeo] to Canada's rodeo "greats" of today. It covers every aspect of the sport, from what to look for in a bronc ride, to the sometimes glamorous, sometimes dirty, world of the cowboy'. Included also is a dictionary of rodeo terms, a who's who in Canadian rodeo and a statistical compendium.

1192   **Eskimo Inuit games.**
Compiled by F.H. Eger.   Vancouver: X-Press, [1981]. 2nd ed. 96p.
The native cultures of Canada are rich in their own games, some of which, like lacrosse, the European settlers came to appreciate, enjoy and eventually play. Although Inuit Games are not well known by Canadians, let alone by those outside the country, they are nevertheless an integral part of our identity as a nation. This slim volume provides the interested reader with a sense of the techniques involved in these games.

1193   **Everybody's hockey book.**
Stan Fischler, Shirley Fischler.   New York: Charles Scribner's Sons, 1983. 384p.
Stan Fischler is one of the more prolific hockey writers; he might also be named one of the best. Certainly his knowledge of the game is without equal. This work, co-written with his wife, provides a good general overview of the game. Here in capsule form is a history of hockey, the equipment requirements, a series of training and conditioning recommendations, an analysis of hockey skills, the tactics of the game, as well as other technical matters of interest. Fischler's previous works are also recommended. Among these are: *Offside: hockey from the inside.* (Toronto: Methuen, 1985); *Hockey's 100: a personal ranking of the best players in hockey history* (Toronto: Stoddart, 1984); *Those were the days: the lore of hockey by the legends of the game* (New York: Dodd, Mead, 1976); and Fischler's own autobiography entitled *Slapshot* (New York: Grosset & Dunlap, 1973).

Sport and Recreation. General

1194 **The canoe and white water: from essential to sport.**
C.E.S. Franks. Toronto: University of Toronto Press, 1977. 237p.
A work recommended as recreational reading as well as recommended as a useful guide for recreational canoeing. The author presents a well written, finely illustrated guide to the sport, interweaving into the text: the history and development of the sport; a commentary on the techniques necessary for success; such arcane topics as the methods for analysis of river conditions and river grading; and recommendations with regard to the planning and preparation for canoe trips. Appendices provide additional information on canoeing rivers, recommended works on canoeing and necessary equipment. Recommended also for the canoeing enthusiast is the beautiful work edited by James Raffan, *Wild waters: canoeing Canada's wilderness rivers* (Toronto: Key Porter Books, 1986).

1195 **Canadian sport: sociological perspectives.**
Edited by Richard S. Gruneau, John G. Albinson. Don Mills, Ontario: Addison-Wesley, 1976. 433p.
The editors' aims were two-fold: to provide a text for the sociology of sports courses and to create a general reference book for in-depth information on Canadian sporting activities. The work is in six parts: Part I looks at sport as an area of sociological study; Part II examines the growth and institutionalization of sport in the nineteenth century; Part III focuses on the democratization of sport; Part IV deals with the formalization of sport, particularly professional sport; Part V looks at voluntary participation in sport and recreational activity; and Part VI considers values and the underlying 'moral order' of competitive sport. A work intended for the academic reader.

1196 **Introduction à l'histoire des sports au Québec.** (Introduction to the history of sport in Quebec.)
Donald Guay. Montreal: VLB Éditeur, 1987. 294p.
This history explores specific themes relating to sport in Quebec since 1880. Beginning with the origin of physical activity, the author goes on to examine the first sporting activity and its development and attendant problems. Also included here are sports organizations and other relevant institutions, and québécois participation. All sporting venues are addressed, including baseball, billiards, lacrosse, cycling, fencing, hockey, swimming, skating, racquet sports and riflery. See also by the same author *L'histoire de l'éducation physique au Québec: conceptions et événements* (1830-1980) (The history of physical education in Quebec: beginnings and developments [1830-1980]. Chicoutimi, Quebec: Gaëtan Morin, 1980).

1197 **An unbroken line.**
Peter Gzowski. Toronto: McClelland & Stewart, 1983. 241p.
The Queen's Plate, first run on 27 June 1860, and considered the premier thoroughbred horse race in Canada, is the background for an examination of horse racing in this country, by one of Canada's best known radio hosts. Chiefly by way of anecdote the reader of this popular, journalistic account comes away with some knowledge of horse racing, considerable appreciation of the players and characters associated with the sport, and, a curiosity as to the motivation behind it all. See also the entertaining work by Trent Frayne, entitled *The Queen's Plate* (Toronto: McClelland & Stewart, 1971).

1198   **Bright waters, bright fish: an examination of angling in Canada.**
Roderick Haig-Brown.   Vancouver: Douglas & McIntyre, 1980.
142p.
This is a work not only about sport fishing in Canada, but it is a work also about the preservation and development of the natural resources of the country. More yet, it is a work about the highly individualized experiences of Canadian anglers. The work is illustrated with coloured photographs. Anglers, who are not already familiar with the works of Haig-Brown should also consult: *The western angler* (1981), *Return to the river* (1982) and *Fisherman's fall* (1982), published in Toronto by Totem, and *Fisherman's spring* (1988), *Fisherman's summer* (1989) and *Fisherman's winter* (1988), published by Douglas & McIntyre (Vancouver).

1199   **Not just a game: essays in Canadian sport sociology.**
Edited by Jean Harvey, Hart Cantelon.   Ottawa: University of
Ottawa Press, 1988. 323p. bibliog.
An anthology of essays which touch on a great many dimensions of sport, including: the historical antecedents of sport; the organizational structure of sport; the ideology of sport; and, the social determinants of sports participation. Includes a selective bibliography.

1200   **Hockey night in Canada: the Maple Leafs' story.**
Foster Hewitt.   Toronto: Ryerson Press, 1956. 211p.
Many popular accounts have been published of the Maple Leaf hockey club. This particular early work recounts the formative years of the club by Canada's then premier sports journalist, broadcaster and hockey expert. This is a work as much about Hewitt as it is about hockey.

1201   **The complete encyclopedia of hockey.**
Edited by Zander Hollander, Hal Bock.   Toronto: Doubleday, 1983.
3rd ed. 466p.
There are several encyclopedic works about hockey. The edition in hand includes historical information about the National Hockey League, a statistical register on more than 3,000 NHL players, reflections on eleven of hockey's most 'memorable moments', and a glossary of terms and a reprint of the 'Official NHL Rules'. Material is included on other major leagues of hockey as well as on the Olympic Games, world championships and collegiate championships. Earlier editions of this work were entitled: *The complete encyclopedia of ice hockey*. Hockey enthusiasts are directed also to *The hockey encyclopedia: the complete record of professional ice hockey* compiled by Stan Fischler and Shirley Walton Fischler (New York: Macmillan, 1983). This work is comprised almost totally of a variety of statistical tables. Of interest also is Gary Ronberg's *The illustrated hockey encyclopedia* (New York: Balsam, 1984).

1202   **History of sport in Canada.**
Maxwell L. Howell, Reet A. Howell.   Champaign, Illinois: Stipes,
1985. rev. ed. 477p.
Taking the view that sport mirrors society, the authors attempt to identify and characterize that which is different with regard to sport in Canada. The work provides much basic information and is useful to the researcher in this manner. The text,

regrettably, offers little to engage the reader. It is ordered chronologically, and it draws heavily from doctoral dissertations produced under the supervision of the authors.

1203   **Sports and games in Canadian life 1700 to the present.**
Nancy Howell, Maxwell L. Howell.   Toronto: Macmillan, 1969. 378p.

Canada's contribution to the world of sports include the creation and development of lacrosse and ice hockey, the increase in popularity of canoeing and snowshoeing, and the beginnings of rugby in the United States, leading to American football. This volume is a general survey of sports and games in the culture of Canada.

1204   **Cheering for the home team: the story of baseball in Canada.**
William Humber.   Erin, Ontario: Boston Mills Press, 1983. 150p

Baseball is a sport that Canadians have played since the 1850s. This is a look at Canada's baseball heritage, from its beginnings in the province of Ontario and its spread across the country, to the entry of two Canadian teams, the Toronto Blue Jays and the Montreal Expos, into the modern major leagues.

1205   **Alpine huts in the Rockies, Selkirks and Purcells.**
Herbert G. Kariel.   Banff, Alberta: Alpine Club of Canada, 1986. 183p.

This is a guide to Alpine huts in Canadian mountains, covering their origin and design, environment and current status. On a more whimsical note, the author provides stories of their 'moments of glory and sadness, moves, additions, and occasional demises, fiery or otherwise,' plus background information on the surrounding peaks, mountaineering, and wildlife of the environs. The volume is illustrated with photographs, maps, and floor plans.

1206   **The complete guide to backpacking in Canada.**
Elliott Katz.   Toronto: Doubleday, 1985. rev. ed. 261p.

Divided into two sections, this book covers firstly the basic equipment and practical skills necessary before heading out on the trail in Canada. The second part of the book is a comprehensive guide to backpacking opportunities in Canada, a landscape which offers everything from gentle rambles to rugged treks in the wilderness. The volume is a useful general guide, but the enthusiast is advised to look for local guides for those areas which are to be visited. A large literature of hiking trail publications has been produced.

1207   **The complete guide to bicycling in Canada.**
Elliott Katz.   Toronto: Doubleday, 1987. 231p.

Information for the serious cyclist. Included are detailed route descriptions and planning maps, suggestions on campsites, accommodation, recreation areas and sightseeing. The history of cycling in Canada can be found in William Humber's *Freewheeling: the story of bicycling in Canada* (Erin, Ontario: Boston Mills Press, 1986).

1208 **History of golf in Canada.**
L.V. Kavanagh. Toronto: Fitzhenry & Whiteside, 1973. 207p.
A well illustrated historical overview of the development of the game of golf in Canada. Includes a large section which documents Canadian and provincial golf records, listing tournament and championship winners.

1209 **Sport and politics in Canada: federal government involvement since 1961.**
Donald Macintosh, Tom Bedecki, C.E.S. Franks. Kingston, Ontario; Montreal: McGill-Queen's University Press, 1987. 210p.
The question of government involvement in athletics, particularly federal government involvement, has recently been the topic of some considerable and heated debate in Canada. No more so than since the troublesome events which surrounded Canadian athletes at the Olympics in Seoul, Korea in 1988. The work in hand provides more than interesting reading within the above context, although it predates the 1988-89 controversy. Here the authors provide a broad framework for a more detailed study of the many areas of federal government involvement in sport. The primary purpose of the work is 'to explain why the federal government changed its focus from the original intent of the act [Bill C-131 passed in 1961], which was to encourage participation in amateur sport and fitness, to concentrate on the development of a corps of élite "state" athletes.' Why indeed!

1210 **The first fifty: a nostalgic look at the Brier.**
Doug Maxwell. Toronto: Maxcurl Publications, 1980. 120p.
Canada claims three major sporting championships: the Stanley Cup in hockey; the Grey Cup in football; and the Brier which is the Canadian curling championship. This is the story of the latter.

1211 **Canada's international equestrians.**
Zita Barbara May. Toronto: Burns & MacEachern, 1975. 219p.
Canada boasts a distinguished history in equestrian sports. Regrettably much of the documentary record of these developments, if it ever existed, has not been preserved. Here the author, drawing extensively from an oral record, with the assistance of newspaper reports, has put together a credible history of the sport. While anecdotal, the framework of the record is in place in this interesting account. The text is amply illustrated with black-and-white as well as colour plates.

1212 **For the record: Canada's greatest women athletes.**
David McDonald. Toronto: Mesa Associates, 1981. 270p.
An extensive record of the accomplishments of thirty-seven Canadian women athletes, representing most sports at both the professional and amateur levels. A separate section is devoted to each athlete, with an appendix listing award winners. The work is well researched and incorporates into each biography, when possible, personal comment by the athlete. See also *Women in Canadian sports* (Toronto: Fitzhenry & Whiteside, 1977).

1213   **60 years of hockey: the intimate story behind North America's fastest, most exciting sport.**

Brian McFarlane.   Toronto: McGraw-Hill Ryerson, 1976. 269p.

A general overview history of the sport, concluding in the mid-1970s, written in journalistic style by one of the sport's most respected commentators. A number of earlier editions of this work carried similar titles.

1214   **The Stanley Cup: the story of the men and the teams who for half a century have fought for hockey's most prized trophy.**

Brian McFarlane.   Toronto: Pagurian Press, 1978. 192p.

The Stanley Cup, hockey's most coveted award, is the oldest trophy competed for by professional athletes. In 1893 it was donated by the then Governor-General, Lord Stanley and was presented to the amateur hockey champions of Canada. It has been presented every year since with the exception of the 1918-19 season (because of the great influenza epidemic). In 1926 it came to be the championship symbol of the professional National Hockey League. Noted sports journalist McFarlane tells the Cup's story year by year. The final chapter provides an interesting statistical record of the Stanley Cup and the records and awards related to the annual series. See also the earlier work by Henry Roxborough entitled *The Stanley Cup story* (Toronto: McGraw-Hill Ryerson, 1964).

1215   **Canada learns to play: the emergence of organized sport, 1807-1914.**

Alan Metcalfe.   Toronto: McClelland & Stewart, 1987. 243p.

(Canadian Social History Series).

Few works of social history introduce, let alone discuss, the integral rôle of organized sport within the context of the development of the country. Metcalfe attempts to place the emergence of forms of sport within the framework of the changes which occurred in Canadian society during the nineteenth and early twentieth centuries. In this examination he looks at such dominant factors as changing demography, the ethnic composition of the population, the economy and relationship of Canada to Britain and the United States.

1216   **A concise history of sport in Canada.**

Don Morrow, Mary Keyes (et al.).   Toronto: Oxford University Press, 1989.

A scholarly, but exceptionally readable historical overview of sport in Canada. The chronology ranges essentially from the early nineteenth century to the events surrounding Canada's involvement in the Seoul Olympics, including the discoveries of the Dubin Inquiry, which was set up in order to investigate the use of performance-enhancing drugs by Canadian athletes. The organization tends to be thematic dealing with major changes in selected organized, competitive sports, such as hockey, football, baseball, and lacrosse. A work which should be considered essential reading in this area of social history.

1217   **The mountains of Canada.**

Randy Morse.   Edmonton, Alberta: Hurtig, 1978. 144p. bibliog.

The mountain ranges of Canada, with their yawning fissures and crevasses, their cruel storms and precarious surfaces, present such a challenge to the adventurous that some climbers never return. Those who do are never quite the same again. Seventy-three peaks are presented in beautiful coloured photographs. Accompanying text describes particular features of the mountain from the climber's perspective, and notes the first or significant ascents. Included is a climber's glossary and a selected bibliography. This is a work as much about physical geography as about mountaineering. See also Phil Dowling's *The mountaineers: famous climbers in Canada* (Edmonton, Alberta: Hurtig, 1979).

1218 **The Montreal Canadians: an illustrated history of a hockey dynasty.**
Claude Mouton. Toronto: Key Porter Books, 1987. 208p.

A richly illustrated popular history of one of the premier teams in Canadian hockey. The development of the club is traced from the early days, as the Montreal Maroons, through to the 1980s. Considerable emphasis is given to the stars of the team through the years. Final chapters are devoted to 'Records and Honours', 'Rosters and Personnel' and 'Player Statistics'. Sports trivia galore! See also Chrys Goyens and Allan Turowetz's *Lions in winter* (Scarborough, Ontario: Prentice-Hall, 1986).

1219 **Canoe Canada.**
Nick Nickels. Toronto: Van Nostrand Reinhold, 1976. 278p.

An essential work for the canoeist. The author provides detailed information on over 600 canoe routes in Canada. The work is organized by province or territory. Each chapter includes a general description of the physical characteristics of the region, a short history of the province, as well as information on climate and fishing. The canoe routes are grouped by drainage basin. Maps are provided to indicate the route, and to identify important lakes and waterways. Listed also are map sources, outfitters and air charter companies. This latter information is dated.

1220 **The complete guide to cross-country skiing in Canada.**
John Peaker. Toronto: Doubleday, 1986. 246p.

Two-thirds of the *Guide* is devoted to providing information on the sport of cross-country skiing in Canada, including advice and recommendations on equipment, waxing, training, technique, touring and racing. The remainder of the book provides information on where to ski in Canada, providing descriptions of trails, facilities, instruction, lodging, and equipment rentals for more than 400 locations all across Canada. Of use also is Michael Keating's *Cross-country Canada: handbook and trail guide for cross-country skiers* (Toronto: Van Nostrand Reinhold, 1977).

1221 **The sporting Scots of nineteenth-century Canada.**
Gerald Redmond. London; Toronto: Associated University Presses, 1982. 347p.

The Scots' contribution to Canadian life has been significant, particularly so in the nineteenth century. They were prominent in such activities and institutions as the fur trade, the financial houses, the development of the railroads, education, and government. It is therefore not surprising that their contribution to Canadian sport was also of major proportions. Sporting contributions of particular note were: the development of curling in Canada (Scots established the first organized sports club in British North America – the Montreal Curling Club in 1807); the popularization of golf (Scots founded the first permanent golf club in the Western Hemisphere – the Royal Montreal Golf Club in 1873); and, the promotion of athletic contests such as the Highland Games (referred to in Canada as the Caledonian Games as they were usually sponsored by the local Caledonian Clubs). Also, the Highland game of 'shinty' was popular in Canada and is often referred to as the forerunner of ice hockey.

1222 **Canada at the Olympics.**
Henry Roxborough. Toronto: McGraw-Hill Ryerson, 1975. 3rd ed. 200p.
While this work is somewhat dated, it does achieve its purpose of supplying a popular history of the Olympic Games and Canadian participation in them. It concludes with the XX Olympiad in Munich in 1972 and thus does not deal with the Montreal Summer Olympics nor the Calgary Winter Olympics, both of which the national bibliography, *Canadiana*, shows to have generated a considerable literature unto themselves. Neither does it deal with the period to date, although the author's preface is disturbingly ironic in the light of the Dubin Inquiry. He writes 'our representation has been large, our contingents have been smartly outfitted and well-behaved. Canadian athletes have performed creditably, and Canadian leaders have enhanced Olympic prestige.'

1223 **One hundred – not out: the story of nineteenth-century Canadian sport.**
Henry Roxborough. Toronto: Ryerson Press, 1966. 252p.
A pioneering work in the field of Canadian sports history. Here the author attempts, with some success, to explore and explain the origins and growth of Canadian sport during the nineteenth century. A readable book, but more for the serious student or researcher.

1224 **Memoirs of a mountain man.**
Andy Russell. Toronto: Macmillan, 1984. 305p.
Russell's experience in the mountains as a trapper and guide belong to a totally different era, so radical have been the changes affecting the Rockies, and his account reads like an adventure story. Most of the work is taken up with his experiences as a trail guide taking hunters into the mountains of Alberta and British Columbia, and his transformation from hunting animals to filming and photographing them as one of Canada's most committed naturalists. This is as much a wilderness adventure as it is a commentary on the outdoors as recreation.

1225 **Canadian football: the view from the helmet.**
Robert A. Stebbins. London: Centre for Social and Humanistic Studies, University of Western Ontario, 1987. 207p. (Culture and Performance).
According to this study, Canadian football accurately 'depicts recurrent themes of Canadian life: imported symbols, unique rules, east-west conflict, compromise between English tradition and American innovation, a shifting balance of smugness and inferiority, and the sense of an elusive identity and uncertain future'. A serious sociological study which would, however, be as interesting to the general reader as it is to the informed. Interesting also is Jeffrey Goodman's *Huddling up: the inside story of the Canadian Football League* (Toronto: Fitzhenry & Whiteside, 1981).

1226 **The Grey Cup story: the dramatic history of football's most coveted award.**
Jack Sullivan. Toronto: Pagurian Press, 1970. 199p.
Since 1909, the year the cup was donated by Governor General Lord Grey, the Grey Cup has been emblematic of the champions of Canadian football. In its early years

(1909-24) it was presented to amateur teams, usually varsity football clubs. From 1925 to the late 1940s the Cup champions were taken from senior city leagues, and from the 1950s forward the Cup has been awarded to a professional team from the Canadian Football League, the winner, in fact, of the League's annual championship game.

1227 **Where to run in Canada.**
Bob Tewsley. [Ottawa]: Deneau & Greenberg, 1980. 181p.
A book for the runner describing running routes in twenty-three cities across Canada. The descriptions include type of terrain, the scenery, listings of hotels and public transportation, the addresses of athletic facilities, clinics, etc. Route maps are included. A book for the traveller.

1228 **Winners: a century of Canadian sport.**
Toronto: Grosvenor House; Canadian Press, 1985. 146p.
This is a testimonial tribute, produced on the 200th anniversary of Molson Breweries of Canada Limited, to a selection of Canadian athletes who have excelled at their sport. Despite the commercial nature of the volume, it provides useful information for the sports enthusiast, as well as the interested but uninformed reader.

1229 **Canada's sporting heroes.**
S.F. Wise, Douglas Fisher. Don Mills, Ontario: General Publishing, 1974. 338p. bibliog.
By way of the talents of an accomplished Canadian historian, and a noted syndicated sports journalist, this work fulfills two purposes. Firstly, it chronicles the achievements and exploits of those athletes who had been inducted, at least to 1974, into the Canadian Sports Hall of Fame. But secondly, the authors have successfully been able to group these biographies into sections, complete with introductory chapters and historical prefaces, which together result in a credible general sports history of Canada.

1230 **Walk into winter: a complete snowshoeing & winter camping guide.**
Gerry Wolfram. Toronto: John Wiley, 1977. 127p.
Winter sports are integral to the Canadian psyche. Snowshoeing, while not as popular as hockey or skiing, still commands a significant number of enthusiasts. This work is a basic introduction to the sport and includes tips on equipment selection, technique and style, as well as information on outdoor survival. The work is well illustrated and incorporates also a history of the sport.

1231 **The golden age of Canadian figure skating.**
David Young. Toronto: Summerhill, 1984. 200p.
A chronicle of Canadian figure skating from 1947 when Barbara Ann Scott won the World Championship, to 1973 (although the final chapters discuss various events and achievements up to the date of publication). Appendices list World Championships and Olympic medals won by Canadians, as well as Canadian champions from 1905 to 1984.

Libraries, Museums
and Archives

1232   **Archivaria: the Journal of the Association of Canadian Archivists.**
Ottawa: Association of Canadian Archivists, 1975- . semi-annual.
Devoted to the scholarly investigation of archives in Canada and internationally.
Articles explore the history, nature, and theory of archival activity and equally, the use
of archives. News notes in relation to the Canadian archival community can be found
in *ACA Bulletin* (Toronto: Association of Canadian Archivists, 1979-).

1233   **Canadian Library Journal.**
Ottawa: Canadian Library Association, 1944- . bi-monthly.
Provides a forum for the discussion, analysis and evaluation of issues in librarianship.
News notes related to Canadian libraries can be found in such publications as: *Feliciter*
(Ottawa: Canadian Library Association, 1956-).

1234   **Canadian Library Yearbook = Annuaire des Bibliothèques
Canadiennes.**
Toronto: Micromedia, 1985- . annual.
Brings together information on libraries, information and resource centres, learning
centres, archives, and library associations, as well as an updated list of library science
periodicals in print. Includes also a section on library vendors (publishers, suppliers,
etc.), library trends and library statistics.

1235   **The museum makers: the story of the Royal Ontario Museum.**
Lovat Dickson.   Toronto: Royal Ontario Museum, 1986. 214p.
A history of the largest museum in Canada, amongst the three largest in North
America. Contains much of interest about the development of museology and related
disciplines in Canada.

1236 **Directory of Canadian archives = Annuaire des dépôts d'archives canadiens.**
[Ottawa]: Bureau of Canadian Archivists/Bureau canadien des archivistes, 1986. 176p.
Records information on 540 archival repositories in Canada. Comprises a description of each repository, including name, address, person responsible, summary description of holdings, and a bibliographic entry for a personal guide to the holdings. Includes a name index and a thematic index by main categories of repositories.

1237 **The National Library of Canada: a historical analysis of the forces which contributed to its establishment and to the identification of its role and responsibilities.**
F. Dolores Donnelly. Ottawa: Canadian Library Association, 1973. 281p.
'As stated in the introduction: 'the purpose of this study is (1) to reconstruct the historical development of the National Library of Canada and to relate it to its present status; (2) to identify the chief factors that led to the establishment of the National Library and to the eventual understanding of its role and responsibilities; (3) to determine the relationships of the National Library with other agencies performing related functions, particularly with other federal libraries in Ottawa; (4) to identify the present role and responsibilities of the National Library as they have emerged from formulated policies, programs and recommendations, and from the statements of the National Librarian'. Also provides considerable insight into the general development of library services in Canada.

1238 **Beyond four walls: the origins and development of Canadian museums.**
Archie F. Key. Toronto: McClelland & Stewart, 1973. 384p.
An historical overview of museum development in Canada. Scholarly yet readable and entertaining.

1239 **Readings in Canadian library history.**
Peter F. McNally. Ottawa: Canadian Library Association, 1986. 258p.
Eighteen papers which reflect various aspects and issues in Canadian library history. See also Loraine Garry and Carl Garry's *Canadian libraries in their changing environment* (Toronto: Centre for Continuing Education, York University, 1977).

1240 **Muse.**
Ottawa: Canadian Museums Association/Association des musées canadiens, 1983- . quarterly.
The journal of the Association which includes feature articles on topics related to museology, Canadian museums and their collections, etc. Also includes: museum profiles; news and descriptions of exhibitions; and, book and video reviews. See also *Museum Quarterly: the Journal of the Ontario Museum Association* (Toronto: Ontario Museum Association, 1971-).

Libraries, Museums and Archives

1241 The official directory of Canadian museums and related institutions =
Répertoire officiel des musées canadiens et institutions connexes.
Ottawa: Canadian Museums Association/Association des musées
canadiens, 1987-88. 276p.
This presents information on 1,893 institutions in Canada. Entries include institution
name, year of opening, address, name of director, staff members, collection
description, publications, governing authority and hours. The *Directory* also includes a
listing of museum associations, related organizations and government agencies.

1242 **Report and recommendations of the Task Force charged with
examining federal policy concerning museums.**
Otttawa: Minister of Supply and Services Canada, 1986.
This federal Task Force was established to examine and make recommendations on the
state of museum institutions devoted to the collection, conservation, classification and
presentation of movable cultural property. The mandate included looking at an
institution's premises, collections, staff, financing, and all the formal and informal
working arrangements and facilities which permit the delivery of services. Recommendations tended to concentrate on actions required by the federal government in
support of the museum's community.

1243 **Union list of manuscripts in Canadian repositories = Catalogue collectif
des manuscrits des archives canadiennes.**
Ottawa: Public Archives of Canada, 1976- .
A comprehensive list of significant manuscripts and records in Canadian archival
institutions which attempts to provide basic information in order to enable researchers
to determine the usefulness of materials.

1244 **Project progress: a study of Canadian public libraries.**
Urban Dimensions Group.   Ottawa: Canadian Library Association,
1981. 120p.
The report identifies the most critical problems facing public library service in Canada.
Particular issues upon which the investigators focused include: inter-library cooperation;
the education and training of personnel; and, the implications of socio-demographic
changes for purposes of planning. Other questions of interest were the changing
political environment, social, technological and economic changes, and the general
objectives of public libraries.

Book Industries and Trade

1245 **Those amazing people! the story of the Canadian magazine industry 1778-1967.**
Noel Robert Barbour.   Toronto: Crucible Press, 1982. 198p.
A somewhat anecdotal, but useful, introduction to the development of the magazine publishing industry in Canada.

1246 **Books in Canada.**
Toronto: Canadian Review of Books, 1971- . nine times a year.
A book review magazine, containing reviews, author profiles, interviews, columns and features on the book trade.

1247 **Canadian Bookseller: the Magazine of Book Retailing.**
Toronto: Canadian Booksellers Association, 1983-. ten times a year.
This trade magazine reflects the news and opinions of the bookselling community, as well as including feature articles.

1248 **Canadian Printer and Publisher.**
Toronto: Maclean Hunter Limited, 1892- . monthly.
A trade publication in magazine format relating to issues of interest to the publishing and printing industries.

1249 **Scholarly publishing in Canada: evolving present, uncertain future = L'édition savante au Canada: tendances actuelles et perspectives d'avenir.**
Edited by Patricia Demers.   Ottawa: University of Ottawa Press, 1988. 244p.
This volume looks at various aspects of the scholarly publishing process, from the generation of research results to the production of the printed book, the marketing and

distribution of same and the implications of various government policies on the publishing industry. The papers included represent the Proceedings of a conference held in Edmonton, Alberta, in March, 1988.

1250   **The Thomson empire.**
Susan Goldenberg.   Toronto: Methuen, 1984. 260p.

Chronicles the fascinating story of the Thomson family and their business exploits, particularly in the areas of publishing and newspapers – a segment of their holdings comparable in size to that of internationally known major media personalities such as Robert Maxwell. Written for the fiftieth anniversary of the founding of the company, this work provides little analysis, but extensive detail, of the growth and development of the Thomson organization.

1251   **Fun tomorrow: learning to be a publisher and much else.**
John Morgan Gray.   Toronto: Macmillan, 1978. 347p.

Canada can claim only a handful of publishers whose biographies or autobiographies would offer much to the literature of publishing and *belles lettres*. John Gray is one of these. This text tells us much about a remarkable man, but it tells us also of the world of Canadian publishing through the 1930s to the mid-1940s. Regrettably, the book concludes with Gray's appointment as General Manager of Macmillan of Canada in 1946. A second volume was planned but, on 9 August, 1978 Gray died. We can only hope that a chronicler as able as Gray himself will complete the biography.

1252   **Book reading in Canada: the audience, the marketplace, and the distribution system for trade books in English Canada.**
James Lorimer.   Toronto: Association of Canadian Publishers, 1983. 448p.

This commissioned report provides hard data, and interpretation of that data, on the audience for trade books in English Canada, on the functioning of the marketplace and on the operation of the channels of distribution. Information is provided on audience makeup and demographics, reader attitudes toward Canadian books, the rôle of bookstores, the rôle of libraries, and the rôle of book clubs.

1253   **Papers of the Bibliographical Society of Canada = Cahiers de la Société bibliographique du Canada.**
Toronto: Bibliographical Society of Canada/La Société bibliographique du Canada, 1962- . annual.

This publication contains articles relating to bibliography and the book arts.

1254   **The beginnings of the book trade in Canada.**
George L. Parker.   Toronto: University of Toronto Press, 1985. 346p.

This is the first extensive history of the book trade in Canada. Regrettably, the work concludes at 1900 thus leaving for a future volume the development of the trade in the twentieth century. Parker's contribution touches on many topics, including copyright, commercial ventures, literary tastes, and intellectual history. The work contains a number of interesting, statistical appendices, as well as many valuable bibliographical notes.

1255 **Royal Commission on Book Publishing: background papers.**
Province of Ontario. [Toronto]: Queen's Printer and Publisher, 1972. 395p.

These nineteen papers were commissioned by the Royal Commission on Book Publishing as a series of background papers, by knowledgeable commentators, to fill in gaps in the available literature on book publishing. The pieces are wide-ranging, covering many aspects of trade and educational publishing, specialized publishing, book distribution, the concerns of writers, relations between libraries and publishers, government assistance to publishers and writers and copyright. Most of the articles deal with English language publishing and related issues. Together the collection serves as a monographic study of publishing in Canada, at least to the date of its publication, independent of its original purpose.

1256 **Royal Commission on Book Publishing: Canadian publishers & Canadian publishing.**
Province of Ontario. [Toronto]: Queen's Printer for Ontario, 1973. 371p.

This Province of Ontario Royal Commission on Book Publishing was, and remains, one of the best and most thorough examinations of the industry. The Commission was appointed in December 1970, to study and report on the industry in terms of its contributions to the cultural life and education of the people of Ontario and Canada. It also examined the economic, cultural, social or other consequences for the people of Ontario and Canada of the control of publishing firms by foreign-owned corporations and non-Canadians. The report encompasses a comprehensive examination of the different areas of book publishing, including the organization of the industry and the status of Canada at that time in world publishing. Particular attention was given to educational book publishers and the questions of financial viability and ownership. The Commission made some seventy specific and wide-ranging recommendations relating to the industry, and the nurturing of a distinctive Canadian identity for indigenous publishers. The report should be consulted in concert with separately published *Background papers* (q.v.).

1257 **The publishing industry in Canada: (with particular reference to newspaper and magazine publishing).**
Oakville, Ontario: AKTRIN Research Institute, 1987. 316p.

A thorough overview of the industry through a consultant's eyes, which includes sections relating to the importance and structure of the industry, governmental intervention and the legal framework, the process and method of production, the market and marketing, financial management, and, labour and employment.

1258 **Quill & Quire.**
Toronto: Key Publishers Company, 1935- . monthly

This is the key journal of the book trade in Canada. It is read and used widely by publishers, booksellers, librarians, writers and teachers, and contains feature articles, trade news, book reviews and advertising. Of interest also, particularly for reviews, is *Books in Canada* (q.v.).

1259 **Scholarly Publishing: a Journal for Authors & Publishers.**
Toronto: University of Toronto Press, 1969- . quarterly.
Of interest to those engaged in the publication of scholarly and academic works, the articles included are wide-ranging, dealing with subjects such as book production, marketing, design, and copyright.

1260 **The Book Trade in Canada With Who's Where = L'Industrie du Livre au Canada Avec Où Trouver Qui.**
Compiled and edited by Eunice Thorne, Ed Matheson. Caledon, Ontario: Ampersand Communications Services, 1985- . annual.
This publication provides information on publishers, agents, wholesalers, book manufacturers, printers, designers, agents, etc., who comprise the book trade in Canada.

1261 **A study of the Canadian periodical publishing industry.**
Woods Gordon Management Consultants. Ottawa: Department of Communications, 1984. 2 vols.
This study was commissioned by the Department of Communications with the aim of developing a solid information base on the industry, of reviewing federal government policies and programmes affecting the industry, and of recommending and developing new policy options. It includes an introduction to periodical publishing, identification of issues important to the industry, policy and strategic concerns, and possible future options for policy and support programmes.

Mass Media

1262 **Journalism, communication and the law.**
Edited by Stuart G. Adam. Scarborough, Ontario: Prentice-Hall, 1976. 245p. bibliog.
This anthology of previously published articles attempts to place a body of knowledge concerning journalism, its history, its practitioners and institutions, its issues as well as its social, economic and legal qualities within the Canadian experience. The work is organized around three primary themes: 'The Nature of Journalism'; 'Politics, Media and Communication'; and 'Journalism and the Law'. There is an extensive bibliography.

1263 **Documents of Canadian broadcasting.**
Edited by Roger Bird. Ottawa: Carleton University Press, 1988. 756p.
An indispensable reference collection for those in the fields of mass communications, broadcasting policy and media history, as well as broadcasters and those who deal with questions of broadcasting and culture. Here are all the documents (primarily government reports, laws, court decisions, etc.), which are key to the development of broadcasting in Canada, as well as those which control or govern the industry today. Documents are presented in chronological order, but have been organized into four sections: the pre-broadcasting era; the radio age; the arrival of television; and the CRTC (Canadian Radio-Television Commission) years. Each document is introduced by remarks intended to indicate the significance of the item and to place it within an historical context.

1264 **Closed circuits: the sellout of Canadian television.**
Herschel Hardin. Vancouver: Douglas & McIntyre, 1985. 339p.
This is a useful, but one-sided, history of television politics, beginning with the establishment of the Canadian Radio-Television Commission (CRTC) in 1968. The author's subtitle exposes his bias, for the work is an indictment of the regulatory process in Canada. For the author, Canadian television has been betrayed by the

Commission, by cable and pay-TV operators, by advertisers, by public administrators, and most particularly, by governments.

1265 **The tangled net: basic issues in Canadian communications.**
M. Patricia Hindley, Gail M. Martin, Jean McNulty. Vancouver: J. J. Douglas, 1977. 183p.

The contributors involved in the creation of this general text were part of the research group in the Department of Communications Studies at Simon Fraser University in Burnaby, British Columbia. Designed as an introductory textbook but written from a distinct Canadian perspective, it includes chapters on all communications media: publishing, film, broadcasting, cable television, telephone, data transmission, and satellite communication. The reader comes away with a good overview of the state of these sectors as well as with a view of the issues and questions which beset each in turn. Incidentally, the perceptive reader will learn much about the uniqueness of the Canadian situation, coexisting within a continental communications environment so dominated by the United States.

1266 **A history of journalism in Canada.**
W. H. Kesterton. Toronto: McClelland & Stewart, 1967. 304p. (Carleton Library, vol. 36).

This was the first comprehensive history of journalism in Canada and remains today one of the best sources of information on the development of the medium. The work is divided into two sections: the first section develops the story chronologically dividing the period 1752 to 1967 into four 'press periods'; the second and much larger section is thematic, analysing various topics such as the history of key journals and the contribution of noteworthy journalists, the qualities of Canadian daily newspapers and how these have changed during the twentieth century, the changes in the content of newspapers during the same period, the development of radio and television, and Canadian press freedom in the twentieth century. The interested reader is also directed to the two other volumes: *A history of Canadian journalism in the several portions of the Dominion with a sketch of the Canadian Press Association 1859-1908* (New York: AMS Press, 1976), and *A history of Canadian journalism II: last years of the Canadian Press Association 1908-1919 with a continuing record of the Canadian Daily Newspaper Publishers Association 1919-1959* (Toronto: Ontario Publishing Company, 1959).

1267 **The law and the press in Canada.**
Wilfred H. Kesterton. Ottawa: Carleton University Press, 1984. 242p. bibliog. (Carleton Library Series, vol. 100).

This is a scholarly treatment of the law and the press as it relates to the Canadian journalist. It emphasizes the 'rudimentary concepts, practices and prohibitions that the "front-line" journalist should know about'. Coverage includes: issues of contempt of court; the question as to the revealing of sources; civil defamation; criminal libel; obscenity and censorship; copyright; privacy laws; and government secrecy and the dissemination of information. An appendix outlines the nature of the legal cases discussed in the book. A bibliography is included. See also G. S. Adam and R. Martin's A *sourcebook of Canadian media law* (Ottawa: Carleton University Press, 1988), Philip Anisman and A. M. Linden's *The media, the courts and the charter* (Toronto: Carswell, 1986), and Clare F. Beckton's *The law and the media in Canada* (Toronto: Carswell, 1982). The working journalist is also directed to Stuart

Robertson's *Media law handbook: a guide for Canadian journalists, broadcasters, photographers, and writers* (Vancouver: International Self-Counsel Press, 1982).

1268 **Inside seven days: the show that shook the nation.**
Eric Koch. Scarborough, Ontario: Prentice-Hall, 1986. 272p.
This is a work as much about television journalism generally, the ethics of same and the relationship between journalism and a political authority, as it is about a particular television programme. 'This Hour Has Seven Days' was a news magazine programme, specializing in investigative journalism, which uncovered many key stories. The show was short-lived; fifty episodes were produced over two years. Its content, however, was provocative and controversial; its impact on subsequent journalists and current affairs programming was profound.

1269 **Communication Canada: issues in broadcasting and new technologies.**
Edited by Rowland M. Lorimer, Donald C. Wilson. Toronto: Kagan & Woo, 1988. 308p.
This anthology of commissioned essays explores the implications of Canada's communication system and some of the changes which may be expected to that system in the light of recent policy initiatives as well as emerging technologies. The book presents its theme primarily within the social context; for example, the editors asked their contributors the following questions: 'Does Canada's communication system really bind the nation together? If it does, in what manner does it perform this function? Does it contribute to the development of a Canadian imagination? Does it create unnecessary vulnerabilities to an uncertain future?'.

1270 **Mass communication in Canada.**
Rowland Lorimer, Jean McNulty. Toronto: McClelland & Stewart, 1987. 334p.
This is an introduction to the field of mass communication, from print journalism to satellite communications, as seen from the Canadian perspective. While designed as a textbook, it is also of interest and use to the general reader. A number of topics are treated in depth, among these are communication and Canadian culture, the media and Canadian society, the media and government, the techniques of journalism, the audience, media ownership, the function of media professionals, the geopolitics of information, and new communications technologies and the information age.

1271 **Canada's video revolution: pay-TV, home video and beyond.**
Peter Lyman. Toronto: James Lorimer in association with the Canadian Institute for Economic Policy, 1983. 173p.
New technologies such as satellites, optical fibres, the digitizing of information and others are creating new delivery systems for cultural products and information. Lyman outlines the impact of the new technologies on Canada's cultural industries and proposes strategies to make these industries viable in the cultural/entertainment/information marketplace. Many of his recommendations relate directly to shifts in federal government policies and attitudes. This is a technical book generally of interest to the informed reader.

1272   **Canadian broadcasting: market structure and economic performance.**
Stuart McFadyen, Colin Hoskins, David Gillen.   Montreal: Institute
for Research on Public Policy/L'Institut de Recherches Politiques,
1980. 277p.
The 1980s has seen considerable policy discussion with regard to the consolidation of
ownership within the media. As described in the preface, this study 'examines the
structure of radio, television and cable television markets and its impact on such
measures of economic performance as the pricing of advertising and profitability. Of
particular interest is the assessment of the impact of multiple and cross-media
ownership on the economic performance of broadcasting enterprises'.

1273   **Signing on: the birth of radio in Canada.**
Bill McNeil, Morris Wolfe.   Toronto: Doubleday, 1982. 303p.
This oral history was compiled to celebrate the fiftieth anniversary of radio
broadcasting in Canada (1932-82). One hundred and twenty-five interviews with
broadcasters, producers, technicians, entrepreneurs and listeners were recorded and
have been edited and reproduced. Despite the resultant anecdotal nature of the work,
it contains significant substance to be of interest both to the general and serious reader.
It is considerably enhanced by many period illustrations, including advertisements,
licenses, photographs, radio listings and rate cards.

1274   **The politics of Canadian broadcasting 1920-1951.**
Frank W. Peers.   Toronto: University of Toronto Press, 1969. 466p.
A scholarly treatment of the development of Canadian broadcasting from the
beginnings of radio to the advent of television. The story is one of technological
development, political intrigue, and personal drama. From the narrative emerges an
understanding of the unique circumstances leading to the mixed system of private
(following the American model) and public (the Canadian Radio Broadcasting
Commission – later the Canadian Broadcasting Corporation) ownership which Canada
enjoys.

1275   **The public eye: television and the politics of Canadian broadcasting
1952-1968.**
Frank W. Peers.   Toronto: University of Toronto Press, 1979. 459p.
A sequel to Peer's *The politics of Canadian broadcasting 1920-1951* (q.v.). Here the
development of broadcasting is brought forward from the inception of television in
1952 to the passing of the Broadcasting Act of 1968. This study, in large measure, deals
at length with government policy decisions as well as those of broadcasting authorities
and regulatory agencies. The work might be characterized as dry reading, suitable for
an academic audience. It is however thorough and a recommended work as a
background source.

1276   **Report of the Task Force on Broadcasting Policy.**
Ottawa: Minister of Supply and Services Canada, 1986. 731p.
This comprehensive review of broadcasting policy forms the foundation for present
federal policy and law which guides the industry at this time. The mandate of the Task
Force was inclusive; that was 'to make recommendations to the Minister of
Communications on an industrial and cultural strategy to govern the future evolution
of the Canadian broadcasting system through the remainder of this century'. The Task

Force members demonstrated the magnitude of their investigation by the thoroughness of their *Report*. The serious researcher will gain much from this work, whether interested in the development of the industry to date, regional broadcasting, the public and private sectors, programming, or issues of ownership and copyright.

1277 **Royal Commission on Newspapers.**
Hull, Quebec: Minister of Supply and Services Canada, 1981. 296p.
The ongoing consolidation of newspaper ownership in Canada was brought dramatically to the public's attention with the simultaneous closure of two newspapers, the *Winnipeg Tribune* and the *Ottawa Journal*, as a result of the culmination of a series of takeovers involving the major newspaper chains, Thomson and Southam, in the country. The Kent Commission (chaired by Tom Kent) was formed in response, to 'inquire generally into the newspaper industry in Canada', and look specifically into the concentration of the ownership and control of the industry. The report of the Commission reviewed the condition of the industry; it considered the responsibility of the press in an open society; examined the law as it relates to newspapers; studied the economics of the industry and provided comment on the trade-off between profitability and the fulfillment of a responsibility to the public; and looked at the processes of gathering and disseminating news. The Commission also studied the changing technologies relating to newspaper publishing, particularly in relation to new forms of electronic communication.

1278 **The making of the Canadian media.**
Paul Rutherford. Toronto: McGraw-Hill Ryerson, 1978. 141p.
bibliog. (McGraw-Hill Ryerson Series in Canadian Sociology).
This work is important in that it begins to outline the development and rôle of the mass media in Canada, a story which even today remains not conclusively told. Rutherford, by his own admission, is a media 'addict' and not a critic of mass communication. He presents a sympathetic appraisal, preferring to present the media as being and remaining 'on the side of the angels' and thus justifying his own addiction. This story is organized into three essays: 'The Rise of the Newspaper' which is a general history; 'The Golden Age of the Press' which discusses the supremacy of the big city daily; and 'The Triumph of the Multimedia', an examination of the impact taken together of the press, radio, television and the cinema. The bibliography will provide a good guide to further sources for the interested reader.

1279 **Politics and the media in Canada.**
Arthur Siegel. Toronto: McGraw-Hill Ryerson, 1983. 258p.
Siegel's study examines the Canadian media which provides information, opinion and entertainment on a daily or regular basis in relation to the political, social and economic context in which they function. The study analyses and comments on the impact of the media on politics and policy formulation, particularly with relation to the transmission of information and the setting of agendas for public discussion. Within this context he is able also to explain to the reader the present legal, legislative and parliamentary restraints on the media with regard to the dissemination of information. See also Mary Anne Comber and Robert S. Mayne's *The newsmongers: how the media distort the political news* (Toronto: McClelland & Stewart, 1986), *Media & elections in Canada* (Toronto: Holt, Rinehart & Winston, 1984), Marc Raboy's *Movements and messages: media and radical politics in Quebec* (Toronto: Between the Lines, 1984), and Edwin Black's *Politics and the news: the political functions of the mass media* (Torono: Butterworths, 1982).

Mass Media

1280 **Communications in Canadian society.**
Edited by Benjamin D. Singer. Don Mills, Ontario: Addison-Wesley, 1983. 342p.

Intended as a text for communications studies, this work is nonetheless most useful and informative for the general reader. Twenty-seven articles examine various aspects of the mass media in Canada, ranging from the historical development of the various media forms, to questions of policy and government control of communications media, to the rôle of the Canadian media in questions of national unity and identity, to the issue of the media as an agent of social change. The articles are written by some of the best known media commentators in the country.

1281 **From coast to coast: a personal history of radio in Canada.**
Sandy Stewart. Toronto: CBC Enterprises; Montreal: Les Entreprises Radio-Canada, 1985, 191p.

A veteran of radio and television programming has produced a most readable illustrated history of radio. Its focus is on the Canadian Broadcasting Corporation, but does give considerable treatment to the period before CBC, as well as to private broadcasting. Stewart discusses the decline of radio in relation to the introduction of television, but also speculates with optimism about the revival of radio in the forthcoming years.

1282 **Here's looking at us: a personal history of television in Canada.**
Sandy Stewart. Toronto: CBC Enterprises, 1986. 272p.

A profusely illustrated personal history of television in Canada, written by one of Canada's most successful creators and producers of television programming. The nostalgic narrative traces the development of Canadian television from the early 1950s through to the 1980s. This work has been aptly described as a book about personalities and programmes.

1283 **Canadian newspapers: the inside story.**
Edited by Walter Stewart. Edmonton, Alberta: Hurtig, 1980. 256p.

A collection of anecdotal, article length accounts about newspapers, and the people who work at them, written by some of Canada's better-known journalists.

1284 **The struggle for national broadcasting in Canada.**
E. Austin Weir. Toronto: McClelland & Stewart, 1965. 477p.

This story is well told by a pioneer in Canadian broadcasting. Weir worked initially as a journalist for a series of western-based agricultural journals. In 1929 he was appointed the Director of Radio for the Canadian National Railways – a position he held until 1937 when he was appointed Commercial Manager for the nascent Canadian Broadcasting Corporation. He served the CBC in a number of capacities until 1956. The work outlines radio operations during the 1920s and 1930s; it devotes some considerable space to the Aird Commission of 1928, the first Royal Commission on Broadcasting; and it discusses the forces leading to the establishment of the CBC in 1936. The latter portion of the work reviews the Broadcast Act of 1958.

1285   **Jolts: the TV wasteland and the Canadian oasis.**
Morris Wolfe.   Toronto: James Lorimer, 1985. 139p.

For seven years the author was a monthly television columnist for *Saturday Night* (q.v.). From this base he has written a work which attempts to examine the differences between English-Canadian and American culture 'as one would perceive them simply by looking at TV'. The author explores, at some length, the rôle of the Canadian Broadcasting Corporation (CBC) within the Canadian cultural fabric. Using his knowledge of American and Canadian television he is able throughout to illustrate his arguments with examples from television programming.

1286   **The news: inside the Canadian media.**
Edited by Barrie Zwicker, Dick MacDonald.   Ottawa: Deneau, [1982]. 356p. bibliog.

The magazine *Content* is devoted to information and constructive criticism about journalism in Canada. This publication is an anthology of articles selected from the magazine between 1970 and 1981. Some of the country's best journalists are represented, and they write about issues and concerns which, taken together, provide the reader with much information about the media and the working concerns of journalists in this country. A selective bibliography is included.

General Periodicals and Newspapers

1287 L'Actualité.
Montreal: Maclean Hunter, 1976- . monthly.
A general interest news magazine for French-Canada. Includes feature articles, news and columns on wide-ranging topics and complements *Maclean's* (q.v.).

1288 Chatelaine.
Toronto: Maclean Hunter, 1928- . monthly.
A national women's magazine, including feature articles and news on topics such as lifestyle, fashion, food, homemaking, careers, etc. See also: *Canadian Living* (Toronto: Telemedia Publishing, 1976- . monthly).

1289 Le Devoir.
Montreal: L'Imprimerie Populaire, 1910- . daily.
This is Canada's premier French-language newspaper.

1290 The Globe and Mail.
Toronto: Globe and Mail, 1844- . daily.
Although the newspaper is Toronto-based, a national edition of *The Globe and Mail* can arguably be claimed to be Canada's national newspaper, even though its coverage remains focused on central Canada. Canada boasts any number of fine daily papers, all representative of regions of the country. Key papers, and those indexed in the *Canadian News Index*, include: the *Calgary Herald*; the *Halifax Chronicle-Herald*; the *Montreal Gazette*; the *Toronto Star*; the *Vancouver Sun*; and the *Winnipeg Free Press*.

1291 Maclean's: Canada's Weekly Newsmagazine.
Toronto: Maclean Hunter, 1905- . weekly.
Canada's premier magazine of news, feature articles and columns on a wide range of topics, both national and international. It constitutes essential reading for all those interested in contemporary Canada.

1292   **Saturday Night.**
Toronto: Saturday Night Magazine Inc., 1887- . monthly.
Feature articles on a wide range of topics including politics, education, science, literature, business, and sports are to be found in this periodical. It includes book and film reviews as well as short fiction and caters to Canada's literati and intelligentsia.

General Reference
Works

1293 **Canada year book: a review of economic, social and political developments in Canada.**
Ottawa: Minister of Supply and Services, 1972- .
Continuously published from 1905 under various titles, this publication is a key reference source. It contains statistical and other information on all aspects of Canadian life, including information on federal and provincial governments, demography, and all educational/industrial/business sectors. Until recently volumes included a useful selective bibliography of books on Canada, compiled by the National Library of Canada. In its entirety the work provides a 'composite portrait of Canada in all its diversity and richness' and is supported by a detailed index. A French edition is also available.

1294 **Canadian Almanac & Directory.**
Toronto: Copp Clark Pitman, 1848- . annual.
Canada's premier directory, with the recent edition containing more than 50,000 indexed entries. Information is organized under seven major sections representing some seventeen subject divisions. The information in the compilation does not concentrate so much on quick reference and fact, as other almanacs tend to, instead it focuses on various sectors of Canadian society such as associations, churches, business and finance, culture, education and government. See also *The Canadian world almanac* (Toronto: Global Press, 1987-); and *The Corpus almanac & Canadian sourcebook* (Don Mills, Ontario: Corpus Information Services, 1966-).

1295 **Canadian Book Review Annual.**
Toronto: Simon & Pierre, 1975- . annual.
An evaluative guide to Canadian English-language publications. CBRA provides 200-500 word reviews of trade books carrying a Canadian imprint. Also reviewed are reprints of books originally published ten years before the current review year; paperback editions of books that were not reviewed when initially published in hardcover; selected federal government publications; English translations of French-

322

Canadian and foreign-language titles; and, selected educational titles with trade appeal. The reviews are organized by broad subject; each entry provides full bibliographic data, including ISBN and price. The main body of each volume is supported by author, title and subject indexes.

1296   Canadian Books in Print: Author and Title Index.
Toronto: University of Toronto Press, 1967- . annual.
Issued quarterly in microfiche with a hardcopy edition annually, CBIP is compiled from listings obtained from Canadian publishers. Efforts have been made to include all titles bearing the imprint of Canadian publishers or originated by the Canadian subsidiaries of international publishing firms. It is basically a listing of books in the English language, but it includes French-language titles published by predominantly English-language Canadian publishers, as well as titles from French-language publishers outside Quebec. CBIP is divided into three sections: an author index; a title index; and a publisher index. See also *Canadian books in print: subject index* (Toronto: University of Toronto Press, 1973-).

1297   Canadian Magazine Index.
Toronto: Micromedia, 1985- . monthly.
Cumulated annually, this reference guide provides details of popular, special interest and academic magazines. It indexes more than 350 periodicals in a broad range of subjects including the arts, business, children's literature, computers, cookery, education, geography, health, history, hobbies, nature, recreation, regional interest, science, and social sciences. Magazines have been chosen according to their availability in libraries and also with an eye to regional and subject coverage. A selection of key United States magazines are also covered. Entries contain standard index information. The publication is divided into two sections: the subject index which arranges articles alphabetically according to subject terms, corporation, government department and organization names; and the personal name index which arranges articles alphabetically by personal name, both by author and by subject. The *Magazine Index* and the *Canadian Periodical Index* (q.v.) have considerable overlap in coverage.

1298   Canadian News Facts: the Indexed Digest of Canadian Current Events.
Toronto: Marpep, 1967- . fortnightly.
This looseleaf publication is issued twice monthly with quarterly and annual cumulations. It provides an indexed digest of Canada's day-to-day news, taken from nineteen of the nation's newspapers including the papers of the provincial capitals and the nationally recognized major papers. Also indexed is the *New York Times* for news involving Canada on the international scene. It gives the user fully indexed reports of current events in the country.

1299   Canadian News Index.
Toronto: Micromedia, 1977- . monthly.
Published monthly and cumulated annually, this reference guide covers the contents of seven major English-Canadian newspapers: the *Calgary Herald*, the *Globe and Mail* (q.v.), the *Halifax Chronicle–Herald*, the *Montreal Gazette*, the *Toronto Star*, the *Vancouver Sun*, and the *Winnipeg Free Press*. The papers chosen represent geographic regions of the country. The publication attempts, within the bounds of practicality and economy, to be an index not only to Canadian news, but also to Canadian newspapers as well. The *Index* does not cover every article published in the papers covered;

instead, a selection is made by the indexers of the items deemed of significant reference value. The *Globe and Mail*, arguably considered Canada's national paper, is given more in-depth treatment than the other papers. The entries include standard information.

1300 Canadian Periodical Index.

Toronto: Info Globe, 1986- . monthly.

Published monthly and cumulated annually, the *Canadian Periodical Index* is an academic and scholarly journal 'published for the purpose of disseminating to the public the location of articles of comment on or analysis of the news, and articles with respect to other topics of interest to the general public'. It provides access to a wide variety of Canadian, and a few American, periodicals, covering English and French journals and indexing in excess of 370 periodicals. Entries contain standard index information. *CPI* was published continuously from 1961 to 1985 by the Canadian Library Association. A retrospective index was published by the Association in 1962 entitled: *Canadian index to periodicals and documentary films: an author and subject index, January 1948-December 1959*. In 1966 CLA published *The Canadian periodical index: an author and subject index, January 1938-December 1947*, and in 1988 a further supplement was produced entitled *Canadian periodical index 1920-1937: an author and subject index*. With these cumulations coverage is complete from 1920 to the present. *CPI* and the *Canadian Magazine Index* (q.v.) have considerable overlap in coverage.

1301 Canadian selection: books and periodicals for libraries.

Compiled by Mavis Cariou, Sandra J. Cox, Alvan Bregman.

Toronto: University of Toronto Press, 1985. 2d ed. 501p.

First published in 1978 with a *Supplement* appearing in 1980, *Canadian selection* is designed 'to meet the need for a selective guide to significant Canadian books and periodicals for adults'. The work is intended to be used as a collection development and reference tool in Canada and abroad. The works listed therein are chosen 'to reflect and foster the growing interest in Canadian authors, publishers, subjects, and styles of literature'. *CS* is divided into three parts: part I lists, in a classified arrangement, over 5,000 English-language books, originals and translations, published in Canada, about Canada, or written by Canadians. Within this context compilers have attempted to choose a selection of titles balanced in subject matter and treatment of subject. All entries are annotated for the purpose of providing descriptive and critical information as an aid for selection purposes. Part II lists current, special interest and hobby-related periodical materials, while part III provides a list of Canadian literary awards. An author/title and subject index supports the work. This is a must for all libraries, in Canada or abroad, as well as the interested student, researcher or general reader in the field of Canadian studies.

1302 Canadian Who's Who.

Toronto: University of Toronto Press, 1910- . annual.

This is the largest of the biographical reference sources for living Canadians. The current year provides standard biographical information on more than 9,000 Canadians, who are chosen on merit. *Canadian Who's Who* has been published annually since 1980, prior to this date it was published triennially with five supplements between editions. See also *Who's who in Canada* (Toronto: Global Press, 1922-), and Evelyn de R. McMann's *Canadian who's who index 1898-1984* (Toronto: University of Toronto Press, 1986).

1303   **Canadiana: Canada's National Bibliography = Canadiana: la Bibliographie Nationale du Canada.**
Ottawa: National Library of Canada/Bibliothèque nationale du Canada, 1951- . eleven times a year.

Canadiana is perhaps the most important bibliographic source of information on publications of Canadian origin or interest. In addition to material published in Canada it includes material published in other countries if the author is a Canadian citizen, a resident of Canada, or if the publication has Canadian subject matter. Types of material listed include monographs, serials, pamphlets, theses, atlases, microforms, kits, sheet music and scores, sound recordings, and, federal/provincial/municipal government publications. The compilation is arranged in Dewey decimal classified sequences, with a variety of indexes, such as author, title, series, and subject. Although Quebec publications appear in Canadiana, they can also be found in the *Bibliographie du Québec* (Montreal: Bibliothèque nationale du Québec, 1968-). In addition, both of these national agencies continue to compile and produce retrospective bibliographic compilations, such as Milada Vlach's *Laurentiana parus avant 1821* (Montreal: Bibliothèque nationale du Quebec, 1976); *Bibliographie du Québec, 1821-1967* (Montreal: Bibliothèque nationale du Québec, 1980-); and, *Canadiana, 1867-1900: Monographs, Canada's national bibliography = Canadiana, 1867-1900: monographies, la bibliographie nationale du Canada* (Ottawa: National Library of Canada, 1980-).

1304   **Colombo's Canadian quotations.**
John Robert Colombo.   Edmonton, Alberta: Hurtig, 1974. 735p.

Some 6,000 quotations arranged alphabetically by author (2,500 contributors in total) constituting a 'repository and an inventory of lore and learning'. Bibliographic references are provided for each quote, with additional information where necessary or when the significance of the passage so prescribes. The main body of the text is supported by a substantive index of twenty-thousand keywords and subject entries. Each quotation has been indexed under keyword, subject word and a combination of the two. Supplementing this work is the author's *New Canadian quotations* (Edmonton, Alberta: Hurtig, 1987) which offers some 4,000 new quotations.

1305   **Colombo's Canadian references.**
John Robert Colombo.   Toronto: Oxford University Press, 1976. 576p.

A quick reference tool or mini-encyclopaedia intended to introduce various aspects of Canada that are likely to be encountered by the average person in reading or conversation. Some 6,000 entries are included covering fifty topics ranging, for example, from agriculture, to art, education, film, mining, ships, theatre, and war.

1306   **Dictionary of Canadian biography.**
Toronto: University of Toronto Press, 1966- . bibliog.

The *DCB* is an on going project, eleven volumes of which have been published to date, with a twelfth expected soon. Twenty volumes are projected in total. The twelve volumes will complete the coverage of the project to the end of the nineteenth century. This monumental work of scholarship falls into the tradition of the *British dictionary of national biography*, or the United States' *Dictionary of American biography*. Articles range in length, depending upon the stature of the individual, and place each subject within the context of the period and events in which he or she participated.

Biographers provide equitable and discriminating evaluation as to the contribution made to Canada by their subjects. *DCB* is noted for meticulous scholarship by authoritative scholars and researchers. The articles include useful bibliographical references.

1307 Doctoral research on Canada and Canadians = Thèses de doctorat concernant le Canada et les Canadiens 1884-1983.
Jesse J. Dossick. Ottawa: National Library of Canada, 1986. 559p.

An inventory of doctoral dissertations concerned with Canada and Canadians, in which over 12,000 works are listed, representing research concluded at institutions in Canada and abroad (over one-third of the theses were produced outside of the country). The arrangement is by subject, with a name index. Each subject division is introduced with a brief statistical analysis of the research completed. Incorporated into the index of names are the microfiche numbers of theses for which the National Library of Canada holds copies. Copies of theses on microfiche are available for sale from the Library's Canadian Theses on Microfiche Service. Useful also is Donald M. Tupling's *A dissertation bibliography = Une bibliographie de dissertations* (Ann Arbor, Michigan: University Microfilms International, [1980]), which lists dissertations produced between 1884 and 1979. The researcher should be aware also of subject listings of theses (doctoral and master's) in various subject areas, e.g. Canadian literature.

1308 Canadian books for young people = Livres canadiens pour la jeunesse.
Edited by André Gagnon, Ann Gagnon. Toronto: University of Toronto Press, 1988. 4th ed. 186p.

An inclusive listing of the 'most informative, relevant, and excellent books for young people'. Included are books suitable for pre-school and ranging up to the young adult reader. Each entry contains full bibliographic information, a brief annotation, and a suggested reading level (i.e. younger, middle, older, and young adult). The work is divided into two primary divisions – English- and French-language materials. Each section is subdivided in turn by broad subject classification. Included also are sections covering reference materials, magazines for young people, publishers' series, award books and professional media. This work, together with the previous editions, is essential for the teacher, librarian or concerned parent. Se also Irene E. Aubrey's *Notable Canadian children's books* (Ottawa: National Library of Canada, 1989); Jane McQuarrie and Diane Dubois' *Canadian picture books/Livres d'images canadiens* (Toronto: Reference Press, 1986); Jon C. Stott and Raymond E. Jones' *Canadian books for children: a guide to authors & illustrators* (Toronto: Harcourt Brace Jovanovich, 1988); and, *CM: a reviewing journal of Canadian materials for young people* (Ottawa: Canadian Library Association, 1971-).

1309 The dictionary of Canadian quotations and phrases.
Robert M. Hamilton, Dorothy Shields. Toronto: McClelland & Stewart, 1979. rev. ed. 1063p.

In 1982 this edition was reprinted in hardback and reduced to a more convenient desk size. Some 10,300 quotations and phrases taken from Canadian sources are arranged under almost 2,000 subject headings which are in turn listed alphabetically. Under the subject heading the arrangement is chronological. A list of subjects with cross-references appears at the beginning of the volume. The index to the work is by author or source, then subject heading and date. This edition supersedes the 1953 edition.

1310 **Bibliography of Canadian bibliographies = Bibliographie des bibliographies canadiennes.**
Compiled by Douglas Lochhead.   Toronto: University of Toronto Press, 1972. 2nd ed. 312p.

Published in association with the Bibliographical Society of Canada, this bibliography of bibliographies is a fundamental guide to scholarship. It serves the purpose for Canadian studies and while it is regrettably dated (a third edition is currently under preparation and should be published in 1992), it remains a useful starting point for the researcher or student. Bibliographies listed have some Canadian connection, either by subject, compiler, or geographical location. The entries are arranged alphabetically. A well-produced index locates entries by subject and by compiler. A similar listing for works dealing with Quebec or French Canada can be found in *Bibliographie de bibliographies québécoises* (Bibliography of Québécois bibliographies. Montreal: Bibliothèque national du Québec, 1979) with the *Premier supplement* (1980).

1311 **The Canadian encyclopedia.**
Edited by James H. Marsh.   Edmonton, Alberta: Hurtig, 1988. 2nd ed. 4 vols.

This comprehensive, illustrated reference work provides a detailed picture of Canada, by its finest scholars and writers encompassing a time scale from the prehistoric geological formation of the ancient rocks of the Shield up until the present. The second edition is in four large volumes and has been reviewed as a triumph of concise expression. There are more than 9,700 entries, which include over 3,500 biographies, representing the work of some 2,500 authorities. The *Encyclopedia* is supported by a comprehensive 370 page index. The first edition of the *Encylopedia*, still useful, was produced in three volumes and was published in 1985. A French-language edition is also available, and a juvenile version is under preparation.

1312 **Quick Canadian facts: the Canadian pocket encyclopedia.**
Surrey, British Columbia: Canex Enterprises, 1945- .

Provides ready reference information on a variety of areas including geography, government, the provinces, census, sports, statistics, the people, election records, transportation and communication, trade and industry, finance and taxation, social security, and, health and welfare. Other such compilations are more thorough, but this work lives up to its claims of convenience combined with quick information.

1313 **Canadian serials directory = Répertoire des publications sériées canadiennes.**
Edited by Gordon Ripley.   Toronto: Reference Press, 1987. 3rd ed. 396p.

A bibliographic listing of 'periodicals and serials presently being published in Canada'. The tool is a reference and finding aid aimed at librarians and scholars, but it also provides an order guide for subscription agencies and booksellers. Periodicals, magazines, newsletters, daily newspapers, annuals, yearbooks, journals, proceedings and transactions of associations and societies, are included in the *Directory*. Excluded are general interest weekly newspapers, monographic series, annual reports, company reports and financial statements, university and school calendars, city and telephone directories and government publications. Arrangement is alphabetical by title and cross-references are provided. Each entry is described in the language of publication.

General Reference Works

A subject index lists serials by subject category, while a publisher and sponsor index gives access by official publisher or corporate body or association.

1314 Canadian reference sources.
Dorothy E. Ryder. Ottawa: Canadian Library Association, 1981. 2nd ed. 311p.

A selective guide to Canadian reference material published to December 1980. Items are organized by broad subject discipline and then subdivided in a manner appropriate to that discipline. Entries include standard bibliographic information, as well as brief descriptive annotations including antecedent and related works. Although dated, the work is a standard tool for libraries and a valuable guide for researchers at all levels. Plans are underway by the National Library of Canada to update and publish a new and revised edition. A similar listing for works dealing with Quebec or French Canada can be found in *Les ouvrages de référence du Québec* (Reference works of Quebec. Montreal: Ministère des Affaires culturelles du Québec, 1969), including its various supplements: . . . *Supplement 1967-1974* (1975), and . . . *Supplement 1974-1981* (1984).

1315 The Macmillan dictionary of Canadian biography.
Edited by W. Stewart Wallace, W. A. McKay. Toronto: Macmillan, 1978. 4th ed. 914p.

Long a key reference source, this dictionary provides standard biographical entries for all those who have held important offices of state, such as governors, lieutenant-governors, administrators, ministers of the Crown, speakers of the House of Commons, and other politicians, such as senators and provincial cabinet ministers, when especially notable. An attempt is always made to include also outstanding Canadian jurists, scholars, scientists, artists, explorers, soldiers, and capitalists.

1316 Who's Who of Canadian Women.
Toronto: Trans-Canada Press, 1984- . annual.

This reference book contains standard biographical information about leading business and professional women. Also included is an index to the entries by company/firm/organization.

Indexes

There follow three separate indexes: authors (personal and corporate); titles; and subjects. Title entries are italicized and refer either to the main titles, or to other works cited in the annotations. The numbers refer to bibliographic entries, not to pages. Individual index entries are arranged in alphabetical sequence.

Index of Authors

331

Index of Titles

343

E

Early Canadian court
  houses 832
Early Indian village
  churches: wooden
  frontier architecture in
  British Columbia 846
Early painters and
  engravers in Canada
  1059
Early Ukrainian settlements
  in Canada 1895-1900
  221
Early voyages and northern
  approaches 1000-1632
  121
Earth sciences in Canada: a
  centennial appraisal
  and forecast 966
Ecology versus politics in
  Canada 891
Economic analysis and
  Canadian policy 578
Economic and social
  history of Quebec,
  1760-1850: structures
  and conjonctures 570
Economic development of
  Canada 573
Economic growth:
  prospects and
  determinants 574
Economic history of
  Canada 566
Economic history of
  Canada: a guide to
  information sources
  548
Economic impacts and
  linkages of the
  Canadian mining
  industry 733
Economic policies in
  Canada 553
Economic resurgence and
  the constitutional
  agenda: the case of the
  east coast fisheries 698
Economics in Canadian
  society: principles and
  applications 578
Economics of industrial
  policy and strategy 635

Economics of the Canadian
  financial system:
  theory, policy &
  institutions 600
Economie du Québec 578
Economie et société en
  Nouvelle-France 570
Economy of Canada: a
  study of ownership
  and control 652
Educating Canadians: a
  documentary history of
  public education 902
Education and social
  change: themes from
  Ontario's past 904
Education, change and
  society: a sociology of
  Canadian education
  916
Education in Canada: a
  bibliography=
  L'éducation au
  Canada: une
  bibliographie 898
Education in Canada: an
  analysis of elementary,
  secondary and
  vocational schooling
  913
Education in Canada: an
  interpretation 906
Education law in Canada
  922
Education of immigrant
  students: issues and
  answers 908
Education: Ontario's
  preoccupation 914
Educational administration
  in Canada 917
Educational digest 911
EDUQ 897
Egerton Ryerson and his
  times 904
Église catholique au
  Canada (1604-1886)
  325
Église et le loisir au Québec
  avant la révolution
  tranquille 1187
Église et le théâtre au
  Québec 1136
1885 and after: native

society in transition
  250
Eldorado: Canada's
  national uranium
  company 716
Embattled shadows: a
  history of Canadian
  cinema 1895-1939 1166
Emergence of social
  security in Canada 354
Empire of the St. Lawrence
  148
Empire of wood: the
  MacMillan Bloedel
  story 709
Employment law in
  Canada 784
Encyclopedia of music in
  Canada 1085, 1092
Endangered spaces: the
  future for Canada's
  wilderness 74
Enduring witness: a history
  of the Presbyterian
  Church in Canada 331
Enemy that never was: a
  history of the Japanese
  Canadians 228
English fact in Quebec 464
English-Canadian literature
  to 1900: a guide to
  information sources
  989
English-Canadian theatre
  1121
Enjoying Canadian
  painting 1058
Entering the eighties:
  Canada in crisis 556
Enterprise and national
  development: essays in
  Canadian business and
  economic history 632
Environment and good
  sense: an introduction
  to environmental
  damage and control in
  Canada 885
Environmental impact of
  mining in Canada 733
Environmental rights in
  Canada 894
Equality rights and the
  Canadian Charter of

354

357

361

367

369

377

Index of Subjects

Canadian Labour Congress
794, 798
Canadian Labour Congress
Political Education
Department 796
Canadian Mental Health
Association 385
Canadian National
Committee for the
International
Hydrological Decade
51
Canadian National
Railways System 757
Canadian Nature
Federation 72
Canadian Northern see
Railways
Canadian Opera Company
1105
Canadian Pacific 752
Canadian Pacific Railway
see Railways
Canadian Permanent
Committee on
Geographical Names
13
Canadian Radio-Television
Commission 1263-64
Canadian Seamen's Strike
807
Canadian Shield 32, 75
Canadian Society of Civil
Engineers 948
Canadian Sports Hall of
Fame 1229
Canadian Wheat Board
677
Canadian Wildlife
Federation 697
Canadian-Arab Relations
Conference 532
Canals 750
Cancer 390
Canoeing 1194, 1203, 1219
Cape Breton 42, 806
Capital punishment 347
Capitalism 652, 714
Cars 777
Cartier, Jacques 325, 330
Cartography 49, 50-53, 59,
61-62, 70
see also Bibliographies
under maps, History

under maps, Province
by name, e.g.
Newfoundland
Cathedrals 852
Catholicism 325, 327
and education 926
and theatre 1136
see also History
Centennial see History
Charlottetown Festival
1128
Charter of Rights and
Freedoms 404-05, 411,
415, 417, 422, 788, 915
Chemistry 974
see also Science
Chicago Architecture
Award 835
Child abuse 385
Children's literature 1004,
1308
Children's theatre 1126
Chinese 209, 220
and racism 208, 220
and bilingualism 223
Chiriaeff, Ludmilla 1110
Cholera see History
Church architecture 833,
839, 841
Churches 313-15, 317, 322,
326, 335, 348
and education 329
see also Bibliographies,
Denominations by
name, e.g. Methodists
Cinema see Film
Cities see History, Urban
life, City by name,
e.g. Quebec
Civil service 73, 457, 496-
97, 499
Clarke, Cecil 1140
Climate 11, 16-17, 53, 76,
661
Coal 732
Cobalt Lake 715
Cockayne, George 1047
Cod 695
Code Napoleon 423
Cold War see History
Columbia Icefield 58
Colville, Alex 1056
Commission on Lead in
the Environment 890

Commission on the
Mackenzie Valley
Pipeline 571
Committee of Visual Arts
Ontario 843
Communications 27
Communism 541, 781
Communist Party 789
see also History
Community colleges 939
Companies 620
Companion of the Order
of Canada 835
Company of New France
see French Canada
Composers 1088, 1094,
1104, 1106
Computers see
Microtechnology
Confederation see History
Conference on the Study
of the History of
Canadian Science and
Technology 961
Congress of International
Organizations 782
Conscientious objectors
333
Conservation 74, 77, 571,
703
see also Ecology
Conservatism 447, 453,
694, 883, 893
Conservatives 435
Constitution 6, 314, 396-
423, 440, 448, 458-59,
503, 788
and the courts 421
new Constitution 404
see also History
Consumer loan 579
Consumer protection 413
Contraception 362
Cooperative
Commonwealth
Federation 449
Courthouses 832
Creighton, Donald 138
Crime 348, 355, 356, 359-
61, 446
violence 370
see also History,
Statistics
Croatians 209

381

387

Map of Canada

This map shows the more important towns and other features.

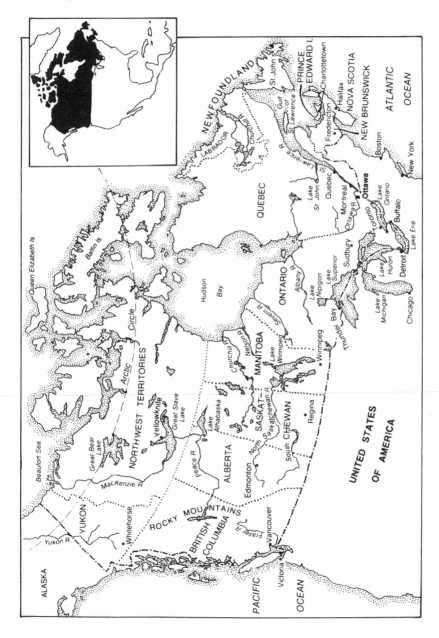